P9-AFA-937

DATE DUE

AG 8 '97			
DE 19 '97			
AR 5 '98			
AP 2 '98			
MY 26 '98			
JY 22 '98			
OC 22 '98			
NO 17 '98			
JY 13 '99			
OC 25 '99			
DE 9 '99			
MY 4 '00			
OC 29 '0			
JE 9 '0			
JY 29 '04			
JE 6 '0			

DEMCO 38-296

MUSIC OF THE TWENTIETH CENTURY

ß

Music of the Twentieth Century

Style and Structure

Second Edition

BRYAN R. SIMMS

University of Southern California

SCHIRMER BOOKS
An Imprint of Simon & Schuster Macmillan
New York

PRENTICE HALL INTERNATIONAL
London   Mexico City   New Delhi   Singapore   Sydney   Toronto

Riverside Community College
Library
4800 Magnolia Avenue
Riverside, California 92506

Copyright © 1996 by Bryan R. Simms

ML 197 .S585 1996

Simms, Bryan R.

Music of the twentieth
   century

s book may be reproduced or transmitted in any
or mechanical, including photocopying, recording,
retrieval system, without permission in writing

Macmillan

Library of Congress Catalog Number: 96–2063

Printed in the United States of America

Printing number:
1 2 3 4 5 6 7 8 9 10

Library of Congress Cataloging-in-Publication Data

Simms, Bryan R.
   Music of the twentieth century : style and structure / Bryan R.
Simms. — 2nd ed.
      p. cm.
   Includes bibliographical references and index.
   ISBN 0-02-872392-9
   1. Music—20th century—History and criticism.   2. Musical
analysis.   I. Title.
ML197.S585   1996
780´.9´04—dc20
                                                          96-2063
                                                          CIP
                                                          MN

Acknowledgment is gratefully made to the following sources for the portraits of
composers appearing within the text:

Malcolm Crowthers: Olivier Messiaen, © 1982 Malcolm Crowthers

Arnold Schoenberg Institute: Alban Berg, Pierre Boulez, Arnold Schoenberg, Roger
Sessions, Anton Webern

G. Schirmer, Inc.: Arthur Honegger, Dimitri Shostakovich

Regional History Collection, University Library, University of Southern California:
Aaron Copland, Roy Harris, Walter Piston, Sergei Prokofiev, Igor Stravinsky

BMI Archives: Eliott Carter, Paul Hindemith

Music Division, The New York Public Library at Lincoln Center, Astor, Lenox and
Tilden Foundations: Samuel Barber, Benjamin Britten, John Cage, Claude Debussy,
Manuel de Falla, Charles Ives, Gustav Mahler, Darius Milhaud, Francis Poulenc,
Maurice Ravel, Erik Satie, Alexander Scriabin, Jean Sibelius, Karlheinz Stockhausen,
Richard Strauss, Virgil Thomson, Edgard Varèse, Ralph Vaughan Williams.

The Bettmann Archive: Béla Bartók

This paper meets the requirements of ANSI/NISO Z39.48-1992 (Permanence of
Paper).

To Shelley

Contents

Repertory

The following are the musical works that receive primary attention in this book.

Chapter 1
  Chopin, Prelude in A minor Op. 28, No. 2
  Liszt, "Nuages gris"
  Schoenberg, "Lockung" Op. 6, No. 7
  Schubert, "Mignon"
  Wagner, Prelude to Act 3 from *Parsifal*

Chapter 2
  Schoenberg, Piano Piece Op. 23, No. 4

Chapter 4
  Boulez, *Structures Ia*
  Schoenberg, String Quartet No. 4, Op. 37

Chapter 5
  Berg, Monoritmica from *Lulu*, Act 1
  Stravinsky, Sacrificial Dance from *The Rite of Spring*

Chapter 6
   Bach, Ricercar from *The Musical Offering*, arranged by
      Anton Webern
   Schoenberg, Orchestral Piece Op. 16, No. 3

Chapter 7
   Berg, Four Songs Op. 2
   Berg, "Lied der Lulu" from *Lulu*, Act 2
   Busoni, *Sonatina secunda*
   Mahler, Symphony No. 10, Adagio
   Reger, String Quartet No. 5, first movement
   Schoenberg, String Quartet No. 1, Op. 7
   Schoenberg, String Quartet No. 4, Op. 37, first movement
   Richard Strauss, *Salome*
   Webern, Second Cantata Op. 31, fifth and sixth movements

Chapter 8
   Debussy, *Jeux*
   Debussy, *Pelléas et Mélisande*
   Debussy, "Placet futile" from *Trois poèmes de Stéphane Mallarmé*
   Debussy, Saraband from *Pour le piano*
   Fauré, "Dans la forêt de septembre"
   Musorgski, "With Nurse" from *Nursery*
   Prokofiev, Piano Sonata No. 7, finale
   Ravel, *Jeux d'eau*
   Ravel, "Méfiez-vous des blancs" from *Chansons madécasses*
   Ravel, "Placet futile" from *Trois poèmes de Stéphane Mallarmé*
   Satie, Saraband No. 1
   Scriabin, Piano Sonata No. 10
   Shostakovich, *Lady Macbeth of the Mtsensk*
   Stravinsky, *L'Histoire du soldat*
   Stravinsky, *Les noces*
   Stravinsky, *Petrushka*
   Stravinsky, *The Rite of Spring*

Chapter 9
   Bartók, Bagatelles Op. 6
   Bartók, "Fekete föd" from Eight Hungarian Folk Songs
   Bartók, *Improvisations on Hungarian Peasant Songs* Op. 20, No. 7
   Bartók, String Quartet No. 3
   Copland, *Appalachian Spring*
   Falla, *Fantasía baetica*
   Milhaud, "Botafogo" from *Saudades do Brazil*
   Milhaud, *La création du monde*

Introduction

This book is a study of musical culture in the twentieth century presented through the examination of its outstanding works. No period in history exceeds our own in the diversity of its music: in it we will find much that is both sublime and unsettling. We will be invited to hear in new ways and sometimes even required to redefine our notions of the function and limitations of music. But, in whatever may present itself as controversial in modern musical thought, we will look to the music itself as our true guide.

The discussion of music in this book will emphasize style and structure and the ways in which these two are related. What are style and structure? The totality of distinguishing features of a musical work or of a group of works constitutes its style. Style calls our attention to the differences among pieces of music; it brings into view the uniqueness of a language and the thumbprints that great composers leave within their works.

Structures, on the contrary, tend to be common property. They are often shared by many composers—even those living in different historical eras—and the same structures recur time and again in large musical repertories. A musical structure embodies a principle of expansion—that is, an underlying rationale for how and why the parts of a composition belong together. Structure in music is often perceived as an alternation of contrasting or similar parts. If we observe that a piece has the form A B A, we make just such a perception about similarity and contrast among its principal sections. But other compositional elements also act as structural components of a less schematic sort. Conventional harmonic progressions, tonal plans, and techniques of counterpoint and fugue, for example, provide structural frameworks in which pieces can be expanded.

Major changes in musical style during the twentieth century have been provoked by a series of "emancipations"—a term used by Arnold Schoenberg to describe his treatment of dissonance—by which new musical materials became available to the composer. The first of these seminal emancipations was of dissonance and key, followed by similar revolutions in rhythm, sound, and texture. Each of these liberations necessitated new structural principles which can be revealed by a careful examination of outstanding musical works.

This book is divided into three parts: the first is a survey of compositional materials and current analytic principles by which structures of twentieth-century music can be perceived; the second and third parts examine the activities of major composers and masterpieces of their music in approximately chronological order. The theoretical part can function either as a preliminary to the later chapters or in coordination with them. The musical survey emphasizes original developments in style. Discussion concentrates on a few exemplary works of major composers; the analyses are intended to provide only a starting point for more detailed investigations. Sketches of the life and works of major composers are set apart from the text for easy reference.

It is strongly advised that readers of this book be provided with excerpts from the scores of works which are discussed. A representative sample of these is found in the Anthology which accompanies this volume. It is also recommended that the text be supplemented by readings from essays by major composers. A brief sketch of literature (emphasizing sources in English) is placed at the conclusion of each chapter. The writings of some composers—among them Bartók, Cage, Carter, Copland, Hindemith, Messiaen, and Schoenberg—are especially valuable to a better understanding of their music and of the issues that have motivated them.

A single date given in parentheses after the title of a composition is its date of completion. Works that underwent an unusually long period of composition are identified by the dates when work on them was begun and ended.

The revised edition of this book is identical in overall outline to the first edition of 1986. A new chapter (Chapter 11) is added, dealing with neoclassical and populist composers in America between the world wars. This allows for a discussion of music by Roy Harris, Virgil Thomson, Samuel Barber, Walter Piston, Roger Sessions, and David Diamond, none of whom were covered in the earlier edition. The final chapters have been expanded to include an enlarged discussion of contemporary music, especially works by Alfred Schnittke, Sofia Gubaidulina, Arvo Pärt, John Adams, Conlon Nancarrow, and György Ligeti. These additions have necessitated the rearrangement of some existing material.

The author is deeply grateful for the advice and support of several colleagues who have read and commented upon the manuscript. Special thanks go to my wife, Charlotte Erwin, who read the entire manuscript and made invaluable suggestions, and to Donald Crockett, Janet Schmalfeldt, William Robinson, and Dean Suzuki.

PART ONE

Structural Principles and Compositional Materials of Twentieth-Century Music

1

Tonality in Transition

Music in the first decade of the twentieth century experienced a profound upheaval which has proved to be one of the most momentous in the entire history of music. It was an eruption that soon reshaped the external physiognomy of music and established new principles for its internal organization. This transformation was felt throughout the world; it was precipitated by such diverse figures as Arnold Schoenberg in Vienna, Charles Ives in America, Alexander Scriabin in Russia, and Béla Bartók in Hungary. In the chapters that follow, we shall trace the contribution of these pioneers and the legacy of their innovations.

We can appreciate the profound newness of the musical world that they helped to create by comparing two works of the same genre and country of origin from before and after this stylistic change: Gustav Mahler's Symphony No. 8 (1906–1907)—called *Symphony of a Thousand*—and Anton Webern's Symphony Op. 21 (1928). The differences are pronounced. Mahler's symphony is gigantic in medium and length, its texts address no less an issue than the destiny of human spirit, and its musical argument is affirmative both in its purely musical sense of triumph and in its implicit statement about mankind. Webern's symphony, on the contrary, is by comparison diminutive of proportion, understated in content, and linked overtly to no subject outside of itself. Mahler's work breathes the air of romanticism in its celebration of the heroic; Webern's work inhabits an intensely introspective musical world far removed from Mahler's grandiloquence.

These outward distinctions in style reflect many technical differences separating Mahler's musical language from Webern's. None is more striking than the use of *tonality* or *key* in the former and its absence in the latter. Mahler's work is in the key of E♭, a tonal focus that lends comprehensibility and unity to its diverse musical elaborations. Webern's symphony has no key and it relies for its understanding on other compositional principles. We turn our attention in this first chapter to the matter of key and its progressive reinterpretation by composers of the nineteenth and early twentieth centuries.

COMMON-PRACTICE TONALITY

Tonality in the common-practice period (roughly, the eighteenth and nineteenth centuries) was a system that guided and coordinated harmony and melody and that influenced rhythm, meter, form, and other elements of a composition. It was a common system to which virtually all major composers of this time subscribed, despite their differences in style. The central elements of a tonality are a fundamental tone (which identifies the key), the major or minor scale having it as tonic, and triads and seventh chords built upon these scale tones. Via generally accepted harmonic and contrapuntal principles, these chords are cast into recurrent circular progressions passing from a tonic to a dominant by way of one or more chords that prepare the dominant, finally returning to a tonic. This conventional pattern of harmonic motion creates a syntax by which a composer's musical argument can be understood.

Let us first examine a piece in which principles of tonality are normative and clearly in evidence. Schubert's song "Mignon" ("Kennst du das Land," D. 321) is one of many settings by composers of the romantic period of this text by Goethe. Its three stanzas are set to music by Schubert in a nearly strophic manner; the identical first two stanzas are shown in Example 1-1.

This song expresses the key of A by its harmonic and melodic components. We shall focus first upon harmony. The basic chords of the work are triads whose tones are drawn from scales of A major or minor (the parallel modes are used interchangeably by Schubert). These are organized into circular progressions both on a large and small scale. One large progression spans the entire stanza: its tonic chord occurs at the beginning, the dominant triad toward the mid-

Example 1-1. Schubert, "Mignon," stanzas 1 and 2.

dle (measures 18 and following), and the tonic triad in the final two measures. Tonic and dominant harmonies are primary elements in the expression of key, and the large progression from I to V to I creates a harmonic superstructure that organizes and directs all of the other harmonic motions. This "tonic-dominant axis," as we shall call it, is a fundamental expression of tonality in a piece of music.

The space between these pillars of the superstructure is filled with other chords, briefer circular progressions, and temporary tonics. Between measures 1 and 18, for example, these intermediary chords guide our attention toward the dominant by a combination of melodic and harmonic processes. The harmonies that we encounter consist primarily of the submediant F major (measures 12–15), prefixed by its dominant C major (measures 8–11). Both of these are drawn from the parallel minor, which prepares the listener for an overt turn to A minor at the beginning of the third stanza.

Example 1-1. continued.

Although we may consider the arrival in F major in measure 12 to
conclude a modulation to a new key, we still remember the home
tonality of A. F major, although a temporary tonic, owes its harmonic meaning to the key of A, in which it functions as a preparation of the dominant.

The large-scale circular progression that organizes the entire stanza is also reproduced on a smaller scale. Harmonies supporting the opening period (measures 1–8), for example, progress from tonic (measure 1) to dominant (measure 4), which marks off a space filled by other triads that function as dominant preparations. The progression is completed in measure 8 by the arrival on a new tonic triad, C major. The dominant chord in measure 4 has a different structural role from the dominant in measure 18: the first is a local point of arrival while the second is a major structural juncture, indeed, the overriding harmonic goal of the entire first half of the stanza.

Melodic motion reinforces harmonic progressions by outlining supporting chords. But the melody also undergoes a large-scale stepwise descent which helps to express the key in a more fundamental way. This motion is from scale degree 3 (C♯), which occurs as the first melodic tone in measure 1, down to scale degree 2 (measure 18), and finally to the tonic scale degree at the end. At this point of conclusion, Schubert thrusts the vocal melody into a higher register to underscore the child-like eagerness of the speaker of the poem. This fundamental melodic path and its supporting harmonic progression I–V–I create the most basic expression of the key of A as it extends through the entire work. (Example 1-2 represents this structure in musical symbols.) Similar patterns were discovered at basic levels of structure in a variety of tonal works by the Viennese theorist Heinrich Schenker (1868–1935), who called them *Ursätze* ("fundamental structures").

The form of the work is clearly articulated by harmonic components of the key. The stanza begins with an expository period (measures 1–8), which concludes at the arrival of C major. The next phrase (measures 9–11) ends with a half cadence in the home key of A, which then moves quickly to F major and to the structural dominant at measure 18.

scale
degrees: 3   2   1

A: I   V   I
meas.   1   18   39

Example 1-2. Fundamental harmonic and melodic motion in Schubert's "Mignon."

The relation of consonance and dissonance in this example is also a basic element of common-practice tonality. Consonant chords are those that contain consonant intervals; these harmonies are thus limited to major and minor triads in root position and first inversion. They are the building blocks of tonal harmony. All other chords are dissonant; they add to music a rich variety of sound and an increased sense of propulsion through time.

In tonal music, dissonant chords serve the function of prolonging or connecting other chords. A typical example is the dissonant French augmented sixth in measure 17. The function of this chord is to connect the submediant harmony that precedes it to the dominant harmony which is the goal of the progression. This role is fulfilled by stepwise voice leading in all parts. The sketch in Example 1-3, which simplifies rhythm and register, will clarify the way in which the French sixth arises. Between measures 15 and 18 there is a chromatic ascent in an inner part from C to E. This linear motion is supported in measure 17 by the familiar French sixth, which intensifies movement to the dominant, making it more urgent, just as the speaker of the poem at this point impatiently inquires, "Do you truly know it?" Although the tone D♯ does not occur in A major or minor, its presence in no way weakens the sense of key. Chromatic tones, even used in large numbers, are features of voice leading that do not in themselves threaten the coherence of a tonality.

In summary, then, let us bear in mind that traditional expression of key is accomplished by a number of coordinated events. Among the most fundamental is a large-scale harmonic progression from tonic to dominant to tonic. Cadential progressions in the smaller scale reinforce local elements of the larger progression. Dissonant chords are a motoric force in music. They serve primarily to connect diatonic, consonant triads. We turn now to ways in which composers of the nineteenth and early twentieth centuries reinterpreted these general principles of tonality.

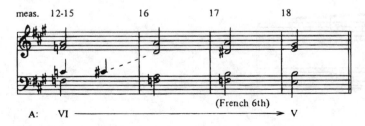

Example 1-3. Harmonic reduction of measures 12–18 of Schubert's "Mignon."

DISRUPTIONS OF THE TONIC-DOMINANT AXIS

The tonic-dominant axis, which we observed in Schubert's "Mignon" is a means by which a single key exerts an influence throughout a piece or movement of a larger work. This typical unity of key may also be observed beyond a single movement in multi-movement instrumental genres. In symphonies, string quartets, sonatas, and similar genres of the classical era, for example, entire works revolve about a home key. First and last movements are invariably in this tonality, and interior movements are either in the home key or in a closely related one such as the subdominant.

In the instrumental music of Beethoven and in a few works of his predecessors in the classical era, there is often a change of mode in the finale. Beethoven's Fifth Symphony, for example, moves from a first movement in C minor to a finale in C major, a transition that conveys a sense of triumph over adversity. The Ninth Symphony moves from D minor to D major, with the suggestion of triumph made explicit by the text from Schiller's "Ode to Joy." These alterations of mode were expanded in the symphonies of Gustav Mahler into outright changes of key. In Mahler's Second Symphony (1894) there is a progression from C minor at the opening to its relative major E♭ at the end. As is the case with Beethoven's symphonies, this change has a clear connection to the program of the work, which traces man's conversion from pessimism to triumphant confidence in God's love. In later symphonies, Mahler makes the progression of keys more remote. The Ninth Symphony (1908–10) begins in D major, moves to C major in the second movement, to A minor in the third, and, finally, to D♭ major in the finale. This work, furthermore, does not have overt programmatic associations, which earlier supplied a rationale for nonconcentric tonal plans.

Single movements composed in the nineteenth century also underwent disruptions in the unity of key associated with the tonic-dominant axis. This new tonal diversity was prefigured by remote modulations in classical developmental or transitional passages as well as by introductions often encountered in the first movements of works by Haydn and Beethoven. Harmonic motion in the typical classical introduction prepares or prolongs the dominant, giving the initial tonic a dramatic arrival. These introductions do not in themselves disrupt the tonic-dominant axis—they solely act as a prefix to the initial statement of the tonic.

Later in the nineteenth century, however, the introduction was often extended and made more remote to a central tonality, thus creating intentional ambiguity of key. By this time, the opening or introduction of a work often replaced the development as the area where a break with conventional tonality was most likely to occur.

The opening of Debussy's Prelude to *The Afternoon of a Faun* (1894) is magically remote from the primary tonality of E major, which is hinted at in the opening measures but confirmed only later. The opening flute melody outlines the tritone—an interval as ambiguous in its tonality as are the nymphs in the mind of the faun as he awakens from his dream (see Chapter 8).

The opening of the Adagio from Mahler's Tenth Symphony (1910) creates tonal ambiguity by its emphasis on chromatic embellishing tones. This fifteen-measure introduction in the violas (Example 1-4) leads the ear away from the underlying F♯ tonic harmony by elongating neighboring tones and placing them on strong parts of the measure. We are at first invited to hear the opening as a preparation of the dominant of B♭ minor, begun by outlining its submediant harmony G major and then moving to its dominant F major. But when the first theme enters in F♯ major at measure 16, we must reevaluate the passage and hear the first fifteen measures as an adumbration of an F♯-major triad. In the first half of the introduction, the composer emphasizes the upper chromatic neighboring tones of this triad, and in the second half the lower chromatic neighbors. We shall see later in this chapter that Mahler's unusual treatment of embellishing tones is continued throughout this movement and becomes an important means by which key is obscured.

Another means by which the tonic-dominant axis was disrupted is the omission of one or more of its elements. An example of such an incomplete structure is Chopin's Prelude in A minor Op. 28, No. 2 (1838; Example 1-5). This work is unusual, especially with respect to tonal plan, voice leading, and treatment of dissonance. The key of

Example 1-4. Mahler, Symphony No. 10, Adagio, measures 1–15. UN: upper neighbor; LN: lower neighbor. Copyright 1951 by Associated Music Publishers, Inc. Reprinted by permission.

Example 1-5.   Chopin, Prelude in A Minor Op. 28, No. 2.

A is not apparent until it is suggested by the cadential six-four chord in measure 15, which leads to the first statement of the tonic chord in the very last measure. The first fourteen measures can be interpreted as a long extension of the dominant triad, first heard as an E-minor chord in measures 1–4 and then prolonged by an involved process of bass arpeggiations until it arrives at the cadential progression of the last nine measures. The entire piece is thus in the key of A minor, but the expected statement of a tonic at or near the beginning is omitted.

A more complex disruption of axis tonality is found in Schoenberg's song "Lockung" ("Lure," 1905) Op. 6, No. 7. The composer refers to this work in both his *Theory of Harmony* and *Structural Functions of Harmony* as an example of extended and suspended tonality. He defines the former as an idiom in which nondiatonic chords and progressions may still be considered to be within one prevailing key. "They function chiefly as enrichments of the harmony," he wrote in *Structural Functions*, "and, accordingly, often appear in a very small space, even in a single measure. . . . Their functional effect is, in many cases, only passing and temporary." Suspended tonality occurs when a tonic chord is nowhere clearly stated. Schoenberg's analysis of "Lockung" in *Structural Functions* shows that he considered two tonalities to be in effect simultaneously for most of the song: Eb (the principal key) and C (its submediant).

Both of these keys are represented almost solely by their dominants; the tonic triad of Eb, for example, occurs only in passing, but its dominant Bb extends through long spans. Typical of the Wagnerian harmonic style, these dominants often do not progress to tonics; rather than setting up complete progressions that firmly establish a key, they are broken off abruptly or lead to deceptive continuations. An example is the juncture of the opening section with the contrasting passage beginning at measure 32 (Example 1-6). The Bb dominant of measure 31 leads directly to a tonicization of B major (or Cb, equivalent to bVI). This passage then leads to its dominant F♯ (measures 39–41), which is again left unresolved, leading to a section in Db.

"Lockung" in fact transforms the tonic-dominant axis almost beyond recognition. The tonal regions of Cb, C, and Db are reminiscent of dominant preparations, the dominant of Eb is much in evidence, and the tonic is sometimes touched upon, but their proportions and syntax are so distorted and the chords themselves so interpenetrated by nondiatonic tones that traditional key is scarcely—if at all—perceptible.

Harmonic *sequences* were also used in new ways to diminish the strength of a prevailing key. Harmonic sequences are repeated patterns consisting of recurrent bass figures and chordal successions. In classical instrumental music they are most often encountered in developmental or transitional passages; there they prolong a diatonic chord or connect two basic harmonies within a larger tonal plan. The boundary points of the sequence normally clarify its harmonic meaning within a prevailing key.

In the later nineteenth century, especially in the music of Richard Wagner, the occurrence of sequence was more widespread, and its role in the expression of a key was diminished or eliminated. This phenomenon can be observed in the Prelude to Act 3 of *Parsifal*

Example 1-6.   Schoenberg, "Lockung" Op. 6, No. 7, measures 11–39.

(1877–82, Example 1-7). Let us first examine the section from measures 12–16, in which sequence is clearly evident. Both the upper and lower parts elaborate upon a diminished seventh chord, which moves upward sequentially from the bass note G in measure 12 to Bb in measure 16, where the pattern is broken. This interval does not

Example 1-7. Wagner, Prelude to Act 3 of *Parsifal*.

reinforce or link any diatonic triads, nor does it depart from, or arrive at, diatonic harmonies.

A more covert harmonic sequence may be observed in the introductory passage of measures 1–11. The first four measures contain an incomplete progression in B♭ minor from I to V^7, which then dissolves into a diminished seventh chord. This pattern of dominant seventh followed by diminished seventh is repeated a semitone higher in measures 6–7 and another semitone higher in measures 9–11. Again, the boundary points of the sequence have no function in any prevailing key; the logic of the passage relies instead upon the ascending chromatic pattern itself. The suspension of key that

Wagner accomplishes in this prelude by the use of chromatic sequences and diminished chords serves an important dramatic role in the opera, as it portrays the aimless wanderings of Parsifal prior to his return to the Kingdom of the Grail in Act 3.

IRREGULAR TREATMENT OF EMBELLISHING TONES AND THE FREEING OF DISSONANCE

Embellishing tones are melodic notes, or tones arising from voice leading, that are not part of a supporting harmony. These result primarily from rhythmic displacements such as suspensions, passing or neighboring motion, and appoggiaturas. Their preparation and resolution in music of the common-practice period were strictly regulated. In the nineteenth and early twentieth centuries, however, composers greatly expanded the ways in which such tones were used. Sometimes their resolutions were delayed, ornamented, or simply omitted, and the dissonant chords produced by the embellishing motion were sustained to the point where their diatonic source was obscured. It was in this way that dissonance took its boldest strides toward "emancipation," a phenomenon that will be addressed further in Chapter 2.

Arnold Schoenberg articulates this new emphasis on dissonant chords in his *Theory of Harmony*, where he insists that chords containing nonharmonic tones must be incorporated into harmonic theory and recognized as valid musical materials. "Non-harmonic tones," he wrote, "form chords, hence they are not non-harmonic; the musical phenomena they help to create are harmonies, as is everything that sounds simultaneously."

The music of Gustav Mahler contains numerous examples of irregular treatment of embellishing tones. Example 1-8 is a reduction of the main theme of the Adagio of his Tenth Symphony (measures 16–23) showing the principal melody in the first violin and its underlying harmonies. The harmonic progression reflects the tonic-dominant axis of F♯ major as it moves from tonic (measures 16–18) to dominant (measures 22–23) and then returns to the tonic in measure 24 as the next musical unit begins. But the melody is highly irregular. Not only does it contain drastic disruptions in register, but its embellishing tones are handled with great freedom. On the downbeat of measure 19, for example, the melodic tone E♯ is an incomplete neighbor to the underlying F♯ in a B-minor chord. The E♯ is neither prepared nor resolved. The chord thus formed is one of the "triadic tetrachords" (to be discussed in Chapter 3) which was favored by early atonal composers. Here it maintains a diatonic

Example 1-8. Mahler, Symphony No. 10, Adagio, measures 16–23. Copyright 1951 by Associated Music Publishers, Inc. Reprinted by permission.

function, however tenuous. On the third beat of measure 21, the melodic tone Eb displaces the implicit chordal tone D. Its resolution is delayed well into the following bar, after the harmony has changed. The chord that is formed with the Eb in measure 21 is a subset of the whole-tone scale, one of a family of chords much in currency among the early atonalists.

In Schoenberg's early songs, irregular embellishing tones are found simultaneously in several strands of voice leading. Let us return to "Lockung" (Example 1-6) and examine the first vocal phrase in measures 11–15. The underlying harmony of the entire passage is a dominant ninth in the key of Eb. It is typical of this song, however, that the dominant chord does not progress to any diatonic goal in this key. The notes F# and C# in measure 11 are upper neighbors to the chordal tones F and Cb (B), respectively. The chord thus formed is another triadic tetrachord much favored by Schoenberg in his atonal period.

EXPERIMENTAL HARMONY AND TONALITY

In the later nineteenth century, harmonic experimentation characterized the works of several major composers. A group of musicians in St. Petersburg called "The Five" (see Chapter 8) began to adapt nondiatonic scales and a remarkably free use of dissonance to their works. Among Western composers, the innovations in harmony and tonality of Franz Liszt (1811–86) strikingly prefigure twentieth-century developments. Liszt's harmonic innovations are evident throughout his career as a composer, and they became pronounced in a series of compositions for piano and for chorus after about 1870. The late piano works are especially innovative and markedly different from his earlier virtuosic music for that instrument. They are usually short and spare in texture, and they apply a repertory of harmonies not normally part of tonal music. In these works major and minor triads are often outweighed by diminished chords, augmented triads and other whole-tone configurations, octatonic sets (see Chapter 2), bitriadic chords, and pentatonic figures. Axis tonality and the customary relationship of consonance and dissonance are little in evidence.

Throughout his life Liszt maintained a keen interest in ways by which traditional tonality could be expanded or reinterpreted. His imagination was fired by lectures given in Paris in 1832 by the Belgian theoretician François-Joseph Fétis (1784–1871), who spoke of a forthcoming "omnitonic" era in music history. A work of this period, Fétis theorized, would not be governed by a single key; tonality would instead fluctuate freely among keys linked by diminished chords. At some unknown date, Liszt composed a "Prélude omnitonique" which may have applied Fétis's ideas, but this work is now presumed lost. In 1885 he sketched an incomplete "Bagatelle Without Tonality": a highly simplified and repetitive work which mingles whole-tone, diminished, and octatonic configurations of pitches.

"Nuages gris" ("Grey Clouds," 1881; Example 1-9) is a more artistic example of Liszt's experimental style. This starkly abstract work makes no use of a traditional key, despite its key signature and emphasis on the notes of a G-minor triad. These three pitches—G, B♭, and D—are boundary points for the melodic lines, as in the opening figure in measures 1–2. But the G triad asserts its centricity no more than do the augmented triads that saturate measures 11–20 or the four-note dissonant figure that opens the work: D G C♯ (D) B♭ (G). The principles of harmonic organization of "Nuages gris" are not referable to those of common-practice tonality; they rely instead upon new methods of association to which we turn in the next chapter.

Example 1-9. Liszt, *Nuages gris*, measures 1–20. From the *Late Piano Works*, Vol. 1. © 1952 Schott & Co Ltd., London. All rights reserved. Used by permission of European American Music Distributors Corporation, sole U.S. agents for B. Schott's Soehne.

BIBLIOGRAPHY

Principles of tonal harmony are addressed in numerous textbooks on this subject, among which those by William Mitchell, Allen Forte, and Edward Aldwell and Carl Schachter are especially recommended. The Schenkerian view of tonality is outlined in Oswald Jonas's *Introduction to the Theory of Heinrich Schenker*, trans. and ed. John Rothgeb (New York, 1982) and in Adele Katz's *Challenge to Musical Tradition* (New York, 1945). Detailed guidelines for Schenkerian analyses are given in *Introduction to Schenkerian Analysis* by Allen Forte and Steven E. Gilbert (New York, 1982).

Schoenberg's two textbooks on harmony—*Theory of Harmony*, trans. Roy E. Carter (Berkeley, 1978) and *Structural Functions of*

Harmony, rev. ed. (New York, 1969)—deal primarily with tonal principles. The first of these is especially valuable for its exercises and examples of harmonic successions in the post-Wagnerian style.

The extent to which Schenker's unified conception of tonality is operative in works of the twentieth century is a matter of debate. Aspects of his analytic method are applied to post-tonal music by Felix Salzer in *Structural Hearing: Tonal Coherence in Music*, 2 vols. (New York, 1952) and by Robert Morgan in his article "Dissonant Prolongations: Theoretical and Compositional Precedents," *Journal of Music Theory*, 20 (1976). Also see James M. Baker, "Schenkerian Analysis and Post-Tonal Music" in *Aspects of Schenkerian Theory*, ed. David Beach (New Haven, 1983). Harald Krebs discusses nineteenth-century works that do not appear to be governed by a single tonic-dominant axis in his article "Alternatives to Monotonality in Early Nineteenth-Century Music," *Journal of Music Theory* 25 (1981).

Jim Samson's *Music in Transition: A Study of Tonal Expansion and Atonality, 1900–1920* (New York, 1977) is a valuable pioneering study of the transition of music from tonality to atonality. It covers a broad segment of musical literature from the early part of the century.

2

Harmonic and Motivic Associations and the "Emancipation of Dissonance"

Works discussed in the previous chapter show the gradual change in the role of dissonance during the second half of the nineteenth century. Its traditional function of prolonging or connecting consonant chords began to give way to a style in which dissonances were the central and referential units. This change contributed to the elimination of key and with it the chief unifying element in music of the preceding 200 years.

Prominent composers early in the twentieth century had a keen awareness of their place in the establishment of a new compositional order, and they also perceived that a new treatment of dissonance was the fulcrum by which the old order was to be toppled. In his Norton Lectures at Harvard University (1939–40), Igor Stravinsky called attention to this expanded role of dissonance:

> For over a century music has provided repeated examples of a style in which dissonance has emancipated itself. It is no longer tied down to its former function. Having become an entity in itself, it frequently happens that dissonance neither prepares nor anticipates anything. Dissonance is thus no more an agent of disorder than consonance is a guarantee of security. The music of yesterday and of today unhesitatingly unites parallel dissonant chords that thereby lose their functional value, and our ear quite naturally accepts their juxtaposition.

[From *Poetics of Music*. See the bibliography to Chapter 8 regarding the authenticity of this work.]

Arnold Schoenberg asserted the "comprehensibility" of dissonance in his lecture "Composition with Twelve Tones" (1941): "The term *emancipation of the dissonance* refers to its [dissonance's] comprehensibility, which is considered equivalent to the consonance's comprehensibility. A style based on this premise treats dissonances like consonances and renounces a tonal center."

In this chapter we shall survey aspects of structural unity in music where dissonance is "emancipated" and in which traditional key is absent. We shall first examine an atonal work by Schoenberg, but the analytic techniques that will be developed are general enough to apply to a broader geographical and chronological spectrum of modern music.

THE ROLE OF THE MOTIVE

Schoenberg, despite his extensive theoretical writings, did not make detailed or systematic explanations of the techniques of harmonic unity in his works characterized by the emancipation of dissonance. He was inclined instead to emphasize only one aspect of their construction, recurrent motivic variation, which was a feature they shared with earlier tonal composition. Schoenberg discusses the nature and use of motives in tonal music in his textbook *Fundamentals of Musical Composition*; these remarks serve equally well to describe his use of the motive in atonal music.

> The *motive* generally appears in a characteristic and impressive manner at the beginning of a piece. The features of a motive are intervals and rhythms, combined to produce a memorable shape or contour which usually implies an inherent harmony. Inasmuch as almost every figure within a piece reveals some relationship to it, the basic motive is often considered the "germ" of the idea. Since it includes elements, at least, of every subsequent musical figure, one could consider it the "smallest common multiple." And since it is included in every subsequent figure, it could be considered the "greatest common factor."
>
> However, everything depends on its use. Whether a motive be simple or complex, whether it consists of few or many features, the final impression of the piece is not determined by its primary form. Everything depends on its treatment and development.
>
> A motive appears constantly throughout a piece: *it is repeated.* [But] repetition alone often gives rise to *monotony*. Monotony can only be overcome by *variation*.

Example 2-1.   Schoenberg, Piano Piece Op. 23, No. 4. © 1923, renewed
1951, by Edition Wilhelm Hansen, Copenhagen. Reprinted by permission.

The main motives in a piece by Schoenberg are in themselves
unstable: they demand, as it were, to be varied and to spawn a network of interrelated forms such that any one occurrence will be a
variant of its preceding versions. A web of organically connected
statements of the basic motives is spun in a manner that Schoenberg
elsewhere termed "developing variations."

Schoenberg's Piano Piece Op. 23, No. 4 (1920–23; Anthology no.
6) will provide examples of his use of the motive in atonal composition. Three principal motives are found in the first measure, of
which the right-hand figure is most important. This central idea
returns in a series of exceedingly remote forms, of which one of the
most straightforward is in measures 12–13. Its relationship to the
original, illustrated by the juxtaposition of the two figures in
Example 2-1, is through its similar intervals, contour, and rhythm.
The right-hand motive of measure 2 is a varied recurrence of the
opening left-hand motive of measure 1, since they share similar
intervals and rhythms (Example 2-2). The succession of three pairs
of thirds which characterizes the second left-hand motive of the first
measure recurs in many varied forms, for example, the left-hand
part in measures 2–3, where the major thirds of measure 1 are con-
tracted to minor thirds or their inversion (Example 2-3).

Example 2-2.   Schoenberg, Piano Piece Op. 23, No. 4. © 1923, renewed
1951 by Edition Wilhelm Hansen, Copenhagen. Reprinted by permission.

m. 1

m. 2-3

Example 2-3.   Schoenberg, Piano Piece Op. 23, No. 4. © 1923, renewed 1951, by Edition Wilhelm Hansen, Copenhagen. Reprinted by permission.

HARMONIC RELATIONSHIPS

The harmonic logic of this work is more difficult to perceive, partly because the composer did not leave specific guidelines for its understanding and because there was no widely accepted or common harmonic practice at this time. Indeed, our first impression of the Piano Piece may well be that its pitches were chosen randomly or that the composer was guided solely by his desire to avoid conventional chords. There are no prominent triads or seventh chords in the entire work, and only fleetingly do we hear other dissonant combinations familiar from music of the past. The difficulty of comprehending harmonic relationships is made more acute by the dense and complicated texture, a rhythmic style that does not project a firm sense of pulse or stable metric organization, and the absence of clear sectional repetitions.

Nevertheless, Schoenberg frequently alluded to the presence of harmonic logic in his atonal works, although he was inclined to see this dimension as the product of an "unconscious" intuition rather than a systematic technique. He wrote of his nontonal musical style in his *Theory of Harmony*: "Every chord I put down corresponds to a necessity, to a necessity of my urge to expression; perhaps, however, also to the necessity of an inexorable but unconscious logic in the harmonic structure. I am firmly convinced that logic is present here too, at least as much so as in the previously cultivated fields of harmony."

In order to understand Schoenberg's harmonic language, we must first expand our idea of a "harmony" beyond its conventional meaning in the analysis of earlier music. Rather than a chord that can be arranged in superimposed thirds, a harmony (or *set*) will refer here to a collection of pitches that are associated by *adjacency* in some musical context—normally adjacent pitches found in a melodic idea or motive, a vertical chord, or a combination of the two.

This integration of vertical and linear structures is found in tonal music as well, but it is made more explicit in works of the post-tonal era. In his article "My Evolution," Schoenberg wrote, "A melodic line, a voice part, or even a melody derives from horizontal projections of tonal relations. A chord results similarly from projections in the vertical direction. . . . The main difference between harmony and melodic line is that harmony requires faster analysis, because the tones appear simultaneously, while in a melodic line more time is granted to synthesis, because the tones appear successively, thus becoming more readily graspable by the intellect."

Let us return to the principal motive of the right hand in measure 1 of Schoenberg's Piano Piece Op. 23, No. 4. In addition to presenting the potential for motivic development by virtue of its distinctive rhythm, meter, and contour, this linear element also represents a harmonic entity, which is characterized solely by its content of pitches and which will, like its motivic aspect, be subject to continuous "developing" variations.

Recurrence of Harmonies: Restatement, Transposition, Reordering, Inversion

The simplest form in which this harmony recurs is a *restatement*. In Example 2-4 we can compare the restatement in measures 33–34 to the original in measure 1. The pitches of both are identical, with the exception of the final E and G in measure 34, which appear an octave lower than before. Changes of register of this type produce at most a disruption in the motivic contour; they do not alter the underlying harmony. We shall consider all notes an octave apart to be structurally equivalent and introduce the term *pitch class* to refer to a representation of all notes of the same or enharmonically equivalent spelling.

We may now define the harmony of our basic motive by its six pitch classes: D♯ B B♭ D E G. Any set of six different pitch classes will be called a *hexachord*; a set of four, a *tetrachord*, and so forth. An atonal harmony is an abstraction since it has no musical contour or rhythmic shape. It takes on these features, however, when it is brought to life as a motive.

Example 2-4. Schoenberg, Piano Piece Op. 23, No. 4 © 1923, renewed 1951, by Edition Wilhelm Hansen, Copenhagen. Reprinted by permission.

A second means of varying the harmony is by *transposition*. Let us return to Example 2-1, in which we will see a recurrence in measures 12–13 of the principal set transposed up two semitones. This new version of the harmony is also assigned a musical configuration that strongly resembles the original motive in rhythm and contour.

A third and more remote method of variation of the basic harmony is accomplished by *reordering* its notes. In Example 2-5 we see the notes of the main set reordered in the right-hand figure in measure 24. One of the main compositional and structural changes in music by Schoenberg and others after about 1921 was the preservation of a fixed order within the linear presentation of a harmonic unit. Music of this type is said to be *serialized*, and it will be discussed in Chapter 4. But in the post-tonal idiom prior to 1921 and in nonserialized music after that time, reordering is a basic means of achieving variety.

The fourth principal means of harmonic variation is *inversion*, which will refer to a symmetric intervallic rotation about a fixed pitch within a set. An inversion of the basic harmony D♯ B B♭ D E G can be obtained, for example, by allowing the note D♯ to remain fixed and rotating the other elements around it symmetrically. Thus D♯ remains constant, B (four semitones below D♯) now becomes G (four semitones above D♯); B♭ (five semitones below D♯) becomes A♭ (five semitones above D♯), and so forth:

Basic Harmony

| B | D | E | A♭ | G | ⌐D♯⌐ | B | B♭ | D | E | G⌐ |

Inversion

Schoenberg makes little significant use of inversions of the basic harmony in the Piano Piece, but for purposes of illustration let us observe a group of pitches found in measures 4–5 (Example 2-6). The six pitch classes of this adjacency, with reordering for easier comparison, are B D E A♭ G D♯, thus the inversion of the basic harmony shown above.

m. 1

Principal Motive

m. 24

Reordering

Example 2-5.   Schoenberg, Piano Piece Op. 23, No. 4. © 1923, renewed 1951, by Edition Wilhelm Hansen, Copenhagen. Reprinted by permission.

Example 2-6. Schoenberg, Piano Piece Op. 23, No. 4. © 1923, renewed 1951, by Edition Wilhelm Hansen, Copenhagen. Reprinted by permission.

These four operations upon basic collections of pitches—restatement, transposition, reordering, and inversion—are manifested time and again not only in the music of Schoenberg, but also in works by Bartók, Scriabin, Stravinsky, and other masters of the atonal language. In fact, they are so commonly encountered that we may postulate that two collections of notes will be harmonically *equivalent* if the pitches of one collection can be made identical to those of the other collection by transposition, reordering, inversion, or a combination of these. (The identity of sets related by restatement is obvious.) This postulate of equivalence greatly simplifies the task of the analyst who seeks principles of harmonic unity in atonal music, since it reduces the number of families of equivalent sets to approximately 220—a sufficiently small number to allow their recurrence and interaction to be observed and interpreted.

Additional Harmonic Relationships:
Complementation, Inclusion, and Similarity

Schoenberg's Piano Piece provides excellent examples of relationships that can exist among nonequivalent harmonies. One of the strongest such relationships is *complementation*. Two sets are complementary if they have no pitch classes in common but together encompass the entire chromatic set. The complement of the basic harmony D♯ B B♭ D E G will be the hexachord C G♯ F♯ C♯ A F, since these pitches are precisely those six not found in the original set. Schoenberg clearly exploits the complement of the basic harmony near the beginning of the piece, in the right hand of measure 3 (Example 2-7).

An important relation that may obtain between sets of different sizes is *inclusion*. If the pitches of a smaller set are contained among those of a larger one, forming a *subset* of the larger collection, then the two are related in this way. The left-hand figure in measure 13 consists of the four notes B♭ G♭ A F. This tetrachord is contained in an accompanimental figure from measure 1, as is shown in Example 2-8.

Basic Set: D♯ B B♭ D E G

Complement: C G♯ F♯ C♯ A F

Example 2-7. Schoenberg, Piano Piece Op. 23, No. 4. © 1923, renewed 1951, by Edition Wilhelm Hansen, Copenhagen. Reprinted by permission.

Principal Accompanimental Set:
A♭ C G♭ B♭ A F

Subset: B♭ G♭ A F

Example 2-8. Schoenberg, Piano Piece Op. 23, No. 4. © 1923, renewed 1951, by Edition Wilhelm Hansen, Copenhagen. Reprinted by permission.

Nonequivalent harmonies may also be *similar* if they share common or equivalent subsets. In Schoenberg's Piano Piece, the three hexachords that underlie the three basic motives of measure 1 are similar in this way. In Example 2-9 these sets and their motives are labeled A, B, and C. The first four notes of motive A, the lowest four notes of motive B, and the last four notes of C are all transpositionally equivalent, which can readily be seen by comparing them in the reorderings that follow:

$$B♭ \; B \; D \; D♯ \text{ (from A)}$$
$$A \; B♭ \; D♭ \; D \text{ (from B)}$$
$$F \; G♭ \; A \; B♭ \text{ (from C)}$$

This family of equivalent tetrachords plays a central role in the Piano Piece, sometimes drawing more attention to itself than to the parent hexachords from which it emanates.

Schoenberg's Piano Piece is a remarkable example of the penetration of a few harmonies throughout an entire atonal composition. Virtually all pitches of the work can be divided into segments that are equivalent to hexachords A, B, C, or their complements. The recurrences of these sets within a complete section of the work—the coda-like passage in measures 29–35—are shown in Example 2-10. A few notes that would complicate the appearance of

A   D♯ B B♭ D E G

B   D B♭ A C F D♭

C   A♭ C G♭ B♭ A F

Example 2-9.   Schoenberg, Piano Piece Op. 23, No. 4. © 1923, renewed 1951, by Edition Wilhelm Hansen, Copenhagen. Reprinted by permission.

this example are not analytically interpreted, but these as well as all other pitches in this section are constituents of sets that are varied forms of A, B, or C. This coda contains a preponderance of sets that are identical in their content of pitches to measure 1, perhaps as an analogy to a tonal piece that returns at the end to its original tonic key.

TYPES OF HARMONIES

The harmonic languages of major atonal composers each contain distinctive and favored vocabularies of sets. Some of these musicians, including Hindemith, Stravinsky, and Britten, maintained triads and other conventional chords in their parlance. We shall return to these composers and their harmonic practice in Chapter 3.

We focus now on atonal works which rely upon harmonies that do not have a prominent place in tonal music. Probably more than any major composer of the first half of the century, Schoenberg avoided triadic sonorities. In his *Theory of Harmony* he describes his reluctance to use traditional chords in his post-tonal music, and he also betrays his excitement in the sheer number and diversity of harmonies newly available to the modern composer:

> There is perhaps also an instinctive (possibly exaggerated) aversion to recalling even remotely the traditional chords. For the same reason, apparently, the simple chords of the earlier harmony do not appear successfully in this environment. I believe, however, that there is another reason for their absence here. I believe they would sound too cold, too dry, expressionless. Or perhaps, what I mentioned on an earlier occasion applies here. Namely, that these simple chords, which are imperfect imitations of nature, seem to us too primitive. That they lack

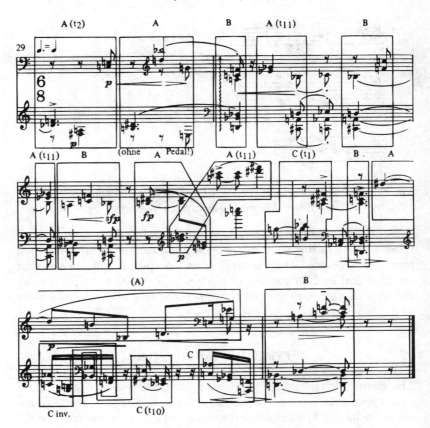

Example 2-10. Schoenberg, Piano Piece Op. 23, No. 4. Sets that are transposed relative to their first occurrence (see Example 2-9) are indicated by *t*, followed by the number of semitones above this first occurrence. © 1923, renewed 1951, by Edition Wilhelm Hansen, Copenhagen. Reprinted by permission.

something, which, for example, Japanese painting lacks when compared with ours: perspective, depth. Perspective and depth of sound could be what we find wanting in the simple three and four-part harmonies. And as in a picture one section can hardly show regard for perspective while another disregards it, without impairing the effect, so perhaps, analogously, these somewhat empty sounds cannot appear alongside those full, sumptuous sounds; whereas the exclusive use of the one *or* the other assures coherence, hence the right effect.

The survey of harmonies that follows is limited to the most distinctive and easily recognizable types. As such, it omits many of the favored harmonies of composers like Schoenberg who avoided musi-

Arnold Schoenberg, autograph sketches to the Piano Piece Op. 23, No. 4.
Schoenberg's analytic annotations are of special interest. (Courtesy of
Lawrence Schoenberg and the Arnold Schoenberg Institute.)

cal materials that might seem commonplace. One of Schoenberg's
most characteristic sets, for example, is the principal harmony of the
Piano Piece Op. 23, No. 4 (D♯ B B♭ D E G). His emphasis on this and its
equivalent sets may derive in part from the musical letters of his name:

S c h ö n b e r g outlines the German pitch names Es C H B E G, that is, E♭ C B B♭ E G. These notes are equivalent by inversion and transposition to the principal set of Op. 23, No. 4.

Symmetric and Quasi-Symmetric Sets: Whole-Tone and "Nearly-Whole-Tone" Hexachords, Octatonic Scales, and the Major/Minor Tetrachord

Among the various categories of dissonant harmonies that characterize atonal music, symmetric sets are some of the most important. A symmetric harmony is one whose pitches can be ordered so that they create the same succession of intervals read from either left or right. Although some such collections of notes (such as the diminished seventh chord) have use in tonal music, most tonal harmonies are asymmetric in their intervallic makeup.

Symmetric sets present the composer with restrictive harmonic resources. Some intervals may be entirely lacking in them and others all the more strongly represented. The augmented triad—a widely used symmetric set—illustrates this point. As shown in Example 2-11, the intervals of an augmented triad consist solely of major thirds or their inversions, minor sixths. The whole-tone scale, another familiar symmetric structure, contains only major seconds, major thirds, tritones, and their inversions, but no minor seconds, minor thirds, or perfect fourths. Thus any motive made up of notes from a whole-tone scale will be decidedly limited in the intervals available to it and all the more distinctive in its sound.

Symmetric sets are also more limited in their transpositional resources than diatonic collections. They are comparable to what Olivier Messiaen has called "modes of limited transposition," which are seven symmetric sets discussed further in Chapter 16. Each can be transposed to alternative pitch levels only a few times before the set repeats itself. The whole-tone scale, Messiaen's first mode of limited transposition, is a simple example: it can be transposed up one semitone and render a new set of six pitches, as shown below. But if it is transposed up two (or any even number) of semitones, it will produce the same collection of pitches as the original:

Whole-tone scale:	C	D	E	F♯	G♯	A♯	(C)
Transposition up one semitone:	C♯	D♯	F	G	A	B	(C♯)
Transposition up two semitones:	D	E	F♯	G♯	A♯	C	(D)

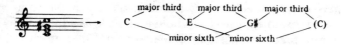

Example 2-11. Intervallic content of the augmented triad.

Each of the diatonic scales, on the contrary, can be transposed to all twelve pitch levels without replicating itself completely.

Symmetric sets, finally, do not produce distinct inversional forms; that is, any inversion of a symmetric set can also be generated by transposition. These restrictions on intervallic content, transposition, and inversion contribute to the relatively unvaried or static harmonic quality of music in which symmetric collections are central. But as the principal harmonic elements in a composition, these sets are powerful means by which the traditional expression of a key and the harmonic idiom of tonal music can be eliminated while still maintaining tonal coherence.

Composers of atonal music have used many different symmetric collections. We shall focus only on the most important and widespread of these—whole-tone and related sets, octatonic sets, and the major/minor tetrachord. We shall also describe subsets of these formations as parts of the same family of chords, although these subsets will not themselves always be symmetrical. The reader may be surprised to find the chromatic scale—a familiar symmetric formation—missing from this group. The chromatic scale or its contiguous segments have relatively little use as central elements in atonal music. The chromatic scale is too unrestrictive in its intervallic contents, since all intervals are contained in it at the maximum possible frequency. It has central importance only in experimental music such as tone-cluster compositions or in idioms where the harmonic principles outlined so far in this chapter are not operative. Chromatic clusters, however small, are rarely basic to the harmonic structure of an atonal composition: instead, they usually function as motivic details that often hide the more fundamental units.

The whole-tone scale and its subsets were increasingly in evidence in tonal music of the nineteenth century. The whole-tone set is encountered in this literature mainly through two of its subsets—the augmented triad and the French augmented sixth chord. These two chords continued to be used outside of a tonal context by early atonal composers. These and other whole-tone formations are seen as extensions of diatonic progressions in music by Russian composers of the nineteenth century (see Chapter 8) and by Western European composers, including Debussy, Dukas, Liszt, Strauss, Schoenberg, Mahler, and Berg.

Whole-tone sets continued to enjoy primacy in early atonal compositions. Berg, for example, uses the whole-tone scale as a means of unifying an entire piece in his song "Schlafend trägt man mich in mein Heimatland" Op. 2, No. 2 (ca. 1908–10). An excerpt from the beginning is shown in Example 2-12. Three- and four-note subsets of the whole-tone scale constitute every vertical chord. Occasionally, these dissonant chords will take on a decidedly familiar sound, as in the last measure of the song, where the bass note Eb supports a sonority identical to a dominant seventh without its fifth. Berg, unlike his teacher Schoenberg, did not reject the use of familiar triadic harmonies in his atonal music; such chords, however, have no traditional tonal function. They are integrated with other chords in the song by the operations of reordering and transposition, and, by the inclusion relationship, they derive their meaning from the master whole-tone set that dominates the entire harmonic dimension of the work.

Related to the whole-tone scale is a hexachord commonly used by composers of the modern French and Russian school as well as by the Viennese avant-garde. For lack of a better term, it will be called the "nearly-whole-tone hexachord." It is derived from a whole-tone scale by raising or lowering any one pitch. Its relationship to a whole-tone scale is shown in Example 2-13.

This collection is one of the harmonic trademarks of the music of Alexander Scriabin composed after about 1908. Its use in his sym-

Example 2-12. Berg, "Schlafend trägt man mich in mein Heimatland," Op. 2, No. 2, from *Vier Lieder für eine Singstimme mit Klavier.*

Example 2-13. Derivation of the "nearly-whole-tone" hexachord.

phony *Prometheus* (1910) has led to its being dubbed the *Prometheus* or "mystic" chord. The collection is sometimes described as a series of superimposed fourths, a conception that is doubtful since the fourth is not at all strongly represented in its total intervallic content and is far outweighed by whole-tone intervals of the major second, major third, and their inversions.

Scriabin's Piano Sonata No. 10 (1913) is based upon subsets of this harmony or of other sets similar to it. The principal theme of the work is heard in measures 1–8: at the midpoint of the theme (Example 2-14) a five-note figure is presented, which lacks only B♭ to make up an inversion of the "mystic" chord. The B♭ is then added at the cadence of this phrase in measures 7–8 (Example 2-15), making the central hexachord explicit.

The nearly-whole-tone hexachord also plays a central role in Berg's opera *Wozzeck*. Acts 1 and 3 are ended by the sonority F G A B C♯ D, which is a form of this hexachord (compare it to the set in Example 2-15 transposed down one semitone). In a lecture on *Wozzeck*, Berg likened this chord to a cadential or tonic point of rest in a tonal composition. It functions in this way not only in the absolute musical sense, but also as a dramatic-musical summation

F♯ A♭ [B♭] C D E♭*

Example 2-14. Scriabin, Piano Sonata No. 10. *Henceforth, sets will be stated in their *normal order*, which is a scalewise representation covering the smallest possible total span.

F♯ A♭ B♭ C D E♭

Example 2-15. Scriabin, Piano Sonata No. 10.

of the story of the opera. The harmony is used elsewhere as an asso-
ciative reference to the character Wozzeck, and its component pitch
classes and intervals are referentially linked to the main events of
Wozzeck's downfall.

The *octatonic* set may be viewed as a scalewise alternation of half
and whole steps; one such form of this collection is illustrated in
Example 2-16. The octatonic scale has many distinctive properties. It
contains, for example, all of the intervals, although the minor third
and its inversion are most frequently represented. It also contains a
large inventory of subsets, including familiar diatonic chords
(major, minor, and diminished triads; dominant, diminished, half-
diminished, and minor sevenths).

Octatonic scales were used in passing in music by several major
nineteenth-century composers, including Liszt, Mikhail Glinka,
and Nikolai Rimski-Korsakov, among whom it usually functioned
as a colorful embellishment of diatonic music. Octatonic sets
became central to the harmonic organization of music by numerous
early atonal composers, for example, Stravinsky and Scriabin, and
they were also prominent in atonal works by Busoni, Bartók,
Debussy, and Ravel. Among later figures, Messiaen has emphasized the octatonic collection, which he calls the second mode of
limited transposition. It has also been adopted by modern jazz
musicians, who sometimes refer to it as a "diminished" scale. It has
much less use, on the other hand, in the music of Schoenberg or his
followers.

An example of a work based upon predominantly octatonic
structures is Bartók's Piano Suite Op. 14, third movement (1916).
This fiery perpetuum mobile opens with fragments of two octatonic
collections in counterpoint (Example 2-17); these lines subsequently
flesh out more of their underlying scales. The contrasting middle
section (measures 60–84) is introduced by a passage in measures
50–59 with a ringing succession of F♯-, A-, and C-minor triads. These
arise as subsets of a transposition of the octatonic set shown in
Example 2-18. This transposition accounts for virtually every note of
the middle section until measure 80.

The octatonic scale contains a four-note subset that is often
encountered in atonal music, either in the context of this larger set or
independent of it. This harmony will be called the *major/minor tetrachord*, since it may be viewed as a statement of both major and minor

Example 2-16.   The octatonic scale.

Example 2-17. Bartók, Suite Op. 14, third movement. Copyright 1918 by Universal-Edition. Renewed 1945. Copyright and renewal assigned to Boosey & Hawkes, Inc. Reprinted by permission.

Example 2-18. Octatonic source of triads in Bartók's Suite Op. 14, third movement.

Example 2-19. The major/minor tetrachord

forms of a single triad (Example 2-19). One attraction of this collection for the early atonal composers was its strong aural relation to
the triad. It is used prominently by Igor Stravinsky in his cantata
Zvezdoliki (1912). The piece begins with a motto-like succession of
three chords setting the word "Zvezdoliki" ("the starry-eyed one")
(Example 2-20). The first of these chords is the major/minor tetrachord, which subsequently recurs with its pungent sonority at the
end of the first line of text (measure 7) and repeatedly among the
powerfully scored verticalities accompanying the prophecies of this
"king of the stars" (measures 27–33).

All-Interval Tetrachords, Fourth Chords, and Pentatonic Scales

All-interval tetrachords have proved to be among the most favored
harmonies of atonal composers from early in the century to the present day. These collections derive their name from the fact that they
contain each of the six basic intervals (minor second, major second,
minor third, major third, perfect fourth, and tritone) or their inversions. All-interval tetrachords may be reduced in number to only
two nonequivalent types, which are shown in Example 2-21. Let us

Example 2-20.   Stravinsky, Le roi des étoiles.

focus on type A to illustrate how this set contains all of the basic intervals. If we pair off each of its notes with each other note, we will see the six basic intervals:

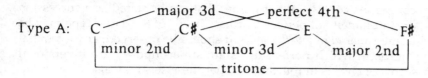

Both types of all-interval tetrachords have been frequently employed by the contemporary American composer Elliott Carter. His First String Quartet (1951) in fact uses these sets as elements of focus throughout the entire work. Their occurrence in the opening measures is illustrated in Example 2-22.

In "Shop Talk by an American Composer," Carter describes his application of an all-interval tetrachord in this work; although he recognizes the use of only one of the two types, both are in evidence:

> In my First String Quartet, I did use a "key" four-note chord, one of the two four-note groups, that joins all the two-note intervals into pairs, thus allowing for the total range of interval qualities that still can be referred back to a basic chord-sound. This chord is not used at

Example 2-21. The all-interval tetrachords.

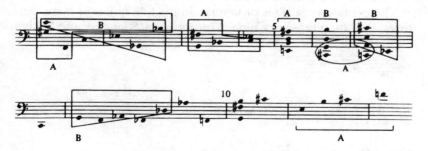

Example 2-22. Carter, First String Quartet, first movement, measures 1–12 (cello), rhythm omitted. Copyright 1955, 1956 by Associated Music Publishers, Inc. All rights reserved. Reprinted by permission.

every moment in the work but occurs frequently enough, especially in important places, to function, I hope, as a formative factor.

A family of sets that had particular importance to early atonal composers consists of harmonies that can be stated as a succession or simultaneity of perfect fourths. Chords of this latter type may be termed *quartal* or *fourth chords*. It should be observed, however, that chords in which perfect fifths are superimposed are inversional forms of chords in fourths and that these sets may also be encountered in motives that move through intervals other than fourths. Quartal harmonies had a broad currency among transitional composers to the atonal idiom and among neoclassicists in Europe and America in the period between the world wars. They are occasionally found in tonal music, where they displace triads. A memorable example of the latter is the introduction to the finale of Beethoven's *Pastoral* Symphony (measures 5–8) where the superimposed fifths in the cello, viola, and horn are created by suspension between a dominant and a tonic harmony.

If the interval class of the fourth is compounded, it will duplicate the entire chromatic set before repeating any pitches. For practical reasons, we will limit our discussion to three-, four-, and five-note quartal harmonies, which are those most frequently encountered. These are shown in Example 2-23. The first two measures of Paul Hindemith's "Ragtime" from his Suite "1922" are made up from fourth chords of the three-note type or its subset, the minor seventh (Example 2-24). The quartal trichord is heard throughout the piece, although Hindemith also exploits whole-tone sets, bitriadic chords (see Chapter 3), and diatonic harmonies in this work.

The *pentatonic scale* consists, as its name suggests, of five notes (Example 2-25); its intervals may be easily recalled since an equivalent set is created by any five adjacent black keys on the piano. It is also a subset of both the major and minor scales.

The pentatonic scale is prominent in the folk music of many cultures, including those of China, Africa, Russia, Scotland, and Native

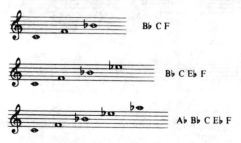

Example 2-23.   Quartal harmonies.

Example 2-24. Hindemith, 1922: *Suite für Klavier.* © B. Schott's Soehne, Mainz, 1922; © renewed Schott & Co, Ltd., London, 1950. Used by permission of European American Music Distributors Corp., sole U.S. agent for B. Schott's Soehne.

Example 2-25. Pentatonic scale.

America. It colors many well-known melodies of Western music, often lending them the flavor of folk song. The pentatonic scale and its subsets became a great harmonic and melodic resource in music of the twentieth century by Bartók, Debussy, and Ravel. For Bartók it established a link between his own work and peasant songs of Eastern Europe, in which this scale was very common. The pentatonic element in Debussy and Ravel may reflect their interest in Russian and other exotic folk cultures.

The pentatonic set is related to diatonic harmony since it is a subset of diatonic scales. It is also closely allied to quartal harmony, since the five-note fourth chord (see Example 2-23) is a pentatonic collection. These relationships were exploited by several major composers of the twentieth century, for example, by having a pentatonic melody accompanied by a succession of fourth chords. The opening of the middle section of Debussy's Saraband from *Pour le piano* (Anthology no. 2, measures 23–26) contains a straightforward example.

Not all major composers of the twentieth century have shared Schoenberg's enthusiasm for the resources and richness of dissonant harmony. Others have maintained the necessity of preserving the triad as the harmonic basis for music in this century. On this matter Paul Hindemith wrote in his *Craft of Musical Composition*, Volume 1:

> Music, as long as it exists, will always take its departure from the major triad and return to it. The musician cannot escape it any more than the painter his primary colors or the architect his three dimensions. In composition, the triad or its direct extensions can never be avoided for more than a short time without completely confusing the listener.

Thus we turn in Chapter 3 to the subject of triadic harmony and tonality.

BIBLIOGRAPHY

The conception of harmonic relationships described in this chapter is largely derived from Allen Forte's *Structure of Atonal Music* (New Haven, 1973). Numerous applications of this approach to twentieth-century music may be found in periodicals such as the *Journal of Music Theory*, *Music Theory Spectrum*, *Music Analysis*, *Perspectives of New Music*, and *Musical Quarterly*. Forte's article "Schoenberg's Creative Evolution: The Path to Atonality," *Musical Quarterly*, 64 (1978), is especially recommended, as is Janet Schmalfeldt's chapter "Pitch-Class Set Theory: Historical Perspective" from her book *Berg's* Wozzeck (New Haven, 1983). Joel Lester's *Analytic Approaches to Twentieth-Century Music* (New York, 1989) deals with pitch structures in post-tonal and serial music.

Schoenberg's observations on the structure of his atonal works are found in various essays and lectures in *Style and Idea*, ed. Leonard Stein (Berkeley, 1984) and in *Arnold Schönberg Gesammelte Schriften*, Vol. 1, ed. Ivan Vojtěch (n.p., Fischer, 1976). Schoenberg's analysis of his Orchestral Songs Op. 22 is typical of his approach to the discussion of his post-tonal works; an English translation by Claudio Spies is found in *Perspectives of New Music*, 3 (1965). Schoenberg's *Fundamentals of Musical Composition* (New York, 1967) deals with tonal composition, but it is also a valuable guide to post-tonal musical form. His article "My Evolution" appears in *Musical Quarterly*, 38 (1952), and the concluding chapters to his *Theory of Harmony* touch upon aspects of early atonal composition.

Major writings by the following composers on their own music are cited in bibliographies to these chapters: Stravinsky (Chapter 8); Bartók (Chapter 9); Messiaen (Chapter 16); Carter (Chapter 13). Alban Berg's lecture on *Wozzeck* is found in Hans F. Redlich, *Alban Berg: The Man and His Music* (London, 1957).

3

Triadic Harmony, Diatonic Collections, and Tonality

Schoenberg's rejection of triads, familiar seventh chords, and diatonic scales proved the exception rather than the rule in the twentieth century. By far the majority of composers have maintained
familiar chords in their harmonic vocabulary, even though their customary diatonic functions have often been ignored or reinterpreted.

In the work of composers who continue to write tonal music in
the twentieth century, triads and seventh chords are to be expected.
But the triad and its extensions are also found repeatedly in music of
this century that uses dissonance in a liberated manner and that
bypasses the tonic-dominant axis and other trappings of common-
practice tonality. We focus first upon the use of these harmonies
where they do not primarily express key.

TRIADS AND TRIADIC EXTENSIONS

Triads are especially prevalent in works by turn-of-the-century composers such as Debussy or figures such as Hindemith, Stravinsky,
Satie, or Prokofiev, whose music maintains contact with traditional
tonality and form. They may also be found as central harmonies in
music that is entirely atonal. A common function of the triad in such

works is to mark the beginning or end of major sections of a piece. The familiar sound of the triad thus articulates the structure of a work much as perfect consonances did in early polyphony.

A striking example of a triad signaling the end of an entire atonal composition is the conclusion of Scriabin's symphonic poem *Prometheus*. This esoterically programmatic work emphasizes the nearly-whole-tone hexachord mentioned in the previous chapter, a harmony commonly known as the *Prometheus* or "mystic" chord after its appearance in this work. Example 3-1 shows the string parts at the end of this symphony. At rehearsal 63 we hear the nearly-whole-tone set (F Gb Ab Bb C D), which moves by the end to an F#-major triad. This is the first occurrence in the entire piece of a major or minor triad, which—by its uniqueness—emphatically marks the end of the work.

All forms of *seventh chords* continue to play an important part in music of this century. Five types of diatonic seventh chords were inherited from common-practice music: the dominant seventh (for example, C E G Bb), minor seventh (C Eb G Bb), major seventh (C E G B), diminished seventh (C Eb Gb Bbb), and half-diminished seventh (C Eb Gb Bb). With the removal of tonality, new relationships among these chords emerge. The half-diminished seventh, for example, is related to the dominant seventh by symmetric inversion, as illustrated in Example 3-2. This intervallic kinship has no analogy in tonal harmony, since the chords have very different functions in the expression of key.

Of the five types of seventh chords, the dominant is least often encountered in atonal twentieth-century music, probably because of the directness by which it defines a key. Chains of parallel dominant sevenths are nevertheless common in the music of Debussy, where they usually serve to enhance a melodic line.

The half-diminished seventh was exceedingly prominent in music around the turn of the century, both in late romantic music and in early or transitional atonal works. This chord is one of the mainstays of Wagner's harmonic language; perhaps its best-known occurrence in his work is the so-called *Tristan* chord, from the Prelude to Act 1 of *Tristan und Isolde* (1857–59). The *Tristan* chord is enharmonically equivalent to the half-diminished seventh (Example 3-3). Its memorable sound and well-known association with the dramatic basis of the opera—the yearning for fulfillment of love—made it and its like-sounding seventh chord fundamental to music of the generation after Wagner.

The half-diminished seventh plays a leading role in tonal music of the early years of the twentieth century. Yet only rarely does it fulfill its normative diatonic function as a seventh chord on the second

Example 3-1. Scriabin, *Prometheus*, conclusion.

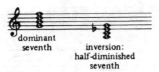

Example 3-2. Inversional relationship of dominant and half-diminished seventh chords.

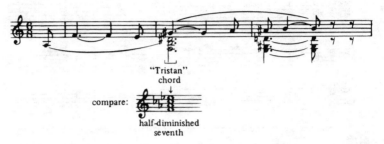

Example 3-3. Tristan chord and half-diminished seventh.

scale degree in minor, preparing the dominant. Instead, it is most often encountered as a harmony produced by stepwise or common-tone connection within parts which prolong an earlier diatonic chord. In measure 6 of Fauré's song "Dans la forêt de septembre" (Anthology no. 10), the half-diminished seventh (ø7) serves to prolong the dominant harmony as the bass moves down by step in parallel tenths with an inner voice (Example 3-4).

A work in the post-Wagnerian idiom which makes even more extensive use of the half-diminished seventh is Schoenberg's "Song of the Wood Dove" from *Gurrelieder* (1900–11). This chord harmonizes the motive of Tove's death (Example 3-5), which recurs throughout the song in rondo fashion amid stretches that freely express a succession of keys. The chord is only weakly related to any diatonic function. It serves instead as an independent motto or "emancipated" dissonance.

The minor seventh chord is often encountered outside of a tonal context in music using pentatonic melodies or harmonies, since it is a subset of the pentatonic scale. A typical occurrence in early twentieth-century French music is in Debussy's piano prelude "La fille aux cheveux de lin" ("The Girl with the Flaxen Hair"). A minor seventh chord is spelled out melodically as the initial motive of the main theme (Example 3-6). But this chord has no traditional tonal function as a seventh chord. Instead it represents a conflation of triads of the two primary tonal centers of the piece, Gb and Eb. It also creates a four-note subset of the pentatonic scale, which would be

Example 3-4.   Fauré, *Dans la forêt de septembre*, measures 6–8.

Example 3-5.   Schoenberg, "Song of the Wood Dove," from *Gurrelieder*, part I. Copyright 1912 by Universal Edition for world excluding U.S.A. Copyright renewed 1940. All rights reserved. Used by permission of European American Music Distributors Corporation, sole U.S. agent for Universal Edition. Used by permission of Belmont Music Publishers, Los Angeles (U.S.A.).

Example 3-6.   Debussy, "The Girl with the Flaxen Hair," from *Préludes*, book 1, measures 1–3.

completed by adding to it the note A♭. The pentatonic scale and its subsets subsequently underlie all melodic material (and much of the harmony) of the entire piece.

The major seventh chord has great prominence in the music of Igor Stravinsky. In the Credo from his Mass (1944–48, Anthology no. 23), virtually all cadences of the middle section (rehearsal 27–32) settle on this harmony in the form D F♯ A C♯.

Seventh chords are familiar four-note extensions of the triad. They are examples of a larger group of four-note harmonies containing triads that will be termed *triadic tetrachords*. Many such tetrachords are encountered in atonal music, so many, in fact, that a systematic examination of them is in order. Imagine a composition that ends with the chord C E G D. This has a euphonious sound devoid of minor seconds, tritones, and major sevenths. Think of how different the effect would be if the composer ended the same work with the chord C E G C♯. This sonority, although it contains a C-major triad like the previous one, has an entirely different and more biting effect on account of the presence of the minor second C–C♯ and the tritone G–C♯. It would be useful to distinguish these triadic tetrachords based on such intervallic properties.

We can, in fact, make distinctions among categories of tetrachords by returning to the notion, introduced in Chapter 2, of families of equivalent sets. Recall that sets can be thought of as equivalent if their tones can be made identical by some combination of transposition, symmetric inversion, or reordering. If the chord C E G D mentioned above were transposed and reordered to become D F♯ E A, it would still have the same quality of sound as before, devoid of minor seconds, tritones, or major sevenths. If this chord is further varied by symmetric inversion—giving it, for example, the form G C B♭ D—it still maintains this same sonorous quality. It is reasonable to assign all three of these tetrachords to a single family.

The hundreds of possible triadic tetrachords can be reduced by the principle of equivalence to only nine families, which are synoptically illustrated in Example 3-7. One harmony within each family—the one having a C-major triad embedded in it—is used in this example to illustrate its entire class. The C-major triad is shown in white noteheads; the fourth note in a black notehead. An inversion of this representative member is then shown after the broken bar line, specifically, the inversion that has a C-minor triad within it. Although inversion does not change the family of a set, the inverted forms are shown separately in the diagram since they often have a distinct quality of sound. Consider family 1 as an example of how these inversions are obtained. Begin with the tetrachord C E G B

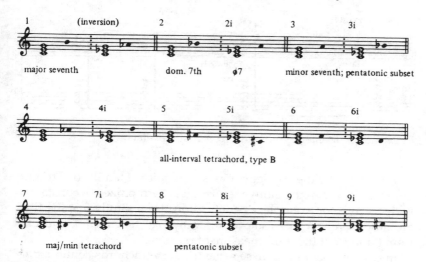

Example 3-7. The nine families of triadic tetrachords.

and allow the tone C to be fixed. An inversion can be produced (see Chapter 2) by symmetrically rotating the three higher pitches below the fixed C. The set C A♭ F D♭ results. By reordering the tones of this inversion as F A♭ C D♭, it is apparent that the inversion is equivalent to the one labelled 1i (C E♭ G A♭). They are related by reordering and transposition at the interval of a fourth or fifth. In fact, any inversion of a tetrachord containing a major triad will contain a minor triad, since major and minor triads are themselves inversionally related.

Many familiar triadic tetrachords are found in the nine families. The families numbered 1, 2, and 3 in Example 3-7 contain seventh chords. Family 5 consists of forms of all-interval tetrachords (see Example 2-21, type B), family 7 contains major/minor tetrachords, and families 3 and 8 contain subsets of the pentatonic scale. All of the nine types were basic to the harmonic practices of composers of early atonal music. Families 4 and 9, for example, are especially prominent in the music of Schoenberg, Berg, Webern, and Bartók.

The historical process by which triadic tetrachords became established in atonal harmony shows the importance of melodic embellishing tones in the new harmonic order. A motive near the opening of Mahler's Symphony No. 3 (1895–96) contains an appoggiatura figure that creates triadic tetrachords that call attention to themselves as quasi-independent harmonies. This reveille motive is first heard at rehearsal 4, pitting a C♯ in the trumpets against an underlying tonic D-minor chord (Example 3-8). The appoggiatura tone is extended to nearly three measures before resolving to D, and the

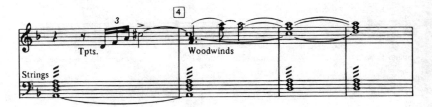

Example 3-8.   Mahler, Symphony No. 3, first movement.

chord created by the appoggiatura is a member of family 4i of triadic tetrachords. When the motive returns, it is harmonized in constantly varied ways, for example, as a tetrachord from family 5 at the fifth measure of rehearsal 7, one from family 7 at rehearsal 9, and one from family 9 at the third measure of rehearsal 17.

In early atonal music these same triadic tetrachords continued to be employed, but usually without resolution to underlying diatonic triads. An atonal work almost totally built on triadic tetrachords is Scriabin's Piano Prelude Op. 74, No. 4 (1914). The first four measures (Example 3-9) show the rich intervallic variety that the composer achieves by moving quickly among five different families of triadic tetrachords. Beneath this highly differentiated surface, however, lies a strict homogeneity and coherence provided by the ever-present triadic subset. Family 7 (containing major/minor tetrachords) plays a central articulative role in this piece, as it is heard at the beginning and end of the first phrase and also at the end of the work. The middle section (measures 11–17) dwells upon tetrachords from family 4.

Triadic tetrachords are also basic to the harmonic vocabulary of composers such as Berg and Hindemith, who maintained a strong allegiance to the triad. They are among the most prominent harmonies described in Hindemith's *Craft of Musical Composition*, Volume 1, in which the author attempts to devise a unified conception of harmony that includes both traditional chords and the expanded harmonic resources of the twentieth century. Hindemith derived six groups of chords with varying degrees of "harmonic tension." Five triadic tetrachords appear in his Group III, which plays an especially large role in his music.

Bitriadic harmonies create another category of atonal sets based upon the triad. A bitriadic harmony is one in which two triads (or seventh chords) are heard simultaneously or closely associated, these triads made distinct by separation of register or difference in timbre. Such chords held a great attraction for atonal composers who wished to keep the triad as a sonorous reference. They are prominently used in the early ballets of Stravinsky. The *Petrushka*

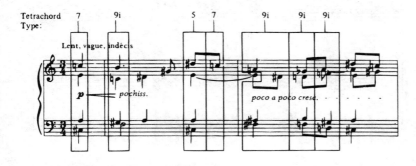

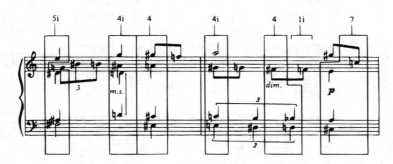

Example 3-9.   Scriabin, Prelude Op. 74, No. 4, measures 1–4.

chord, heard in this work at rehearsal 49 and elsewhere, combines major triads on C and F♯, and the "Augurs of Spring" chord from *The Rite of Spring* (rehearsal 13) joins an F♭ triad in the lower register to an E♭ dominant seventh in a higher register. Stravinsky's use of these two chords will be discussed further in Chapter 8. Just as the appearance of a triad does not in itself establish a tonality, the occurrence of bitriadic chords does not alone posit "bitonality," a phenomenon to be discussed shortly.

Charles Ives's song "From *Paracelsus*" (Anthology no. 12) uses a bitriadic harmony as a means of transition. This song begins with densely scored dissonances, which give way in the middle to a progression in G major. The linking of these two sections in measure 15 is facilitated by a chord made up of C- and D-minor triads (Example 3-10).

This transitional passage includes two other chords which are harmonically equivalent to the bitriadic formation of measure 15. These are heard on the words "blind" (measure 13) and on "shun" (measure 14). The diagram in Example 3-11 shows the relationship of the three chords, which are equivalent by transposition or inver-

Example 3-10. Ives, "From *Paracelsus*," © 1935 by Merion Music Inc. Used by permission of the publisher.

measure 13

measure 14

(inversion)

bitriadic
harmony:

measure 15

Example 3-11. Harmonic equivalences in Ives's "From *Paracelsus.*" © 1935
by Merion Music, Inc. Used by permission of the publisher.

sion. Ives's presentation of them helps to accomplish an orderly
transition from the dissonance of the opening to the triadic middle
section. The appearance of the chord in measure 13 is ordered in
such a way that its triadic subsets are not readily audible. In its second appearance in measure 14, we find its two triads separated in
register but still closely positioned. By measure 15, the equivalent
chord is stated as a true bitriadic configuration, with its constituent
triads clearly audible as separate units.

MODALITY

In twentieth-century composition, *modality* refers to the occurrence of
a set of pitches of which one is asserted as central or "tonic." *Modes*
are synonymous with the collection of pitches in effect, provided that
one note is shown (often as the first note in a scalar arrangement) as
central. Modes thus join two independent structural principles of
modern music: the pitch-class set and pitch centricity. This latter phenomenon will be discussed shortly under the rubric of "tonality."

Any set can be treated modally by consistently emphasizing one
of its pitch classes. The pentatonic set in music by Zoltán Kodály, for
example, is often encountered in a musical context where one of its

pitch classes is emphasized. This note is usually the one falling a minor third below the cluster of two whole steps found in all penta-tonic sets (Example 3-12). Kodály's use of this pentatonic mode reflects his study of Hungarian peasant music, in which repertory it underlies the oldest melodies.

But modality in the twentieth century is most important among diatonic sets, that is, among collections of seven pitch classes equiv-alent to the notes of a major or minor scale. Since there are seven pitch classes in the diatonic set, there can be seven modes created from it by asserting each of its elements as tonic.

These seven modes are often called the "church modes" because of their similarities to the modes of medieval and Renaissance music. Contemporary terminology regarding the modes, however, has relatively little historical basis. We shall focus now solely upon the twentieth-century idea of the church modes.

The most common names currently in use to designate the seven church modes are Dorian, Phrygian, Lydian, Mixolydian, Aeolian, Locrian, and Ionian. Each refers to a scale duplicating the order of half and whole steps occurring without accidentals above the tonics D, E, F, G, A, B, and C, respectively (Example 3-13).

These modes are encountered in the work of composers such as Béla Bartók, Claude Debussy, Ralph Vaughan Williams, Jean Sibelius, and Carl Nielsen, all of whom sought to imitate early music or folk song. In their works modality is primarily a melodic phe-nomenon. The finale of Vaughan Williams's *Pastoral* Symphony, for example, contains a principal theme in the Dorian mode on D

Example 3-12.   The pentatonic mode of old Hungarian peasant music.

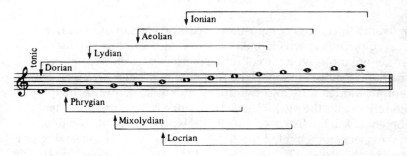

Example 3-13.   The seven diatonic modes.

(Example 3-14). Despite the chromatic inflection of the note B♭ near the end of the melody, its pitch content generally duplicates that of the natural diatonic set. The note D is heard as a tonic because of its frequency of recurrence, its use as the last note, and its metric emphasis in several measures; D is also reinforced by the prominence of its dominant note, A, toward the beginning.

Modality in twentieth-century music normally exerts less influence on the harmonic than on the melodic dimension. Modal melodies are sometimes harmonized by triads within the mode, which may be strung together in root position. The opening of Bartók's Bagatelle Op. 6, No. 4 (Example 3-15), is of this type. Its theme is a folk song in the Aeolian mode on D, which is harmonized in the first two measures by a succession of root position triads. These chords express the centricity of D much more dimly than does the melody, since the mode lacks a dominant chord with leading tone which could strongly direct the harmonic motion toward a cadential tonic. The next phrase (measures 3–4) uses the same outer voices for the first two measures, only enriching the sound of the triads by the addition of sevenths and ninths.

Other harmonizations of modal themes by twentieth-century composers make few references to the structure of the melody. They are instead entirely atonal. In Bartók's *Improvisation* Op. 20, No. 7 (Example 9-2), a Hungarian peasant melody in the Phrygian mode on C is elaborated by a harmonic setting that does not refer to the modality of the theme. The accompanimental chords draw freely upon all chromatic pitches, and the note C does not receive special

Example 3-14. Vaughan Williams, *Pastoral* Symphony, fourth movement, finale, measures 21–28. Copyright 1924 by J. Curwen & Sons Ltd. U.S. copyright renewed 1952. Used by arrangement with G. Schirmer, Inc., U.S. agent for J. Curwen & Sons Ltd., London.

Example 3-15. Bartók, Bagatelle Op. 6, No. 4, measures 1–4.

emphasis. The principal chords, furthermore, are not subsets of the diatonic collection.

A phenomenon related to modality is the use of a diatonic set—normally the notes of a C-major scale—without the assertion of a clear and stable tonic which would posit a mode. The term *pandiatonicism* was coined by Nicolas Slonimsky to identify this technique, which was prefigured in works by Debussy and Satie and used extensively in music of Stravinsky and other neoclassicists in the 1920s and 1930s.

The opening of Debussy's piano prelude "La cathédrale engloutie" ("The Sunken Cathedral") uses all notes of the C-major scale, but projects no tonic note by which a key or mode could be inferred (Example 3-16). As in much of Debussy's diatonic music, pentatonic subsets are emphasized (for example, the quarter notes of the first measure constitute one of the three pentatonic sets—D E G A B—contained in a C-major scale). These pitches are arranged into chords in open fourths and fifths, which help to create the effect of a "gently sonorous mist" mentioned at the beginning of the score. The pandiatonic collection of pitches is not at all static. Harmonic motion is strongly directed by the bass line, which moves inexorably downward by step from the initial bass note G to B at the beginning of the middle section (measure 16).

Example 3-16. Debussy, "La cathédrale engloutie" ("The Sunken Cathedral") from *Préludes*, book 1, measures 1–6.

TONALITY AND ATONALITY

There is no term in twentieth-century musical theory that has received more varied interpretations than *tonality*. The word is most commonly used in two ways, one specific, the other general. In the former sense it refers to the expression of key by methods that were common among composers of the eighteenth and nineteenth centuries. Some of these techniques were outlined in Chapter 1. In the latter and more general sense, it refers to the power of one or a few pitches to be heard through some span of a piece as central to its organization.

Common-practice tonality has continued to exist in this century, although as a relatively minor phenomenon. Many composers who were trained in the nineteenth century, such as Richard Strauss, chose to continue their earlier approach to key rather than to follow the more general trend away from traditional tonality. Certain works by European and American neoclassicists of the years between the world wars are also of this type, and in the 1970s, 1980s, and 1990s composers such as David Del Tredici and George Rochberg have written tonal music.

Music that does not express a key by these compositional principles is *atonal*. This term was first used in German musical criticism shortly before 1920 to refer pejoratively to a variety of modern works. The definition given shortly thereafter by the Viennese composer and theorist Josef Matthias Hauer in his *Lehrbuch der atonalen Musik* (1923) is still usable: "In atonal music there is no longer tonic, dominant, subdominant, scale step, resolution, consonance, or dissonance: instead, only the twelve intervals of equal temperament. Its 'scale' consists of twelve tempered semitones."

Although Hauer readily accepted the term "atonal" to describe his music, it was rejected by Schoenberg and his circle because of its negative connotation. In a radio dialogue titled "What is Atonality?" (1930), Alban Berg deemed the term "diabolical" since it falsely implied a rejection of all older musical values and structural principles. Berg concluded that much atonal music was unpopular not because of its lack of key, but because of the absence of triadic consonances. Schoenberg, the first important composer to be closely associated with atonal music, did not settle upon any special term to designate it. His description of what others called atonality (see the quotation near the beginning of Chapter 2) was simple and succinct: it was a style in which dissonance is used like consonance and in which there is no tonal center. Atonality is nevertheless a useful term, and it has long shed whatever pejorative connotations it possessed earlier. It will be used in this book to designate twentieth-century music that is nontonal and nonserialized.

In a more general sense, tonality refers to the centricity of one or a few pitches in parts of a musical work. Under this definition, virtually all music in Western history is to some degree tonal. The most common way such tonality is expressed in the twentieth century is by *assertion*, that is, by repeating a central pitch or otherwise emphasizing it by means of instrumentation, register, rhythmic elongation, or metric accent. Tonality by assertion is normally heard in the thematic or linear dimension of an otherwise "atonal" work. The third movement of Bartók's Piano Suite Op. 14 (opening measures in Example 2-17) strongly asserts the note D as its tonic by frequent recurrences, metric emphasis, placement in the lowest register of the piano, and by priority of place as the first and last note of themes and accompanimental lines.

Other twentieth-century works express a "key" by maintaining vestiges of common-practice tonality, for example, beginning and ending on the same triad, references to dominant or tonic pedal points, or contrapuntal motion within or around some central chord (often a triad). Such references are usually insufficient to establish a key in the traditional manner, and the musician must rely upon careful listening to judge whether the work is tonal or atonal. No single approach to tonality by assertion has become widespread in this century.

Key signatures may be found in twentieth-century music that is either tonal or atonal. A key signature does not create a key. It only simplifies notation, reducing the need for accidentals. Signatures imply that a diatonic collection of seven pitch classes has greater frequency or priority over the remaining five pitch classes. In atonal music that avails itself freely of all twelve pitch classes—as in the post-tonal works of Schoenberg—key signatures are usually not found. But works that emphasize a single diatonic set or subset may use a signature to simplify notation despite little or no reference to a key. The "Augurs of Spring" from Stravinsky's ballet *Rite of Spring*, for example, uses a signature of three flats, despite its lack of significant references to a key. The bass line at rehearsal 16 and 28 dwells on the notes B♭ and E♭, but this suggestion of an E♭ triad is temporary and confined entirely to this one voice.

Other occurrences of key signatures in the atonal literature are intentionally enigmatic. The first three of Alban Berg's Four Songs Op. 2 use signatures despite Berg's application of an accidental to every note. His purpose for this apparent superfluity may have been programmatic rather than purely musical—in this case, a secretive homage to his teacher Arnold Schoenberg which is explained in Chapter 7.

Bitonality refers to the superposition of two different diatonic collections in different strata of a piece, each of which makes an allusion to a different key. This device was fashionable among composers living in France early in the century, especially Charles Koechlin (1867–1950), Igor Stravinsky, and Darius Milhaud. In his article "Polytonalité et atonalité" (1923), Milhaud traces this tonal device back to the canons of Bach, in which a consequent voice at the interval of a fifth is superimposed over a leading voice. Milhaud's dance for piano "Botafogo" from *Saudades do Brazil* (Anthology no. 5) begins with an F-minor collection in the left hand, which accompanies a melody in the right hand in F♯ minor. These two strata maintain distinct harmonic relations: the left hand reiterates a tonic-dominant-tonic motion in its key, and the melody in the right hand emphasizes scale degrees one and five, reinforcing its key of F♯ minor.

BIBLIOGRAPHY

An early study of the relationship between tonal and atonal music in the twentieth century is Rudolph Réti's *Tonality, Atonality, Pantonality: A Study of Some Trends in Twentieth-Century Music* (New-York, 1958). Réti's view of atonality is somewhat more narrow than the one advanced in this book, and he supplements it with the notion of "pantonality"—brought to twentieth-century music by Debussy—in which a purely melodic type of tonality is made pervasive. Early theoretical writings on atonality are generally unavailable in English; important among them are Josef Matthias Hauer's *Vom Wesen des Musikalischen: Ein Lehrbuch der atonalen Musik* (Leipzig, 1920; rev. Berlin, 1923), Herbert Eimert's *Atonale Musiklehre* (Leipzig, 1924), and Edwin von der Nüll's *Moderne Harmonik* (Leipzig, 1932).

Discussions of polytonality by two composers who used this technique are Darius Milhaud's "Polytonalité et atonalité," *Revue musicale*, 4 (1923), and Charles Koechlin's "Evolution de l'harmonie: période contemporaine," in the *Encyclopédie de la musique et dictionnaire du conservatoire*, ed. Albert Lavignac and Lionel de La Laurencie (Paris, 1923). Koechlin's lengthy study also emphasizes the application of modes to late-nineteenth- and early-twentieth-century French music.

Differing views on how triadic harmony can relate to twentieth-century practices are put forth by Paul Hindemith in his *Craft of Musical Composition*, Vol. 1, trans. Arthur Mendel (New York, 1942), and by Felix Salzer in *Structural Hearing: Tonal Coherence in Music*, 2 vols. (New York, 1952). Arnold Whittall's *Music Since the First World War* (London, 1977) emphasizes the ways in which triadic harmonies can create tonality in modern music. John Clough's articles "Aspects of Diatonic Sets," *Journal of Music Theory*, 23 (1979), and "Diatonic Interval Sets and Transformational Structures," *Perspectives of New Music*, 18 (1980), present technical discussions of diatonic sets.

Nicolas Slonimsky's discussion of pandiatonicism is located in his *Music Since 1900* (5th ed., New York, 1994).

4

Serialism

Serialism is a method of composition by which the order of occurrence of one or more musical elements is determined by a preexistent arrangement. The musical elements that can be disposed serially include pitch, duration, attack, instrumentation and timbre, and overall form. Serialism was applied to music of the twentieth century at first to compensate for the absence of common-practice tonality. Like tonality, it produced unity of design and offered the composer a practical guide to musical expansion. After the Second World War, it was applied in a broader way to the compositional process. Serialism is thus a structural element and compositional method that does not produce any single musical style.

Antecedents of serialism exist in common-practice music. For example, the order of notes in a motive influences the order in which the tones recur when the motive is brought back. The order of harmonic functions that underlies a circular harmonic progression—tonic, dominant preparations, dominant, tonic—suggests a fixed series of events that guides the composer in organizing musical space. After twentieth-century composers had ceased using tonal progressions, many still felt the need for a compositional method that would guide them in choosing the order in which elements occurred and thus provide the basis for unity throughout a composition.

We shall begin our discussion of serialism by an investigation of the twelve-tone method: a way of serializing pitch introduced by Arnold Schoenberg and freely adapted by other composers. Subsequently, we shall turn to non-twelve-tone serialization of pitch, a technique that was used in music both before and after the development of the twelve-tone method, and, finally, to "integral serialism," in which musical elements other than pitch are predetermined in their order of appearance.

THE TWELVE-TONE METHOD

In a lecture on "Composition with Twelve Tones" (1941), Schoenberg stated:

> After many unsuccessful attempts during a period of approximately twelve years, I laid the foundations for a new procedure in musical construction which seemed fitted to replace those structural differentiations provided formerly by tonal harmonies. I called this procedure Method of Composition with Twelve Tones which are Related Only with One Another. This method consists primarily of the constant and exclusive use of a set of twelve different tones.

According to Schoenberg's method, most or all pitches of a composition occur in an order derived from forms of a *row* (or *series* or *set*). This "basic set," as it was called by Schoenberg, is a predetermined ordering of the twelve pitch classes, each occurring once. The term *dodecaphonic* also designates music composed according to this method. In the following discussion, the terms "row" and "series" will be used synonymously, but we shall avoid the term "set," since it has been used earlier to refer to a collection of tones that has no fixed precompositional order.

Schoenberg's method was applied tentatively in movements of his Suite for piano Op. 25 in 1921, and it was more fully developed by 1923. Most (but not all) of his compositions after that time use the method, although his interpretation of it later changed in several fundamental ways. In his 1941 lecture, Schoenberg stated that his first thought or inspiration for a piece of this type was motivic in nature, from which the basic row could then be extracted. "The basic set functions in the manner of a motive," he said. "This explains why such a basic set has to be invented anew for every piece. It [the motive] has to be the first creative thought."

The basic series is abstracted from its motivic origins and then generates as many as forty-eight related *row forms*. These are derived, first, by performing three operations upon the basic series:

retrograde arrangement, (symmetric) inversion, and retrograde arrangement of the inversion. Let us illustrate these operations by considering the basic series of Schoenberg's Fourth String Quartet Op. 37 (first movement, Anthology no. 25). The motivic shape in which the row was conceived is heard in the first violin in measures 1–5. From this line we can readily extract the order of twelve pitch classes that constitutes the basic series. We shall call this basic series the *prime* form of the row, abbreviated P. (These abbreviations, by the way, are not widely standardized.)

P: D C♯ A B♭ F E♭ E C A♭ G F♯ B.

The *retrograde* of P (abbreviated RP) may be obtained by reading the series from right to left:

RP: B F♯ G A♭ C E E♭ F B♭ A C♯ D.

The *inversion* of the prime form (abbreviated I) may be obtained by intervallic rotation about some fixed pitch class within P. We shall allow the first pitch class D to remain fixed as the first pitch class within I. The second pitch class of P is one semitone *below* D, so the second pitch class of I will be one semitone *above* D, that is, E♭. The third pitch class is a fifth above D, so the third pitch class in I will be G, a fifth below D—and so forth through all pitch classes of the prime form:

I: D E♭ G F♯ B C♯ C E A♭ A B♭ F.

The *retrograde inversion* (abbreviated RI) can be obtained by reading the inversion from right to left:

RI: F B♭ A A♭ E C C♯ B F♯ G E♭ D.

The four basic forms of the row—P, RP, I, and RI—can then spawn a total of forty-eight forms by transposition of each to all of the twelve available levels of pitch. The prime form of the row from the Fourth String Quartet, for example, can be transposed up three semitones to render a new row form. We shall use the abbreviation P_3 to identify this transposition and refer to the basic (untransposed) form as P_0:

P_0: D C♯ A B♭ F E♭ E C A♭ G F♯ B
P_3: F E C C♯ G♯ F♯ G E♭ B B♭ A D.

These forty-eight forms of the basic series are available to the composer for the purpose of establishing the order in which pitches will occur in a twelve-tone piece. The forms are closely related. The intervals between pitch classes in the prime form recur in all of the other forms, although they may be reversed in order. Thus a work based on the twelve-tone method will have a powerful intervallic unity.

Before continuing with a survey of Schoenberg's applications of the row, we shall briefly examine the circumstances that led him to his method. It will be especially instructive to compare the premises of twelve-tone composition with Schoenberg's compositional procedures in his "atonal" period, the latter extending from about 1908 to 1921. Many of the same techniques and assumptions underlie both types of composition. In both, dissonance is emancipated and suggestions of a keynote are usually suppressed. In both, transpositions and inversions of sets of pitches contribute to diversity and unity among lines and chords. In most respects, the twelve-tone method only provides more "conscious control" (to use Schoenberg's terms) over the materials of composition than was the case in his largely intuitive atonal language.

The twelve-tone method differs from atonal composition primarily in two ways: it guarantees a more complete recirculation of all twelve pitch classes, and it applies a rigorous criterion of order to pitches as they unfold in the music from the background chromatic set. The first of these phenomena continues a pronounced historical trend toward chromaticism, especially among German and Austrian composers of the generation after Wagner. Numerous works of the late nineteenth and early twentieth centuries contain themes that touch upon every note of the chromatic scale. The beginning of Liszt's *Faust* Symphony (1854), the fugal subject "On Science" from Strauss's *Also sprach Zarathustra* (1895), and the passacaglia theme from Act 1 of Berg's *Wozzeck* (1917–22) are important examples.

In the early decades of the twentieth century, this trend toward chromaticism led to systems that were intended to insure total chromatic saturation of themes. While these techniques are related to Schoenberg's twelve-tone method only in the most superficial way, they are evidence of a broad concern for total chromaticism. The Viennese composer Josef Matthias Hauer (1883–1959), for example, devised a "law" governing atonal melody: "Within a given [melodic] succession of pitches," he stated in his *Vom Wesen des Musikalischen* (1923), "no pitch may be repeated and none may be omitted. . . . Over and over again, all twelve pitches of the tempered scale must be heard." By 1924 Hauer had further refined his method for insuring complete chromatic recirculation by basing his works upon one or more "tropes." These were divisions of the chromatic set into forty-four different pairs of complementary, unordered hexachords. Hauer's tropes contain no system of order within the twelve-tone set, and his music is not closely related to Schoenberg's twelve-tone works.

The twelve-tone method differs most strikingly from atonal composition by its principle of order. The row establishes an unvarying succession of intervals, which is repeatedly presented, either directly, in inversion, or in retrograde. Schoenberg found a historical precedent for this intervallic order in the strict motivic practices of Beethoven. In his lecture of 1941, Schoenberg called attention to the primary motive from the finale of Beethoven's String Quartet in F major Op. 135. After its initial presentation, Beethoven subsequently varied the motive by inversion and free retrograde motion. Schoenberg must also have been aware that a strict principle of intervallic order was desirable in music whose basic linear materials were to be twelve-note sets. An unordered twelve-note set is, in fact, very limiting. It has no inversion, no transpositions, no complement, and it possesses an undistinctive intervallic content. To use such sets as Hauer did—as ever-present unordered collections—might have produced music that was monotonous and unstructured. So Schoenberg added a principle of order to his basic sets, thus creating a new dimension of variety and differentiation.

Schoenberg's method was later adopted by many composers, including Alban Berg, Anton Webern, Ernst Krenek, Luigi Dallapiccola, and a large group of avant-garde musicians in Europe and America after the Second World War. Among them the method has proved enormously flexible. Other than the necessity of deriving the order of most pitches from preconceived arrangements of the total chromatic set, there are few if any firmly established principles that have been widely and consistently observed. The method has instead become a general approach to order and chromatic pitch content. It will be useful, nevertheless, to survey various interpretations of the method in works of major composers, focusing primarily upon the twelve-tone compositions of Schoenberg.

Construction of the Row

The row of Schoenberg's Fourth String Quartet—D C♯ A B♭ F E♭ E C A♭ G F♯ B—is typical of his series in its succession of intervals. There is diversity of intervallic content and avoidance of triadic or diatonic segments. Some interval classes, here the semitone and major third, are emphasized. Schoenberg's construction of rows after about 1925 was guided by the principle of combinatoriality, which will be discussed shortly.

Other composers deliberately incorporated diatonic shapes into their rows, giving their music more familiar sonorities. The series of Berg's Violin Concerto consists of interlocking major and minor triads concluded by three whole tones: G Bb D F♯ A C E G♯ B C♯ D♯ F. One of the rows from his opera *Lulu* begins with the first six notes of an F-minor scale: F G Ab Bb C D (F♯ D♯ E A B C♯).

The rows employed by Webern are often made from segments with the same succession of intervals. An example is the row of his String Quartet Op. 28: Bb A C B D♯ E C♯ D Gb F Ab G. Its first four notes (spelling BACH in German) are identical at I₅ to the second four notes and, if transposed up eight semitones, to the final four notes. A row of this type, which can be generated by operations on an initial segment, is said to be *derived*: its symmetry reduces its number of different intervals—this series contains only minor seconds, minor thirds, major thirds, and their inversions. Derived series present the composer with many possibilities for motivic relationships within different segments of different row forms.

An opposite tendency from Webern's reduction of intervallic variety is found in rows that state every interval. The row from the first movement of Berg's *Lyric* Suite is such an *all-interval series*: F E C A G D Ab Db Eb Gb Bb B. If we count the number of semitones from each pitch class upward to the next pitch class, we obtain the intervals 11 8 9 10 7 6 5 2 3 4 1, which shows that each interval within the octave occurs once. Several composers after World War II favored all-interval rows of symmetrical construction. The row of Luigi Nono's *Il canto sospeso* (1956) expands chromatically in both directions to form an all-interval series. Its shape can be observed in the staff notation in Example 4-1.

Supplementary Row Forms

Composers of twelve-tone music have felt the need in some works to expand the number of forms of a row beyond the forty-eight variations upon a single basic series posited by Schoenberg. A sim-

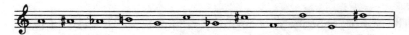

Example 4-1.   Basic series of Luigi Nono's *Il canto sospeso*.

ple way to accomplish this expansion is to use more than one basic
series in a composition. Schoenberg—who generally opposed the
use of more than one basic row in a work—resorted to several
interrelated basic series in his Third String Quartet Op. 30 and
String Trio Op. 45. Berg used several rows in his *Lyric* Suite and
opera *Lulu*. The rows of *Lulu* are each associated with a character
in the drama. In a letter to Schoenberg of 1928, Berg stated that
these rows were derivable from one central series by a variety of
imaginative procedures. The row associated with the character
Alwa, for example, is constructed from every seventh note of the
basic series, the latter identified with Lulu. But, regardless of their
method of derivation, these rows function as mutually independent elements.

Another way to expand the number of row forms is to devise
operations on a basic series that supplement inversion and retrograde arrangement. The most common and widespread of these
additional operations has been *cyclical rotation* (sometimes called
cyclical permutation). A row form is cyclically rotated when one or
more consecutive pitch classes at the beginning are made to go, as it
were, to the end of the line. Consider as an example the following
row form from Berg's "Lied der Lulu" (Anthology no. 20), which is
I_{10} of the basic series of the work:

$$I_{10}: \text{Bb Gb F Ab D♯ C♯ E D B C G A.}$$

There can be as many as eleven additional cyclical rotations of
this row, beginning with Gb, F, Ab, and so forth, rotating preceding
pitch classes in order to the end. We shall designate these rotations
by two numbers in parentheses, the first showing which pitch class
begins the rotation, the second designating which pitch class ends
the new row form. Thus, I_{10} (5–4) refers to the rotation which begins
with the fifth note of I_{10} (D♯) and ends with the fourth (Ab):

$$I_{10} \text{ (5–4): D♯ C♯ E D B C G A Bb Gb F Ab}$$

Berg uses cyclic rotations of basic series in his opera *Lulu* in
addition to the normal forty-eight forms. The first vocal phrase of
the "Lied der Lulu" begins with a statement of the central series at
P_0, which is then followed by the rotation of I_{10} shown above. A
subsidiary line in the celli and bass clarinet uses I_7 (Example 4-2).
This passage is typical of music from *Lulu* and of Berg's twelve-
tone music in general in that subsidiary inner parts (and some
important lines) may be atonal rather than dodecaphonic. Most of
the chords of measures 492–97 are whole-tone subsets, which are

Example 4-2. Berg, *Lulu*, Act 2. Copyright 1936 by Universal Edition, © renewed 1964 by Universal Edition, all rights reserved. Used by permission of European American Music Distributors Corp., sole U.S. agent for Universal Edition.

not segments of any tone rows in this work. In measures 495–96 the basses and piano repeat the notes D G Ab Db, which is a primary set in the opera representing Lulu's seductivity. It is not part of a tone row. A further discussion of this aria will be found in Chapter 7.

A special way of using cyclic rotations was devised by Ernst Krenek in his *Lamentatio Jeremiae* (1941) and used later by Igor Stravinsky beginning with his *Movements* (1959). According to this procedure, the composer supplements the forty-eight basic row forms and their cyclic rotations by four matrices, each consisting of six hexachords. The hexachords within each matrix are transposed rotations of the first and last hexachords of the basic series and its inversion.

Let us illustrate with the basic series of Stravinsky's Variations for Orchestra by constructing a matrix from its first hexachord:

$$P_0: D\ C\ A\ B\ E\ A\sharp\ (G\sharp\ C\sharp\ D\sharp\ G\ F\sharp\ F)$$

This hexachord is first rotated its maximum of five times:

D	C	A	B	E	A♯
C	A	B	E	A♯	D
A	B	E	A♯	D	C
B	E	A♯	D	C	A
E	A♯	D	C	A	B
A♯	D	C	A	B	E

The rotations are then transposed so that they will all begin with the first pitch class of the source hexachord (in this case D):

D	C	A	B	E	A♯
D	B	C♯	F♯	C	E
D	E	A	D♯	G	F
D	G	C♯	F	D♯	C
D	G♯	C	A♯	G	A
D	F♯	E	C♯	D♯	G♯

The matrix is used by Stravinsky in various ways in his Variations, especially to guide him in constructing chords by duplicating the content of pitches found in vertical columns of the matrix. These verticalities greatly expand the harmonic vocabulary derivable from the row. The third and fifth columns of the matrix, for example, form major/minor tetrachords—a set that had long been favored by Stravinsky.

Combinatoriality and Invariance

The terms combinatoriality and invariance, both brought into the study of music by Milton Babbitt, refer to properties of twelve-tone rows and relationships among row forms that have proved to be of great consequence to many twelve-tone composers. *Combinatoriality* is the capacity of a segment of a series to form a collection of all twelve pitch classes when it is combined with the corresponding segment of one or more of its row forms. The basic series of Schoenberg's Fourth String Quartet is combinatorial, since its first hexachord combines with the first hexachord of I_5 to form the chromatic set (which Babbitt has dubbed the *aggregate*):

	first hexachord:						second hexachord:				
P_0:	D	C♯	A	B♭	F	E♭	(E	C	A♭	G	F♯	B)
I_5:	G	G♯	C	B	E	F♯	(F	A	C♯	D	D♯	B♭)
	aggregate						aggregate					

It will be obvious from this example that the second hexachord must also be combinatorial with the second hexachord of the related row form (I_5). Furthermore, any transposition of P will be combinatorial with the same transposition of I plus five semitones. P_3, for example, will be combinatorial at I_8. And, finally, it can be observed that combinatoriality does not depend upon the order of pitch classes within the hexachord—only upon its total content of pitches. In other words, any reordering of the notes D C♯ A B♭ F E♭ will also form an aggregate when combined with its transformation at I_5.

Combinatoriality has been extensively exploited in the music of Schoenberg, Babbitt, and other contemporary Americans. Schoenberg focused solely upon inversional, hexachordal combinatoriality as illustrated above. Combinatorial relations have been applied much more broadly in Babbitt's music, where they are central to its construction and meaning. Combinatoriality had a decisive influence on Schoenberg's construction of rows beginning with his Suite Op. 29 (1924–26). A few years thereafter his selection of basic series became even more restrictive as he only used rows whose hexachords were combinatorial at I_5.

Schoenberg stated in his 1941 lecture that his purpose in using combinatorial row forms was to insure that no pitch class would inadvertently be doubled if, for example, a hexachord from one form were accompanied by the corresponding hexachord from the related row form. His use of combinatorial series, however, is more extensive than this fundamental circumstance. Combinatoriality became Schoenberg's primary criterion for *association* of row forms, that is, which of the forty-eight forms should be used in the same region of a composition or used at the same time. In the Fourth String Quartet we see a P form consistently paired with its combinatorial I form, the two heard either simultaneously or in succession.

Schoenberg's later twelve-tone music reveals a fascination with the creation of aggregates by combinatorial conjunction of hexachords such that the principle of order in a twelve-tone series plays a decidedly secondary role. In works such as the String Trio Op. 45 and the Violin Fantasy Op. 47, the unordered hexachord becomes the primary structural unit.

Invariance refers in general to the existence of elements of a series that remain unchanged subsequent to the operations of inversion, transposition, or retrograde arrangement. An example of this phenomenon is the preservation of certain pitch classes at the same position in the row after it is inverted. Any row will maintain two pitch classes in the same position if it is inverted and transposed to an even number of semitones (I_0, I_2, I_4, and so forth). These invariant pitch classes will always be a tritone apart:

P_0:	D	C♯	A	B♭	F	E♭	E	C	A♭	G	F♯	B
I_2:	E	F	A	G♯	C♯	E♭	D	F♯	B♭	B	C	G

tritone

This type of invariance has compositional significance in the Musette from Schoenberg's Piano Suite Op. 25, in which a P form is associated with an I form at an even-numbered transposition level. The two invariant pitch classes are reiterated in a very prominent manner.

More important for the later twelve-tone music of Schoenberg and for the works of Berg and Webern is segmental invariance. This type of invariance obtains when a continuous segment of two or more notes reappears as a segment in another row form. Any of the prime forms of the row of Schoenberg's Fourth String Quartet contains two trichordal invariants in comparison with the corresponding RI form five semitones higher. Let us illustrate by comparing P_1 to RI_6.

P_1:	E♭	D	A♯	B	F♯	E	F	C♯	A	G♯	G	C
RI_6:	B	E	E♭	D	A♯	F♯	G	F	C	C♯	A	G♯

These invariant segments are used to construct principal lines and to bring about motivic continuity despite changes in row forms. In measures 153–54 of the first movement of the Fourth String Quartet, the principal line in the viola consists of these two disjunct trichords in P_1, while the other parts fill in the remaining pitch classes of this row form. The next two measures unfold RI_6, and the same line is heard an octave higher in the first violin. This recurrence is possible since the two trichords that underlie this line are still available in that row form.

Application of the Row to Lines and Chords and Choice of Row Forms

The twelve-tone method is most applicable to the melodic lines of a composition. Schoenberg usually began his twelve-tone works with a principal melody which unambiguously states the basic series while the subsidiary parts unfold the same or another row form. Immediate repetitions of notes or groups of notes are common since these are motivic details that cause no fundamental distortion in the order in which a row form is presented. The opening of Schoenberg's Fourth String Quartet unfolds the basic series in the principal line (first violin) while segments of the same row form are heard simultaneously in the accompanimental chords. The composer also initiates in these first measures a characteristic division of the row—four segments of three notes each—which will be continued throughout the entire movement. In the diagram that follows, it will be seen that these trichords (labelled *a, b, c,* and *d*) subdivide both vertical and horizontal dimensions:

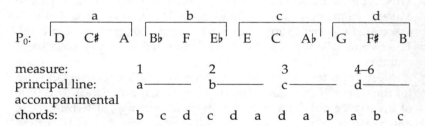

In measure 6 the principal line passes to the second violin, which then unfolds I_5. Schoenberg's decision to follow P_0 with I_5 is no doubt based on the fact that these two row forms are combinatorial. His selection of forms later in the work is also influenced by motivic considerations. The basic shape of the Fourth String Quartet strongly emphasizes the descending semitone, two occurrences of which are marked by rhythmic elongations (Example 4-3). When this theme makes its first important return at measure 165, Schoenberg chooses to state it at P_6 so that the figure Ab–G will then be thrust into the leading position.

descending
semitone D-C♯

descending
semitone A♭-G

Example 4-3. Schoenberg, Fourth String Quartet Op. 37, first movement. Copyright 1939, by G. Schirmer, Inc. International copyright secured. Reprinted by permission.

Other composers such as Berg and Webern often choose row forms that elide with one just heard. In other words, they select a form whose first pitch class is the same as the last pitch class of the row just concluded. In the sixth movement of Webern's Second Cantata Op. 31, for example, the soprano line begins with a prime form which is followed by the prime form six semitones distant. The composer has P_6 follow P_0 since in that succession they share the note C:

P_0

| F♯ A F E G♯ D♯ G B B♭ D C♯ | C E♭ B B♭ D A C♯ F E G♯ G F♯ |

P_6

Another consideration guiding composers in their choice of row forms is their desire to create certain harmonic sonorities. At the beginning of the fifth movement of Webern's Second Cantata (Anthology no. 22) the four choral parts simultaneously state P_0, P_2, P_5, and P_6 (Example 4-4). Webern probably chose these transpositions because they create a succession of all-interval tetrachords of type A, which we hear as the six verticalities of this opening passage. The all-interval tetrachord, which was prominent in Webern's vocabulary of atonal harmonies, does not occur as a segment of the row used by the composer in this piece, but it is brought nonetheless into the music as a prominent sonority by the choice of row forms.

The derivation of chords from row forms is often less systematic than the construction of melodies. Schoenberg usually creates chords from segments of a row, that is, from two or more consecutive pitch classes. But their vertical order does not consistently reflect the intervallic order of the series. In music by Milton Babbitt, on the other hand, the vertical arrangement of chordal pitches is strictly determined by serial order. In many cases, chords will be made from invariant segments of two row forms that are operative in the same area of a work, or, as we have seen in the

Example 4-4. Webern, Second Cantata Op. 31, fifth movement, measures 1–3, rhythm omitted. Copyright 1951 by Universal Edition, Wien. Copyright renewed. All rights reserved. Used by permission of European-American Music Distributors Corp., sole U.S. agent for Universal Edition.

whole-tone harmonies in Berg's "Lied der Lulu," they may be independent of the row.

NON-TWELVE-TONE SERIALISM

Series of more or fewer than twelve pitch classes were important elements in the organization of music by Schoenberg and Stravinsky prior to their adoption of the twelve-tone method. Nondodecaphonic serialism also plays a role in music by the American composer Carl Ruggles (see Chapter 12). Schoenberg began to apply series of this type in several incomplete works around 1915 and later in his Piano Pieces Op. 23 (1920–23) and Serenade Op. 24 (1920–23). Stravinsky's music from the Cantata (1952) to his first twelve-tone composition, *Threni* (1958), mixes atonal and nondodecaphonic serial procedures.

Schoenberg's Serenade for seven instruments and bass voice is in seven movements grouped symmetrically about a vocal setting of a Petrarchan sonnet. Two experimental approaches to serial composition are encountered in this work: one in the sonnet, where the vocal part reiterates an untransformed twelve-note row, and the other in the third movement, Variations, which is based upon a fourteen-note series. The theme of the Variations (Example 4-5) consists of this row joined to its retrograde, in imitation of the antecedent and consequent phrases of a classical period. Compared to Schoenberg's later twelve-tone procedures, application of the row in the five variations and coda that follow is decidedly primitive. Only the untransposed prime form, untransposed inversion, and their retrogrades are used, and, toward the middle of the movement, these row forms are scattered in free order among several contrapuntal lines.

Igor Stravinsky's *In Memoriam Dylan Thomas* (1954) is a work in three movements which uses a five-note set: E E♭ C C♯ D. The outer movements, "Dirge-Canons," imitate instrumental *equali* of the eighteenth century, of which Beethoven's *Three Equali for Four Trombones* are the best known examples. The middle movement is a

Example 4-5. Schoenberg, *Serenade* Op. 24, third movement, measures 1–11. Copyright 1924 by Wilhelm Hansen, Copenhagen. Reprinted by permission.

setting for tenor and string quartet of Thomas's "Do not go gentle into that good night."

Several transpositions of all four basic transformations of the row are strictly applied to the polyphonic lines. Stravinsky's elisions of row forms reflect the row technique of Webern; as in the music of Webern, these elisions often encompass larger segments. The first vocal phrase of the second movement (Example 4-6) is an illustration. Despite the chromatic content of the row, the composer's choice of row forms insures that diatonic subsets will be evident, especially as harmonies at major cadences. The brass cadences in the first movement and string cadences in the finale are mainly on triads. Other passages come to a rest on diatonic segments such as C–D–E or (in the song) B–D–E.

INTEGRAL SERIALISM

Shortly after the conclusion of World War II, the revival of a musical avant-garde stimulated renewed interest in serial composition. In Europe the long suppressed twelve-tone works of Schoenberg, Webern, and Berg were performed and studied, and the method underlying their composition was spread by former students of Schoenberg including René Leibowitz and Josef Rufer. In America a younger generation of composers including Milton Babbitt and Gunther Schuller had become devoted and resourceful serialists.

There arose among musicians on both sides of the Atlantic similar though independent movements to extend the serial principle to embrace multiple elements of a composition, such as duration, placement of attacks, dynamics, tempo, and timbre. This application of serialism to several dimensions of a work will be called total or integral serialism.

Postwar integral serialism was prefigured by the twelve-tone works of Schoenberg, Berg, and Webern. The row in Schoenberg's music strongly (although unsystematically) influences melodic

Example 4-6. Stravinsky, *In Memoriam Dylan Thomas*, second movement (song, "Do not go gentle," poem by Dylan Thomas) © Copyright 1954 by Boosey & Hawkes, Inc.; renewed 1982. Reprinted by permission. From *Collected Poems of Dylan Thomas*, by permission of J.M. Dent and Sons.

phrasing, rhythm, meter, attack, register, timbre, and form. The influence of the row on these elements is more systematically explored in works of Webern, whose desire to achieve the greatest possible conciseness of materials led in some pieces to a consistent interrelation of intervallic structures with other musical elements. His sparse and disconnected textures were also very appealing to the postwar European avant-garde.

Music by Olivier Messiaen of the late 1940s was also influential upon the emerging movement of European serialism. In his piano prelude "Mode de valeurs et d'intensités" (1949), Messiaen devised a way to integrate the different elements of a work, although these were not disposed serially. In this piece an unchanging dynamic level, duration, type of attack, and register are assigned to each pitch class in each of three strata. These pitch classes are not deployed in a serial order, but their prearranged integration with other variables of composition was an idea that Messiaen's students (including Pierre Boulez and Karlheinz Stockhausen) soon allied to serial methods.

Systems of integral serialism did not attain widespread standardization. We shall thus focus on two representative approaches: those of Milton Babbitt and Pierre Boulez. By the late 1940s, Babbitt had devised a mathematical model that concisely represents the manipulations of pitch in a twelve-tone piece. He used these same numerical operations to generate rhythm and dynamics in his Three Compositions for Piano (1947), which reveals a highly integrated structure. His goal in this and later compositions, as he wrote in the article "Some Aspects of Twelve-Tone Composition" (1955), is "a completely autonomous conception of the twelve-tone system, and . . . works in which all components, in all dimensions, would be determined by the relations and operations of the system."

Babbitt begins by constructing a basic series that is rich in structural relationships. Some series, as in the first of his Three

Compositions for Piano, are all-interval rows. Most of Babbitt's basic series are what he calls *all-combinatorial*: their hexachords can create aggregates when combined with at least one transposition each of P, RP, I, and RI.

Babbitt then extends the structural features of the row to other aspects of composition by interpreting pitches and their relationships in terms of modular arithmetic and mathematical group theory. The pitch classes of a tone row are represented by integers from 0 to 11, each corresponding to the number of semitones of a pitch class above the initial one in the basic series, which is postulated as 0. Row forms can then be derived by simple arithmetic functions. The inversion of the row can be obtained by subtracting each number from 12 (the first element remains 0). Transpositions are figured by adding the number of semitones by which the row is to be transposed to each integer, reverting to 0 when 12 is reached. The basic series of Schoenberg's Fourth String Quartet, its inversion, and the inversion transposed up five semitones, for example, would be represented:

(P$_0$: D	C#	A	Bb	F	Eb	E	C	Ab	G	F#	B)
P$_0$: 0	11	7	8	3	1	2	10	6	5	4	9
I$_0$: 0	1	5	4	9	11	10	2	6	7	8	3
I$_5$: 5	6	10	9	2	4	3	7	11	0	1	8

These arithmetic procedures simultaneously underlie the construction and application of rhythms, successions of dynamics, and overall form. We shall return to Babbitt's serialized music in Chapter 5 to explain how rhythms are derived from his mathematical model.

Pierre Boulez's involvement with integral serialism was more short-lived than Babbitt's. Boulez's *Structures Ia* for two pianos (1952) was his most detailed essay in this method of composition, and it will show both the similarities and differences of European postwar serialism with its American counterpart.

Boulez's basic series in *Structures Ia* is borrowed from one of the "modes," or sets, used by Messiaen in his "Mode de valeurs et d'intensités." Boulez, like Babbitt, uses the series in the forty-eight classical transformations, and, also like Babbitt, he relates these rows to the serialization of other elements of the work by mathematical means. Boulez's system, however, is entirely different from Babbitt's. Boulez assigns the numbers 1 to 12 to each pitch class in the basic series in the order of their occurrence:

P$_0$: Eb	D	A	Ab	G	F#	E	C#	C	Bb	F	B
1	2	3	4	5	6	7	8	9	10	11	12

He then constructs two twelve-by-twelve matrices of numbers, each of whose rows represents a transposition of either the P or I forms of the basic series. In the P matrix, for example, a transposition of P_0 up one semitone results in a number series representing how this transposition changes the *order* of elements in P_0.

P_0:	1	2	3	4	5	6	7	8	9	10	11	12
P_1:	7	1	10	3	4	5	11	2	8	12	6	9
	(E	D♯	A♯	A	G♯	G	F	D	C♯	B	F♯	C)

The first integer of P_1 is 7 because its first pitch class, E, is numbered 7 in P_0. The matrices are then completed in this way:

P Matrix

	1	2	3	4	5	6	7	8	9	10	11	12
[P_0]	1	2	3	4	5	6	7	8	9	10	11	12
[P_{11}]	2	8	4	5	6	11	1	9	12	3	7	10
[P_6]	3	4	1	2	8	9	10	5	6	7	12	11
[etc.]	4	5	2	8	9	12	3	6	11	1	10	7
	5	6	8	9	12	10	4	11	7	2	3	1
	6	11	9	12	10	3	5	7	1	8	4	2
	7	1	10	3	4	5	11	2	8	12	6	9
	8	9	5	6	11	7	2	12	10	4	1	3
	9	12	6	11	7	1	8	10	3	5	2	4
	10	3	7	1	2	8	12	4	5	11	9	6
	11	7	12	10	3	4	6	1	2	9	5	8
	12	10	11	7	1	2	9	3	4	6	8	5

I Matrix

[I_0]	1	7	3	10	12	9	2	11	6	4	8	5
[I_1]	7	11	10	12	9	8	1	6	5	3	2	4
[I_6]	3	10	1	7	11	6	4	12	9	2	5	8
[etc.]	10	12	7	11	6	5	3	9	8	1	4	2
	12	9	11	6	5	4	10	8	2	7	3	1
	9	8	6	5	4	3	12	2	1	11	10	7
	2	1	4	3	10	12	8	7	11	5	9	6
	11	6	12	9	8	2	7	5	4	10	1	3
	6	5	9	8	2	1	11	4	3	12	7	10
	4	3	2	1	7	11	5	10	12	8	6	9
	8	2	5	4	3	10	9	1	7	6	12	11
	5	4	8	2	1	7	6	3	10	9	11	12

By certain precompositional decisions based on these matrices, the order of occurrence of durational values, dynamics, types of attacks, and row forms is established. Other precompositional decisions dictate the order of tempi, texture, and overall form. Some elements of the piece—such as the succession of meters—are freely or intuitively chosen. In his application of structures of pitch to the other variables of composition, Boulez's method differs strikingly from Babbitt's. Boulez makes no attempt to establish a logical connection between these components: they are all interrelated, but in an essentially arbitrary way. We shall illustrate this point in Chapter 5, where we shall see how the matrices of *Structures Ia* dictate its rhythmic structure.

BIBLIOGRAPHY

An authoritative introduction to serialism is provided by Ernst Krenek in his article on this subject in the *Dictionary of Contemporary Music*, ed. John Vinton (New York, 1974). Josef Rufer's *Composition with Twelve Notes*, trans. Humphrey Searle (London, 1954) focuses on the music of Schoenberg, and it also contains a detailed analysis (emphasizing motivic and formal matters) of Schoenberg's Fourth String Quartet (pp. 140–54). Ethan Haimo's *Schoenberg's Serial Odyssey: The Evolution of his Twelve-tone Method, 1914–1928* (Oxford, 1990) contains a clearly stated exposition of the composer's serial method and its historical development. Also see George Perle, *Serial Composition and Atonality*, 6th ed. (Berkeley, 1991), Reginald Smith Brindle, *Serial Composition* (London, 1966), and Joseph Straus, *Introduction to Post-Tonal Theory* (Englewood Cliffs, N.J., 1990).

The article by Brian Fennelly on "Twelve-Tone Techniques" in the *Dictionary of Contemporary Music* is a concise and lucid explanation of concepts put forth by Milton Babbitt. Babbitt's ideas also underlie Charles Wuorinen's *Simple Composition* (New York, 1979).

Among composers' descriptions of twelve-tone tecniques, see Arnold Schoenberg, "Composition with Twelve Tones," in *Style and Idea*, ed. Leonard Stein (Berkeley, 1984), Ernst Krenek, "Extents and Limits of Serial Techniques," in *Problems of Modern Music*, ed. Paul Henry Lang (New York, 1960), and Pierre Boulez, "Eventually . . ." (1952), in *Notes of an Apprenticeship*, trans. Herbert Weinstock (New York, 1968). Most of Milton Babbitt's writings deal with compositional resources of the twelve-tone system, but they also have extensive analytic applications. He discusses the phenomenon of invariance in "Twelve-Tone Invariants as Compositional Determinants," in *Problems of Modern Music*, and combinatoriality in

"Set Structure as a Compositional Determinant," in *Perspectives on Contemporary Music Theory*, ed. Benjamin Boretz and Edward T. Cone (New York, 1972). A concise overview of his goals in twelve-tone music is found in "Some Aspects of Twelve-Tone Composition," *Score*, 12 (1955). Babbitt's interpretation of the twelve-tone idea is surveyed in the first chapter of Andrew Mead's *An Introduction to the Music of Milton Babbitt* (Princeton, 1994). A detailed analysis of compositional method in Boulez's *Structures Ia* has been made by György Ligeti in *Die Reihe*, 4 (1958; English trans., 1960).

5

Rhythm and Meter

The revolution in musical style of the early years of the twentieth century had no less effect upon rhythm and meter than it did upon harmony and tonality. The emancipation of dissonance that we have observed in music of the late nineteenth and earn twentieth centuries was accompanied by a freeing of regular beat and an unsettling of stable metric organization in music of the same period. In this chapter we shall sketch some features of this disruption of earlier conventions of rhythm and survey some notable constructive systems devised by major twentieth-century composers to reorganize the dimension of time in their music.

THE EMANCIPATION OF RHYTHM

In music of the common-practice period, rhythm is organized essentially in three interconnected levels. The central level is a regularly recurring beat or pulse. Beat is expressed in music primarily by a regular onset (or "attack") of notes; the beat may also be clarified by frequent occurrence of note values that extend without interruption from one beat to the next.

Let us see how a pulse is expressed musically by observing the rhythm of the main theme of Schubert's song "Mignon" (Example 5-1). The score of the first two stanzas of this song is found in Example 1-1. If this rhythm is performed at a moderate tempo, the listener will hear the recurrence of a beat as shown in the lower line of Example 5-1. The beat is expressed by the regular pattern of recurrent attacks and by the prominence of the quarter-note value—a duration, that is, which spans without interruption the distance from one beat to the next. Frequency of beat also depends upon tempo. If the speed of this passage were very slow, for example, beats would be heard twice as often as would occur if the tempo were fast.

A lower level of rhythmic organization in music is created by a characteristic *division* of the beat into groups of either two or three values or their multiples. A beat in the rhythm shown in Example 5-1 has a characteristic *duple* division on account of the many eighth and sixteenth notes—in other words, values that divide the beat into subgroups of twos and fours.

A third and higher level of temporal organization is a recurrent *grouping* of beats into larger units of the same size. This characteristic grouping and its expression in music is called *meter*. The first four measures of "Mignon" reveal that the recurrent metric group consists of two beats (Example 5-2). This grouping is expressed musically by several factors. At the beginning, a recurrent pattern is established which consists of a quarter note followed by two eighths. This pattern spans two beats, which tells us that the metric unit will probably be of this duration. Another factor that articulates meter is an emphasis on the first note of the metric group. In Schubert's song the emphasis is created by elongation of the initial note of the metric pattern, as we see in the opening figure quarter-eighth-eighth.

Example 5-1.   Rhythm and beat in Schubert's "Mignon."

Example 5-2.   Metric grouping in Schubert's "Mignon."

In order to clarify the rhythmic-metric structure of a piece, performers often make the beginning of a metric group even more emphatic by adding to it a slightly percussive accent. This practice coincides with a widespread belief among musicians that the very beginning of a metric group is "stronger" than the remaining beats in the group.

Time signatures are chosen to conform to this three-level rhythmic structure: the time signature of $\frac{2}{4}$ in "Mignon" acknowledges that the metric group consists of two beats and that the characteristic division of the beat is duple. Music in which the metric group consists of two beats with a triple division of the beat is normally given a $\frac{6}{8}$ signature; metric groups of three beats having a duple division of the beat normally call for a $\frac{3}{4}$ signature; and so forth.

A time signature is a practical notational device assisting the performer to read note lengths and to visualize (by virtue of bar lines) the metric group. It is analogous to key signature. Both reflect structures of pitch or time that predominate in the music, but neither type of signature creates these structures nor does it rule out temporary deviations from them.

Just as music in a key normally passes through other temporary tonics, music with a prevailing rhythmic-metric organization frequently undergoes temporary or superficial metric changes. In the common-practice period, these deviations include flexible or rubato tempo, syncopation, and hemiola. An example of the last of these—a simultaneous duple and triple division of the beat—occurs in "Mignon" at measure 8 and following. In these measures the voice and left hand of the piano express primarily a duple division of the beat; the right hand of the piano, primarily a triple division. The fluttering motion that results graphically captures the meaning of the words of measures 8–11 of the first stanza: "a gentle breeze wafts from the blue heavens." It is also entirely typical of tonal music that this change of rhythmic design coincides with and underscores an important harmonic and structural juncture—the end of the expository thematic period and the beginning of a passage where a harmony preparing the dominant is in effect.

In late-nineteenth- and early-twentieth-century music, conventions of rhythmic organization were increasingly disregarded. Perhaps the most radical innovation in rhythm of this time was the suspension or outright avoidance of a clear beat, without which regular meter cannot exist. The opening of Ravel's ballet *Daphnis et Chloé* (1909–12, Example 5-3) depicts a fanciful scene from Greek mythology. To capture its supernatural aura, Ravel avoids a clear beat by entrances of parts at irregular intervals of time and by syncopated or irregularly divided note values. The chimerical quality of

Aristide Maillol, *Daphnis Plays to his Goats*. (Courtesy of the Print Collection, The New York Public Library, Astor, Lenox and Tilden Foundations.)

the scene is further enhanced by its lack of triadic harmonies and the use instead of chords in superimposed fourths and fifths.

Music by German and Austrian composers such as Max Reger, Schoenberg, and Alexander Zemlinsky at the turn of the century often had a dense and hyperactive texture that obscured the beat. In his essay "Brahms the Progressive," Schoenberg referred to works of this type as "musical prose," since they are dense in texture and asymmetrical in phrasing. Schoenberg's atonal music continued to incorporate prose-like textures. The perception of a beat in his Piano Piece Op. 23, No. 4 (Anthology no. 6), for example, is made dim by

Example 5-3. Ravel, *Daphnis et Chloé*, measures 1–11. © 1910 Durand S.A.
Editions Musicales, Editions Arima and Durand S. A. Editions Musicales.
Joint Publication. Used by permission of the publisher. Theodore Presser
Company, Sole Representative U.S.A. and Canada.

a busy texture in which different divisions of the beat often conflict, by the large number of changes of tempo, and by frequent placement of rests on downbeats.

The atonal and twelve-tone music of Webern is even more radical in its elimination of beat through its sparse texture and profusion of rests. The rhythm of the opening measures of the fifth movement of his Second Cantata (Anthology no. 22) is shown in Example 5-4; regular pulse plays only a minor role in these figures due to the use of rests on downbeats, syncopation, and irregular accents.

Avant-garde composers after the Second World War intensified Webern's disruption of pulse as a perceptible means of rhythmic measurement. In the "pointillist" style of Stockhausen, Boulez, Messiaen, and other European serialists (see Chapters 6 and 13), regular beat is completely absent. The music of Elliott Carter intensifies the turgid polyphony of Schoenberg's musical prose. Other experimental trends in composition after the war—including the textural compositions of Krzysztof Penderecki and György Ligeti, the studies in sound of Morton Feldman, and the rhythmically indeterminate works of Earle Brown and John Cage—are also generally devoid of conventional pulse.

But a majority of twentieth-century composers have maintained beat and metric organization in their music, albeit in a freer way than their forebears. Music in which a beat is strongly evident may still bypass the conventions of common-practice music by employing rapidly changing meters, irregular placement of the beat, or both simultaneously. Changing meters were prefigured in the nineteenth century by the appearance of themes having five or seven beats per metric unit. Composers who quoted folk songs or who were influenced by folk music—including Brahms, Tchaikovsky, and Musorgski—often used such meters. The Hungarian theme quoted by Brahms in his Variations for piano Op. 21, No. 2, consists of a metric group of seven beats, which Brahms notates by alternating measures of $\frac{3}{4}$ and $\frac{4}{4}$. The Scherzo of Tchaikovsky's Sixth Symphony uses a meter with five beats, which reflects the profile of certain Russian folk songs.

Example 5-4. Rhythmic elements in Webern's Second Cantata, fifth movement, measures 1–6.

The "Sacrificial Dance" from Stravinsky's *Rite of Spring* is a monumental and widely imitated example of irregular beat and changing meter in twentieth-century music. Example 5-5 shows a composite of the rhythm of the opening twenty measures, using Stravinsky's time signatures and note values from the original score of 1921. An interpretation of the location of beats and metric groups is placed below and above this rhythm. The unit of measurement is not the beat, but instead the small value of the sixteenth note; these particles are joined in various quantities to make up beats, whose occurrence is made more asymmetrical by the placement of rests. The beats are gathered into metric segments in a highly irregular manner that is open to various interpretations. The analysis of meter found in Example 5-5 is based upon the opening idea in measures 2–5, which is repeated almost exactly in measures 6–9. The figure that terminates this group (measures 4–5) is interpreted as the closing of metric groups for the remainder of the passage. Stravinsky's choice of time signatures and placement of bar lines in this dance does not directly correspond to the perception of pulse or meter; the arbitrariness of notation is confirmed by his revision of the score for publication in 1943, in which the music remains the same but the barring and time signatures are revised.

An innovation often seen in music by Stravinsky, Ives, Carter, and Copland is *polyrhythm*, or the simultaneous use of two or more distinct modes of rhythmic-metric organization. Polyrhythms are encountered occasionally in music of the nineteenth century. In the finale of Berlioz's *Symphonie fantastique*, for example, the orchestra is divided at measure 399 into two groups, which express conflicting locations of

Example 5-5. Rhythm and meter in Stravinsky's *Rite of Spring*, "Sacrificial Dance."

the beat (Example 5-6). Passages with more than two simultaneous meters are common in Stravinsky's *L'histoire du soldat* (1918). At rehearsal 10 in the first Soldier's March, for example, four simultaneous lines incorporate either different meters or different placements of the pulse. The score to this passage is shown in Example 5-7, after which is an interpretation of the different meters in its four strata.

The diversity of approaches to rhythm among composers early in the twentieth century has not led to a reconsolidation into a common rhythmic practice. Several major composers of the century have nevertheless pursued their own systems of rhythmic and metric construction. We shall now survey three of the most important of these new avenues of temporal organization.

SYSTEMATIC CHANGES OF TEMPO AND METER: BERG, IVES, AND CARTER

Twentieth-century composers have generally been more specific in their indications of tempo than have earlier musicians. Rather than allowing the performer the traditional selection of tempo within general guidelines, composers of this century have been inclined to dictate precise metronomic speeds. These speeds are sometimes linked to a large-scale plan according to which every tempo has a simple numerical relationship to its neighboring tempos.

Alban Berg was a pioneer in such proportional systems of tempo. The changes of speed in his opera *Wozzeck* are normally linked by ratios that facilitate smooth transitions. A change of tempo in the tavern scene of Act 2, scene 4, between a *Ländler* rhythm and a passage of drunken philosophizing among apprentices, is accomplished in several stages. An irregular division of the beat (eighth-note triplets) is first established (measures 447–55), through which a ritardando slows the tempo by measure 455 to a metronomic marking of 54. The irregular division of the beat—an eighth note within a triplet—then becomes at the same speed a regular division of the beat in a new meter and rhythmic design. These relationships are shown schematically in Example 5-8; they directly prefigure the method of changing tempo used later by Elliott Carter, which will be described shortly.

Example 5-6.   Berlioz, *Symphonie fantastique*, fifth movement, measures 399–403.

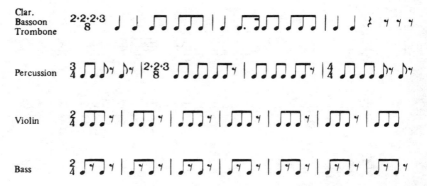

Example 5-7.   Stravinsky, *L'histoire du soldat*. Reprinted by kind permission of the copyright owner J & W Chester/Edition Wilhelm Hansen London Ltd.

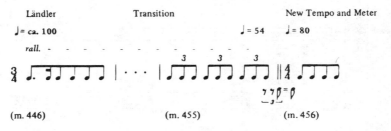

Example 5-8.   Systematic change of tempo in Berg's *Wozzeck*, Act 2.

A passage in Act 1, scene 2 of Berg's opera *Lulu* (measures 669–956), in which the Painter commits suicide, is labeled by Berg a "Monoritmica." This term refers to the use of a single rhythmic motive, which recurs in various guises throughout the passage. This figure—symbolic of fate and violent death—is shown in Example 5-9. Berg organizes tempos in the Monoritmica in a symmetrical manner reminiscent of the symmetrical shapes that are pervasive elsewhere in this work. The first half of the Monoritmica (measures 666–842, including its three-measure introduction) consists of eighteen sections, which increase in tempo from an eighth note at the metronomic rate of 76 to a half note at 132. The second half (measures 843–956) reverses the eighteen tempos, but links them by a gradual ritardando rather than by stepwise changes.

Berg's sketch for the metronomic speeds of this passage (Vienna, Austrian National Library) shows that he was guided in constructing the tempos by a numerical sequence in which the difference between any two adjacent terms is one greater than the preceding difference. His sequence begins with the number forty—usually the

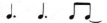

Example 5-9. Motive of fate and violent death in Berg's *Lulu*.

slowest tempo available on a common metronome. He then derives tempos by approximating the terms of the sequence by even numbers with which metronomes are calibrated:

original numerical sequence:
40 42 45 49 54 60 67 75 84 94 105 117 130 144 159 175 192 210
metronomic approximation (♩ =):
38 42 46 50 54 60 66 76 86 96 106 118 132 152 172 192 224 264.

He begins the Monoritmica with the eighth note as the temporal unit and changes to quarter and half notes as the speeds increase.

Independently of the Europeans, Charles Ives devised related methods for linking changes of tempo in his music composed before the First World War. His *Robert Browning* Overture (1911) contains a change of speed akin to the one we observed in Berg's *Wozzeck*. At measure 55 (Example 5-10) the tempo slows by allowing the quarter-note beat in the old tempo to remain at the same duration and as the same value in a quarter-note triplet in the new tempo. The new tempo is thus one-third slower than the old tempo.

This change of tempo ushers in a polyrhythmic passage of two distinct speeds. Example 5-11 shows the location of the beat and metric groupings of the two strata, which begin in measure 55. The upper line represents the principal beat and meter, which proceeds at the slower rate of 66. At the same time other instruments play, in Ives's words, "a kind of fast march" in a different meter and at a quicker speed. The march is represented by the lower line in Example 5-11.

Ives's use of polyrhythms linked by fractional changes of tempo was developed and refined in the music of Elliott Carter beginning in the late 1940s. Carter's Cello Sonata (1948) was his first major work to apply the device that he termed *metric modulation* (which Carter later called "tempo modulation"). A metric modulation is a change of tempo (often accompanied by a change of meter) in which an irregular division of the beat in the previous tempo becomes a regular division and remains at the same durational length in the new tempo. Metric modulations consist of three stages, which are illustrated by the paradigm in Example 5-12. The first stage is characterized by a regularly divided beat; the second stage, which we shall call the "transition," establishes an irregular division of the beat. The final stage completes the modulation, as a note value within the irregular

Example 5-10. Ives, *Robert Browning* Overture. © 1959 by Peer International Corp. International copyright secured. Reprinted by permission.

division of the beat becomes part of a regular division of a new beat and maintains its earlier duration, thus bringing about a new tempo.

In his lecture "The Time Dimension in Music" (1965), Carter remarked that metric modulations were analogous to modulations

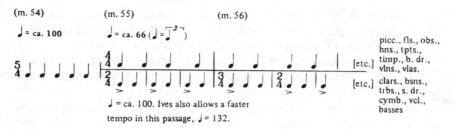

Example 5-11. Change of tempo in Ives's *Robert Browning* Overture.

Example 5-12. Metric modulation.

in key in earlier music. He pursues this analogy in his First String Quartet, for example, by returning near the end to the tempo of the beginning, just as a tonal work returns to the tonic at its conclusion. In his interview *Flawed Words and Stubborn Sounds*, Carter elaborates on his purposes behind the use of metric modulations:

> I tried to think in larger-scale time-continuities of a kind that would be still convincing and yet at the same time new in a way commensurate with, and appropriate to, the richness of the modern musical vocabulary. This aim led me to question all the familiar methods of musical presentation and continuation—the whole so-called musical logic based on the statement of themes and their development. In considering constant change-process-evolution as music's prime factor, I found myself in direct opposition to the static repetitiveness of much early twentieth-century music, the squared-off articulation of the neoclassics, and indeed much of what is written today in which "first you do this for a while, then you do that." I wanted to mix up the "this" and the "that" and make them interact in other ways than by linear succession.

Carter's First String Quartet is one of his earliest essays in these "larger-scale time-continuities." In this work two independent temporal devices are explored: polyrhythm and metric modulation. Each of the four instruments follows its own tempo, meter, and rhythm, only occasionally merging into unified structures. The polyrhythmic aspects of this quartet are discussed further in Chapter 13.

Let us focus upon the initial metric modulation, which occurs in the cello part in measure 17. Carter's notation of this part in measures

13–22 is shown in Example 5-13, below which a revision of the time signatures and bar lines is added in order to clarify its rhythmic structure. The first thirteen measures establish a regular quarter-note beat at the metronomic rate of 72. Measures 14–16 constitute the transition, during which the beat is divided into groups of five equal values. Modulation to the new tempo is completed at measure 17 as the sixteenth note within the quintuplet becomes the eighth note in $\frac{6}{8}$ meter, thus producing a tempo of 120. A change from $\frac{6}{8}$ to $\frac{4}{4}$ in the next few measures adds a complication the third stage in this passage, but it does not involve a change of tempo, which remains at 120.

THE RHYTHMIC LANGUAGE OF MESSIAEN

The music of Olivier Messiaen contains many works without a perceptible pulse or regular meter. In order to avoid these conventional modes of temporal organization, he uses rhythms that are sometimes borrowed from preexistent sources (such as Indian talas), rhythms constructed from series of numbers, or those freely devised

Example 5-13. Carter, First String Quartet. Copyright 1955, 1956 by Associated Music Publishers, Inc. All rights reserved. Reprinted by permission.

according to self-imposed guidelines. These principles of rhythmic construction—upon which we shall focus in this section—have been imitated by several of his students, including Pierre Boulez. They are outlined in Messiaen's *Technique of My Musical Language* (ca. 1942), upon which this survey is based.

Messiaen's rhythmic style is aimed at dispelling regular pulse and its conventional division into smaller values. "We shall replace the notions of 'measure' and 'beat,' " he writes, "by the feeling of a short value (the sixteenth note, for example) and its free multiplication, which will lead us toward a music more or less 'ametrical.' " Messiaen found a model for this freely multiplicative rhythm in Stravinsky's *Rite of Spring*, a work whose analysis was a fundamental part of his teaching.

Messiaen's music consists of short rhythmic figures that are superimposed or pieced together. These figures are often built from a prime number (five, seven, and so forth) of small values. The basic figures are then varied or reshaped by a combination of four processes: retrograde arrangement, added values, augmentation, and diminution. An *added value* is produced by interpolating a brief rest, a dot of augmentation, or an additional small note value into the basic figure. Illustrations of added values are seen in Example 5-14. Augmentation (or diminution) can be either exact, in which all note values of the basic figure are increased or decreased by the same multiple, or inexact, in which the values are increased or decreased by differing multiples (Example 5-15).

Although Messiaen uses retrograde arrangement as a means of varying rhythmic figures he also favors rhythms that are palindromic, that is, those whose retrogrades are identical to their original shapes. He calls such figures "nonretrogradable rhythms" and describes the limitations that constrain their variation as having the

Example 5-14. Added rhythmic values.

Example 5-15. Rhythmic augmentations.

"charm of impossibilities." They are rhythmic equivalents to his "modes of limited transposition" (see Chapter 16), which similarly contain restrictions upon the ways in which they can be varied.

SERIALIZED RHYTHM

Music in Europe and America following World War II emphasized experimental styles that were often organized by serial procedures. The twelve-tone method at this time became a widespread compositional technique, and the serial idea upon which it is based was often applied systematically to patterns of attack, durational successions, and metrical groups.

In Chapter 4 we sketched two approaches to "integral" serialism: Pierre Boulez's highly automated technique of composition in his *Structures Ia* and the mathematical model of Milton Babbitt. Let us now continue that discussion to explore ways in which Boulez and Babbitt use a series of pitches to influence the creation of rhythmic ideas. The methods of Boulez and Babbitt are representative of techniques of serialization among their fellow composers in Europe and America, respectively; their rhythmic styles are similarly representative. Boulez—like many European composers after the war—uses serial procedures to obliterate pulse and meter. Babbitt—like many of his American colleagues—uses serialism to produce rhythms in which traditional means of organization are still much in evidence.

In Chapter 4 we saw that the basic series of Boulez's *Structures Ia* is used to construct two twelve-by-twelve matrices of numbers. Each row of numbers in these arrays may be used to create a rhythmic pattern. A number in a row represents a multiple of a thirty-second-note value. The number one, for example, signifies a thirty-second note; the number two, a sixteenth note; and so forth. The rhythmic figure corresponding to the first row in the I matrix, for example, is shown in Example 5-16. The rhythms that result from this method are plainly devoid of regular beat or meter, thus accomplishing by an arithmetic method what Messiaen accomplished in his music of the 1930s and early 1940s by intuitive processes.

The order in which these rhythmic series occur is determined in advance by an arbitrary plan. In piano I, for example, the durational rows are used at first in the order in which they appear in the I matrix, moving from bottom to top and read in retrograde from right to left. The rhythm in the first piano part in the opening section (Example 5-17) can be seen to derive from the numbers 12 11 9 10 3 6 7 1 2 8 4 5, which is the retrograde of the bottom row in the I matrix. A similar plan governs the order of durational row forms of piano II.

Example 5-16. Rhythmic construction in Boulez's *Structures Ia.*

Example 5-17. Boulez, *Structures Ia,* measures 1–7. Copyright 1955 by Universal Edition (London) Ltd., London. Copyright renewed. Used by permission of European American Music Distributors Corp., sole U.S. agent for Universal Edition.

Milton Babbitt's system differs from Boulez's primarily in Babbitt's attempt to establish a more logical connection between transformations of rows of pitches and those of rhythms. He was critical of the procedures of European serialists, who, like Boulez, manipulated rhythms by what seemed to Babbitt to be arbitrary decisions. Babbitt's Three Compositions for Piano (1947) contain early examples of his closed system. In the first piece in this set, Babbitt derives rhythms from the numerical row 5 1 4 2. Each number is interpreted as a group of that number of sixteenth notes or its equivalent; the group is terminated by a rest, a longer value, a new phrase mark, an accent, or some other means of articulation. The rhythmic row is "inverted" by subtracting each number from the value 6, just as a row of pitches in Babbitt's system is inverted by subtracting the integer by which a pitch class is represented from 12. Retrogrades of these P and I forms and cyclic rotations of all forms are also available.

While this method of serializing rhythm has analogies in operations of the twelve-tone system, it did not completely satisfy "the necessity of temporal interpretation translating completely the attributes of the pitch system into temporal terms," upon which Babbitt insisted in his article "Twelve-Tone Rhythmic Structure and the Electronic Medium" (1962). Therefore, in certain instrumental and electronic compositions of the 1950s and later, he used what he called the *time-point* system of serializing attacks. A time-point row consists of twelve integers, each of which governs the place in a measure where an attack may occur. The basic time-point row is identical to a row of numbers expressing the intervals between pitch classes of the basic (pitch) series. The first element of this intervallic or time-point row is postulated to be 0, and each number that follows is the number of semitones from a pitch class upward to the next pitch class. If the basic series is an all-interval row, the intervallic series will contain all of the integers from 0 to 11. Let us illustrate with the basic series of Babbitt's Three Compositions for Piano, No. 1:

P_0:   Bb   Eb   F   D   C   Db   G   B   F#   A   G#   E
        0   5   2   9   10   1   6   4   7   3   11   8

The composer then picks a basic note value (such as the sixteenth note) and a measure length (such as $\frac{3}{4}$) which will contain twelve basic values. Let us use the assumption of a basic value of the sixteenth note to illustrate how the intervallic or time-point row determines where in a measure a note can begin. Example 5-18 shows how the integers from 0 to 11 correspond to a point in a $\frac{3}{4}$ measure. Since the first element of the time-point row is 0, the first note will begin on the downbeat of the first measure; the next integer of the row (5) commands that the next attack be on the fifth sixteenth of the measure; the next element (2) requires the next attack on the second sixteenth of a following measure. One rhythmic interpretation of the intervallic row is shown in Example 5-19.

Example 5-18. Rhythmic "time points."

Example 5-19. Rhythm derived from a numerical series.

The time-point series does not literally control durations, only points of attack within the measure. The space between attacks can be filled freely by a sustained tone or by a shorter value followed by a rest. Attacks do not have to occur in each measure; for example, the second element of the time-point row (5) can be realized by an attack in the second measure, thus allowing for a more sparse texture. The time-point series can be transformed by "transposition," "inversion," or "retrograde" arrangement through arithmetic functions analogous to those used on numerical representations of pitch series. An inversion is obtained by subtracting each of the integers of the time-point row from twelve, and "transposition" delays the onset of the first attack point by some number of basic values. Babbitt's system, unlike Boulez's, produces music with a definite pulse and the potential for conventional metric organization.

BIBLIOGRAPHY

The issue of musical rhythm in a broad sense, with much attention to modern music, is taken up by Jonathan Kramer in *The Time of Music* (New York, 1988). Rhythm from the performer's perspective is treated in Arthur Weisberg's *Performing Twentieth-Century Music: A Handbook for Conductors and Instrumentalists* (New Haven, 1993). Howard E. Smither's article "Rhythm" in the *Dictionary of Contemporary Music*, ed. John Vinton (New York, 1974) is a concise introduction to rhythmic innovations in the twentieth century. It distills ideas more fully presented in his "Rhythmic Analysis of 20th-Century Music," *Journal of Music Theory*, 8 (1964), which is drawn from his dissertation entitled "Theories of Rhythm in the Nineteenth and Twentieth Centuries" (Cornell University, 1960). Also see Arnold Elston, "Some Rhythmic Practices in Contemporary Music," *Musical Quarterly*, 42 (1956). General theories of rhythm are contained in books on this subject by Paul Creston (New York, 1964) and Grosvenor Cooper and Leonard Meyer (Chicago, 1960).

Regarding rhythmic procedures in Berg's *Lulu*, see Douglas Jarman, "Some Observations on Rhythm, Metre and Tempo in *Lulu*," in *Alban Berg Studien*, Vol. 2, ed. Franz Grasberger and Rudolf Stephan (Vienna, 1981). Carter's innovations are discussed by David Schiff in his book *The Music of Elliott Carter* (London, 1983) and in Richard Franko Goldman's contribution to the Current Chronicle (regarding Carter's Cello Sonata) in *Musical Quarterly*, 37 (1951). Also see Carter's lecture "The Time Dimension in Music" (1965), in *The Writings of Elliott Carter*, ed. Else and Kurt Stone (Bloomington, 1977) and his article "The Rhythmic Basis of American Music", *Score*, 12 (1955). The latter article discusses innovations in rhythm in music by Ives, but it does not mention Ives's experiments with metric modulation.

The concept of a musical prose has long been used by German writers on musical form. It is discussed by Carl Dahlhaus in his article "Musikalische Prosa," *Neue Zeitschrift für Musik*, 125 (1964). Messiaen's doctrine of rhythm in his music of the 1930s and early 1940s is given out in Chapters 2–7 of his *Technique of My Musical Language*, 2 vols., trans. John Satterfield (Paris, ca. 1956).

Babbitt's proposal for his time-point system of rhythmic serialization is contained in his article "Twelve-Tone Rhythmic Structure and the Electronic Medium" (1962), in *Perspectives on Contemporary Music Theory*, ed. Benjamin Boretz and Edward T. Cone (New York, 1972). It is more clearly stated by Charles Wuorinen in *Simple Composition* (New York, 1979) and by Andrew Mead in Chapter 1 of *An Introduction to the Music of Milton Babbitt* (Princeton, 1994). The rhythmic construction of Boulez's *Structures Ia* is analyzed by György Ligeti in *Die Reihe*, 4 (1958; English trans., 1960).

6

Orchestration, Tone Color, and Texture

We turn in this chapter to a primary element in twentieth-century composition: sound. Modern composers have made many efforts to refine and diversify the audible fabric of music. Increasingly throughout the century, distinctive qualities of sound have become basic compositional materials and structural components, at times outweighing in importance the more traditional elements of pitch, interval, line, and chord.

The primacy of this "sonorous image" in modern music is underlined by Aaron Copland in his book *Music and Imagination*:

> The sonorous image is a preoccupying concern of all musicians. In that phrase we include beauty and roundness of tone; its warmth, its depth, its "edge," its balanced mixture with other tones, and its acoustical properties in any given environment. . . . A deliberately chosen sound image that pervades an entire piece becomes an integral part of the expressive meaning of that piece.

To Copland's list of constituents of the sonorous image, we may add the broad and interrelated areas of orchestration, tone color, and texture. *Orchestration* is the art of realizing a musical idea for a specific group of instruments. *Tone color* or *timbre* is the distinctive quality of a musical sound, and *texture* refers to the sonorous aggregate of lines, chords, or other audible events as they interact with one another.

ORCHESTRATION

The orchestra of the later nineteenth century underwent an expansion in size that gave it greater force and diversity and enabled its basic subdivisions—choirs of brass, woodwinds, and strings—to be deployed independently. But, more often than not, this enlarged and diversified medium was used to create a relatively limited range of homogenized sounds. Like the painter who mixes his primary colors prior to putting them on the canvas, the nineteenth-century orchestrator was inclined to blend the pure colors of his instruments into a much smaller number of composite hues.

Multiple doublings of essential parts, especially in passages where the full orchestra plays, create a uniformity of timbre in the nineteenth-century symphony. Among German composers such as Richard Wagner, a line or chord is often taken simultaneously by instruments from two or even three of the principal choirs. French and Russian symphonists, on the other hand, typically doubled parts among instruments of the same family or choir. We see the Germanic style of orchestration at the beginning of Anton Dvořák's Symphony in G major Op. 88 (1889), shown in Example 6-1. The melody is played in unison by selected woodwinds, brass, and strings (clarinets, bassoon, horns, and cellos); no one instrument stands out as a distinctive color, and the line is heard instead as a blended composite. The underlying harmonies are realized similarly by other members of all three choirs.

Nineteenth-century standards of orchestration endured well into the twentieth century in symphonic works by Shostakovich, Prokofiev, Bartók, Hindemith, Sibelius, and Vaughan Williams. But a new handling of the orchestra, which would be immensely influential upon early twentieth-century composers, was initiated at the end of the romantic period by Claude Debussy and Gustav Mahler. Debussy wrote for an orchestra of moderate size, often omitting instruments that did not contribute to the image which his music was to evoke. In *Nocturnes* (1893–99), for example, the gray sameness of "Nuages" is suggested by its ensemble of woodwinds, horns, and strings; the brilliant revelry of "Fêtes" by the addition of a band of trumpets, trombones, tuba, and percussion; and the mysterious seascapes of "Sirènes" by the unexpected appearance of a female chorus.

The full orchestra in Debussy's scores rarely plays loudly for long stretches, seeking instead a refined understatement which is characteristic of all of his music. Debussy lavishes great attention upon the woodwinds, which often replace the strings as primary bearers of melodic material. In soft or thinly scored passages, Debussy usually avoids doubling melodic lines, preferring the pure colors of solo instruments. Only in passages where the full orchestra plays are doublings common, as at the beginning of the middle section (measure 55) of the Prelude to *The Afternoon of a Faun*.

Among German and Austrian composers of the later nineteenth century, Mahler was unrivaled as an innovator in orchestration. Each of his symphonic works uses orchestral devices uniquely geared to express the idea of that piece. The triumph of human spirit depicted by the end of the Eighth Symphony is expressed by the force of its gigantic orchestra and chorus. And how poignantly do the cowbells in the Sixth Symphony express the isolation of the artist, which prefigures his destruction—symbolized by blows of a hammer—in the finale of that work. The audience of the Second Symphony is itself brought into the grim procession of mankind toward its final judgment by Mahler's diverse placement of brass instruments offstage.

Mahler's manipulation of spatial effects and his use of unorthodox instruments anticipated developments in orchestration after the Second World War. Of even greater importance to the direction of orchestration in the early twentieth century, however, was his tendency to use small, heterogeneous subdivisions of the orchestra independently and to clarify the contrapuntal content of his scores by fewer doublings and more clearly etched soloistic timbres. These practices are seen in the opening of his Ninth Symphony (1908–10), illustrated in Example 6-2. This passage, which introduces motives upon which the first movement is based, contains no doublings. It consists of a disjunct and fragmentary play of rhythms, colors, and intervals, in a manner that is remarkably akin to the "pointillistic" textures later developed by Anton Webern.

The relatively small number of instruments that Mahler usually calls into play at any one time—as at the beginning of the Ninth Symphony—marks a transition between the large orchestra of the nineteenth century and a widespread preference for the *chamber ensemble* among composers of the first quarter of the twentieth century. European composers of the modern period turned to small ensembles for many reasons: rebellion against romantic overstatement and giganticism, economic deprivation which descended upon Europe after the First World War, the tastes and requirements of several influential patrons, interest in popular music, a revival of the sonority of music of the baroque and early classical periods, and the need for a medium that could best convey clear and concise polyphonic fabrics or lightness of spirit.

Example 6-1. Dvořák, Symphony in G major Op. 88, first movement, measures 1–15.

After *The Rite of Spring* (1911–13), Stravinsky made a clean break with the large orchestra, to which he did not return until the late 1920s. Between 1913 and 1917 he composed a series of songs on Russian words—*Three Japanese Lyrics*, *Pribaoutki*, and *Cat's Cradle Songs*—each accompanied by diverse chamber groups. The orchestration of the first of these, which is for voice, piano, woodwinds, and strings, may have been influenced by Schoenberg's *Pierrot lunaire*, which Stravinsky had heard in 1912 in Berlin and later deemed a "brilliant instrumental masterpiece." Stravinsky's ensemble songs were much admired by the Viennese atonalists, who heard them between 1919 and 1921 in Schoenberg's Society for Private

Example 6-1. continued.

Musical Performances (a Viennese concert organization dedicated to performances of modern music). In a letter to Berg dated June 9, 1919, Webern describes a performance by the Society:

> Stravinsky was magnificent. These songs are wonderful. This music moves me completely beyond belief. I love it especially. The cradle songs are something so indescribably touching. How those three clarinets sound! And "Pribaoutki." Ah, my dear friend, it is something really glorious. [From Hans Moldenhauer, *Anton Webern* (New York: Alfred A. Knopf, 1979), p. 229.]

Example 6-2. Mahler, Symphony IX, first movement. Copyright 1912 by Universal Edition A. G. Wien. Copyright renewed 1940, assigned 1952 to Universal Edition (London) Ltd., London. This edition revised by the Internationale Gustav Mahler-Gesellschaft, Copyright 1969 by Universal Edition A. G. Wien and Universal Edition (London) Ltd., London. All rights reserved. Used by permission of European American Music Distributors Corporation, sole U.S. agents for Universal Edition.

It is likely that Webern's predilection for the song with accompaniment by chamber ensemble (used in his Opp. 8, 13, 14, 15, 16, 17, and 18) stems from his enthusiasm for these works by Stravinsky.

Toward the end of the First World War, Stravinsky also composed several dramatic works for small ensemble. The first of these was *Reynard* (1915–16) for fifteen instrumentalists, singers, and actors, followed by *Les noces* and *L'histoire du soldat. Reynard* owes its medium in part to the wishes of the French-American patron Princess Edmond de Polignac, who commissioned the work. She writes in her *Memoirs*:

> My intention at that time was to ask different composers to write short works for me for a small orchestra of about twenty performers. I had the impression that, after Richard Wagner and Richard Strauss, the days of big orchestras were over and that it would be delightful to return to a small orchestra of well chosen players and instruments. [*Horizon: A Review of Literature and Art*, 12 (1945).]

The Princess de Polignac—who, ironically, was one of the leading enthusiasts in France in the 1880s and 1890s for the music of Wagner—catalyzed the French change of taste after the First World War in favor of small orchestral ensembles. In addition to Stravinsky's *Reynard*, she commissioned Satie's *Socrate* (1918), Falla's puppet show *El retablo de Maese Pedro* (1919–22), and Milhaud's chamber opera *Les malheurs d'Orphée* (1924).

No two of Stravinsky's works involving small orchestras in the decade following the war use the very same instrumentation. During these years he explored a series of novel orchestral combinations, which have in common the clear outlines and rhythmic drive created by his emphasis upon woodwinds, brass, and percussion. His style of orchestration was influential upon native French composers of the 1920s and 1930s, who found in it a model for the clarity, lightness, and unemotional objectivity that they sought in their own works. In an article on Stravinsky written in 1922, Erik Satie praises the "extraordinary cleanness" of Stravinsky's orchestrations. Satie continues:

> One of the characteristics of the music of Stravinsky is its sonorous transparency. This quality is always found among pure masters, who never allow residue in their sonorities—residue which you will always find in the musical substance of impressionist composers and even in that of certain romantic musicians. [Erik Satie, *Ecrits*, ed. Ornella Volta, rev. ed., Paris, 1981.]

Stravinsky's emphasis upon percussion and his other innovations in orchestration found a fertile ground in the music of Darius Milhaud at about the time of the First World War. Milhaud was the earliest major composer to use the percussion as an independent choir within the orchestra. In sections of his music (1913–22) to Paul Claudel's translation of the *Oresteia* by Aeschylus, striking dramatic effects are produced by narration joined to music solely for percussion ensemble. Edgard Varèse's emphasis upon percussion—most notably in his *Ionisation* (1931)—reflects Milhaud's innovations.

Music for percussion ensembles was also written by American composers on the West Coast such as John Cage and Lou Harrison in the 1930s and 1940s. These works are informed by a resourceful interest in new sounds and formal experimentation as well as by Asian music, in which percussion plays a large role.

Arnold Schoenberg was especially devoted to the chamber orchestra, for which he composed two Chamber Symphonies, a Serenade, Suite, and numerous works using voices. In these pieces Schoenberg's mature style of orchestration is most evident: there is little octave doubling of parts, a rapid change of colors, and, in general, an attempt to clarify and differentiate contrapuntal or motivic elements. Schoenberg writes in his *Interview mit mir selbst*:

> My goal has for some time been to find for my orchestral structures a form such that the fullness and saturation of sound shall be obtained only through the use of relatively few voices. . . . Coloristic changes serve, while animating the expression, to clarify the musical idea. That is their principal function.

In music by American composers such as Charles Ives, Henry Cowell, Edgard Varèse, Harry Partch, and John Cage, the chamber orchestra became a medium of experimentation with new sounds, textures, and structural principles. Ives composed over twenty-five works for small ensembles between 1900 and 1917. In his *Memos* he refers to them as "sound-pictures": "Some of these . . . chamber music pieces were in part made to strengthen the ear muscles, the mind muscles, and perhaps the Soul muscles too. . . . [They] gave the ears plenty of new sound experiences."

A major development in orchestration after the Second World War was the exploitation of *spatial effects*: dividing the orchestra into several groups which play from different parts of the stage or auditorium. The use of multiple sources of sound in music has a history dating from the Renaissance. In nineteenth-century music, offstage instruments were frequently used to create realistic effects. The offstage trumpet in Beethoven's *Fidelio* and offstage brass in requiems by Berlioz and Verdi are stirring examples of the nineteenth-century composer's use of multidimensional space.

Charles Ives applied these dramatic spatial devices in his *Unanswered Question* (ca. 1906). In the foreword to the score, the composer states that the strings are to be offstage and separated physically from the other instruments, which consist of a solo trumpet and a choir of flutes. The music played by these three orchestral groups is also made independent in character and relatively uncoordinated in time. Each of the three strata represents an actor in a metaphysical drama in which mankind (flutes) is confronted by recurrent existential doubt (the "question" stated by the trumpet) within the continuum of space and time represented by the offstage strings.

In his *Music for Strings, Percussion, and Celesta* (1936) Béla Bartók indicates a detailed seating plan in which two small string ensembles flank the percussion and keyboard instruments. These resources are then treated with great attention to the opposition, alternation, and union of bodies of sound. Unlike Ives's *Unanswered Question*, however, the spatial element in Bartók's work has no overt programmatic meaning.

Following the Second World War these initiatives in spatial arrangement were developed in many experimental directions both by European and American composers. Boulez manipulates divided orchestral groups in his *Doubles* (1958), *Domaines* (1968–69), and *Rituel* (1974) in which ensembles of various sizes engage in antiphonal repartee. Stockhausen's use of divided orchestras in *Gruppen* and *Carré* was anticipated by the spatial effects in his electronic work *Gesang der Jünglinge*, whose original version called for five distinct channels of sound to surround the audience. Stockhausen makes a grandiose extension of spatial effects in his *Sternklang* (1971), in which five ensembles perform in distant locales of an outdoor park.

A series of orchestral works by Iannis Xenakis beginning with *Terretektorh* (1966) calls for the instrumentalists to be scattered throughout the audience. These pieces extend the spatial effects used by this composer in his earlier *Duel* (1959) and *Stratégie* (1962), in which two orchestras engage in a game-like competition.

Spatiality has been a major concern of the Canadian-American composer Henry Brant (1913–). Virtually all of his orchestral music since the early 1950s uses multiple ensembles situated in different areas of an auditorium. Each ensemble carries on its own distinct musical discourse. In his article "Space as an Essential Aspect of Musical Composition" (1967), Brant investigates the ways in which unorthodox placement of performers can create novel acoustic effects. Unlike Ives's *Unanswered Question* (which Brant cites as his model), Brant's orchestrational medium does not suggest dramatic or theatric ideas. Placement of the instrumentalists is intended instead to enhance the acoustic experience of the listener. He writes:

> The spatial elements in concert music, if exploited fully and expressively, could make their points much more strongly if the sounds could be heard in complete darkness, without the disturbing and confusing intervention of merely functional visual impressions . . . that are irrelevant to the actual communication of the music in terms of its sound.

TONE COLOR

At the conclusion of his *Theory of Harmony* (1911), Arnold Schoenberg enters into a speculative discussion on the role of tone color in music of the future. He states:

> It must also be possible to make [melodic] progressions out of tone colors . . . , progressions whose relations with one another work with a kind of logic entirely equivalent to that logic which satisfies us in the melody of pitches. That has the appearance of a futuristic fantasy and is probably just that. But it is one which, I firmly believe, will be realized. I firmly believe it is capable of heightening in an unprecedented manner the sensory, intellectual, and spiritual pleasures offered by art. . . . Tone-color melodies [*Klangfarbenmelodien*]! How acute the senses that would be able to perceive them! How high the development of spirit that could find pleasure in such subtle things!

As Schoenberg predicted, the importance of tone color rose to unprecedented heights later in the twentieth century. In addition to the creation of tone-color melodies which Schoenberg advised, composers have increasingly called upon the voice and traditional instruments to produce unorthodox sounds, to play in registral extremes, and to master high levels of technical complication. The twentieth century has also witnessed a revolution in musical instruments in which electronic devices for the production of sound have supplemented conventional instruments. The percussion has undergone a dramatic increase in its variety and independent use, and other sources of noise or sounds of unfixed pitch have lent their timbres to the modern composer. In experimental compositions by European and American composers before and after the Second World War, timbre has sometimes become the sole compositional material.

Klangfarbenmelodie ("tone-color melody") is a term coined by Schoenberg, who suggests by it (see the preceding quotation) that melodic elements can be created by successions of different colors as well as by different pitches. The third of Schoenberg's Five Pieces for Orchestra Op. 16 (1909)—which he alternately titled "Chord Colors," "Colors," "Summer Morning by a Lake," and "The Changing Chord"—is Schoenberg's primary example of this concept. The movement is in a ternary form in which the outer sections (beginning at measures 1 and 32) contain relatively long-held notes which dovetail into a kaleidoscope of changing colors and chords. The middle section (measures 12–31) is animated by a filigree of short figures in a more pointillistic texture. Although the mottled play of colors of this orchestral panorama first captures our attention, the work is structured by recurrent harmonies and brief motives. The principal chord is the initial pentad G♯ A B C E, which returns transposed at the end of the first section and in the reprise; the primary motive is the figure A B♭ A♭, heard in long values and in different transpositions in all parts in the A section and in fleeting diminutions in the middle part. This movement, accordingly, is not a pure exercise in timbral composition, but it is indeed unusual in Schoenberg's music in the degree to which normal motivic exposition and development are hidden by rhythmic and coloristic devices.

The music of Anton Webern contains a different type of tone-color melody. Webern's lines are often constructed of small segments which are passed among several instruments, with further variety added by a large number of rests and disjunctions in register.

Webern's orchestration of the subject of the six-voice ricercar from Bach's *Musical Offering* (Example 6-3) illustrates his use of changing colors within a single theme. The line is passed back and forth among three muted brass instruments and punctuated by the harp harmonic in measure 5 before it is turned over to the contrasting colors of flute and violin in measure 9. In a letter to Hermann Scherchen dated January 1, 1938, Webern states that in his Bach arrangement the "instrumentation attempts to reveal motivic coher-

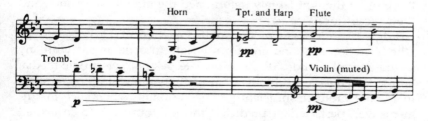

Example 6-3. Bach *Fuga (Ricercata) no. 2 aus dem "Musikalischen Opfer" von Joh. Seb. Bach.* Transcribed for orchestra by Anton Webern. Copyright 1935 by Universal Edition. Copyright renewed 1963. All rights reserved. Used by permission of European American Music Distributors Corporation, sole U.S. agents for Universal Edition.

ence." Webern asserts, in other words, that color serves to clarify structures of pitch; it is not an independent element.

Each change of color occurs at a point at which Webern perceived a juncture in the motivic structure of the theme. In his letter to Scherchen, Webern explains that he considered the opening of the theme to consist of three groups of five notes each: C E♭ G A♭ D / G F♯ F E E♭ / (E♭) D D♭ C B. The first group—terminated by a rest—is given to a single instrument. Each of the pairs of descending semitones of the second group is emphasized by alternative statements in the horn and trumpet. This second group overlaps with the third segment on the note E♭, a juncture that Webern underscores by doubling the note with a harp harmonic. The beginning of the next structural unit of the fugue—the answer and countersubject in measure 9—is signaled by contrasting string and woodwind sonorities.

Experiments and innovations in musical sound were in abundance in Europe in the early years of the twentieth century. The Italian Futurist artist and composer Luigi Russolo (1885–1947) used noise to create musical works that celebrate the machine and life in an industrial society. Bartók, Schoenberg, Berg, and Stravinsky devised new playing techniques on traditional instruments, which provided these composers with a more diverse palette of colors. But it was among experimental composers in America that sound was used in the most original way. In works by Edgard Varèse, Henry Cowell, John Cage, Morton Feldman, George Crumb, and others, a movement was established in which tone colors were freed from their traditional role of clarifying structures of pitch and rhythm and became instead independent structural elements. George Rochberg alludes to this development in his article "The New Image of Music" (1963): "Today, the sound material of music enjoys an autonomy never before accorded it. . . . This liberation permits sounds to create their own context, a reversal of the traditional procedure in which the train of thought largely determined the individual sounds and their succession."

Edgard Varèse was a pioneer of this movement. He crusaded for "the liberation of sound and for my right to make music with any sound and all sounds." Prior to his late pieces in electronic media, Varèse felt constrained by the unavailability of musical instruments that could produce sufficiently varied sounds. When such instruments were perfected, he predicted, musical forms would be shaped solely from the manipulation of masses of sound. In a lecture at Santa Fe in 1936, he said: "The role of color or timbre [will] be completely changed from being incidental, anecdotal, sensual or picturesque; it [will] become an agent of delineation like the different colors on a map separating different areas, and an integral part of form."

Varèse's ensemble music of the 1920s and 1930s contains vivid timbral elements, such as the appearance of sirens in his *Ionisation* and the dramatic climaxes for *ondes Martenot* in *Ecuatorial*. Varèse's theories regarding the liberation of sound were fully realized only at the end of his career in his electronic works, of which *Poème électronique* (1958) is the masterpiece.

A series of experimental works by Henry Cowell written for the strings of a piano prefigure the liberation of sound of electronic music. Cowell's *Banshee* (1925, Anthology No. 7) is typical of these studies. Noise from the piano strings creates an eerie effect, which forms a backdrop to short melodic motives made by plucking the strings.

Among American composers after World War II, Morton Feldman (1926–87) typifies the fascination with sound that had long characterized his American forebears. His music consists primarily of studies in contrasting timbres, normally in hushed dynamics and devoid of motivic development, regular pulse, or dramatic climaxes. Feldman's devotion to sound led him to bypass systematic constructive methods of composition and, in their place, to embrace indeterminate procedures. "An indeterminate music can lead only to catastrophe," he writes in the article "Pre-Determinate/Indeterminate" (1966). "This catastrophe we allowed to take place. Behind it was sound—which unified everything. Only by 'unfixing' the elements traditionally used to construct a piece of music could the sounds exist in themselves—not as symbols, or memories which were memories of other music to begin with."

Certainly, the most important outcome of the liberation of sound in the twentieth century is the medium of electronic music—a development beginning about 1950 which is surveyed in Chapter 15. The electronic experience influenced the works in nontaped media by American composers, who continued to seek new vistas in the art of sound. The music of George Crumb, for example, combines a panoply of conventional and unorthodox instruments and innovative vocal techniques to create his vivid and dramatic soundscapes.

Yet other composers in America have remained aloof from the revolution in new timbres. Schoenberg—who, ironically, had eagerly foretold the liberation of sound in his *Theory of Harmony*—later recanted and proclaimed that color was not basic to the vocabulary of musical thought. In his essay "Composition with Twelve Tones" he writes: "More mature minds resist the temptation to become intoxicated by colors and prefer to be coldly convinced by the transparency of clear-cut ideas." Similarly, Elliott Carter has stated in the interview *Flawed Words and Stubborn Sounds*: "As far as color goes, I still believe that the real interest of music lies in its organization. . . . I don't believe in novelty of sound for its own sake; that is always the easiest thing to bring off and loses its interest very quickly."

TEXTURE

Western music prior to the twentieth century utilized three primary textures: *monophony*, which consists of a single melodic line; *homophony*, in which one predominant line stands forth from a backdrop of chords or other accompanimental strata; and *polyphony* or *counterpoint*, in which two or more distinct lines are heard simultaneously. Throughout the classic and romantic periods, homophonic textures were most common. These endured in the twentieth century, especially in the hands of composers for whom clarity and lightness of spirit were paramount.

In the late nineteenth and early twentieth centuries, there began a revival of polyphonic writing among composers in several different styles. In works by neoclassicists such as Paul Hindemith and Stravinsky, counterpoint often evoked baroque music. Hindemith took the orchestral music of Bach as a point of departure for his busy, linear *Kammermusik* series (1924–27)—a cycle of concertos for different instruments and chamber orchestra. Counterpoint in Stravinsky's neoclassic works served to dispel pictorial connotations within the music and to create the unemotional and objective tone that he intended his music to convey. In an article entitled "Some Ideas about my Octuor [Octet]" (1924), Stravinsky writes: "Form in my music derives from counterpoint. I consider counterpoint as the only means through which the attention of the composer is concentrated on purely musical questions. Its elements also lend themselves perfectly to an architectural construction" (from Eric Walter White, *Stravinsky* [Berkeley and Los Angeles, 1969], p. 530).

German and Austrian modernists beginning with Gustav Mahler and Richard Strauss adopted the dense part writing of Brahms and contrapuntal passages from Wagner's works such as *Die Meistersinger* and *Siegfried Idyll* as models for further development. The texture of Mahler's later symphonies is dominated by a free and dense polyphony. Principal melodic lines are commonly accompanied by one or more subsidiary lines, all of which share common motivic elements. This style of polyphony was developed by Schoenberg and his school. "It is apparent and will probably become increasingly clear," Schoenberg writes in his *Theory of Harmony*, "that we are turning to a new epoch of polyphonic style, and as in the earlier epochs, harmonies will be a product of voice leading." Schoenberg's polyphony may be studied in his First String Quartet, of which the opening ten measures are shown in Example 6-4. The principal line is contained in the first violin, with important subsidiary lines presented in the viola and cello. Later in this work, motives and shapes from all three lines recur in new forms within densely polyphonic textures. In most such passages one line is still predominant. Schoenberg and his student Alban Berg later used the notation H⌐ (for *Hauptstimme* or "principal voice") and N⌐ (*Nebenstimme*, "subsidiary voice") to clarify the relative importance of the lines within their complicated polyphony.

Example 6-4. Schoenberg, First String Quartet, measures 1–10.

The strict imitative forms of canon and fugue have been maintained or reinterpreted by twentieth-century composers. Canon has proved to be a basic means for contrapuntal elaboration in modern music, especially in works that use the twelve-tone method. The sixth movement of Webern's Second Cantata Op. 31, for example, is a four-voice canon in which the lines are interrelated by inversion and retrograde. Schoenberg's "Mondfleck" from *Pierrot lunaire*—an atonal, pre-twelve-tone composition—combines canonic lines in the strings and woodwinds with a fugue in the piano.

Fugue—more than canon or free polyphonic writing—is intimately related to traditional tonality. All the same, modern musicians have mingled traditional elements of fugue—subject and answer separated by the interval of a fifth, alternating statements of subjects and episodes, and stretti, to name a few—with a liberated harmonic and tonal idiom. Stravinsky, for example, writes fugues and fugatos in his Octet, *Symphony of Psalms, Dumbarton Oaks* Concerto, and *Orpheus*. Hindemith's *Ludus tonalis* for piano (1942) contains a cycle of twelve three-part fugues which integrate traditional and nontraditional features. The first movement of Bartók's *Music for Strings, Percussion, and Celesta* (1936) is an especially ingenious adaptation of fugal principles to liberated tonality and symmetrical form. The subject—a chromatic figure beginning on the note A—is answered first on E and then on D, and it continues to reappear through a cycle of fifths both above and below the starting point. The second half of the movement introduces freely inverted forms of the subject, which return through a cycle of fifths to the central "tonic" A.

A momentous change in twentieth-century musical style occurred when composers began to dispense with the traditional textures of homophony and polyphony and to experiment with various alternatives. Americans such as Varèse and Cowell were pioneers in this stylistic revolution as they delved into textures made from masses of sound rather than from intervals, lines, and chords. In Europe, Anton Webern was pivotal in the "liberation of texture" which characterized postwar European developments.

Webern's instrumental music disguises polyphonic textures beyond recognition. The beginning of his Symphony Op. 21 (Example 6-5) illustrates this phenomenon. The texture consists of several lines, each of which is made discontinuous by the placement of rests, large leaps, disjunctions in register, and rapid changes of color. It is, in fact, difficult to perceive any lines in the traditional sense, and the listener's attention is at first drawn to a mottled array of individual sounds or intervals. Webern's textures of this kind may be described as *pointillistic*. This term comes from art criticism,

*) Sounds as written

Example 6-5. Webern Symphony Op. 21, first movement. Copyright 1929 by Universal Edition. Copyright renewed 1956. All rights reserved. Used by permission of European American Music Distributors Corporation, sole U.S. agents for Universal Edition.

where it refers to a technique of painting used by Georges Seurat (1859–91) and Paul Signac (1863–1935), in which subjects are represented by a multitude of dots of pure color. The mosaic of dots appears at a distance to merge into recognizable forms.

Although it is unlikely that Webern intended works such as the Symphony to obliterate conventional textures, these pieces guided European composers after the Second World War in their elimination of traditional musical argument based on thematic statement and elaboration. György Ligeti writes in his article "Weberns Melodik" (1966) that Webern's fragmentation of line created a new "global" texture in which the mosaic of independent colors and intervals is amalgamated into a large static mass. "Global form has no characteristics of traditional musical form because of the relative autonomy of its constituent parts. In it there is no longer a flow of music through time. It has no real termination; rather, it is summation and structure made from individual moments. The music appears to stand still, to effect a stoppage in the stream of time."

Ligeti, Stockhausen, Boulez, and many of their European contemporaries eagerly adopted into their own music the global texture made from autonomous moments of sound which they found in

Pointillism in nineteenth-century French painting: Georges Seurat, *Bridge and Quays at Port-en-Bessin*. (Courtesy of The Minneapolis Institute of Arts.)

Webern. Stockhausen's *Kreuzspiel* (1951, excerpt in Anthology no. 26) is an example of postwar pointillism. In this music there is no line, accompaniment, counterpoint, or motivic development in the traditional sense (although the part for tumbas at the beginning provides a linear measurement of durational values). The texture instead projects a maximal differentiation of pitches, durations, registers, colors, and other musical elements, which focuses our attention upon isolated moments rather than upon linear continuities.

By the later 1950s many among the European avant-garde had become concerned that their pointillistic textures were too uniform. Composers such as Ligeti recognized that the maximum differentiation and variety that they sought had ironically produced a deadening sameness. While figures such as Stockhausen and Boulez were bringing indeterminacy to their music for the sake of variety, others such as Ligeti and Krzysztof Penderecki developed new ways to govern masses and textures of sound. Their experiments in *textural composition* were widely imitated in both Europe and America, and they represent the outcome of an evolution of texture begun by Webern.

Ligeti's music beginning with his orchestral studies *Apparitions* (1958–59) and *Atmosphères* (1961) is concerned primarily with textures. The specific intervals, lines, and colors from which they are made are subsumed into a totality of sound which becomes the elemental compositional material. The textures are created mainly by sustained chromatic clusters or by busy chromatic figures distributed over fifty or more orchestral voices, and these masses then interact by collision, penetration, dissipation, merging, or other vividly dramatic gestures.

In his article "Zustände, Ereignisse, Wandlungen" (1967), Ligeti writes: "The transformation of optical and tactile sensations into acoustic phenomena often occurs to me involuntarily. I almost always associate sounds with color, form, and consistency, and, conversely, every acoustic sensation has form, color, and material qualities."

His *Apparitions* is a musical interpretation of the texture of a vast web of filaments, which is transformed into new shapes by a series of sonic jolts. *Volumina* for organ (1961–62) uses graphic notation (see Chapter 14) to represent its textures and their transformation. In later works such as the wordless dramas of *Aventures* (1962) and *Nouvelles aventures* (1962–65), Ligeti returns to textures of a more pointillistic type.

BIBLIOGRAPHY

Theories of musical sound are advanced by Wayne Slawson in *Sound Color* (Berkeley, 1985), Robert Cogan in *New Images of Musical Sound* (Cambridge, Mass., 1984), and Robert Erickson in *Sound Structure in Music* (Berkeley, 1975). Extended playing techniques are surveyed in Gardner Read's *Compendium of Modern Instrumental Techniques* (Westport, Conn., 1993). General historical surveys of orchestration are found in Gardner Read's *Style and Orchestration* (New York, 1979); the book-length article "Histoire de l'orchestration" by Gabriel Pierné and Henry Woollett in the *Encyclopédie de la musique et dictionnaire du conservatoire*, ed. Albert Lavignac and Lionel de La Laurencie, Part 2, Vol. 4, 2215–2286 and 2445–2818 (Paris, 1929); and Egon Wellesz's *Die neue Instrumentation*, second ed. (Berlin, 1928). Aaron Copland's discussion of the sonorous image of modern music is found in *Music and Imagination* (Cambridge, Mass., 1952).

The autobiographical "Memoirs of the Late Princesse Edmond de Polignac" are found in *Horizon: A Review of Literature and Art*, 12 (1945). Charles Ives's Memos (ed. John Kirkpatrick, New York, 1972) were written in 1931 and 1932 as a private rejoinder to journalistic critiques of his music. A list of published music for chamber orchestra is given by Cecilia and Henry Saltonstall in their *New Catalog of Music for Small Orchestra* (Clifton, N.J., 1978).

Henry Brant's "Space as an Essential Aspect of Musical Composition" is in the collection *Contemporary Composers on Contemporary Music,* ed. Elliott Schwartz and Barney Childs (New York, 1967). The untitled article by Satie on Stravinsky is published in French in Satie's *Ecrits,* ed. Ornella Volta, rev. ed. (Paris, 1981). Varèse's lecture in Santa Fe in 1936 is excerpted in "The Liberation of Sound," *Perspectives of New Music,* 5 (1966). Schoenberg's "Interview mit mir selbst" is in the Schoenberg *Gesammelte Schriften,* ed. Ivan Vojtěch, Vol. 1 (n.p., Fischer, 1976).

Ligeti's article "Weberns Melodik" is in *Melos,* 33 (1966), and "Zustände, Ereignisse, Wandlungen" by the same author is in *Melos,* 34 (1967). Morton Feldman's remarks on the purity of musical sound are found in "Pre-Determinate/Indeterminate," *Composer,* 19 (1966). In Allen Edwards's *Flawed Words and Stubborn Sounds: A Conversation with Elliott Carter* (New York, 1971), Carter speaks slightingly about timbral composition. George Rochberg's article on the liberation of sound and the "spatialization" of new music, entitled "The New Image of Music," is in *Perspectives of New Music,* 2 (1963).

PART TWO

Music from 1900 to 1945

7

Avant-Garde Composition in Germany and Austria

At the turn of the twentieth century, German musical culture was preeminent in the Western world. German music was widely admired and imitated by composers of virtually every Western nationality. The works of Richard Wagner had become a beacon of modernism, an inspiration for a generation of young writers and artists as well as musicians. The music of Brahms honored a distinguished past by preserving traditional forms and genres, but transformed them in such a way as to defy distinctions between old and new. As the twentieth century began, there was great confidence that Germany would continue to be the source of new musical ideas.

Modern music, like modern developments in the other arts, was centered mainly in the large cities of the German-speaking world, especially Vienna and Berlin. Vienna, or the "Music City," as it was known, was by longstanding reputation conservative in its tastes, and here modernism had the tinge of a youthful rebellion against values of the older generation. Stefan Zweig writes in his memoirs *The World of Yesterday*:

Suddenly the old, comfortable order was disturbed, its former and infallible norms of the "aesthetically beautiful" (Hanslick) were questioned, and while the official critics of our correct bourgeois newspapers were dismayed by the often daring experiments and sought to dam the irresistible stream with such epithets as "decadent" and "anarchistic," we young ones threw ourselves enthusiastically into the surf where it foamed at its wildest. We had the feeling that a time had set in for us, our time, in which youth had finally achieved its rights.

In Berlin, on the other hand, experiment was tolerated, so that many of Vienna's younger musicians looked enviously across the border at a more sympathetic atmosphere for their endeavors. In 1904 a number of young Austrian musicians—among them Arnold Schoenberg and Alexander von Zemlinsky—set about to create a society for the advancement of modern music. The organizers presented their case to the conservative Viennese theorist Heinrich Schenker:

Whoever compares the musical situation in Vienna with that in even the smaller cities of Germany will recognize that the "Musikstadt" has for a long time lagged behind. It has lacked that minimal progress which one demands of all cultural centers, even those that rest on their laurels of yesteryear. Those who suffer most for this are the young creative artists, the rising generation of composers, not only of Vienna but of the Empire. In Germany the public and the press regard serious modern artists not simply with snobbish condescension, but show their favor with warmth and high regard. Here their efforts are greeted at all times with silence. [Oswald Jonas Memorial Collection, University of California, Riverside.]

Developments in modern music in Germany and Austria were closely allied to modernism in the other arts, an affinity that was stimulated by the unusually close personal contact among younger musicians, architects, writers, and painters. The architectural style of Adolf Loos (1870–1933), for example, with its austere geometrical shapes and rejection of ornament, has much in common with the musical idiom of his close friend Arnold Schoenberg, who similarly eliminated all but the essentials of musical expression. The operas of Alban Berg deal with themes of social criticism, sexuality, and the degradation of the individual, which were matters addressed by contemporary Expressionist playwrights. Schoenberg's aesthetics of intuitive subjective expression are remarkably akin to those of Expressionist painters such as his friend Vasili Kandinski (1866–1944).

This chapter will follow the musical accomplishments of a group of German and Austrian composers who placed great value on the progress of style. They formed an avant-garde in that they consciously sought to expand and reinvigorate their inherited musical language. Yet none of them was an experimentalist: their innovations and artistic outlook were grounded instead in their musical past.

Their movement may be divided into three chronological and stylistic phases. The first is an extension of progressive tendencies among German composers of the late nineteenth century; the second, atonality and its associated styles; and, third, a postwar stylistic consolidation which coincided with the early years of twelve-tone composition. The avant-garde movement in Germany and Austria was brought to a decisive halt in the 1930s by the Nazis. From then until the end of the Second World War, only the most traditional composers were tolerated.

THE PROGRESSIVE ROMANTICS

The music of Wagner and Brahms proved to be a compelling model for progressive German and Austrian composers born in the second half of the nineteenth century. The older figures in this group, such as Gustav Mahler (1860–1911), Hugo Wolf (1860–1903), and Richard Strauss (1864–1949), typically singled out Wagner as the spiritual leader of modernism and rejected—often vehemently—what they saw as the conservative direction of Brahms. But the younger composers—Alexander von Zemlinsky (1871–1942), Max Reger (1873–1916), Arnold Schoenberg (1874–1951), and Franz Schreker (1878–1934)—were inclined to see both Brahms and Wagner as models for future developments in music.

From Brahms they inherited a renewed confidence in the power of absolute instrumental music. Also from Brahms came a revival of interest in the string quartet and other chamber genres, notably among the works of Reger, Zemlinsky, and Schoenberg. From Wagner they took their harmonic idiom and attenuated tonality, the leitmotif technique, massive lengths and media, and mythic subjects. Most of their works shared Wagner's affirmation of the power of the individual artist to control his world and destiny. They were progressives in their determination to preserve and advance those ideals of composition which were so strikingly innovative in the music of their models.

The musical idiom of these "progressive romantics" was not limited to the years at the turn of the century. Indeed, in works by Richard Strauss it continued into the 1940s. Thus it existed side-by-side with other styles: atonality, on one hand, and the traditionalism of composers such as Hans Pfitzner (1869–1949) and the German neoclassicists of the 1920s and 1930s on the other. Their idiom has itself been revived in the 1970s by American composers such as Thomas Pasatieri, David Del Tredici, and George Rochberg.

Gustav Mahler's ten symphonies mark the end of a symphonic tradition among Viennese composers which included masterworks by Haydn, Mozart, Beethoven, Brahms, and Bruckner. Although Mahler was an ardent supporter of Wagner and a great conductor of his music, Beethoven was his model for symphonic composition, a model that he enriched by the addition of elements from the music of Bruckner, Wagner, Tchaikovsky, and Liszt, popular Austrian music, and Jewish ghetto music.

Mahler's symphonic genres—the absolute symphony, programmatic symphony, and symphony with voices—all have precedents in the works of Beethoven. The expansive slow movements of the Third, Fourth, and Ninth Symphonies take their departure from the Adagio of Beethoven's Ninth Symphony, and the scherzo with multiple trios, used by Mahler in most of his works, is suggested by the scherzi of Beethoven's Fourth and Seventh Symphonies. Mahler's characteristic juxtaposition of the ecstatic and the mundane is prefigured by passages such as the Turkish march in the finale of Beethoven's Ninth Symphony, and his technique of recapitulating themes from first movements in finales (as in his First, Second, Fifth, Seventh, and Eighth Symphonies) is also seen in Beethoven's Ninth.

Mahler's attitude toward programmatic music was ambivalent. His early symphonies are intensely programmatic, and he remarked in a letter of 1897 to Arthur Seidl that he needed a verbal idea to guide and motivate his work. Nevertheless, he meticulously eliminated programmatic details from the published scores of all of his music, bringing it still closer to the tradition of Beethoven and the Viennese symphony. By doing so, he hoped to bypass the inclination of audiences of his day to invent elaborate verbal explanations of instrumental music. Mahler summarized his views on programmatic music in a letter to Max Marschalk of 1896:

> I know that, so far as I myself am concerned, as long as I can express an experience in words, I should never try to put it into music. The need to express myself musically—in symphonic terms—begins only on the plane of obscure feelings, at the gate that opens into the "other world," the world in which things no longer fall apart in time and space. Just as I find it banal to compose programme music, I regard it as unsatisfactory and unfruitful to try to make programme notes for a piece of music. This remains so despite the fact that the reason why a composition comes into existence at all is bound to be something the composer has experienced, something real, which might after all be considered sufficiently concrete to be expressed in words.

In his Eighth Symphony (1906–1907), dubbed the *Symphony of a Thousand* on account of its immense instrumental and vocal re-

GUSTAV MAHLER
(*Kalište, 1860–Vienna, 1911*)

Mahler was born to the family of a merchant and innkeeper and lived as a child in Bohemia and Moravia, north of Vienna. He exhibited a prodigious talent on piano, which he continued to study at the Conservatory of the Gesellschaft der Musikfreunde in Vienna from 1875 to 1878. He also attended lectures at the University of Vienna, where he became acquainted with Anton Bruckner. After his days as a student, Mahler put aside his plans to be a concert pianist and concentrated instead upon conducting and composition. He served as a conductor in Kassel, Prague, Leipzig, Budapest, and Hamburg before his appointment in 1897 as director of the Vienna State Opera. From 1907 until 1911 he conducted at the Metropolitan Opera in New York and served briefly as conductor of the New York Philharmonic.

SELECTED WORKS

Symphonies. Ten symphonies (1888–1910); *Das Lied von der Erde* ("a symphony for tenor, contralto and orchestra," 1908).
Songs. Cycles: *Lieder eines fahrenden Gesellen* (texts by the composer, 1884) and *Kindertotenlieder* (Rückert, 1904). Other songs on texts from *Des Knaben Wunderhorn* and on poetry by Mahler, Leander, Tirso de Molina, and Rückert. The early songs are for the medium of voice and piano, the later songs for voice and piano or orchestra.

quirements, Mahler returns to a metaphysical theme—the nature of divine spirit—comparable to those that he addressed in his earlier works. This symphony is his swan song to Wagnerian romanticism in its grandiloquence and larger-than-life affirmation. It is in a style to which Mahler did not return: the summer after completing this magnificent statement of faith, he learned that he had an incurable heart ailment that would soon bring about his own death. His works after this time—*Das Lied von der Erde*, Symphony No. 9, and the incomplete Symphony No. 10—reflect the personal anxiety and skepticism that would impel him in new stylistic directions.

The Tenth Symphony was left in a fragmentary state after Mahler's work on it during the summer of 1910. The manuscripts suggest a five-movement piece in F♯ major, of which the first movement (Adagio) was the most completely scored. This movement is often performed alone, although a version of the entire symphony has been successfully reconstructed by Deryck Cooke from the drafts and sketches.

The Adagio from the Tenth Symphony deviates strikingly from the idiom of Mahler's earlier works. Its form is unlike any of his other first movements. Here an introductory viola theme (A) returns in cyclic fashion, alternating with two other principal themes B and C. These themes are shown in Example 7-1. Elements of sonata form are present in the development of themes in measures 112–40 and in the reprise of themes B and C beginning at measure 141.

The modern spirit of the work resides in its abstract mood, wide and angular leaps in the principal themes, intensely polyphonic texture, and chromatic content of both lines and chords. The relationship of lines to underlying harmonies is sometimes remote, as a result of Mahler's typically free handling of embellishing tones (see Chapter 1).

Example 7-1. Mahler, Symphony No. 10, Adagio. Copyright 1951 by Associated Music Publishers, Inc. Reprinted by permission.

Principal melodic ideas of this Adagio are motivically interrelated, which was a feature of much German music of the nineteenth century that would be of immense importance for early atonal composition. All the themes of the movement grow out of motives of the viola's introduction. With respect to contour and rhythm, theme C begins almost identically to A. The head motive of theme B is constructed out of the emphasized notes of A as shown by the bracket in Example 7-1. Themes B and C then become the basis for new variants, some of which for theme B are illustrated in Example 7-2. The head motive of theme B is inverted at measure 20, for example, and its second measure is spun into a diminution at measure 28.

The Adagio of the Tenth Symphony illustrates clearly how Mahler replaces the distinct thematic areas of the classical symphony with a web of themes that derive by motivic variation from a common source. It was precisely this formal procedure that Schoenberg dubbed "developing variation" and that he would apply in all of his own works, whether tonal or atonal.

If Mahler's model as a composer was Beethoven, then Richard Strauss's model was Mozart, with whom he shared an effortless lyricism and great technical virtuosity. Strauss began his career as a composer of tone poems, brilliantly reviving the genre established by Liszt, and lieder, where he was a worthy successor to Schubert and Schumann. After two early operas in the Wagnerian vein,

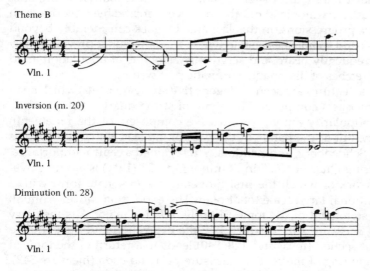

Example 7-2.   Mahler, Symphony No. 10, Adagio. Copyright 1951 by Associated Music Publishers, Inc. Reprinted by permission.

Guntram (1893) and *Feuersnot* (1901), he turned his attention almost exclusively to the stage. His next two operas, *Salome* and *Elektra*, continue to use the Wagnerian technique of the leitmotif, but they are strikingly original in their subject matter, free use of dissonance, and extended tonality.

Strauss then returned to the model of Mozart's Italian operas and *Singspiele* in a collaboration with the Viennese poet and playwright Hugo von Hofmannsthal (1874–1929), first with the immensely popular *Der Rosenkavalier* (1910), which was then followed by five other works. In these and in his later operas, Strauss adopts a tuneful, predominantly consonant, and tonal idiom, with few references to the experimental style of *Salome* or *Elektra*. Later in this chapter we shall return to the opera *Salome* as a forerunner of Expressionist musical theater.

Max Reger's short but prolific career is marked by a multiplicity of stylistic directions. At various times he was an outspoken advocate of conservative trends in late nineteenth-century music and also of the more progressive tendencies associated with Wagner and the "New German School." But Reger was primarily a follower of Brahms, who had once praised his youthful compositions. He returned time and again to genres and media of the classical era—chamber music, the sonata, and variations forms—and his admiration for the music of Bach and earlier contrapuntal masters is shown by his many fugal works. His music, nevertheless, is marked by asymmetric phrasing, irregular rhythm and meter, organically unified motivic work, and, above all, a harmonic idiom that achieves remarkable freedom from diatonic progressions. In this last area he goes considerably beyond Brahms and establishes a style where triads within a prevailing key are infrequently heard and serve only as points of orientation amid long stretches of dissonant, chromatic part writing.

These features are seen in Reger's five string quartets, which span his career as a composer. The genre of string quartet did not enjoy great popularity among progressive composers of the nineteenth century, but at the hands of the post-Brahmsian romantics such as Reger, Schoenberg, and Zemlinsky, it regained a central importance. The String Quartet No. 5 in F♯ minor Op. 121 (1911) is a four-movement work of which the first movement is in sonata form with a conventional large-scale tonal plan. The exposition moves from an initial statement of the tonic F♯ to the relative major A (subsidiary theme, measure 76), in which key the exposition ends. The development section (measures 128–240) leads to a return of the tonic at the beginning of the reprise (measure 241) and coda (measure 342). But between these principal tonal guideposts, the sense of a controlling key is not at all strong.

MAX REGER
(*Brand, 1873–Leipzig, 1916*)

Reger's early years were spent in the Bavarian town of Weiden; his father was a schoolmaster and musical amateur, and Reger received keyboard lessons from a local organist, Adalbert Lindner. In 1890 he moved to Sondershausen to study with the renowned scholar and composer Hugo Riemann, and he followed Riemann shortly thereafter to Wiesbaden. From 1901 to 1907 he lived in Munich, attempting to make his way as a composer and pianist. He subsequently was appointed Professor of Composition and Director of Music at the University of Leipzig and, in 1911, conductor of the orchestra in Meiningen. In 1915 he moved to Jena, but retained teaching duties in Leipzig.

SELECTED WORKS

Orchestral Music. Concertos (violin and piano), overtures, variations, tone poems.

Choral Music. Part songs, cantatas, miscellaneous music for the Latin liturgy.

Chamber Music. Five string quartets (1900–11); sonatas for violin alone, violin and piano, cello and piano, clarinet and piano; Clarinet Quintet (1915).

Songs. Over 250 songs, including the *Schlichte Weisen* Op. 76. Some are orchestrated.

Music for Piano Solo. Variations and fugues on themes by Telemann, Mozart, Beethoven, and Bach; dances; character pieces, études.

Music for Organ. Two sonatas (1899, 1901); chorale fantasies; fugues.

Reger links together a large number of loosely related themes, which project rapidly differing moods ranging from the brief whole-tone idea at measures 10–12 to the *Ländler* at measure 76. The themes are constructed in the manner of a "musical prose"—a characteristic of Reger—in their asymmetrical and nonperiodic phrasing and irregularity of rhythm and meter.

Reger's music often has a singsong quality created by the effusion of themes and sudden changes of mood, sections of turgid counterpoint, and the lack of strongly directed harmonic motion. His music was nevertheless influential upon later German composers such as Schoenberg and Paul Hindemith, who saw in it a logical development for musical style between the age of Brahms and Wagner and the twentieth century.

Arnold Schoenberg is the greatest of the late romantic German composers born into the generation after Strauss and Mahler. Schoenberg's early music draws upon the styles of both Wagner and Brahms, but, unlike his contemporaries Zemlinsky, Reger, and Schreker, he eventually went beyond this hybrid language and transformed it in an entirely new way. We will thus have occasion to return to Schoenberg's music under several different headings in this chapter.

Schoenberg remarked that his works fell into three stylistic periods: extended tonality until about 1908, atonality from 1908 until about 1921, and twelve-tone composition after 1921. We focus now upon the first of these three. Schoenberg's period of tonal composition produced seven published collections of lieder, two programmatic works (the string sextet *Verklärte Nacht* and the symphonic poem *Pelleas und Melisande*), chamber music (two string quartets and a chamber symphony), the chorus *Friede auf Erden*, and the massive cantata *Gurrelieder*. By Schoenberg's admission his models were Brahms and Wagner and, later, Strauss and Mahler. It is unclear whether he knew much of Reger's music early in his career, but he later expressed great admiration for it.

His early style is exemplified by the String Quartet No. 1 in D minor Op. 7 (1905). The key of D had a special importance for Schoenberg at this time. It is also the key of an earlier string quartet (1897), the sextet *Verklärte Nacht*, and the symphonic poem *Pelleas und Melisande*. Later it would be used by him and his students to refer in a general way to his accomplishments of this period.

Even in the first measures of this quartet, Schoenberg's superior command of the late romantic idiom is plain. The impetuous first theme is the start of a breathless inspiration which continues unabated to the end. The work is in one movement, whose sections combine features of both the sonata-allegro form and the movement types of a traditional four-movement quartet or symphony. This formal amalgam is found in the nineteenth century, for example, in Liszt's Piano Sonata in B minor, and it was used in several

ARNOLD SCHOENBERG
(*Vienna, 1874–Los Angeles, 1951*)

Schoenberg was largely self-taught as a musician. He received a few lessons from his future brother-in-law Alexander von Zemlinsky, but otherwise developed his musical skills by an intense and independent study of the works of the masters. Until he was forced to flee Europe for America in 1933, he lived alternately in Berlin and Vienna. His last residence in Berlin was from 1926 to 1933, when he was Professor of Composition at the Academy of Arts. Schoenberg continued his teaching in America, primarily at the University of California, Los Angeles.

SELECTED WORKS

Operas. *Erwartung* (1909), *Die glückliche Hand* (1910–13), *Von Heute auf Morgen* (1929), *Moses und Aron* (1932, incomplete).

Orchestral Music. *Pelleas und Melisande* (1903); Five Pieces Op. 16 (1909); Variations Op. 31 (1928); Concertos for violin (1936) and piano (1942).

Chamber Music. Five string quartets (1897–1936; the earliest has no opus number), sextet *Verklärte Nacht* (1899), two chamber symphonies, Serenade (1923), Woodwind Quintet (1924), Suite (1926), String Trio (1946).

Piano and Organ Music. Five collections for piano solo (Opp. 11, 19, 23, 25, 33 [two versions]), Variations on a Recitative (organ, 1941).

Songs. Eight collections of lieder for voice and piano (Opp. 1–3, 6, 12, 14, 15, 48), orchestral songs (Opp. 8, 22), *Herzgewächse* (1911).

Choral Music. *Gurrelieder* (1900–1911), *Friede auf Erden* (1907), six miscellaneous collections.

Works for Speaker and Instruments. *Pierrot lunaire* (1912), *Survivor from Warsaw* (1947), *Ode to Napoleon* (1942), *Kol Nidre* (1938), *Modern Psalm* (1950).

other works by Schoenberg and his contemporaries. The music to rehearsal E corresponds to the first movement of a traditional quartet and at the same time to the exposition of a sonata form; the music from E to K is both developmental and in the manner of a scherzo; from K to M is the slow "movement" and continued development, and the passage from M to O is a rondo finale. A coda begins at letter O.

Rhythm, meter, and phrase structure in this quartet create examples of "musical prose" also observed in Reger's Fifth String Quartet. The themes are nonperiodic and asymmetrical, rhythm and meter are fluid, and the polyphony restless and turbulent. Periodic themes, which consist of symmetrical antecedent and consequent phrases, are replaced here by freely developmental forms, some of which are examples of what Schoenberg called "sentences" (see his *Fundamentals of Musical Composition*, Chapters 5 and 8). A sentence consists of three parts: an initial phrase containing the basic motive(s) and expressing the tonality, tempo, and meter; a simple or varied repetition of the first phrase; and a continuation which develops the basic motives into more varied shapes and leads to a cadence. The principal theme in the first violin in measures 1–10 (Example 7-3) is such a sentence.

As in Reger's Quartet in F♯ minor, diatonic harmonies support the dissonant voice leading. But basic triads themselves rarely come to the surface of the music, being submerged instead beneath the chromatic counterpoint. In his analysis "Why is Schoenberg's Music So Difficult to Understand?" written for the Festschrift honoring the composer's fiftieth birthday, Alban Berg produced a reduction of the

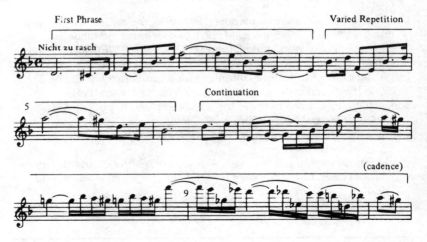

Example 7-3. Schoenberg, First String Quartet, measures 1–10 (violin 1).

chords of the first ten measures of this quartet, intending to show that frenetic rhythmic activity and diminutions of part writing conceal a normal harmonic progression in D minor. The beginning of Berg's analysis (covering measures 1–3 of the quartet) is shown in Example 7-4, which illustrates the harmonic motion from I to V of the first phrase of the sentence.

Harmonic complexities are nevertheless in abundance in the continuation of the sentence. Its cadence in measure 10 occurs upon a whole-tone harmony F♯ D B♭ G♯. This chord may be understood to represent the tonic D-major triad in first inversion. It is typical of Schoenberg's harmonic practice that a literal statement of the triad does not occur. It is instead suggested by an ellipsis—the ear must complete the voice leading hypothetically by imagining the B♭ and G♯ moving to octave A's in order to interpret the diatonic role of the chord.

Perhaps the most remarkable feature of this quartet is the extent to which themes and contrapuntal part writing grow out of motives stated in the principal subject of the first ten measures. Schoenberg's degree of motivic integration goes far beyond Reger and relates more to the music of Brahms, Mahler, and, ultimately, Beethoven. In program notes to his quartets, Schoenberg wrote that he was guided in this work by the "spiritual essence" of the first movement of Beethoven's *Eroica* Symphony. "The *Eroica* was the solution to my problems: how one produces diversity out of unity, how one creates new forms from basic material, and how much can be made from often insignificantly small shapes by small modifications, if not by outright developing variations."

Some of the themes produced by developing variation are illustrated in Example 7-5. Three important motives in the main theme are bracketed and labeled *a*, *b*, and *c*. In a transformation of the theme in measure 85 (part of a passage that Schoenberg would have called a "liquidation" because of its progressive elimination of dis-

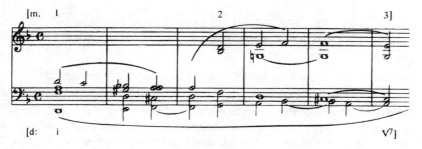

Example 7-4. Schoenberg, First String Quartet, harmonic reduction of measures 1–3.

Example 7-5.   Schoenberg, First String Quartet, motivic development.

tinctive features of the main theme), the head motive *a* is followed immediately by motive *b*, characterized by the descending tritone. The passage at rehearsal A is a transition in the manner of a fugato on two themes—the first is derived from motive *b* and the second from motive *c*—followed by a new motive *d*. The first subsidiary theme (m. 153) picks up motive *d* from the transition and ends with a new motive *e*, which is the basis for the second subsidiary theme (m. 167). Such intense motivic integration was a guiding formal principle in all three of Schoenberg's periods of style, and it was of great importance in leading him finally to his twelve-tone method of composition.

Another way in which Schoenberg attained "diversity out of unity" is his use of varied rather than literal repetitions. All of the recapitulations or restatements of themes in the D-minor quartet are varied by seemingly endless invention. Schoenberg considered repetition to be the basis of all musical form; however, it was his belief that the literal repetitions used by earlier composers were no longer valid means of musical expansion and that they must be replaced by varied repetitions.

Schoenberg may well have been indebted to Mahler for these principles of musical form. Anton Webern noted in his diary in 1905 a discussion between Mahler and Schoenberg:

> The conversation turned to counterpoint, as Schoenberg said only the Germans could write counterpoint. Mahler refers to the old French composers (Rameau, etc.) and will accept only Bach, Brahms, and Wagner as great contrapuntalists among the Germans. "Our model in this matter is nature. Just as the whole universe has developed from the original cell—through plants, animals, men, to God, the highest being—in music too a whole piece should be developed from a single motif, a single theme, which contains the germ of all that is to follow. . . ." Variation is the most important element of musical work, he said. A theme has to be quite exceptionally beautiful—a few by Schubert, for example—to make a repeat of it without alteration successful. [From Kurt Blaukopf, *Mahler: A Documentary Study*, New York and Toronto, 1976, p. 240.]

Alexander von Zemlinsky divided his career between conducting opera, composing, and teaching. In this last capacity he is best known as the teacher of Alma Mahler and Arnold Schoenberg. His compositions—primarily operas, songs, and chamber music—are in the late romantic idiom. The Six Songs Op. 13, on texts by Maurice Maeterlinck; Second String Quartet Op. 15; and *Lyric* Symphony Op. 18 are among his most advanced works. The Second String Quartet was dedicated to Schoenberg, and it utilizes the same one-movement form as Schoenberg's D-minor quartet, to which it is also related in style. The *Lyric* Symphony is a work in the vein of Mahler's *Das Lied von der Erde*, using large orchestra and solo voices on texts by Rabindranath Tagore. Zemlinsky immigrated to America in 1938, where he lived until his death in 1942.

Franz Schreker, like Zemlinsky, was a conductor, teacher, and composer. He was educated at the Conservatory in Vienna, where he lived until his appointment as director of the Hochschule für Musik in Berlin in 1920. His early compositions were mainly songs in the manner of Richard Strauss. Later he turned to operatic composition, a genre in which he completed nine works between 1900 and 1932. The best known is *Der ferne Klang*, whose libretto (written by Schreker) and leitmotif technique are indebted to Wagner, but whose musical style otherwise reflects Schreker's interest in French Impressionism.

ATONALITY

Works of late romantic composers at the turn of the century show that tonality was waning in importance. The tonic-dominant axis (see Chapter 1), which had earlier organized harmonic motion throughout entire pieces or movements, was increasingly disrupted. Dissonant chords were exchanging roles with consonances as central elements in the harmonic vocabulary, and these were often unfamiliar combinations composed of five or more notes. Even in those areas where a diatonic triad was perceptible, its significance tended to be local rather than a guide to the organization of an entire movement. Indeed, it was a relatively short step toward the complete elimination of key. This final step was taken by Arnold Schoenberg approximately in 1907 or 1908, at about the same time as composers elsewhere in the world including Scriabin, Ives, and Bartók had similarly disposed of key. Schoenberg's innovations were quickly adopted by his students Alban Berg and Anton Webern and, at least briefly, by others such as Ferruccio Busoni.

Schoenberg considered atonality a historical necessity—a product of the "evolution" toward dissonant harmony. He wrote in "My Evolution":

> The overwhelming multitude of dissonances [in music at the turn of the century] cannot be counterbalanced any longer by occasional returns to such tonal triads as represent a key. It seemed inadequate to force a movement into the Procrustean bed of a tonality without supporting it by harmonic progressions that pertain to it. This dilemma was my concern, and it should have occupied the minds of all my contemporaries also. That I was the first to venture the decisive step will not be considered universally a merit—a fact I regret but have to ignore.
>
> This first step occurred in the Two Songs, Op. 14, and thereafter in the *Fifteen Songs of the Hanging Gardens* and in the Three Piano Pieces, Op. 11. Most critics of this new style failed to investigate how far the

ancient 'eternal laws' of musical esthetics were observed, spurned, or merely adjusted to changed circumstances. Such superficiality brought about accusations of anarchy and revolution, whereas, on the contrary, this music was distinctly a product of evolution, and no more revolutionary than any other development in the history of music.

A comparison of Schoenberg's music from before and after his decision to forgo the use of key supports his assertion that atonality was not a revolutionary stylistic change. Many features of his music remained unchanged: the contrapuntal textures, motivic unity, avoidance of literal repetitions, and "prose"-like rhythm and meter. But after 1907 he rarely made any further use of triads or other familiar chords, preferring instead to treat dissonances as stable or referential sonorities. He began immediately to settle upon a repertory of favored dissonances that would characterize his style, and he intuitively developed ways of interrelating these dissonant chords so that the unity he had attained in the thematic dimension would also be preserved harmonically. A further examination of his "emancipated" use of dissonance and of techniques of harmonic relation is found in Chapter 2.

Schoenberg's transition to atonality was provoked not only by his view of its historical inevitability, but also by a great personal crisis. In the summer of 1908, his wife Mathilde left him for the painter Richard Gerstl; she subsequently returned, whereupon Gerstl committed suicide. Schoenberg worked out his feelings of betrayal not only by breaking with the idiom of the late romantic period, but also by setting to music several texts that referred to his dilemma, thus undertaking the sort of public self-examination common to Expressionist painters and writers at this time. The most notable of these are his two operas *Erwartung* (1909) and *Die glückliche Hand* (1910–13). Symbolic references to his plight are also found in his choice of song texts, as in the cycle of *Fifteen Poems from The Book of the Hanging Gardens* Op. 15 (1908–1909). These songs, on poetry by Stefan George (1868–1933), were begun at the height of Schoenberg's crisis. The first poem that he set to music, "Du lehnest wider eine Silberweide," speaks of the separation of lovers, and the cycle ends with a piano postlude in a tone of bitter resignation to a fate that had destroyed love.

Schoenberg and others in his circle of composers were strongly attracted to the poetry of George, with its mysterious symbolism, elegant perfection of language, and inherent musicality. George's *Book of the Hanging Gardens* is a cycle of thirty-one poems telling of initiation to love, its consummation, and ultimate destruction. In the eighth poem of Schoenberg's cycle, the initiate has entered the gar-

den sanctuary of love and tells of his tortured anxiety for fulfillment. George's free verse is accentuated by frantic rhythms and dynamic outbursts. The music is through composed, but with a hint of
ternary form. Typically, it contains subtle word paintings in the
piano part, such as the alternation of B and F on the word *wankend*
("wavering") in measure 19. The harmonies make free use of the
whole-tone idea of the opening motive.

The tenth poem ("Das schöne Beet") is the climax of the cycle:
here the lovers consummate their passion, which is expressed poet-
ically by erotic references to flowers of the garden. Schoenberg's
musical treatment makes a startling return to the idiom of late romanticism. The song expresses the key of D major/minor—
Schoenberg's motto key—thus reinforcing his kinship with the
persona of the poem.

Among vocal works of Schoenberg's atonal period, *Pierrot lunaire*
(1912) treats the voice in the most original manner. This is a setting
of twenty-one Expressionistic poems by Albert Giraud for speaker
and mixed instruments. The work captures the atmosphere of the
German artistic cabaret as the speaker evocatively couples the tragic
with the clown-like. The actor is called upon to use a form of recitation called *Sprechstimme* ("speaking voice"), in which rhythmic values are to be strictly observed and pitches approximated.

Of Schoenberg's nine completed works that are entirely atonal
(Opp. 11 and 15 through 22), only three are instrumental: two collections of piano music, Opp. 11 and 19, and Five Orchestral Pieces
Op. 16. The composer remarked in his lecture "Composition with
Twelve Tones" (1941) that he needed a text to guide him in constructing larger forms, since he was using his musical materials intuitively rather than systematically. Schoenberg calls each of the
instrumental collections "pieces": the most neutral and abstract of
titles. Thus he rejects the programmatic implications with which he
imbued much of his own earlier instrumental music, and he suggests that these works will be solely "about" their own compositional content. He was later asked by his publisher Peters to supply
titles to the orchestral pieces of Opus 16. He did so, although he was
"on the whole unsympathetic to the idea. . . . Whatever was to be
said has been said by the music."

Unlike Schoenberg, Alban Berg had only a brief period of tonal
composition behind him when he turned to atonality. His early
works consist of songs reminiscent of the style of Hugo Wolf. In
1904 he began to study with Schoenberg, marking the beginning of
his career as a serious composer, and about 1909 he followed his
teacher on the path to atonality. Berg's studies with Schoenberg

ALBAN BERG
(Vienna, 1885–Vienna, 1935)

Berg's early years in Vienna were largely devoted to his passionate love of literature and music, at which he was self-taught before becoming a private student of Schoenberg in 1904. Prior to the great success of his opera *Wozzeck* in 1925, Berg was virtually unknown as a composer, working instead as a teacher of music, journalist, and consultant for the publisher Universal Edition. Berg was one of the leaders of Schoenberg's Society for Private Musical Performances from its founding in 1918. His final years were devoted to the opera *Lulu*, which was left unfinished, and to his Violin Concerto, which was dedicated to the memory of the daughter of Alma Mahler and Walter Gropius. Much has been written in recent years about Berg's relationship with Hanna Fuchs-Robettin, to which he refers in all of his late works in the manner of secretive programs.

SELECTED WORKS

Operas. *Wozzeck* (1917–22), *Lulu* (incomplete, 1928–1935).

Concertos. Chamber Concerto for piano, violin, and thirteen wind instruments (1925), Violin Concerto (1935).

String Quartets. String Quartet Op. 3 (1910); *Lyric* Suite (1926).

Songs. Seven Early Songs (1905–1908); "An Leukon" (1907); "Schliesse mir die Augen beide" (two versions, 1907, 1925); Four Songs Op. 2 (ca. 1908–10), Five Orchestral Songs Op. 4 (1912); *Der Wein* (concert aria, 1929).

Miscellaneous. Piano Sonata Op. 1 (1908); Four Pieces for Clarinet and Piano Op. 5 (1913); Three Pieces for Large Orchestra Op. 6 (1915); piano-vocal scores prepared for Universal Edition and other arrangements.

Writings. Thematic analyses of Schoenberg's *Pelleas und Melisande*, First Chamber Symphony, and *Gurrelieder*; miscellaneous lectures and essays.

were exceptionally thorough: they began with exercises in harmony and later emphasized tonal counterpoint, at which Berg was especially gifted. He was a slow worker who produced a relatively small number of compositions, but each of great depth and artistry. In the atonal style, which he pursued between 1909 and about 1925, he completed only seven works: chamber music, songs, orchestra pieces, and the opera *Wozzeck*. This masterpiece and its companion *Lulu* will be discussed in the section on Expressionist opera later in this chapter.

Berg's Four Songs Op. 2 were written about 1908–10, toward the end of his period of study, and they exemplify his transition from tonality to atonality. The poetry by Friedrich Hebbel (1813–63) and Alfred Mombert (1872–1942) is unified by images of sleep which increasingly become Expressionistic nightmares. The final poem— Mombert's "Warm die Lüfte" (Anthology no. 11)—also has a general similarity to the text of Schoenberg's opera *Erwartung*, a work that was composed at about the same time as these songs. Both deal with themes of a lover's betrayal, isolation, and death.

Berg's music is also unified as a cycle by the recurrence in the final song of harmonic materials used earlier in the cycle. The first song of Opus 2 begins and ends with D-minor triads, which establish a tonal framework. No other references to the key of D minor are made, however, as the interior regions of the song emphasize all-interval tetrachords (measures 5–10), whole-tone sets linked by a bass in ascending fourths (measures 11–14), and fourth chords (measures 18–19). The second song dwells upon the whole-tone harmonies introduced in the first piece: almost every chord in the accompaniment is a subset of a whole-tone scale. The third song emphasizes the triad: it begins by outlining an Ab-minor chord, passes in measures 4 to 8 through a cadential progression whose goal is D minor, and then moves to an Eb-major triad at the end.

The final song makes no reference to any key or triad, nor does it contain the varied reprise found in each of the earlier songs. The climactic passage from measure 17 to the end recapitulates several of the pitch structures of the first two songs: whole-tone segments (measures 17–19), all-interval tetrachords (20–22), and a bass line ascending in fourths (20–22). The work concludes with the same five-note chord heard in the first song at measure 5, transposed down a minor third.

In the songs of Opus 2 Berg also makes a hidden tribute to his teacher, Arnold Schoenberg. The first song is in an extended D minor, the favored key of Schoenberg's earliest works; the last song is entirely atonal, as are Schoenberg's later compositions. The second song uses a key signature suggesting Eb minor, despite the presence of an accidental on every note and the lack of any reference to a key other than the bass note Eb of the final whole-tone chord. The note Eb (*Es* in German) may be understood symbolically to refer to the first letter of the name Schoenberg. This symbolism is carried into the third song as well, which progresses from a statement of an Ab triad (*As* in German: *Arnold Schoenberg*)—reinforced by an otherwise superfluous key signature—through a progression in D minor, to an Eb triad at the end, thus thrice referring to Berg's mentor.

The atonal compositions of Schoenberg and his students were utterly baffling to most audiences and alienated them even from musicians who had sympathetically followed their achievements up to 1907. Bruno Walter wrote in his memoirs:

> Much as I admired Schoenberg's courage and unwavering attitude, profoundly though I was impressed by his exquisite musicianship, and attracted though I was by much of his later chamber music and vocal compositions, I felt increasingly unable to follow him on his way because I considered it a devious way.... I am quite serious when I say that I should be happy if in a future existence, in which I might have the benefit of superior organs of musical perception, I were to be able to ask his forgiveness for my primitive mundane lack of understanding.

Nevertheless, the strikingly original language of atonality was influential upon certain composers outside of Schoenberg's circle. Alois Hába (1893–1972) became familiar with Schoenberg's music during his period of study with Franz Schreker, and he utilized aspects of the atonal style in his own works prior to his experiments with quarter-tone music. Paul Hindemith took a brief excursion through Expressionism and atonality in the years immediately after World War I in several one-act operas and in his Second String Quartet (1921). This style and its attendant aesthetic were never congenial to his artistic temperament, and he shortly became the leading German neoclassicist. Ernst Krenek (1900–91), like Hába a student of Schreker, wrote atonal symphonies and quartets before turning to neoclassicism and, later, to serialism.

Composers of an older generation were also attracted to Schoenberg's innovations. Giacomo Puccini (1858–1924) was especially supportive and cordial after hearing *Pierrot lunaire* in Florence in 1924. Ferruccio Busoni (1866–1924) also expressed admiration for Schoenberg's atonal works. Busoni was a piano virtuoso in the mold of Franz Liszt, whose accomplishments also included composition, teaching, arranging, and writing on music. His attitude toward modernism was ambivalent. While he supported younger

FERRUCCIO BUSONI
(Empoli, 1866–Berlin, 1924)

Busoni was born in the Tuscan region of northern Italy to a family of professional musicians, and for his entire life he attempted to balance his German and Latin influences. After establishing his reputation as a child prodigy on piano, he took a variety of teaching positions in both Europe and America, settling permanently in Berlin in 1894. From 1919 until his death in 1924 he held the position of Professor of Composition at the Academy of Arts. His repertory as a pianist was based upon works by Bach and Liszt: in his words, the "alpha and omega" of music for that instrument. Although he did not perform piano music by the twentieth-century avant-garde, he greatly encouraged younger composers in all styles, and he conducted a notable series of orchestral concerts featuring modern compositions with the Berlin Philharmonic Orchestra from 1902 until 1909. His essay *Sketch of a New Esthetic of Music* (1907) proclaimed absolute freedom for the composer in materials and approaches—a position that he recanted in later writings. His music is generally tonal, although certain works mirror more experimental directions.

SELECTED WORKS

Operas. *Die Brautwahl* (1910), *Turandot* (1917), *Arlecchino* (1917), *Dr Faust* (incomplete, 1916–).

Orchestral Music. *Nocturne symphonique* (1912), Suites, *Berceuse élégiaque* (1909).

Concertos. Violin Concerto in D (1897), Concerto for Piano and Male Choir, miscellaneous concerted works for piano.

Chamber Music. String quartets (2), sonatas for violin and piano (2).

Piano Music. Sonatinas (6, 1910–20), Toccata in A minor (1921), Exercises, Elegies, *Fantasia contrappuntistica* (1910, later revised), artistic arrangements.

Writings. *Sketch of a New Esthetic of Music* (1907); *Futurism in Music* (1911); miscellaneous essays, reviews, and polemics.

composers with exceptional generosity and conducted new music with the Berlin Philharmonic Orchestra, his own compositions were generally conservative, and he resolutely avoided twentieth-century works in his own piano repertory. Schoenberg's atonal style exerted considerable fascination on him. In 1910 he prepared, an arrangement or "Concert Interpretation" of Schoenberg's Piano Piece Op. 11/2, intending to make the original more idiomatic for the instrument.

Busoni's awareness of new stylistic directions is also apparent in his *Sonatina secunda* of 1912. This powerful and entirely eclectic work for piano shows aspects of the recent music not only of Schoenberg, but also of Alexander Scriabin and Béla Bartók. From Bartók and Scriabin comes the prominent use of the octatonic scale (see Chapter 2), which is laid out in the opening motive. The piece has the flexible, improvisatory élan of the piano music of Scriabin, using the suggestive instructions ("triste," "lamentoso," "pallido") of which Scriabin was fond. The work consists of two large parts, each of several sections; certain themes recur in new guises in the Lisztian manner of thematic transformation. The *Sonatina* is atonal, with the interval of the major seventh the primary integrative detail. The inversion of this interval forms the boundary points (B to C) of the opening theme as well as the final gesture, and the interval is spelled out in various shapes in every section. The octatonic passages alternate with whole-tone motives, chromatic clusters, and, in the Lento occulto, with triads.

CONSOLIDATION: THE TWELVE-TONE METHOD

The First World War led to years of unprecedented social and economic turmoil in Germany and Austria. Famine was widespread, and a period of uncontrolled inflation caused wild inversions in the social order. Stefan Zweig describes the chaos:

> Every descent into the town [Salzburg] at that period was a moving experience; it was my first sight of the yellow and dangerous eyes of famine. The bread crumbled into black particles and tasted like pitch and glue, coffee was a brew of roasted barley, beer like yellow water, chocolate like colored sand and the potatoes were frozen. . . .
> The first sign of distrust [in the value of currency] was the disappearance of hard money, for people tended to value a bit of copper or nickel more highly than mere printed paper. . . . In consequence of this mad disorder the situation became more paradoxical and unmoral from week to week. A man who had been saving for forty years and who, furthermore, had patriotically invested his all in war bonds,

became a beggar. A man who had debts became free of them. A man who respected the food rationing system starved; only one who disregarded it brazenly could eat his fill. [*The World of Yesterday*.]

These disastrous consequences of the war spelled the end of musical progressivism—that tradition of modernism which had reigned supreme in German music from the age of Liszt and Wagner through the time of Mahler and Strauss and which was then carried relentlessly into the realm of atonality by Arnold Schoenberg. After the war this tradition split in two opposing directions: an experimentalism that disdained the moderate values of the earlier progressives and a contrary movement toward retrenchment or consolidation of the stylistic advances of the preceding decades.

Experimentation in Europe in the postwar period did not produce music of lasting value, although the activities of Dadaists, Italian Futurists, and Russian Constructivists of these years prefigured developments among the avant-garde following the Second World War. In fact, artists and musicians in Germany and Austria cast an increasingly suspicious eye at uninhibited experiment and progress. Busoni totally retracted the declaration of artistic freedom that he had made in his pre-war *Sketch of a New Esthetic of Music*, and Hindemith excoriated music that appeared elitist and excessively abstract. This postwar conservativism will be traced more fully in Chapters 10 and 11.

Even the music of Schoenberg—the most steadfast of modernists—entered a phase of consolidation and systematization of his earlier advances. This new period in Schoenberg's work coincides with his adoption of the twelve-tone method of composition, whose technical features are surveyed in Chapter 4. Beginning in the early 1920s, Schoenberg returned predominantly to instrumental composition, and he no longer distilled his music into aphoristic fragments. These new, full-blown instrumental pieces return, furthermore, to the traditional instrumental genres that he had earlier bypassed. No longer were his works called simply "pieces"; instead, he wrote quartets, suites, variations, and concertos. In vocal media he composed operas, choruses, and works for speaker. With only one exception (Op. 48) he avoided lieder, which earlier had been his favored vocal genre. He also renewed his interest in traditional forms, such as the sonata-allegro. In some works such as the Piano Suite Op. 25, he even uses exact sectional repetitions, a formal device that he had absolutely ruled out earlier.

The first movement of the Fourth String Quartet Op. 37 (1936, Anthology no. 25) exemplifies this stylistic retrenchment of the twelve-tone period. Like his Third Quartet, this work was commissioned by Elizabeth Sprague Coolidge (1864–1953), America's greatest patron of modern chamber music. The quartet is in four movements in the classical sequence of sonata form/scherzo/adagio/rondo-finale, and it is entirely based on a single tone row.

The main theme, heard at the outset in the first violin, has a regularity of rhythm and meter that contrasts plainly with Schoenberg's earlier "musical prose." Its structure is reminiscent of the classical small ternary form: it is sixteen measures in length and is divided into three phrases (at measures 6 and 10) which create an A B A' shape. The substance not only of this theme but the entire movement is contained in its first five measures, which the composer would have called the "basic shape" of the composition. From it can be abstracted the tone row, basic rhythms, and fundamental motivic elements.

The rhythm and meter of the main line in these five measures recur first to round off the theme itself (measures 10–14, violin 1) and later to identify reappearances of the theme at major structural junctures (measures 95, 165, 239). The basic shape is made up of several smaller rhythmic motives that are subsequently developed independently. Primary among them is the group of three eighth notes on the note A in measure 2. This rhythmic motive also underlies the rhythm of the accompaniment at the beginning, the triplets in the transitional passage at measure 21, and numerous other developmental areas.

The principal line in measures 1 to 5 also contains two intervallic motives which will become the crux of the musical argument that follows. These frame the line: first, the descending semitone in measure 1 and, second, the ascending fourth (F♯–B) in measure 4. These two intervals are the first and last intervals of the row. But they do not derive their importance from serial considerations, rather, from a more basic conception. These intervals guide, for example, the bass line in each of the first two measures; later, the choice of forms of the row and much of the development of rhythm and meter will be made to assert them and their derivative shapes.

Schoenberg uses a very free adaptation of sonata-allegro form in this movement. The lyrical second theme begins at measure 66, an episode begins at 116, and there are two recapitulations at measures 165 and 239. The composer was faced with a major difficulty in adapting sonata form to the nontonal idiom, since this structure earlier had been delineated more by tonal plan than by theme. As a solution, he uses transposition levels of row forms analogously to relations among keys. The second theme, for example, states the row a fifth "higher" than the main theme, just as the second theme of the classical sonata form is normatively in the dominant. Comparable to the return of the tonic, the untransposed prime form of the row is brought back at the principal reprise in measure 239.

Schoenberg was chary about the importance of row techniques to an understanding of his dodecaphonic music. To Rudolf Kolisch he wrote, "I can't utter too many warnings against overrating these analyses [of row technique], since after all they only lead to what I have always been dead against: seeing how it is *done*, whereas I have always helped people to see what it *is!*" Although Schoenberg may have overstated this point, not wishing the twelve-tone method to be perceived as a preprogrammed way of writing music, he raises an important point: the method does not in itself dictate a style, but is susceptible to widely varying modes of application, which produce music of many different types.

The twelve-tone method was immediately adopted by Schoenberg's leading students, among them Berg and Webern and, prior to the Second World War, by a few other European composers such as Ernst Krenek. In the later music of Berg—*Lyric* Suite, aria *Der Wein*, Violin Concerto, and opera *Lulu*—the method was joined to a renewed emphasis upon tertian harmonies and lyricism of the age of Mahler. Berg's application of the method was relatively free. For example, he made the method accommodate his favored chordal sonorities such as whole-tone harmonies and triadic tetrachords, and he frequently quoted preexistent tonal melodies. His dodecaphonic opera *Lulu* will be discussed in more detail later in this chapter.

The twelve-tone technique found its most devoted follower in Anton Webern. Like Berg, Webern did little serious composition before becoming a private student of Schoenberg in 1904, and both he and Berg turned to atonality in 1909. His music from this time until his definitive adoption of the twelve-tone method in 1924 is about equally divided between songs and instrumental works. The latter are among the most original creations in the entire history of music: their length dwindles often to a few measures, and the customary notions of musical line, pacing, and form are called into question. The composition of brief or "aphoristic" pieces was virtually a compulsion for Webern. Beneath their fleeting surface lie profound networks of structural relations and whirlpools of personal sentiment. Their melodic content is no less original. Melodic ideas are often passed from instrument to instrument and thus completed in a disjunct manner in which rests and changing colors are of heightened importance.

Webern experimented with the twelve-tone method beginning in 1922, and he adopted it as his sole compositional approach in 1924.

ANTON WEBERN
(*Vienna, 1883–Mittersill, 1945*)

As a young man in Vienna, Webern was greatly attracted to the music of Wagner, in whose style he made his earliest essays as a composer. He pursued a Ph.D. degree in musicology at the University of Vienna under the guidance of Guido Adler, which he completed in 1906. During his university studies he became a student of Schoenberg, forming a lifelong friendship.

Webern's career is a study in total dedication to music, despite considerable obstacles posed by the unprecedented originality of his compositions. He lived primarily by teaching, consulting for Universal Edition, and conducting. Toward the end of the Second World War he left Vienna to live with his daughter in the Tyrolean village of Mittersill. On September 15, 1945, he was accidentally shot to death there by an American occupation soldier.

SELECTED WORKS

Orchestral Music. Passacaglia Op. 1 (1908); Symphony Op. 21 (1928); Variations Op. 30 (1940); collections of short pieces (Opp. 6, 10).

Chamber Music. String Quartet Op. 28 (1938); other works for string quartet (Opp. 5, 9); Concerto for nine instruments Op. 24 (1934); Variations for piano Op. 27 (1936).

Songs. Five collections for voice and piano, seven collections for voice and instruments.

Choral Music. Two cantatas (1939, 1943), *Das Augenlicht* (1935).

Works without Opus Numbers. Webern usually conferred an opus number on a completed work with which he was satisfied. There are thirty-one such pieces or collections, some of which were not published during his lifetime. A larger number of compositions have come to light since his death in 1945, and many of these have now been published.

His application even exceeds Schoenberg's in its strictness and in the extent to which the structural potential of a tone row is explored. But, as with Schoenberg, his use of the method also brought about more traditional thematic expansion and the application of conventional forms and genres.

These retrospective features are seen in his Second Cantata Op. 31 (1943), a six-movement work for mixed chorus, soprano and bass soloists, and orchestra. It would be his last completed composition before his tragic death in 1945. The composer selected poetry by his confidante Hildegard Jone, whose work and thought inspired all of his late vocal music. The verses chosen for this work, like much of Jone's poetry, are mystically religious. The fifth movement, "Freundselig ist das Wort" (Anthology no. 22), is an apostrophe to the Christian Logos or "the Word": mankind seeks the Word searching for love, and, though the Word fell silent on the Cross, it is still the source of life. Webern's setting is ternary, with the middle part an aria-like passage for soprano and instruments and the exterior sections for chorus with soprano and instrumental interpolations.

The outer sections are examples of the severe understatement that characterizes all of Webern's music: here the ephemeral gesture, momentary juxtaposition of colors, the concentrated disjunction of line, and spareness of texture project similar moods in Jone's poetry. In the central "aria" the vocal line is more connected, though filled with expressive leaps and nuances of attack, dynamics, and tempo. This music—perhaps more than that of any major composer— stands or falls on how it is performed. It relies heavily upon the sensitivity with which the performer realizes Webern's intentions, to which the written music is at best an imperfect guide.

The sixth movement, dealing with the Epiphany of Christ, is composed in the manner of a Renaissance motet, a genre with which Webern was intimately familiar through his doctoral thesis on the music of Heinrich Isaac. Webern imitates this archaic style by writing *a cappella*. The instruments only double the four vocal lines. Webern also resorts to Renaissance "white notation," using large note values with the half note or "minim" as the metric unit. The movement, furthermore, is in a simple strophic form. But the most antiquated aspect of this music is its absolute linearity. The four lines are strictly canonic in rhythm and meter, and they each enter at the distance of three minims and at the interval of the major third or minor sixth. The canon creates both an inversion and a retrograde, since the alto and bass invert the subject of the tenor and soprano and the alto-tenor and soprano-bass pairs are exact retrogrades of one another.

The logic of the twelve-tone method seemed inescapable to Schoenberg; in his view, the stylistic evolution of music toward greater chromaticism and reliance on theme as the instrument of unification made the method not just a private compositional principle, rather, a historical necessity which in time would have to be realized and embraced. Thus he confided to his student Josef Rufer in 1921 that his discovery of the method would "insure the supremacy of German music for the next hundred years."

But from the perspective of more than seventy years since Schoenberg's bold assertion, it is now clear that musical style has not unfolded with the predictability that he anticipated. The method unquestionably produced masterpieces by European composers between the world wars, and it was taken up by several Americans before and after World War II. In the decade following the war it inspired a more generalized approach to serialism among most of the leading composers around the world. But the evolution of style has since led composers on new paths, pushing twelve-tone composition, at least for the time, into the background.

THE EXPRESSIONIST MUSICAL THEATER

Man screams from the depths of his soul; the whole era becomes a single, piercing shriek. Art also screams, into the deep darkness, screams for help, screams for the spirit. This is Expressionism.

Thus in 1914 the Austrian critic Hermann Bahr sought to define the most original and influential movement in the arts and letters in Germany in the first quarter of the twentieth century. Bahr's image of the scream is especially apt, since Expressionist art turns on emotional exaggeration and lays bare the secret corners of the human psyche.

Expressionism was a diffuse artistic orientation rather than a coherent movement. The term was first used to describe German painting and graphic art in which the natural appearance of objects was to some extent distorted so as to heighten their emotional significance. In the works of painters such as Ernst Ludwig Kirchner (1880–1938) or Erich Heckel (1883–1970), the degree of distortion was relatively small and limited to angular shapes, vivid colors, and bold brush strokes. But in paintings of Vasili Kandinski, abstraction became virtually complete. His works express inner visions, from which they derive their beauty. "The beautiful," wrote Kandinski in *Concerning the Spiritual in Art*, "is that which springs from an inner, emotional necessity. The beautiful is that which is inwardly beautiful."

The Expressionist woodcut: Edvard Munch, *The Scream*. (Courtesy of the National Gallery of Art, Washington, D.C., Rosenwald Collection [B-11, 106].)

The new forms and aesthetic of Expressionist painting found a mirror in German literature. Expressionist drama typically dealt with the grotesque, the erotic, the dehumanizing forces of modern society, or the clash of father and son. Such "distortions" of conventional behavior or reality are comparable to the abstractions of

Nonrepresentational art among Expressionist painters: Vasili Kandinski, *Improvisation* 19. (Courtesy of the Städtische Galerie im Lenbachhaus, Munich. © A.D.A.G.P., Paris/V.A.G.A., New York, 1985.)

Expressionist painting: both allow the artist a more spontaneous statement about the human psyche.

Precursors of the Expressionist theater include Georg Büchner (1813–37), August Strindberg (1849–1912), and Frank Wedekind (1864–1918); later figures include Georg Kaiser (1878–1945), Walter Hasenclever (1890–1940), and Franz Werfel (1890–1945). Characters in their plays often embody principles or generalities, and, for this reason, they often lack names. In Büchner's *Woyzeck* (1837), the basis of Berg's opera *Wozzeck*, we encounter a "Doctor" representing science gone mad, a "Captain" who acts out the hypocrisy of modern society, and a "Drum Major" who symbolizes its brutish elements. Typically, the play is centered on a main character (Woyzeck) who represents all mankind.

In many of these works the theme of sexual perversion was for the first time openly addressed in modern literature. Wedekind's

Earth Spirit (1895), his *Pandora's Box* (1903), and Oskar Kokoschka's *Mörder, Hoffnung der Frauen* (ca. 1907)—all later used as opera libretti—deal with the clash of male and female life principles. August Stramm's *Sancta Susanna* (1914), later adapted as a libretto by Paul Hindemith, deals with the repressed sexual drives of a nun. Indeed, the emphasis on erotic themes in the Expressionist theater echoes Sigmund Freud's contemporary psychoanalytic theories on the role of sexual repression as a cause of neurotic behavior.

All music of the German avant-garde of this period may appear analogous to Expressionist painting and literature. Its liberation of dissonance, angular melodic lines, vivid orchestration, and bombastic dynamics may well be viewed as distortions of a more natural order in music. But such an interpretation is belied by the high degree of organization that we have observed in this repertory and its continuity in style with the later nineteenth century. These characteristics have little in common with the contrived chaos of nonmusical Expressionism. To be sure, some musicians such as Arnold Schoenberg had close personal contact with the Expressionist movement. Schoenberg was himself a painter and was active in the "Blue Rider" group of Expressionists in Munich around 1912. He wholeheartedly embraced Kandinski's aesthetic of beauty arising from the artist's expression of inner necessity. But, as we have seen, his music maintains a strong bond with his forebears, and it projects a logical order that is essentially non-Expressionist.

The main area of contact between musicians and the Expressionist movement was the genre of opera. Between 1909 and 1935 a number of Expressionist plays were fit to music by Schoenberg, Berg, Hindemith, and Kurt Weill. Libretti that reflected Expressionist themes were also used by composers outside of Germany and Austria, as, for example, in Béla Bartók's *Duke Bluebeard's Castle* (1911) and Dimitri Shostakovich's *Lady Macbeth of the Mtsensk* (1932).

Expressionist plays were attractive to musicians for several reasons. Many had the qualities of good libretti: they were usually brief, they presented striking dramatic situations and clearly drawn characters, and they tended toward mythic universality. They also provided younger composers such as Paul Hindemith and Kurt Weill a convenient way to gain attention by shocking the musical establishment.

The prototype of German Expressionist opera is Richard Strauss's *Salome* (1905). Its libretto is based on Oscar Wilde's play *Salomé* (1891–92), which Strauss had seen performed in Berlin in 1903. Wilde's drama was inspired by the Symbolist plays of Maurice Maeterlinck and by the morbid images of humanity presented by a group of late-nineteenth-century French and English writers known as the "Decadents." In its themes and techniques, this play, which

RICHARD STRAUSS
(*Munich, 1864–Garmisch, 1949*)

Strauss's career as a musician was shaped by his childhood in Munich, where his father was an internationally renowned French horn virtuoso. Like Mahler he pursued the dual career of conductor and composer, beginning as an assistant to Hans von Bülow in Meiningen and later holding conducting positions in Munich, Weimar, Berlin, and Vienna. With proceeds from his highly successful opera *Salome*, he built a villa in Garmisch, which would be his main refuge for composition after 1908. He acted briefly as an administrator of several governmental organizations during the early years of the Third Reich, but he was dismissed from these positions when he criticized the Nazi's anti-Semitic policies. He resided primarily in Switzerland after the war.

SELECTED WORKS

Operas. *Guntram* (1893), *Feuersnot* (1901), *Salome* (1905), *Elektra* (1908), *Der Rosenkavalier* (1910), *Ariadne auf Naxos* (1912, revised 1916), *Die Frau ohne Schatten* (1918), *Intermezzo* (1923), *Die Aegyptische Helena* (1923–27), *Arabella* (1932), *Die schweigsame Frau* (1935), *Friedenstag* (1936), *Daphne* (1937), *Die Liebe der Danae* (1940), *Capriccio* (1941).
Orchestral Music. *Don Juan* (1889), *Tod und Verklärung* (1889), *Till Eulenspiegel* (1895), *Also sprach Zarathustra* (1895), *Don Quixote* (1897), *Ein Heldenleben* (1898), *Sinfonia domestica* (1903), *Alpensinfonie* (1915).
Songs. Approximately 200 songs for voice and piano or orchestra.
Miscellaneous. Concertos for horn (2), oboe, and violin; *Burleske* for piano and orchestra; ballet *Josephs-Legende*; *Metamorphosen* for twenty-three strings.

was repeatedly performed in Germany early in the century, formed a link between French Symbolist literature (see Chapter 8) and German Expressionism.

Wilde's story is a grotesque fantasy upon Gospel accounts of the execution of John the Baptist (called by his Hebrew name Jochanaan) at the hands of King Herod, his wife Herodias, and her daughter Salome. In Wilde's play Herod is crazed by superstition, fear, and desire for his stepdaughter, and Salome is swayed by an unquenchable lust for Jochanaan. Herod has promised Salome any wish if she will dance for him. The ensuing "Dance of the Seven Veils," set to music by Strauss in an exotic but arguably facile manner, is frequently performed separately as an orchestral tone poem.

Salome's wish is to have the head of Jochanaan. In the lurid final scene (Anthology no. 18), she sings a rapturous soliloquy to the decapitated head, which she fondles and finally kisses. Herod is at last revulsed and commands that she be killed.

The basic musical idiom that Strauss brings to this disturbing story remains that of Wagner. The work is through composed with a free leitmotif technique dominating the orchestral music. The vocal part leaps over wide, dissonant intervals and demands the power to be heard over a large orchestra. The establishment of keys is still important to the structure of the music, but lines are often highly chromatic and blaring dissonances dominate the harmony.

Strauss goes beyond Wagner, however, by concentrating the action into a relatively brief single act and by intensifying the development of motives into a dense, busy counterpoint. This technique of development may be observed in the handling of Jochanaan's motive (Example 7–6), first heard at the beginning of the third scene when he is fetched out of his prison at Salome's command. The motive then suggests his magisterial self-command and noble purpose. But in the final scene, as Salome gloats over his head, his motive returns (Example 7-7) in a frantic diminution, now contrapuntally subordinated to two of Salome's more expansive motives. Thus, in the orchestral music alone, Jochanaan's grotesque plight and Salome's momentary perverse triumph are made vivid.

The final measures are a famous instance of Strauss's use of harmony and tonality to express Salome's insanity. As the music reaches the central key of C♯ major (rehearsal 359), Salome soars into a triumphant cantilena on the words, "I have now kissed thy mouth Jochanaan." Her music becomes diatonic as she appears victorious over Jochanaan's virtue. But as the orchestra builds to a gigantic cadence, the clash of the nondiatonic chord A C♯ G against the diatonic melodic motion in C♯ (Example 7-8) screams out her derangement.

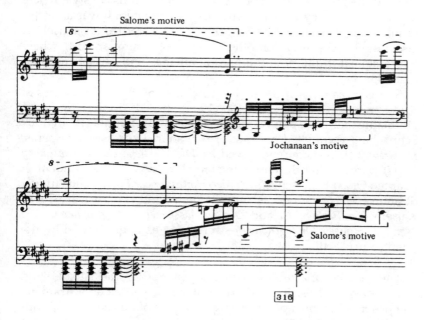

Example 7-6. Richard Strauss, *Salome*, piano-vocal score. © 1905 by Adolf Fürstner. Renewed 1933. Copyright and renewal assigned to Boosey & Hawkes, Inc. Reprinted by permission.

Example 7-7. Richard Strauss, *Salome*, piano-vocal score. © 1905 by Adolf Fürstner. Renewed 1933. Copyright and renewal assigned to Boosey & Hawkes, Inc. Reprinted by permission.

Example 7-8. Richard Strauss, *Salome*, piano-vocal score. © 1905 by Adolf Fürstner. Renewed 1933. Copyright and renewal assigned to Boosey & Hawkes, Inc. Reprinted by permission.

The moon—a recurrent symbol in the play identified with Salome—betrays her by illuminating the ghastly scene. Herod turns and commands that she be killed, and in a tumultuous ten-measure codetta the key shifts without preparation to the distant C minor. With stunning dramatic effect, the older logic of harmonic progression and modulation is cast aside, just as Salome's perversity has shattered the norms of civilized behavior.

Strauss's *Salome* was a milestone in the history of music, for it showed the great dramatic power inherent in a musical style where dissonance and key were to a large extent liberated. It was an inspiration to composers such as Schoenberg, who studied it intensely. It also pointed the way for other operas of a similar sort, where Expressionist drama found a natural alliance with dissonance and atonality.

Strauss was himself the first to capitalize on the great success of *Salome* with his opera *Elektra* (1908), based upon Hugo von Hofmannsthal's adaptation of the tragedy by Sophocles. In 1909 Schoenberg completed his first of two short Expressionist operas, *Erwartung* (*Expectation*), followed by *Die glükliche Hand* (*The Lucky Hand*). Shortly after the end of the First World War, Paul Hindemith adapted Oskar Kokoschka's *Mörder, Hoffnung der Frauen* and August Stramm's *Sancta Susanna* as one-act operas, and two plays by Georg Kaiser—*Der Protagonist* and *Der Zar lässt sich photographieren* (*The Tsar Has Himself Photographed*)—were used as opera libretti by the young Kurt Weill.

The greatest master of Expressionist opera was Alban Berg, whose deep interest in modern theater and genius as a dramatic composer led to the most enduring examples of this genre in his operas *Wozzeck* (1917–22) and *Lulu* (1928–35).

Georg Büchner's play *Woyzeck* is a work of social realism which prefigured the techniques of the Expressionists by almost a century. The main figure Woyzeck (or Wozzeck, as in an edition used by Berg to construct his libretto) is a poor soldier who is assailed by the forces of society and ultimately driven to insanity, murder, and self-destruction. Berg's music is atonal, but it makes passing references to keys and triads and it has a diversity of styles typical of this composer. An elaborate technique of leitmotifs and other musical-dramatic associations helps to give the score its great dramatic power. But Berg dispenses with Wagnerian through composition by using large symmetrical organizations and casting scenes and acts into forms associated with instrumental music.

Many of these techniques recur in the opera *Lulu*, a work of greater abstraction. *Lulu* was left incomplete upon the composer's death in 1935. Only recently has the third act been published (1978) and the complete opera performed (1979), with much of the orchestration of Act 3 realized by Friedrich Cerha.

Berg made up the libretto by joining two related plays of Frank Wedekind, *Earth Spirit* and *Pandora's Box*. The central figure Lulu represents female sexuality in the broadest sense: she enslaves men at will, tyrannically wielding the power of life and death over them. But she is herself ultimately destructible by masculine forces. The three-act libretto is arranged by Berg into a rigidly symmetrical two-part form which emphasizes the alternating dominance of female (part 1) and male (part 2) principles. In the first part Lulu has a succession of three husbands—a medical specialist, a painter, and the editor Dr. Schön. Each is totally in her power, and each is destroyed by jealousy or by a futile attempt to break from her spell.

In the second part of the story, Lulu's fortunes have declined. She is hunted for the murder of Dr. Schön and has fled to Paris and finally to London, where she becomes a prostitute. There she procures three patrons. The last is Jack the Ripper, the notorious murderer of nineteenth-century London, whom Berg identifies by common motives with Dr. Schön. Just as she murdered Schön, symbolically showing the power of her sexuality when it was at its zenith, now he murders her, in an exercise of the brutish power of the male life force.

In this opera as in *Wozzeck*, virtually every detail of musical style and structure is put at the service of the drama. Despite its intense and multifaceted formalism, the listener senses an unbroken continuity through each act. The work reveals a free application of the twelve-tone method, but with many nondodecaphonic elements.

The "Song of Lulu" from Act 2 (Anthology no. 20) is one of over fifty numbers into which Berg divides this opera. Many of these subdivisions are identified as vocal genres or styles; others suggest specific forms. An aria-like song is appropriate at this point as it is an avowal of Lulu's sensuality. Its musical structure is derived from the poetic form, which is a series of five couplets. Each of the five suggests that Schön and Lulu—representing, as they do, male and female—are opposite sides of the same existential principle. In the first half of each couplet, Lulu sings a theme that is answered in the second half by its inversion, thus an echo of the argumentative parallelisms in the text. The inversion in the first couplet is illustrated in Example 4-2.

In the first, second, and fourth couplets, the antecedent themes each state a different twelve-tone row, of which the first and third are associated in various thematic guises throughout the opera with Lulu:

Row I (voice, mm. 491–94)   C E F D G A F♯ G♯ B A♯ D♯ C♯
Row II (mm. 498 ff.)   F♯ D C♯ G♯ E C A B♭ C♭ E♭ G F
Row III (mm. 516 ff.)   F E♭ D C B♭ A♭ E G F♯ C♯ B A

Since row I returns in the fifth couplet, the lied is appropriately a ternary or "song" form:

A—	B—	A'—
Couplets 1, 2	Couplets 3, 4	Couplet 5
Mm. 491–507	Mm. 508–21	Mm. 522–38

The third couplet, which begins the middle section, is not twelve-tone. It instead contains a succession of octatonic, chromatic, and whole-tone passages which contrast with the outer sections also by their more florid vocal style.

After Lulu's Song, Dr. Schön demands that she commit suicide. His music states his own tone row, cast into a motive that piles up in a tumultuous stretto. At measure 548 the orchestra welds itself into a unison rhythm (Example 7-9) that is associated throughout with fate and violent death. As he turns his back, Schön is shot to death by Lulu in an expression of her most violent and destructive power.

Expressionist art, literature, and music were totally suppressed by the Nazis in the 1930s, when they were dismissed as degenerate or as examples of "cultural Bolshevism." This attitude reflected in part Hitler's own tastes, which in music did not extend beyond the style of Wagner. Among the outstanding living German composers, only Hans Pfitzner and Richard Strauss—who had long turned away from the avant-garde direction of *Salome* and *Elektra*—received official support. The others lived like Webern in total obscurity or like Hindemith and Schoenberg in exile.

A limited revival of opera in the Expressionist vein followed World War II, documented by such work as Gottfried von Einem's *Dantons Tod* and *Der Prozess*, Hans Werner Henze's *Ein Landarzt*, and Krzysztof Penderecki's *Devils of Loudon*. But by the 1940s the artistic rebellion that had nurtured Expressionism had waned and could not be revived with the shocking audacity of its earlier years.

Example 7-9. Motive signaling the murder of Dr. Schön in Berg's *Lulu*, Act 2, measures 548–49.

BIBLIOGRAPHY

General studies or reminiscences of the arts in Germany and Austria early in the century may be found in Stefan Zweig's poignant auto-biography *The World of Yesterday* (Lincoln, Neb., 1964), selected essays by Carl E. Schorske in *Fin-de-siècle Vienna* (New York, 1980), Otto Friedrich's study of Berlin during the Weimar Republic *Before the Deluge* (New York, 1972), and *Wittgenstein's Vienna* by Allan Janik and Stephen Toulmin (New York, 1973). Among the many memoirs of German musicians of these years, Bruno Walter's *Theme and Variations* (London, 1947) is especially recommended.

The life of Gustav Mahler to 1904 is traced in detail in Henry de La Grange's two-volume *Gustav Mahler* (Garden City, N.Y., 1973; Oxford, 1995); the complete biography upon which this study is based appeared in three volumes in French in 1979. Donald Mitchell's three-volume study *Gustav Mahler* (Berkeley, 1975–85) contains detailed analyses of selected works. *The Selected Letters of Gustav Mahler* (New York, 1979) is highly informative about the composer's music throughout his life, and Natalie Bauer-Lechner's *Recollections of Gustav Mahler* (London, 1980) gives an insightful first-hand portrait of the composer during his early years. Norman Del Mar's *Richard Strauss* (three vols., 1962–72, reprinted Ithaca, 1986) covers this composer's life and works in detail, and *Gustav Mahler, Richard Strauss: Correspondence, 1888–1911* (Chicago, 1984) contains letters between these two great contemporaries.

Schoenberg's writings are fundamental to an understanding of his music. His theoretical essays, which deal primarily with tonal music, are surveyed in the Bibliography to Chapter 2. His article "My Evolution" is found in *Musical Quarterly*, 38 (1952); this and other articles and lectures are collected under the title *Style and Idea*, ed. Leonard Stein (Berkeley, 1984). Also see his *Letters*, ed. Erwin Stein (Berkeley, 1987) and *The Berg-Schoenberg Correspondence*, eds. Juliane Brand, Christopher Hailey, and Donald Harris (New York, 1987). The most detailed biography of Schoenberg remains H. H. Stuckenschmidt's *Arnold Schoenberg: His Life, World and Work* (New York, 1977), and a detailed study of the early tonal music is provided by Walter Frisch in *The Early Works of Arnold Schoenberg, 1893–1908* (Berkeley, 1993).

General studies of the life and works of Alban Berg are written by Hans F. Redlich (London, 1957) and Mosco Carner (2nd ed. New York, 1983). His music is analyzed by Douglas Jarman in *The Music of Alban Berg* (Berkeley, 1980). Jarman follows the analytic method of George Perle, whose many writings on Berg include books on *Wozzeck* (Berkeley, 1980) and *Lulu* (Berkeley, 1985). The former is complemented by Janet Schmalfeldt's *Berg's "Wozzeck": Harmonic Language and Dramatic Design* (New Haven, 1983), which contains an analysis of pitch sets. Hans and Rosaleen Moldenhauer's *Anton von Webern* (New York, 1979) is an admirably thorough study of this composer, containing much information on the music.

Among Busoni's voluminous writings on music, see his "Sketch of a New Esthetic of Music" in *Three Classics in the Aesthetic of Music* (New York, 1962) and *The Essence of Music and Other Papers* (London, 1957). Biographies of Busoni include one by his friend Edward Dent (London, 1933); his music is analyzed in Antony Beaumont's *Busoni the Composer* (Bloomington, 1985). Christopher Hailey's *Franz Schreker, 1878–1934: A Cultural Biography* admirably assesses this composer's life and cultural milieu.

John Willett's *Expressionism* (New York, 1970) contains an informative account of this movement, emphasizing developments in painting and drama. *Expressionism in Twentieth-Century Music* (Bloomington, 1993), by John C. Crawford, seeks a broad definition of the expressionist spirit in modern music.

8

Avant-Garde Composition in France and Russia

France in the nineteenth century was a center of innovation in literature and the visual arts and the guardian of a distinguished musical culture and tradition. In the second half of the century, poets of the Symbolist movement and Impressionist painters created a revolution in their genres that would be felt throughout the world and endure well into the twentieth century. French composers of this time cultivated traditional idioms, invigorating them with imported stylistic ideas and a native gift for color and vividness. By the turn of the century, French musicians looked increasingly toward developments in modern literature and painting as a stimulus for new directions in their work.

SYMBOLISM AND IMPRESSIONISM

The Symbolist movement in literature is associated primarily with the poetry of Charles Baudelaire (1821–67), Stéphane Mallarmé (1842–98), Paul Verlaine (1844–96), and Arthur Rimbaud (1854–91), and plays by Maurice Maeterlinck (1862–1949). The works of these writers frequently avoid narration in order to allow sensations or objects to symbolize immaterial states of mind. Meaning is typically blurred by irregular syntax, the unexpected metaphor, and emphasis on the sonority and rhythm of words. Mallarmé's dramatic poem "Afternoon of a Faun" (1876), which inspired Claude Debussy's orchestral Prelude (1894), illustrates the network of sensuous associations that underlies Symbolist poetry. This "eclogue" expresses the fantasies of a mischievous faun who has awakened from a dream of erotic adventure with two nymphs:

> I would perpetuate these nymphs.
> So clear,
> Their skin's light bloom, it eddies in the air
> Heavy with tufts of sleep.
> Did I love a dream?
> My doubt, a heap of ancient night, has come
> To rest in many a subtle branch, which, still
> The very woods, proves, me, alas! the fool
> Crowning myself with roses, perfect flaw. . . .

[The remainder may be found in *Mallarmé: The Poems*, trans. Keith Bosley (London, 1977).]

The faun cannot decide if his encounter was real or imagined, but his vivid and sensuous recollection of the experience transcends reality, and he happily goes to sleep again to seek new adventures.

The Symbolists looked with envy upon the art of music, which seemed to them most capable of eliciting a free play of emotions and associations. Musical imagery abounds in their poetry as a means of evoking realms of fantasy. They were especially drawn to Richard Wagner, in whose libretti they found a kindred symbolism and whose writings proclaim the same "total artwork" which was their aspiration. In fact, literary figures were the main contributors to a French journal devoted to the accomplishments of Wagner, the *Revue wagnérienne* (1885–88), which helped to provoke a flurry of interest in this composer among French amateurs and professional musicians alike.

Impressionism is a loosely defined style of French painting of the late nineteenth century associated with works by Edouard Manet (1832–83), Edgar Degas (1834–1917), Claude Monet (1840–1926), Pierre-Auguste Renoir (1841–1919), and others. Their subjects are usually unpretentious scenes from everyday life. Landscapes, which had a particular attraction for the Impressionists, were reproduced to capture the changing effects of light and the dynamic interplay of color. The artist's concentration upon spontaneous light often led to a blurring of the appearance of objects. Impressionism took on greater abstraction and emotion among painters such as Paul Gauguin (1848–1903) and Vincent Van Gogh (1853–90) and from these "post-

Impressionism in French painting: Claude Monet, *Le pont japonais, Giverny*. (Oil on canvas, ca. 1900, 35 ⅛ × 39 ½, Mr. and Mrs. Lewis L. Coburn Memorial Collection. © The Art Institute of Chicago. All rights reserved. Courtesy of the Art Institute of Chicago.)

Impressionists" there is a direct line to German Expressionism of the early twentieth century. The Impressionists were also forerunners of *art nouveau*: a style of illustration and decoration characterized by fanciful organic shapes, often with grotesque or erotic overtones.

Certain composers active in France in the late nineteenth and early twentieth centuries—primarily Claude Debussy, and also Maurice Ravel, Paul Dukas, the Englishman Frederick Delius, and the American Charles Griffes—are commonly referred to as "Impressionists." Some aspects of their music indeed echo the style of the Impressionist painters: a fluidity of rhythm and meter suggestive of the hazy outlines of an Impressionist landscape, melodic arabesques reminiscent of *art nouveau* illustration, a sensitivity to the

Art nouveau illustration: Aubrey Beardsley, illustration for Oscar Wilde's *Salome* (London, 1894).

play of instrumental and vocal color, and, in general, the use of a refined and evocative musical language that expresses the sensuousness of nature and the external world.

But the concept of an Impressionist movement in French music may also be misleading: composers such as Debussy and Ravel created their own independent styles rather than working within a single movement. Debussy strenuously objected to being termed an Impressionist—a word that was at first used pejoratively to describe his music. Regarding his orchestral pieces *Images*, he wrote to his publisher, "What I am trying to do is something 'different'—an effect of reality, but what some fools call Impressionism."

THE FRENCH ROMANTICS

If French musical life of the later nineteenth century was not marked by the originality of German romanticism, it was nonetheless diverse and lively. César Franck (1822–90), Camille Saint-Saëns (1835–1921), and Ernest Chausson (1855–99) produced instrumental works of great tunefulness and color, marked by the cyclic return of themes in different movements. Operas by Emmanuel Chabrier (1841–94) and Vincent d'Indy (1851–1931) reflected the influence of Wagner in their libretti and in certain musical formulas.

Gabriel Fauré (1845–1924) was among the most original voices in French music of the late nineteenth century. He worked in all of the major musical genres of his time. His songs are especially noteworthy, as they reveal his great lyric gift and an imaginative adaptation of the harmonic richness of German music to the understated refinement of modern French poetry. His works were highly influential upon Debussy and later French composers.

In his setting of Catulle Mendès's "Dans la forêt de septembre" (1902, Anthology no. 10), Fauré merges Wagnerian harmony with an atmosphere laden with restrained melancholy. The poem is precise in its language, leaving the impression that the poet is barely able to prevent the emotions from overflowing into sentimentality. The narrator beholds an aging forest that bears signs of long suffering. He gladly enters to escape from life, and a tree sends down a leaf as a token of spiritual kinship in the face of the approaching winter.

Fauré's music matches Mendès's use of direct and precise language to contain an overabundance of emotion. The overall form of the song is entirely regular. The music of the first stanza, solidly in the tonic Gb major, returns in the third and sixth stanzas, and this principal melody is divided into four two-measure phrases. The intervening stanzas move to contrasting tonal areas. Fauré's harmonic language is more daring, as it incorporates hyperexpressive tendencies in German music of the late romantic period. The prevailing circular harmonic progressions are continually expanded by the chromatic alterations of diatonic triads, the use of triads from outside of the key, and the suppression of the dominant, which tends to be absent at major cadences.

DEBUSSY, SATIE, AND RAVEL

The musician who rescued France from the dominance of German music was Claude Debussy (1862–1918). His works are monuments to the power of music to evoke an image or, to use his own words, "an effect of reality." Except for the early String Quartet and three late sonatas, he cultivated those genres that were suited to programmatic association: the character piece for piano, tone poem, and song. In a letter to Emile Baron of February 1887, he expressed "a profound disdain for music which has to follow a little story, which you are given when you arrive at the concert." Debussy's music is not literally programmatic, but seeks instead to capture the immaterial essence, poetry, or emotion of his subjects.

The themes of Debussy's works are sometimes drawn from exotic regions of the world or from fantastic visions of the mind. His most important subject is nature. In an article for the journal *Musica* (1903), he writes: "Music is a mysterious mathematical process whose elements are a part of Infinity. It is allied to the movement of the waters, to the play of curves described by the changing breezes. Nothing is more musical than a sunset!"

Nature is not only a recurrent subject of Debussy's instrumental works, it is also a metaphor for the true nature of music in general. Both are spontaneous, unconstrained, and asymmetrical. In an interview in 1902, Debussy used Baudelaire's notion of "correspondences" between objects, images, and artistic symbols to describe the function of nature in his works: "I should like for music a liberty that is proper to it—more to it, perhaps, than to any other art. It is not limited to a more or less exact reproduction of nature, but to the mysterious correspondences of nature and the imagination" (from Stefan Jarocinski, *Debussy: impressionnisme et symbolisme* [Paris, 1970], p. 122).

Debussy's style is consistently marked by refined understatement and simplicity of means: he rejected music that was formulaic, contrived, or grandiloquent. "Extreme complication is contrary to art," he writes. "Beauty must appeal to the senses, must provide us with immediate enjoyment, must impress us or insinuate itself into us without any effort on our part. Take Da Vinci or Mozart—these are the great artists!" In the *Revue musicale S.I.M.* (1912), he writes: "What one is meant to hear should be apparent at once. The rest is just a matter of environment and other extra-musical considerations."

CLAUDE DEBUSSY
(St. Germain-en-Laye, 1862–Paris, 1918)

Debussy was sent at the age of 10 to study at the Paris Conservatory in the hope that he would become a piano virtuoso. He remained a student there for twelve years. During this time his attention turned increasingly toward composition, which he pursued with Ernest Guiraud. In 1884 he won the Grand Prix de Rome, which made possible a three-year sojourn in Italy. He resigned his stipend after two years and returned to Paris.

During the summers of 1888 and 1889, he traveled to Bayreuth to attend performances there of operas by Richard Wagner. Debussy held a lifelong admiration for Wagner's music, although he had a strong distaste for Wagnerian aesthetics and amateur Wagnerites. At the Paris International Exhibition of 1889 he was fascinated by Javanese gamelan ensembles and traditional Chinese theatrical music. He was closely associated with Symbolist writers in the circle of Stéphane Mallarmé, and at least by 1891 he became a close friend of the eccentric musician Erik Satie.

Debussy's reputation as a composer was initially based upon the success of his opera *Pelléas et Mélisande* (1893–1902). After 1907 he made several tours as conductor of his own music and worked sporadically on two operatic projects based on tales of Edgar Allan Poe. He undertook several commissions by the Russian impresario Sergei Diaghilev, including the score to the ballet *Jeux*. Through Diaghilev he met Igor Stravinsky.

SELECTED WORKS

Dramatic Music. *Pelléas et Mélisande* (opera, 1893–1902), *Jeux* (ballet, 1912), *Khamma* (ballet, 1912, mainly orchestrated by Charles Koechlin).
Orchestral Music *Prélude à l'après-midi d'un faune* (1894), *Nocturnes* (1899), *La mer* (1905), *Images* (1905–12).
Chamber Music. String Quartet (1893); Sonatas for cello (1915), flute, viola and harp (1915), and violin (1917); miscellaneous works for saxophone, clarinet, and flute.

Piano Music. Approximately 100 pieces including the collections *Pour le piano* (1894–1901), *Estampes* (1903), *Images* (two sets, 1905, 1907), *Children's Corner* (1908), Preludes (two books, 1910, 1913), Etudes, *Six épigraphes antiques* (four hands, 1914), *En blanc et noir* (two pianos, 1915).

Songs. Fifty-seven songs published during Debussy's lifetime, some with orchestral accompaniment. Eighteen are settings of poetry by Paul Verlaine.

Technical innovations in Debussy's music include a free use of dissonance where sevenths and ninths no longer require preparation or resolution, new methods of voice leading by which perfect intervals move in parallel, greater freedom in the expression of key, and passing use of nondiatonic harmonies such as the whole-tone set. Although some of his later works are entirely atonal, he rejected the harmonic experimentation of his younger contemporaries. The triad and diatonic scale were his points of orientation. Most of the dissonances that lend a distinctive color to his music are triadic extensions such as seventh and ninth chords. Occasionally these harmonies are decorated by passing use of whole-tone, octatonic, or pentatonic scales and chordal formations, but, with only a few exceptions, these are ways of embellishing a diatonic framework.

Debussy's melodic lines are often spun into eccentric and flamboyant shapes, as in the Prelude to *The Afternoon of a Faun*. Or they may be flexible and chant-like, as in the song "En sourdine." Phrasing is also varied—some works, such as the Saraband from *Pour le piano*, are laid out primarily in multiples of two-measure units. But in pieces such as *Jeux*, periodic phrasing is little in evidence.

An example of Debussy's piano music in his early mature style is the Saraband from *Pour le piano* (Anthology No. 2). This work was composed in 1894 and provisionally titled "Image," but it was revised and retitled for its publication in 1901. It is superficially related to the Sarabands of Erik Satie, works that will be discussed shortly. Like all of Debussy's piano music, the Saraband is a character piece that creates a distinctive mood. The title comes from the work's rhythmic style, which suggests the slow, triple-time sarabands often found in works by seventeenth-century clavecinists, whom Debussy admired. In the original version, the composer states that the work is to be played "in the tempo of a saraband, that is, with a slow and solemn elegance, a bit like an old portrait, a recollection from the Louvre."

The form of the work is ternary. The middle section (mm. 23–41) introduces new motives and contrasts with the outer sections by virtue of its quartal harmonies (mm. 23–28). Perhaps owing to its derivation from a baroque dance, the formal structure of the Saraband is regular: most motives span multiples of two measures, and phrases are built from simple repetitive patterns.

Motives in this work share similarities of interval and rhythm, but they are not developmentally linked as in music of the German and Austrian modernists. Debussy is reported to have rejected conventional exposition and development:

> I should like to attain a music which is truly released from motives or made from one continuous motive that is not interrupted and that never comes back upon itself. Then there will be logical development—compact and deductive. Between restatements of the same motive—typical and characteristic of the work—there will not be a superfluous and unimportant padding. Development will no longer be this amplification of material, this professional's rhetoric learned through excellent lessons. It will instead take on a more universal and ultimately psychic meaning. [From André Fontainas, *Mes souvenirs du symbolisme* (Paris, 1928), pp. 92–93.]

Harmonies of the Saraband do not project the tonic C♯ minor until the reprise at measure 42, and then only indistinctly. Their role instead is to enhance the melody by successions of parallel seventh chords (mm. 35–41), fourth chords (mm. 23–28, 67–70), or by combinations of seventh chords and triads that arise without reference to traditional resolutions of dissonances or harmonic functions within a key. "A chord is an edifice of sound," writes Debussy, "having merely the importance of a stone in a building. Its real value depends on the place it occupies and the support it lends to the flexible curve of the melodic line." Cadences completely avoid the strong dominant-to-tonic forms.

Pelléas et Mélisande, Debussy's first great success as a composer, was premiered in 1902 after a decade in the making. It is based on a Symbolist play by Maurice Maeterlinck in which the youthful lovers Pelléas and Mélisande are destroyed by the jealousy of Golaud, Mélisande's husband and half-brother of Pelléas. The play has a mythic and surrealistic atmosphere in which characters act out their roles as symbols of a morbid but all-powerful fate. It also has connections with Wagner's text to *Tristan und Isolde*. Both are studies of love that is frustrated by existential forces beyond the control of the lovers.

The orchestral part provides an unobtrusive backdrop to the singing, which is predominantly parlando in character, occasionally varied by song-like passages. A very subtle and unsystematic technique of leitmotifs may be discovered in the orchestral music, but the work's severe understatement is virtually the opposite of Wagnerian rhetoric. Toward the end of Act 4, for example, Pelléas and Mélisande declare their love in a scene that parallels the love duet of *Tristan*, Act 2. Wagner's lovers boldly vent their passions for more than a half hour, but Pelléas must confess that he could scarcely hear Mélisande's declaration of love, even though the orchestra had by then dwindled into complete silence.

In his two books of Piano *Préludes* (1910 and 1913), Debussy gives full rein to his musical imagination. The listener is transported to exotic locales in Spain, Greece, India, and Brittany; evocations of nature—mists, wind, dead leaves—give way to images of pure fantasy. These works call to mind those of Robert Schumann in their subtle translation of diverse images into music for piano. At the same time these brief compositions are encyclopedic in their innovative structural resources. Some such as "La cathédrale engloutie" use diatonic scales but avoid the expression of a key; others rely on the whole-tone scale, as in "Voiles," and the octatonic scale, as in "Brouillards." But most retain an orientation to a key by ending with a triad and making at least passing references to diatonic chords and tonic and dominant pedal points.

Debussy's late style may be observed in the song "Placet futile" from the *Trois poèmes de Stéphane Mallarmé* of 1913. This text was also used in a song of the same year by Maurice Ravel, which allows a useful comparison of the works of these two composers. Debussy was a friend of Mallarmé: he took part in literary discussions held weekly at Mallarmé's residence and, to Mallarmé's delight, composed an orchestral Prelude to his dramatic poem "The Afternoon of a Faun."

The text of "Placet futile" is an example of the Symbolists' sacrifice of clear meaning to suggestive metaphors and distorted syntax. The narrator of this sonnet makes his "futile petition" to be appointed "shepherd of the smiles" of the beloved; any more active participation in love must be sublimated beneath a flourish of pastoral metaphors. The central image of the poem is a Sevres teacup, whose naked goddesses are portrayed musically in a slow minuet with rococo ornamentation. As in most of Debussy's later works, tonality plays a minor role. The context is G major/minor, but most of the harmonies are nondiatonic seventh and ninth chords and whole-tone collections.

Debussy's last completed composition for orchestra is his score for the ballet *Jeux* (*Games*, 1912). This work was commissioned by Sergei Diaghilev for the Ballets Russes (see below), by whom it received its premier performance in 1913. The scenario of the ballet was devised by Vaslav Nijinsky (1890–1950), the leading dancer of Diaghilev's company. Debussy succinctly described the scenario in an article for

Le matin written shortly after the first performance: "There was a park, a tennis court, and the chance meeting of two young girls with a young man in pursuit of a lost ball. A mysterious landscape with that slightly evil *je ne sais quoi* that always accompanies twilight. And a lot of leaping and turning in the air, and nimble footwork—all the necessary ingredients for real rhythms to be born."

In fact Nijinsky's scenario is considerably more risqué. A man encounters two ladies at a tennis court. He dances with one—even manages a kiss—which makes the other petulantly jealous. He dances next with the second lady, but the first leaves dejectedly. Now the three dance together a voluptuous waltz, ending in a triple kiss. A tennis ball bounds across the stage and the trio disappears. Nijinsky later wrote that the meaning of the story was that the two ladies represent two boys in a homosexual liaison with Diaghilev, whom the man represents. Regardless, the work is known primarily for its musical setting, which is a masterpiece of motion and color.

The ballet is framed symmetrically by music to the prelude (mm. 1–46), which returns in the epilogue (rehearsal 80). The body of the work consists of a through-composed succession of episodes, which are linked by rhythmic and motivic similarities. Some of the motives recur straightforwardly; others are transformed in shape. The harmonic content of *Jeux* is typical of Debussy's late music. The lines and chords are predominantly diatonic, although they do not dwell upon any single diatonic collection in a manner that defines a key. References to A at the beginning (rehearsal 1) and end, and to the tritone related region of E♭ at rehearsal 41, are brief and superficial. The harmonies that support Debussy's surging motivic arabesques are mainly seventh and ninth chords, occasionally varied by whole-tone formations (rehearsal 5, 61, 81), pentatonic sets and subsets (rehearsal 42), and bitriadic chords (rehearsal 10).

Debussy's wish to reestablish a distinctively French style of composition free of German influences was shared by his friend Erik Satie (1866–1925). Satie's music includes songs, piano pieces, and music for the stage. Most compositions are miniatures, and his works include imitations of the style of the music hall, certain farcical gestures, as well as music of considerable ambition and seriousness. The common threads running through it all are its melodiousness, simplicity, and complete lack of pretense.

An example of his early idiom is the first Saraband (1887, Anthology no. 1). This piece may be compared to Debussy's Saraband in its use of unresolved seventh and ninth chords. Such colorful harmonies are also found in passing in French opera of this

ERIK SATIE
(*Honfleur, 1866–Paris, 1925*)

Satie spent his childhood alternately in Honfleur and Paris. He entered the Paris Conservatory in 1879, but his work there was found unpromising. His earliest compositions were published with assistance from his father in 1887. In the 1880s and 1890s he was active in various unorthodox Christian sects for which he composed music.

He earned his livelihood primarily as a pianist in Parisian cabarets, and he composed several music hall songs for the singers Vincent Hyspa and Paulette Darty. At the age of 40 he entered the Schola Cantorum to study counterpoint, which he did successfully with Albert Roussel. His career as a serious composer received encouragement from Ravel, who played some of his piano pieces in concerts, and from the writer Jean Cocteau. His collaboration with Cocteau on the ballet *Parade* (1917) produced his first major success as a composer. Toward the end of his life he and Cocteau became mentors to a group of younger French composers known as the Six.

SELECTED WORKS

Dramatic Works. Ballets: *Uspud* (1892), *Parade*, (1917) *Mercure* (1924), *Relâche* (1924); incidental music: *Le piège de Méduse* (1913).
Piano Music. Approximately thirty collections including Sarabands (1887), *Gymnopédies* (1888), *Gnossiennes* (1890), Preludes, *Sports et divertissements* (1914), *Avant-dernières pensées* (1914), Nocturnes, *Trois morceaux en forme de poire* (four hands, 1890–1903), and arrangements.
Songs. Four collections for voice and piano, popular songs, *Socrate* for sopranos and orchestra (1918).

time and in popular songs, which Satie accompanied as a cabaret pianist. On the large scale the Saraband expresses the key of A♭ major. But few chords occur diatonically in A♭ and most of them carry unresolved dissonances. The music is highly repetitive, simple in texture and rhythm, and—at least in comparison to Debussy's Saraband—curiously motionless.

Satie's later piano music adopts textures that are spartanly bare, usually consisting of a simple melody above a light accompaniment. The repetitiveness and freedom from diatonic harmony of the Sarabands are retained. Many pieces lack regular meter. Beginning with his first three *Gnossiennes* (1890), Satie's scores for piano contain witty marginalia which contribute a running commentary by the composer upon the work at hand. His collection *Sports et divertissements* (1914) is an especially charming series of fragments, each of which depicts in the space of a minute or less a particular sport or entertainment.

Two of his later works epitomize the different artistic stances that alternate in his music after the First World War. The symphonic drama *Socrate* (1918) is serious and poignantly expressive, while the ballet *Parade* (1917) is high spirited and tongue-in-cheek. The music to *Socrate* comprises solo songs for four sopranos and small orchestra. Its texts are drawn from Plato's *Dialogs*, concluded touchingly by Phaedo's description of Socrates' death. The vocal line is a tuneful recitation; the orchestra, a repetitive and unobtrusive backdrop. It is music that reveals Satie's debt to Debussy and *Pelléas*, where the largeness of sentiment and occasion expressed in the text is intentionally contrasted to the modesty and understatement of musical resources. This divergent relation of text and music was Satie's alternative to Wagnerian music drama and his solution to the question of how a truly French musical idiom should unfold in the modern age.

Parade was Satie's first real success as a composer. It was commissioned by Sergei Diaghilev, who brought Satie into collaboration with the writer Jean Cocteau and the painter Pablo Picasso. The setting is outside of a tent at a fair, where three managers, a juggler, acrobats, and an American girl try to coax the passersby to enter and see the show within. Satie's music is again modest: "a musical background," he said, "for certain noises which Cocteau considers indispensable in order to fix the atmosphere of his characters." The music for the Chaplinesque antics of the American girl includes gun shots and typewriter sounds in the orchestra as well as a ragtime dance.

The premiere of the ballet provoked a disturbance, which, since the scandalous first night of Stravinsky's *Rite of Spring*, had become increasingly obligatory among French audiences of new music. Satie was no doubt pleased with this mark of success, and he

increasingly associated himself with the aesthetics of his collaborator Cocteau. The influence of Satie and Cocteau on French music
after the First World War will be traced later in this chapter and in
Chapter 10. After the death of Debussy in 1918, Satie became mentor
to a new generation of French composers for whom the refined
artistry of the Impressionists was disagreeable. Stravinsky, for
example, credited Satie with "opposing the vagueness of a decrepit
Impressionism by a precise and firm language stripped of all pictorial embellishments." Virtually all of the musicians who met Satie,
regardless of their artistic direction, were captivated by his wit and
generosity, and it was as much by the power of his personality as by
his musicianship that he exerted his influence.

The rejuvenation of modern French music begun by Debussy was
continued by Maurice Ravel (1875–1937). Ravel's early works reflect
the style of Debussy: they are vividly pictorial and expand the
framework of diatonic tonality in ways associated with Debussy.
Ravel's piano works, however, rely to a greater extent on virtuosity
for their expressiveness, and most are appropriate to orchestral tran-
scription, done with unparalleled brilliance by the composer. He
was also more inclined to experiment with new stylistic directions,
as in his Mallarmé songs and in later works such as the *Tombeau de
Couperin*, which is a sympathetic reflection upon the idiom of the
baroque clavecinists.

Ravel's early style may be observed in his piano work *Jeux d'eau*
(1901, Anthology No. 3). This piece was probably inspired by Liszt's
"Les jeux d'eaux à la Villa d'Este" (1877) from the third *Année de
pèlerinage*. In both, the "play of water" mentioned in the title is captured by an effervescence of arpeggios and melodic arabesques. The
spirit of Ravel's piece is suggested by a line added to the score from
the poet Henri de Régnier: "River god laughing from the water
which tickles him." The work avails itself of the repertory of harmonies characteristic of both Debussy and Liszt. It begins and ends
in E major, but all tonic triads are decorated by the major seventh D♯.
The triads of the opening give way to a whole-tone passage in measures 4–6, and the subsidiary theme (mm. 19 ff.) is pentatonic. A
cadenza near the end pits arpeggiated F♯-major triads in the left
hand against C-major triads in the right. This bitriadic passage may
well have been in Stravinsky's ear when he wrote the very similar
opening to the second tableau of *Petrushka* (see below).

During a period of collaboration with Ravel in 1913, Stravinsky
introduced him to his *Trois poésies de la lyrique japonaise* for voice and
chamber orchestra. Stravinsky's work for the medium of vocalist and
diverse instruments was stimulated by Schoenberg's *Pierrot lunaire*,

MAURICE RAVEL
(*Ciboure, 1875–Paris, 1937*)

Ravel's career is to an extent similar to that of the musician with whom he is most often mentioned, Claude Debussy. Both were sent as adolescents to the Paris Conservatory to study piano, and both later turned their attention mainly to composition. Ravel was in the composition class of Gabriel Fauré. Like Debussy, he was stimulated by the music and wit of Erik Satie, by Russian music, and by discussions with artists in other disciplines.

In 1912 Ravel completed *Daphnis et Chloé* for Sergei Diaghilev and the Ballets Russes; Diaghilev also brought Ravel and Stravinsky together to complete Musorgski's opera *Khovantchina*, thus beginning a lifelong friendship of these two musicians. In the 1920s and 1930s Ravel found himself outside of the circle of younger French composers who were actively renouncing the preciosity which they found in musical Impressionism. Ravel undertook numerous tours in the 1920s, including a lengthy visit to the United States in 1928. His work as a composer slowly came to a halt after 1933 because of a degenerative nervous disorder, which would cause his death in 1937.

SELECTED WORKS

Operas. *L'heure espagnole* (1909), *L'enfant et les sortilèges* (1920–25).
Ballets. *Daphnis et Chloé* (1909–12), *La valse* (1920), *Boléro* (1928).
Orchestral Music. Arrangements of piano music (see below).
Concertos. *Tzigane* (violin and piano or orchestra, 1924), Concerto for Left Hand (1930), Piano Concerto in G (1931).
Chamber Music. String Quartet (1903), Trio (piano, violin, cello, 1914), Sonata for Violin and Cello (1922), Violin Sonata (1923–27).
Piano Music. *Pavane pour une infante défunte** (1899), *Jeux d'eau* (1901), *Sonatine* (1905), *Miroirs** (1905), *Rapsodie espagnole** (four hands, 1908), *Gaspard de la nuit* (1908), *Ma mère l'oye** (four hands, 1910), *Valses nobles et sentimentales** (1911), *Le tombeau de Couperin** (1917). The

asterisk (*) indicates works transcribed—at least in part—for
orchestra by Ravel.
Songs. *Histoires naturelles* (1906), *Trois poèmes de Stéphane Mallarmé* (1913),
  Chansons madécasses (1926), *Don Quichotte à Dulcinée* (1933).

---

which he had heard in Berlin the previous year. Ravel now called
upon a similar ensemble in his *Trois poèmes de Stéphane Mallarmé*
(1913). At the very time that Ravel was completing these songs, he
learned that Debussy was also at work on three Mallarmé settings,
and, by a remarkable coincidence, two of them used the same texts.
One of these two, "Placet futile," will show how far Ravel had
departed from the Impressionistic "Debussyism" of his early music.
    In a letter of 1913 to his student Roland-Manuel, Ravel wrote
about his objectives in this song:

> I fully realize the great audacity of having attempted to interpret
> this sonnet ["Placet futile"] in music. It was necessary that the
> melodic contour, the modulations, and the rhythms be as precious,
> as properly contoured as the sentiment and the images of the text. In
> spite of that, it was necessary to maintain the elegant deportment of
> the poem. Above all, it was necessary to maintain the profound and
> exquisite tenderness which suffuses all of this. [Quoted in Arbie
> Orenstein, *Ravel* (New York: Columbia University Press, 1975), pp.
> 128–29.]

    In order to mirror the elegance and tenderness of the poem, Ravel
takes an entirely different approach from that of Debussy. While
Debussy casts the entire poem as an ornate minuet, Ravel calls for
the utmost variety in his musical resources. The tempo is almost
constantly in flux, there is little formal symmetry, and the accompanimental colors change kaleidoscopically. The harmonies, likewise,
move back and forth from triads and triadically based dissonances
to other dissonant collections without triadic suggestions. The dissonant chords at the beginning, such as the all-interval tetrachord on
the downbeat of measure 2, give the work a distinctly German flavor. There is little sense of tonality, other than a hint of D minor near
the beginning (mm. 4–6) and F major at the end. The Mallarmé
songs are Ravel's most difficult and experimental works. They
reflect both Mallarmé's euphuistic poetry and an openness to new
directions which Ravel no doubt discovered in Stravinsky's music
of this time.
    Ravel composed relatively less after the end of the First World
War. But from these years come such works as the opera *L'enfant et*

les sortilèges (The Child and the Magic Spells) on a fairy-tale libretto by Colette. The music makes use of a ragtime dance, and Ravel's fascination with American popular music is also reflected in several later works such as the slow movement ("Blues") of his Violin Sonata (1927). The ever-popular *Boléro* (1928) was conceived as a ballet score for Ida Rubinstein. A simple bolero rhythm and folk-like tunes are repeated as an ostinato, sustaining a continual crescendo. The work was described by the composer as "wholly orchestral tissue without music." Ravel's two piano concertos mix different styles. The first, one of several concertos for left hand written for Paul Wittgenstein after he lost an arm in the war, uses jazz idioms in a somber way. The ensuing Concerto in G major is a lighter work, "in the same spirit," Ravel said, "as those of Mozart and Saint-Saëns."

Ravel considered his *Chansons madécasses* (*Madagascar* Songs, 1926) to be among his greatest works. These pieces, for soprano accompanied by flute, cello, and piano, use texts by Evariste Parny, who claimed that they were from folk songs that he had collected and translated. In fact they were written by Parny, expressing fanciful and evocative images of life among the Madagascans. Ravel's three texts dwell upon love, war, and blissful idleness. The second, "Méfiez-vous des blancs," narrates in prose the arrival of white men to the island, who, proving deceitful and treacherous, are finally slaughtered by the natives.

Lithograph by Luc-Albert Moreau for the first edition of Ravel's "Méfiez-vous des blancs" from *Chansons madécasses* (Paris, 1926). (Courtesy of Durand S.A. Editions musicales.)

The music vividly traces the emotions of the narrator. He begins his tale with seething tension, builds to the frantic war cries at measure 35, and erupts with savage fury as he tells of the destruction of the second wave of settlers. In exhaustion he falls back at the end, confident that "they are no more and we shall live free." The setting is entirely atonal, with only passing reference to triadic harmonies. It is carefully unified by recurrent motives. The printed score makes novel use of conflicting key signatures in the various parts, but these do not reflect traditional tonality.

Among Ravel's contemporaries in France, Paul Dukas (1865–1935) and Albert Roussel (1869–1937) are especially notable. Dukas devoted himself to teaching at the Paris Conservatory; he left a relatively small number of compositions among which the tone poem *Sorcerer's Apprentice* is best known. His opera *Ariane et Barbe-bleue* (1907) on a text by Maurice Maeterlinck was highly regarded both in France and Austria, where it was performed in 1908. It is marked by whole-tone sonorities and a brilliant style of orchestration.

Roussel was a student of Vincent d'Indy and later his colleague on the faculty of the Schola Cantorum. His students there included Erik Satie and Edgard Varèse. Roussel's best-known music is for orchestra, for which he wrote in a powerfully direct manner. His symphonies use the technique of cyclic return of themes as do those of his teacher d'Indy, and they contain a rhythmic vigor and brilliant orchestral color reminiscent of Ravel and Prokofiev.

THE DECLINE OF THE AVANT-GARDE

A significant musical avant-garde did not endure long after the end of World War I in France, despite the rambunctious high spirits of composers who were allied to the versatile Jean Cocteau (1889–1963). Cocteau was a writer who delved into cinema, the visual arts, and music and who catalyzed a generation of French artistic experiment. In a collection of aphorisms on music titled *Le Coq et l'arlequin* (1918), he decried "all music which has to be listened to through the hands. . . . What we need is a music of the earth, everyday music. . . . I want someone to build me music I can live in like a house." For Cocteau the ultimate in "hand music" was the work of Wagner, but Debussy's evocative Impressionism was also tainted in this way. "One cannot get lost in a Debussy mist as one can in a Wagner fog," he quipped, "but it is not good for one."

The antidote for Wagner and the Impressionists, according to Cocteau, was simplicity, an emphasis on straightforward melody, rejection of the colossal, and an art with the immediacy and accessibility of popular entertainment. "The music hall, the circus, and American Negro bands: all these things fertilize an artist just as life does. . . . These entertainments are not art. [But] they stimulate in the same way as machinery, animals, natural scenery, or danger. . . . Do not derive art from art!"

Cocteau enunciated a new taste and direction in French music that was prefigured by Satie and realized between the world wars in different ways by the outstanding French composers of the following generation. This new idiom, which can generally be termed "neoclassicism," will be taken up again in Chapter 10.

THE RUSSIAN AVANT-GARDE: THE FIVE AND SCRIABIN

We turn now to the flowering of a distinguished musical culture in Russia. The development of music in Russia along Western lines was a by-product of liberalization in society and politics during the second half of the nineteenth century. Activities in music were largely centered in the capital St. Petersburg and Moscow. Conservatories were founded in both cities in the 1860s, and these institutions soon produced outstanding orchestras and opera companies. Throughout the nineteenth century Russia had been a center of classical ballet, thanks to the efforts there of the French ballet master Charles-Louis Didelot (1767–1837) and the choreographer Marius Petipa (1818–1910).

As the nineteenth century progressed, two distinct approaches to composition emerged. Figures associated with the Moscow Conservatory such as Nicholas Rubinstein (1835–81), Sergei Taneev (1856–1915), Pëtr Ilich Tchaikovsky (1840–93), and Sergei Rachmaninoff (1873–1943) followed mainly Western models. A circle of composers who gathered around Mili Balakirev (1837–1910) in St. Petersburg, on the other hand, consisted of musical nationalists who felt less constrained by Western notions of musical structure. These composers came to be known as the "Russian Five" and they included, besides their mentor Balakirev, Alexander Borodin (1833–87), César Cui (1835–1918), Modest Musorgski (1839–81), and Nikolai Rimski-Korsakov (1844–1908).

The Westernized tastes of composers in Moscow are reflected in the music of Sergei Rachmaninoff. Moscow was his principal residence until his emigration to the West in 1918, following the Revolution. After this time he lived in both Europe and America, pursuing an international career as a pianist, conductor, and composer. Virtually all of his important works were composed prior to his emigration from Russia. These include symphonies and tone poems, works for chorus, character pieces and sonatas for piano, songs, and four enduringly popular piano concertos. Rachmaninoff was generally aloof from the innovations in musical style of the early years of the century, maintaining instead the romantic tradition.

Composers of the Russian Five, on the contrary, were inclined to move beyond nineteenth-century tastes. Musorgski's song cycle *Nursery* (1868) shows the composer's gift for spontaneous and realistic narration in vocal music, joined to a highly unorthodox tonal and harmonic style. Musorgski's text for the first song of the cycle, "With Nurse," is charmingly naive: a child at first wishes to hear the tale of the wolf who ate naughty children, but then decides that a story about an imaginary king and queen would be more congenial. The melodic line is recitational, moving almost entirely by quarter notes grouped into constantly changing meters according to the length and scansion of the poetic lines. Typical of many songs by Musorgski, the tonic harmony is not heard at the beginning. It is reached only at the end of the first section at measure 13. Before this point of orientation, various triads alternate with whole-tone harmonies, the latter brought in at the mention of the wolf. Throughout the nineteenth century, Russian composers commonly used whole-tone sets to depict images of fear or the unearthly. Musorgski's mentor Alexander Dargomyzhski used whole-tone sonorities to accompany the vivified statue in his opera *The Stone Guest*, an adaptation of the Don Juan legend. After the cadence on the tonic B♭ in measure 13 of "With Nurse," the music shifts directly to a D-major triad, a progression commonly encountered in operatic recitative. The second half of the song contains a comic musical picture of the hobbling king and his sneezing queen, turning finally to a codetta squarely in the tonic key.

About this cycle and its composer, Debussy wrote: "[Musorgski] is unique and will remain so, because his art is spontaneous and free from arid formulas. . . . It is like the art of an inquiring savage discovering music step by step through his emotions." Indeed, it was this model of unaffected simplicity more than any particular technical resources that was Musorgski's primary influence upon composers at the turn of the twentieth century.

Nikolai Rimski-Korsakov was primarily a composer of operas, symphonic works, and songs. His music of the 1870s and 1880s repeatedly incorporates Russian folk song and traditional Russian stories. His brilliant orchestral music reflects the style of Liszt and Berlioz. A feature of much of his music that proved especially important to composers in both France and Russia was the octatonic scale, a formation also prefigured in experimental works by Liszt.

For example, the codetta to the third movement of the symphonic poem *Antar* (1868) (Example 8-1) begins upon a cadence in D major (rehearsal V), which is followed by octatonic movement in the upper strings and woodwinds. For Rimski-Korsakov the octatonic scale was an exotic embellishment to diatonic harmony. It would later be used by Ravel, Debussy, Scriabin, Stravinsky, and Messiaen as a central harmonic resource in the atonal idiom.

From Moscow came one of the most prophetic figures in the transition from romantic to modern music, Alexander Scriabin (1872–1915). Like most of his fellow Muscovites, he did not outwardly adopt Russian folk materials, and he stayed closely in touch with modern developments in Western music. His evolution as a composer is unique among his countrymen at this time in the dispatch with which he embraced modern styles.

His music is almost wholly for orchestra or piano, on which instrument he performed as a virtuoso. The early piano works are based on the idiom of Chopin, and, by the turn of the century, his orchestral music was touched by the harmonic and orchestrational style of Wagner. Between this time and his complete break with tonality about 1908, his music increasingly reflected his devotion to cult and mystic notions of love. Several works are connected with his own poetry, the tone of which can be gathered from lines written to accompany his Fourth Symphony (*Poem of Ecstasy*): "The world is consumed in universal flame. The spirit is on the summit of being. . . . And the world resounds with the joyful cry: I am!" His scores from this time are peppered with exotic instructions suggesting their poetic content: "with profound and veiled ardor," "with a sad voluptuousness," "in a sweet intoxication"—these from the Tenth Piano Sonata. His symphony *Prometheus*, furthermore, calls for a "color organ," an instrument that would regulate colored lights which the composer associated with certain harmonies.

His works after about 1908 maintain the rhapsodic, improvisatory gestures of his earlier music, but they totally dispense with key and triadic harmony. In these pieces dissonance is emancipated as completely as in works by Schoenberg of the same era. But Scriabin favors a repertory of atonal sets quite unlike those embraced by Schoenberg. Most are symmetrical or nearly so. Whole-tone chords, for example, are frequently used before and after his break with tonality. After about 1908 his music is characterized by two other sets: the octatonic scale and the collection that was called the "nearly-whole-tone" hexachord in Chapter 2. Both whole-tone and octatonic collections had a long history in nine-

Example 8-1. Rimski-Korsakov, *Antar*, conclusion of third movement.

ALEXANDER SCRIABIN
(Moscow, 1872–Moscow, 1915)

Scriabin inherited his mother's gift as a prodigious pianist, and he later studied this instrument along with composition at the Conservatory in Moscow. From 1898 he was an instructor of piano at this institution, from which he resigned in 1903 to devote himself to composing. Scriabin enjoyed the support of two influential Russian patrons: the publisher Mitrofan Belyaev and the conductor and publisher Serge Koussevitsky. From 1904 until 1910 he lived in Western Europe, where he toured, composed, and refined an exotic philosophy in which theosophy, Nietzschean ideas, and Eastern religions mingled. He lived primarily in Moscow from 1910, and he continued to travel and perform as an interpreter of his own piano music.

SELECTED WORKS

Orchestral Music. Five symphonies (1900–10) (No. 3 is titled *Divine Poem* [1904]; No. 4, *Poem of Ecstasy* [1908]; No. 5, *Prometheus* [1908–10]); Piano Concerto (1896).
Piano Music. Collections of character piano pieces including études, preludes, *Albumblätter*, dances; ten sonatas (1892–1913).

teenth-century Russian music, but there as exotically colorful embellishments to diatonic scales. In Scriabin's music these formations become central, creating a static harmony that corresponds to the motionless realm of the senses proclaimed in the composer's writings.

These features may be observed in Scriabin's Tenth Piano Sonata Op. 70 (1913). Like all of his later music, it is in one movement. Its surface is characterized by changes of mood in fits and starts, trills in all registers, little feeling of stable meter, and rhythm that changes sud-

nearly-whole-tone hexachords

Example 8-2.   Scriabin, Piano Sonata No. 10.

denly from hymnic slowness to frenetic outbursts. These seemingly improvisatory gestures stand in contrast to the structure of the sonata, which is methodically planned and highly unified. Its form may be described as symmetrical: in the first 99 measures appear a number of distinct motives which are then varied by transposition and reharmonization. These are recapitulated in reverse order toward the end of the work, either at their original pitch or transposed.

The harmonic dimension is marked by recurrences of the nearly-whole-tone set, or, as it is more commonly known, the *Prometheus* or "mystic" chord. This set, as will be recalled from Chapter 2, is synonymous with a whole-tone scale in which any single pitch is raised or lowered a semitone. It occurs most often at structurally important junctures of the Sonata, articulating form just as tonic and dominant harmonies clarify the form of a tonal work. The motive first heard at measures 84–87 (Example 8-2) will illustrate the use of the *Prometheus* chord. This melodic idea is typical of lines in all of Scriabin's late music in its alternation of minor and major thirds. It is harmonized by forms of the basic hexachord, which occur most clearly on the downbeat of each of the last three measures. The chord of the first measure of this example is synonymous with a dominant seventh on the root E♭. This harmony does not suggest a tonicization of A♭ or any other such function. Instead, it is a familiar subset of the nearly-whole-tone hexachord, relating by inclusion to this controlling sonority.

DIAGHILEV, STRAVINSKY, PROKOFIEV, AND SHOSTAKOVICH

Russian music was an important part of French musical life beginning in the last quarter of the nineteenth century. The orchestral works of Tchaikovsky were regularly performed by French orchestras beginning in the 1870s, and, at the International Exhibition of

1889, Rimski-Korsakov came to Paris to lead concerts of music by all of the "Five" in addition to music by several of his students.

French interest in Russian music at this time was also stimulated by close political ties between the two nations. In a great victory of diplomacy, France concluded an alliance with Russia that frustrated the plan of Prussia to isolate France politically and militarily. Tsar Nicholas II visited Paris in 1896 to seal this "Dual Alliance," setting off a burst of enthusiasm there for all things Russian. In that year the songs of Musorgski were heard in recitals by the soprano Marie d'Alheim, and these works greatly attracted Debussy and Ravel with their ingenuous spontaneity. It was only natural that younger Russian composers such as Stravinsky and Alexander Glazunov (1865–1936) should later adopt France as the center of their activities in the West.

Connections between Russian and French music were greatly strengthened by the arrival in Paris of the impresario Sergei Diaghilev (1872–1929). As a young man in St. Petersburg, Diaghilev had briefly studied music with Rimski-Korsakov. But he realized that he would not have the career of a practicing artist; instead, he would become a promoter and propagandist of modern art and music. Supported by royal patronage and an impressive committee of sponsors, he brought a production of Musorgski's *Boris Godunov* to Paris in 1908. The following year he organized a company of dancers from the Maryinsky Theater in St. Petersburg, including the remarkable Vaslav Nijinsky, Anna Pavlova, and Tamara Karsavina, to perform in Paris. Thus began the "Ballets Russes," which continued under Diaghilev's leadership to perform around the world and which almost singlehandedly produced a revival of ballet as a central musical genre in the twentieth century.

Diaghilev favored ballets of a single act, several of which would constitute an evening's entertainment. He was particularly interested in the musical dimension of ballet, and he insisted on scores of high quality, whether orchestrations of preexistent works or new commissions. Increasingly Diaghilev wished to see innovation in all dimensions of his productions: "Surprise me!" was a common directive to the artists with whom he worked.

After their first few seasons in Paris, the Ballets Russes began to shed their connections to Russian art in favor of a more international image. Diaghilev eventually commissioned new ballet scores from most of the leading Western composers, including Debussy, Ravel, Satie, Milhaud, Poulenc, and Strauss. But Diaghilev's accomplishments are inevitably tied to his patronage of the young Russian composer Igor Stravinsky (1882–1971), whom he first brought to the attention of European audiences.

For purposes of discussion, Stravinsky's music may be divided into three chronological periods, each with certain distinctive stylistic features. A period of experimentation extended to about 1920, in which his music had strong connections to Russian folk art and to the musical works of his Russian forebears. A period from about 1920 to the early 1950s is less experimental, more international than Russian, and more concerned with stylistic continuity and tradition. Finally, from the early 1950s to his last composition in 1966, he adopted serial methods associated with the music of Schoenberg and Webern. In this chapter we will deal with the first of these periods, returning to the middle period in Chapter 10 and the serial works in Chapter 13.

The centerpieces of Stravinsky's music during his first period are the first four of five ballet scores that he wrote for Diaghilev. All four are based on Russian tales and myths and make frequent use of Russian or Slavic folk melodies, but each is distinctive in its own way. The earliest, *Firebird* (1910), owes the most in style to Stravinsky's teacher Rimski-Korsakov, with its large, luminous orchestra, sensitivity to color, and passing references to whole-tone and octatonic passages within a tonal context. Stravinsky also uses a dramatic device associated with Rimski-Korsakov in which music depicting diabolical figures is octatonic and music for heroic figures, diatonic. Unlike most ballet music of the nineteenth century, the score is closely tied to the scenario by recurrent motives and passages accompanying pantomimed narrative, rather than stock dancing numbers.

Petrushka (1911) makes greater use of folk song, and it prefigures Stravinsky's later music by dispensing with tonality as a principle of large-scale organization. The octatonic scale now takes on central importance, which it retains in Stravinsky's music throughout the first period. The story of the ballet was conceived by the composer in connection with a concerto-like work for piano and orchestra; it was elaborated upon at Diaghilev's urging as a ballet scenario, on which Stravinsky collaborated with the painter Alexandre Benois (1870–1960).

The story is divided into four connected scenes. At a nineteenth-century Russian Shrovetide fair, a showman of a puppet theater brings to life his puppets: the little clown Petrushka, a ballerina, and a Moor. In the second scene (Anthology no. 19) we encounter Petrushka in his cell, embittered by his fate. He cannot win the affections of the ballerina, and, in the final scene, he is "slain" by the brutish Moor. But, in the end, he elfishly thumbs his nose at the audience, having returned to life by the magic of the fairy tale. In his *Reminiscences of the Russian Ballet* (1941), Benois writes that Petrushka represents "the spiritual and suffering side of humanity."

IGOR STRAVINSKY
(*Oranienbaum, 1882–New York, 1971*)

As a young man in St. Petersburg, Stravinsky frequented performances of opera and ballet at the Maryinsky Theater, where his father was a leading singer. His career as a composer was late in developing, as he first pursued a degree in law. Subsequently, he became the student of Rimski-Korsakov. His music came to the attention of the impresario Sergei Diaghilev in 1909; this led to a series of commissions through which he attracted international attention.

During World War I he lived in Switzerland, moving to France in 1920, where he later became a citizen. After 1924 he was increasingly active as a performer and conductor of his own music, a capacity in which he toured throughout the world. In September of 1939 he immigrated to the United States, settling later in the Los Angeles area and becoming an American citizen. In 1945 he began a series of revisions of many of his earlier works, which were edited by his new publisher Boosey & Hawkes. In 1962, with the assistance of the conductor Robert Craft, he returned to the Soviet Union for a series of concerts. His last years were spent alternately in Europe and New York City. He is buried in Venice, near the grave of his friend and patron Diaghilev.

SELECTED WORKS

Operas and Theater Pieces. *Nightingale* (1908–14), *Reynard* (1916), *L'histoire du soldat* (1918), *Mavra* (1922), *Oedipus rex* (1927), *Rake's Progress* (1948–51).

Ballets. *Firebird* (1910), *Petrushka* (1911), *Rite of Spring* (1911–13), *Les noces* (1914–23), *Pulcinella* (1920), *Apollon musagète* (1928), *Fairy's Kiss* (1928), *Perséphone* (1934), *Jeu de cartes* (1936), *Orpheus* (1947), *Agon* (1953–57).

Orchestral Music. Symphonies of Wind Instruments (1920), Symphony in C (1939–40), Symphony in Three Movements (1945), *Movements* for Piano and Orchestra (1959), Variations (1964).

Concertos. Concerto for piano and winds (1924), Capriccio for piano and orchestra (1929), Concerto in D for violin and orchestra (1931).

Chamber Music. Octet (1923), Concerto in E♭ (*Dumbarton Oaks*, 1937), Concerto in D (*Basle*, 1946), Septet (1953).
Piano Music. *Piano-Rag-Music* (1919), Sonata (1924), Serenade in A (1925).
Songs. *In Memoriam Dylan Thomas* (1954), numerous collections of Russian-language songs with diverse instrumental accompaniments.
Choral Music. *Zvezdoliki* (1912), *Symphony of Psalms* (1930), Mass (1944–48), Cantata (1952), *Threni* (1958), *Requiem Canticles* (1966).

He indeed embodies the idea of the antihero, common to much twentieth-century art and literature.

Stravinsky's music integrates folk song and original material in an alternation of pentatonic, modal, and diatonic passages. The dance of the bear in the fourth scene (rehearsal 100) uses a whole-tone melody, typical of the earlier Russian musician's treatment of fearful objects. Stravinsky's first music for the ballet was a bitriadic figure uniting major triads on C and F♯. This material was later placed in the second scene (rehearsal 49 ff.), where it represents Petrushka and his bitterness toward his lot. The bitriadic "Petrushka chord" has harmonic meaning as a six-note subset of the octatonic scale (Example 8–3), the latter of which plays a large integrative role in the music of the entire ballet.

Le sacre du printemps (*The Rite of Spring*, 1913) portrays scenes among prehistoric Slavonic tribes, gathered to celebrate the coming of spring. In the first of two parts, the choreography represents dances, games, and rituals. The second part focuses upon a single terrifying act: a maiden is chosen to dance herself to death to appease the gods. Stravinsky's music evokes the primitivism of the scenario in part by its quotations of folk melodies, ostinatos, and dissonant atonality. But the feature of *The Rite of Spring* that struck its early listeners as scandalously provocative was its rhythm and meter, whose free shapes were brazenly underscored by a massive orchestration. Sections such as the concluding "Sacrificial Dance," the maiden's frenzied dance of death, consist of rapidly pulsating small values gathered into constantly changing metric groups. Here Stravinsky gives free rein to the orchestra and its bitingly percussive

Example 8-3.   Derivation of the bitriadic "Petrushka" chord.

effects in order to project the tumult and violence that were his recollections of the coming of spring to Russia.

The Rite of Spring is atonal despite the diatonic content of its folk
tunes. The bassoon solo at the beginning of the work, for example,
quotes a Lithuanian folk song suggesting A minor (Example 8-4).
Other themes, whether of folk origin or not, are based typically on
small segments of diatonic scales and treated in a repetitive manner.

The harmonic dimension of this ballet, as in *Petrushka*, makes use
of the octatonic scale and its subsets. Bitriadic collections are also
prominent, as in the seven-note chord underlying the "Augurs of
Spring" section, where an F♭ triad is heard in the lower voices
against an E♭ dominant seventh in a higher register (Example 8-5).
This dark sonority is repeated as an ostinato, interrupted by irregular accents and by brief, undistinctive motives. The "Augurs of
Spring" chord is also very similar to the octatonic collection: only its
pitch class E♭ deviates from an octatonic arrangement of intervals.

Diaghilev referred to *The Rite of Spring* as the "Ninth Symphony"
of the twentieth century. Like Beethoven's late music, it was widely
imitated: to name a few instances, in Prokofiev's *Scythian* Suite,
Samuel Barber's *Medea*, and numerous works by Latin American
composers of the 1930s such as Silvestre Revueltas's *Sensemayá*
(1938). It was not imitated by Stravinsky himself. His next ballet, *Les
noces (The Wedding)*, was of a very different sort.

Les noces was composed between 1914 and 1917, but it was not
definitively orchestrated until 1923. In its final shape it calls for a
chorus and vocal soloists, four pianos, and percussion—an accompaniment that the composer described as "perfectly homogeneous,

Example 8-4. Stravinsky, *The Rite of Spring*. Copyright 1921 Edition Russe
de Musique (Russischer Musikverlag). Copyright assigned 1947 to Boosey
& Hawkes, Inc. for all countries. Reprinted by permission.

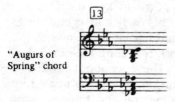

"Augurs of
Spring" chord

Example 8-5. The "Augurs of Spring" chord from Stravinsky's *Rite of
Spring*.

perfectly impersonal, perfectly mechanical." Although *Les noces* was first performed as a ballet, it is more akin to a cantata since there is no scenario beyond the text and since the voices sing from beginning to end. The words were drawn from wedding songs in a nineteenth-century collection of Russian popular poetry. In the first of two parts, the scene alternates between the houses of the bride and the bridegroom prior to their wedding. We hear their expressions of doubt, prayers, testaments, all embraced in busy preparations. Part 2 is the wedding feast. Drink loosens the guests' tongues, some bawdy remarks are heard, a couple is chosen to warm the wedding bed, and, finally, the couple is tucked away as wedding bells toll the happy occasion.

Although the chorus normally takes the role of the wedding party and soloists deliver the lines of the bride, groom, and other important individuals, there is no consistency in such a dramatic arrangement. For example, the groom's last expression of love to his bride is sung by the chorus, since by then the couple is tactfully out of sight in the bed chamber. This antioperatic detachment of drama from musical means characterizes much of Stravinsky's later vocal works; it represents, furthermore, a departure from the intimacy of text and music characteristic of both the romantics and the French Impressionists. "Music is, by its very nature, powerless to *express* anything at all," he wrote in his *Autobiography*. "Music is [instead] the sole domain in which man realizes the present. . . . The phenomenon of music is given to us with the sole purpose of establishing an order in things, including, and particularly, the coordination between *man* and *time*."

In addition to its unusual percussive orchestra, the music of *Les noces* is highly innovative in its treatment of the voices, which are declamatory and nonlyrical. Their patter-like rhythm is grouped in changing meters based upon the poetic structure of the Russian texts. During the wedding feast, the drunken revelers begin to blurt out their exhortations in a pitchless speaking voice—a technique also employed in the choruses of Milhaud's cantata *Les choéphores* (1915).

Toward the end of the First World War Stravinsky's music began to leave behind the Russian influences of his early ballets and songs as well as the experimental directions that had allied him with the musical avant-garde. The first major work reflecting his new internationalism was *L'histoire du soldat* (1918). The story about a soldier's meeting with the devil was of Russian origin, but it was treated by his librettist, Charles Ramuz, in a more general and timeless way. The soldier trades his fiddle, symbolic of his soul, to the devil in return for untold wealth. But he finds that wealth is a curse and gladly rids himself of it. He is then able to cure an ailing princess by the power of his violin playing and claims her as his wife. But he loses all when he tries to return to the land of his childhood. The play is acted out by the devil and soldier, which are speaking roles, and by the princess, who is a dancer, with the story filled in by a narrator. A diverse band of seven musicians sits on stage adding musical commentary. The score contains virtuosic parts for violin, the soldier's instrument, and for the percussion, which represents the devil, who has the last word in both drama and music.

The music has an immediate accessibility. Some of it imitates popular or familiar genres: a march, tango, waltz, ragtime, and hymn. It is predominantly diatonic with the triad as the central sonority, but these elements are not used over large spans in the traditional expression of a key. Its tunefulness, clarity, and simplicity point to a new direction in Stravinsky's work.

This new direction is also apparent in his last ballet for Diaghilev, *Pulcinella* (1920). The music is a masterful arrangement of operatic excerpts by Giovanni Pergolesi (1710–36) and instrumental movements probably composed by Domenico Gallo, an obscure eighteenth-century composer whose music was passed off as Pergolesi's. It was in this ballet that Stravinsky revealed another important new direction—adapting the spirit, if not the music itself, of earlier composers whom he admired. Later he would pay similar homage to Tchaikovsky, Bach, Weber, Beethoven, Verdi, and others.

By 1922 with the completion of his Italianate comic opera *Mavra*, Stravinsky's transition to a new idiom was complete. Its traits were a cosmopolitan tone stripped of folk influence, frequent references to earlier styles of Western music, a predominantly diatonic harmony where the triad was of central importance, and a lean and clear orchestration. In his *Autobiography* he made it plain that he wished to dissociate himself both from his immediate past—Russian music of the later nineteenth century and French Impressionism—and from the avant-garde. "It would be a great mistake to regard me as an adherent of *Zukunftsmusik*—the music of the future. Nothing could be more ridiculous. I live neither in the past nor in the future. I am in the present."

The other outstanding young Russian composer whom Diaghilev brought to the attention of Western Europe was Sergei Prokofiev (1891–1953). His three scores for the Ballets Russes (*The Buffoon*, 1915; *The Steel Step*, 1926; *The Prodigal Son*, 1929) were successful, but they have not had the longevity in the repertory of his later ballets *Romeo and Juliet* (1936) and *Cinderella* (1944). His seven mature operas are among his greatest works, but they are rarely performed in the West

SERGEI PROKOFIEV
(*Sontsovka, Ukraine, 1891–Moscow, 1953*)

Prokofiev's budding talent as a musician received every encouragement from his parents—especially from his mother, who was an amateur pianist. In addition to regular trips to Moscow and St. Petersburg to hear music, Prokofiev had Reinhold Glière as his private tutor in music for two summers at the family's provincial estate. At the age of 13 Prokofiev was enrolled at the St. Petersburg Conservatory where he studied with Rimski-Korsakov, Anatoli Liadov, and Nikolai Cherepnin. In 1914 he visited London to meet Diaghilev, hoping to interest him in his opera *The Gambler*. Instead, Diaghilev put him to work on a ballet score on a primitive subject inspired by Stravinsky's *Rite of Spring*. Although this commission was not completed, Prokofiev later composed three scores for Diaghilev's company.

After the Revolution, Prokofiev immigrated to Western Europe. He resided primarily in Germany from 1922, with many trips elsewhere in Europe and in America. After several visits to the Soviet Union, he returned there permanently in 1936 and settled in Moscow. His music became the object of repeated criticism for its tendencies toward "formalism" and lack of "Soviet realism." After the death of Stalin, however, it was recognized by Soviet authorities for its greatness.

SELECTED WORKS

Operas. *The Gambler* (1916), *Love for Three Oranges* (1919), *Flaming Angel* (1919–23), *War and Peace* (1943).

Ballets. *The Buffoon*, (1915, revised 1920), *Le Pas d'acier* (1926), *The Prodigal Son* (1929), *Romeo and Juliet* (1936), *Cinderella* (1940–44).

Symphonies. Seven symphonies: 1917, 1924, 1928, 1930, 1944, 1947, 1952: *Scythian* Suite (1915).

Concertos. Five piano concertos (1912–32), two violin concertos (1917–35), cello concerto (1933–38), *Sinfonie concertante* for cello (1952).

Chamber Music. Two string quartets (1930–41), Sonata for violin and piano (1938–46), Cello Sonata (1949).

Piano Music. Numerous collections of short works, nine sonatas (1909–47).
Cantatas. *Seven, They Are Seven* (1918), *Alexander Nevsky* (1939).
Miscellaneous. *Lt. Kije* (film score, 1933), *Peter and the Wolf* (narration, 1936).

and only the symphonic suite from *Love for Three Oranges* is well known. His seven symphonies, nine piano sonatas, and five early piano concertos are among the most frequently performed works in their genres from the twentieth-century literature.

Prokofiev did not intend his music to be experimental. He carefully avoided association with any artistic movements, and his musical style did not follow a consistent line of evolution. In his *Autobiography* he defines four features, some of which characterize each of his works: classicism, innovation, toccata-like rhythm, and lyricism. These alternated freely throughout his entire career, and the only characteristics that he considered invariably present in all of his music were clarity and brevity.

Prokofiev's classicism occurs most clearly in works that are based on earlier models, such as his *Classical* Symphony (1917) in which he wrote as he thought Haydn would have had he lived into the twentieth century. Prokofiev rejected the neoclassical movement of many composers of the 1920s and 1930s. He considered such works as the *Classical* Symphony to be isolated within his music as a whole, and he was bitingly critical of Stravinsky's neoclassicism, calling it "Bach on the wrong notes."

Prokofiev said that his innovative contribution was seen mainly in harmony. Indeed, his harmonic idiom is entirely singular. It takes its departure from the triad and common-practice tonality, but it is also pungently dissonant and little constrained by triadic functions within a key or by normative voice leading. He also asserted his harmonic individuality by avoiding the repertory of dissonances that characterize works of the other French and Russian modernists, such as octatonic and pentatonic sets or the strings of seventh and ninth chords of the Impressionists.

Lyricism is the feature most consistently distinguishing Prokofiev's music. His melodic lines are often cast within a diatonic framework, but with chromatic turns of phrase and distinctively large and unexpected leaps. Prokofiev remarked that his many toccata-like piano works took their departure from Schumann's Toccata in C Op. 7, a technical showpiece that was often featured in Prokofiev's concerts as a pianist. An example of this type of music, which also illustrates his harmonic idiom at its most adventuresome, is the finale to the Seventh Piano Sonata (1939–42, Anthology

No. 8). This fiery movement exploits asymmetrical divisions of 7/8 meter. Rhythm is nearly the sole point of focus: there are no important themes and the dissonant harmonies are limited in their variety and return in a highly repetitive fashion. The context of the piece, nevertheless, is the key of B♭. A B♭-major triad opens the movement and the end dwells on a B♭-major scale.

A musical avant-garde flourished in the Soviet Union for over a decade after the Revolution of 1917. For many, the ideals of liberation associated with the advent of communism were consistent with those of artistic experiment. Even before the Revolution there existed in Russia a distinctly experimental movement of which Scriabin was the guiding light. Music by Nikolai Rosslavetz and Yefim Golyscheff, for example, was not only entirely atonal, but systematically exploited the complete chromatic set. Western avant-garde composers were welcomed to the Soviet Union during its early years. Alban Berg, for example, traveled to Leningrad (formerly St. Petersburg) in 1927 to see *Wozzeck* performed. He was fascinated by the great public involvement there in new music and gratified by the high quality of the production.

The ideals of the Revolution fired the imagination of a number of young Russians who experimented with new musical resources hoping to capture the spirit of the times. The tone poem *Iron Foundry* (1928) by the Moscow-trained Alexander Mosolov (1900–73), for example, depicted the glory of labor by using percussive imitations of the factory. Even Diaghilev, no friend of Bolshevism, hoped to capitalize on the artistic ferment in his homeland by commissioning Prokofiev's ballet *Le Pas d'acier* (*The Steel Step*), which extolled the factory and the machine.

The greatest of the younger Soviet composers whose careers were launched during the post-Revolutionary decade was Dimitri Shostakovich (1906–1975). Like Prokofiev he attended the conservatory in St. Petersburg, by then renamed Petrograd, where he was an outstanding pianist and prodigious composer. His First Symphony (1925), composed while he was still a student, brought him worldwide acclamation. In several works for orchestra or piano over the next five years, he experimented with highly dissonant textures and spare counterpoint, reflecting his knowledge of contemporary European developments. During the early 1930s he allied himself with the remarkably innovative Soviet theater by several ballets and operas in which he showed his gift for musical dramatization and witty parody.

But his meteoric rise as a composer was temporarily stayed in 1936 when his opera *Lady Macbeth of the Mtsensk* was chastised by the

DIMITRI SHOSTAKOVICH
(St. Petersburg, 1906–Moscow, 1975)

Shostakovich was one of numerous outstanding Russian musicians to attend the Conservatory in Petrograd, the name given to St. Petersburg in 1914. There he was a student of composition of Maximilian Steinberg, the son-in-law of Rimski-Korsakov. His First Symphony, composed as a graduation work from the Conservatory in 1925, gained him international attention.

His early works for stage emphasized revolutionary themes, but his opera *Lady Macbeth of the Mtsensk* was retracted after criticism by Soviet authorities in 1936. His Fifth Symphony (1937) was his initial attempt to conform to Stalinist guidelines for music, but Shostakovich remained an object of criticism in the Soviet Union for the remainder of Stalin's life. Toward the end of the Second World War he settled in Moscow.

SELECTED WORKS

Operas. *The Nose* (1928), *Lady Macbeth of the Mtsensk* (1932, revised and retitled *Katerina Izmailova* in 1963).
Ballets. *The Golden Age* (1930), *Bolt* (1931).
Orchestral Music. Fifteen symphonies, several of which use voices (1925–71).
Concertos. Concerto for piano, trumpet, and strings (1933), Piano Concerto No. 2 (1957), concertos for violin (2) and cello (2).
Chamber Music. Fifteen string quartets (1935–74), cello sonata (1934), violin sonata (1968).
Piano Music. Two sonatas (1926, 1942), *Aphorisms* (1927), 24 Preludes and Fugues (1951).
Songs. *From Jewish Poetry* (1948), *Song of the Forests* (with chorus and orchestra, 1949), *Satires* (1960), *The Execution of Stepan Razin* (with chorus and orchestra, 1964).

Soviet government. From this point, his career—as well as the careers of all Soviet composers—would be intertwined with political restraints to a degree unprecedented outside of Nazi Germany. Soviet criticism of free artistic expression will be taken up again shortly. After 1936 Shostakovich almost completely avoided dramatic works in favor of instrumental composition, to which he eventually contributed fifteen symphonies and fifteen string quartets.

The opera *Lady Macbeth of the Mtsensk* (1932, revised and retitled *Katerina Izmailova* in 1963), like Hindemith's nearly contemporary *Mathis der Maler*, made its composer an international celebrity because of its suppression by a dictatorial regime. The work is freely based on a story of the same title by Nikolai Leskov (1831–95), which deals realistically with the lascivious and homicidal activities of one Katerina Izmailova. Her murderous nature and certain other themes led Leskov to the reference in the title to Shakespeare's character. Shostakovich's version of the story attempts to shed a sympathetic light on Katerina, showing her as the helpless victim of bourgeois society under the Tsars. In fact Shostakovich planned this as the first in a series of operas dealing with women, tracing their historical debasement by male-dominated society and their ultimate triumph in the Soviet utopia.

Katerina is unhappily married to Zinovy Izmailov, and the two are living with his father, Boris, a wealthy merchant. She has an affair with the dashing serf Sergei, only to be discovered by Boris. Sergei is savagely beaten and saved only by Katerina, who poisons her father-in-law's food. Sergei later murders Zinovy. But Boris's body is found, and the nuptials of Katerina and Sergei are interrupted by the police. The two are condemned to march to a Siberian prison camp. Sergei now curses Katerina and takes up with another lady convict, but Katerina kills her rival and herself.

It is a little wonder that the opera was an instant success in both Leningrad and Moscow, as it had something for everyone: sentimentality, comedy, sex, violence, and clever caricature. The music is direct and eclectic, with touches of Wagner, Offenbach, Mozart, and Russian folk songs, mixed with grand orchestral production numbers and touching songs. Its style is primarily tonal and triadic, varied by scenes of brilliant orchestral dissonance and temporary suspension of key.

Such an area is the orchestral interlude between the fourth and fifth scenes, thus at the very center of the nine-scene opera (Anthology No. 21). Boris has just been murdered, and a priest has intoned an irreverent cavatina over his body. The orchestra then plunges into a dramatic passacaglia: eleven variations upon a ground bass first heard in measures 9 through 17 (Example 8-6). The

Example 8-6.   Passacaglia theme from Shostakovich's *Lady Macbeth of the Mtsensk*, Interlude between scenes 4 and 5. Used by arrangement with G. Schirmer, Inc. U.S. agent for Musikverlag Hans Sikorski, Hamburg.

ground has weak and conflicting tonal implications: D minor at the beginning and C♯ at the end. It is octatonic except for the pitch class C♯. The variations in the upper voices play upon the opening motive of the ground but avoid establishing a key, even though they temporarily dwell upon various triads and diatonic scale segments.

The interlude is followed by Katerina's passionate love song to Sergei—a text that was rewritten by the composer for the 1963 revival to eliminate some of its frankness. It begins on a G-minor triad and the accompaniment continues the dotted figure from the end of the interlude. Although it is basically triadic, no key is established. By its touching lyricism—typical of all of Katerina's music in the opera—it invites the sympathy for her that Shostakovich intended.

The friendly atmosphere for musical experimentation in the 1920s was clouded by the end of the decade in the Soviet Union by the rise of the Association of Proletarian Musicians (RAPM), who demanded a music geared in simplicity to the masses and who rejected works by the Western avant-garde. Although RAPM was disbanded in 1932 and superseded by the Union of Soviet Composers, its doctrines about the role of music in the Soviet state continued to gain importance. In 1934 the writer Maxim Gorky enunciated a doctrine of "socialist realism," by which works of art were to be models of optimism and propagation of communist values. The opposite of this realism was said to be "formalism," a catchall term describing works of art that appeared elitist and abstract.

Any hopes that Soviet musicians may have had for continuing the avant-garde movement were dashed once and for all in 1936. An article—perhaps dictated in part by Stalin himself—appeared in the newspaper *Pravda* at this time condemning Shostakovich's *Lady Macbeth* as "coarse, primitive, and vulgar." "Here is music turned deliberately inside out," the reviewer continued, "in order that nothing will be reminiscent of classical opera or have anything in common with symphonic music or with simple and popular musical language accessible to all." Not only was the subject deemed inappropriate, but the apparent "noise, wild rhythm, vocal shriek-ing, and deliberate dissonance" were henceforth unacceptable in the Soviet Union. Only at the height of World War II was there a mea-sure of relaxation of governmental restraint over the arts, and it was during this time that works such as Prokofiev's Seventh Piano Sonata were composed.

After the war the charge of formalism was made all the more menacing against modernism in the arts. In a Decree on Music issued in 1948, Stalin's advisor Andrei Zhdanov castigated Prokofiev, Shostakovich, and others for their "errors" of atonality, dissonance, and lack of melody. In the years after the death of Stalin in 1953, a cautious measure of artistic freedom returned to the Soviet Union. But by then Stalin's repression had effectively removed Russian composers from their place in the evolution of musical style, a place that they had earlier occupied with great distinction.

BIBLIOGRAPHY

The life and works of several composers treated in this chapter are concisely surveyed in The Master Musician Series (London: J. M. Dent). Especially commendable are books on Debussy by Edward Lockspeiser (1936) and on Musorgski by M. D. Calvocoressi (rev. G. Abraham, 1946). The Oxford Studies of Composers has excellent short books on the music of Debussy by Roger Nichols (1973), Scriabin by Hugh MacDonald (1978), and Shostakovich by Norman Kay (1971). A series of longer technical studies of the music of twen-tieth-century composers by the Yale University Press includes con-tributions on Stravinsky by Pieter C. Van den Toorn (1983), Debussy by Richard S. Parks (1989), and Scriabin by James M. Baker (1986).

The evolution of French avant-garde arts near the turn of the twentieth century is traced in a lively manner in Roger Shattuck's *The Banquet Years* (New York, 1968). The author focuses upon Satie among modern French musicians. Nancy Perloff's *Art and the Everyday: Popular Entertainment and the Circle of Erik Satie* (Oxford, 1991) gives a fascinating account of the taste for popular art among Satie, Cocteau, and the Six, and sympathetic portraits of Satie's life and music are found in studies by Robert Orledge (Cambridge, 1990) and James Harding (London, 1975). Orledge is also the author of an excellent general study of Gabriel Fauré (rev. ed., London, 1979).

Debussy's life and relationship to contemporary artists and French aesthetics are admirably recounted in Edward Lockspeiser's *Debussy: His Life and Mind*, 2 vols. (London, 1962–65) and Stefan Jarocinski in *Debussy: Impressionism and Symbolism* (London, 1976).

Unless otherwise stated, all quotations in this chapter from the writings of Debussy are drawn from *Debussy on Music*, ed. François Lesure, trans. Richard Langham Smith (New York, 1977) or from Léon Vallas, *The Theories of Claude Debussy*, trans. Maire O'Brien (London, 1929). Also see Debussy's *Letters*, ed. François Lesure, Roger Nichols (Cambridge, Mass., 1987). Ravel's life and music is authoritatively studied in Arbie Orenstein's *Ravel: Man and Musician* (New York, 1991).

The writings of Gerald Abraham form an authoritative introduction to modern Russian music. See especially his *On Russian Music* (1939), *Eight Soviet Composers* (1944), and *Masters of Russian Music* (ed. with M. D. Calvocoressi, 1936). Boris Schwarz's *Music and Musical Life in Soviet Russia* (enlarged ed., Bloomington, 1983) is a standard source of information on Russian music and culture from 1917 to 1980. Diaghilev and the Ballets Russes are studied in detail in books by Serge Lifar (New York, 1940), Richard Buckle (rev. ed., New York, 1984), and Lynn Garafola (New York, 1989). Nijinsky's remarks on the scenario of *Jeux* are found in his *Diary*, ed. Romola Nijinsky (New York, 1936). A psychological study of the great dancer is given in Peter Ostwald's *Vaslav Nijinsky: A Leap into Madness* (New York, 1990). Historical background and a study of manuscript materials concerning *Jeux* are found in Robert Orledge's *Debussy and the Theatre* (Cambridge, 1982).

Studies of composers living in the Soviet Union are sometimes clouded by controversies regarding authenticity and viewpoint. The official Soviet account of Prokofiev is found in Izrail Nest'ev's *Sergei Prokofiev* (1946, later revised); it is quite a different portrait from the one found in Victor Seroff's biography of this composer (New York, 1968). Seroff is also the author of popular biographies of Shostakovich (1943), Musorgski, and Rachmaninoff. Prokofiev was the author of two autobiographies: One covers his life in detail to 1909 (*Prokofiev by Prokofiev*, New York, 1979), the other is briefer, covering his life to 1937. The latter is found in his *Soviet Diary 1927 and Other Writings*, trans. and ed. Oleg Prokofiev (Boston, 1991), which also contains a diary-like account of the composer's tour of the Soviet Union in 1927, during his period of Western exile. For a detailed study of Prokofiev's life, with much original material, see Harlow Robinson's *Sergei Prokofiev: A Biography* (New York, 1987).

Boris de Schloezer's *Scriabin: Artist and Mystic* (Berkeley, 1987) first appeared in 1923, setting a precedent for studies of this composer which emphasize his aesthetics and interest in mysticism rather than his music. The excerpt from Scriabin's *Poem of Ecstasy* is drawn from the translation by Hugh MacDonald in *The Musical Times*, 113 (1972). Shostakovich's memoirs, entitled *Testimony*, ed.

Solomon Volkov (New York, 1979), paint a grim portrait of the Soviet artist's relationship with governmental authorities. The authenticity of these memoirs has been disputed. A biography of the composer based on documents and recollections is by Elizabeth Wilson, *Shostakovich: A Life Remembered* (Princeton, 1994), and Ian MacDonald's *The New Shostakovich* gives a broad account of the composer's life. Documents that pertain to RAPM and to Zhdanov's criticism of Soviet composers in 1948 are found in the appendix to Nicolas Slonimsky's *Music Since 1900* (New York, 1971).

It has long been known that Stravinsky solicited editorial assistance in his writings, which include the *Autobiography* (New York, 1936), *Poetics of Music* (Harvard College, 1947), and six volumes of "conversations" with his assistant Robert Craft. It has recently come to light, however, that *Poetics* was ghost written by Roland-Manuel (a student of Ravel), a revelation that casts doubt on the authenticity of all of Stravinsky's writings and vastly diminishes their importance. The literature on this composer is immense. Eric Walter White's *Stravinsky: The Composer and His Works* (Berkeley, 1979) is a standard reference work on the music. Two books by Soviet musicologists emphasize Stravinsky's connections with music of his native land: Mikhail Druskin's *Igor Stravinsky* (Cambridge, 1983) and Boris Asaf'yev's *Book About Stravinsky* (1929; English trans., Ann Arbor, 1982).

9

Musical Nationalism

National or patriotic consciousness exerted its greatest influence on modern music during the second half of the nineteenth century and early decades of the twentieth. An especially notable symptom of this influence was a growing awareness of the artistic value of folk song and its applicability to art music. Collections of folk texts and music began to appear in large numbers in the nineteenth century, some prepared by writers or amateur ethnologists, others by professional composers. Tunes in these collections were normally provided with harmonizations, as in the arrangements of Scottish, Welsh, and Irish songs made by Haydn and Beethoven for the collector George Thomson. The publication of anonymous German folk poetry by Achim von Arnim and Clemens Brentano under the title *Des Knaben Wunderhorn* (1806–1808) was especially influential upon German romantic poetry and was later an inspiration to Gustav Mahler among other musicians.

European composers of the nineteenth century also appropriated folk materials into their original works. Haydn and Beethoven occasionally quoted folk songs in their symphonies, and a folk element in piano works by Chopin and Liszt betrays a nostalgia for their native lands. Many of the strophic songs of Schubert have the foursquare simplicity of German folk music. Brahms was especially indebted to German folk song, which was both a source of inspiration in its artless simplicity and economy of means and also an object of his serious study. For most of these Europeans, folk song imparted spontaneity, color, and robustness to their cosmopolitan musical language.

Folk elements played a relatively minor role in works of German and Austrian composers of the generation after Brahms. Mahler had a great affinity for folk art, but his uses of folk tunes, such as the quotation of "Bruder Martin" ("Frère Jacques") and the evocation of Jewish ghetto music in the third movement of his First Symphony, occur within an intensely autobiographical oeuvre as allusions to his musical past. Quotations of folk song by Schoenberg and Berg invariably had programmatic connotations. Schoenberg, for example, used the tune "Alles ist hin!" ("It's all over!") in his Second String Quartet, probably as a reference to the passing of tonality and to the temporary rupture of his marriage.

The widespread influence of German and Austrian music during the later romantic period helped to provoke a different and more intense form of nationalism among composers working outside of Western Europe. The Czechs Bedřich Smetana (1824–84) and Anton Dvořák (1841–1904), the Russian Five, and the Norwegian Edvard Grieg (1843–1907) infused their music with the spirit and substance of their native cultures. They sought a deeper alliance with their national history and art, and their music often echoed the emotional struggle of their countrymen for national identity. The use or assimilation of folk music was widespread among them. Their nationalism was in part a rebellion against romanticism, which increasingly was identified with German culture.

A similar element of rebellion was carried into the twentieth century by Debussy, Ravel, and Stravinsky in their use of folk materials. These three composers were cited by Béla Bartók as the founders of a new era in the enrichment of art music by folklore:

> In 1907 at the instigation of Kodály I became acquainted with Debussy's work, studied it thoroughly and was greatly surprised to find in his music pentatonic phrases similar in character to those contained in our peasant music. I was sure these could be attributed to influences of folk music from Eastern Europe, very likely from Russia. Similar influences can be traced in Igor Stravinsky's work. It seems, therefore, that, in our age, modern music has developed along similar lines in countries geographically far away from each other. It has become rejuvenated under the influence of a kind of peasant music that has remained untouched by the musical creations of the last centuries. [From the "Autobiography," 1921.]

The continuation of this form of nationalism into the early decades of the twentieth century will be the principal subject of this chapter. We will trace the work of several major composers who were active outside of France, Italy, and Germany and who brought their national folklore and history to bear on their music. Strikingly different modes of national expression will be seen. Bartók and Aaron Copland readily quoted folk music in their original compositions, although their presentation of it differs markedly. Vaughan Williams and Manuel de Falla did not ordinarily quote folk tunes; instead, they assimilated certain features of their native music, which were then expressed in their own distinctive ways. The music of Jean Sibelius, on the other hand, has little connection with Finnish folk song, but he is nonetheless a nationalist by the immediacy with which his musical speech was understood and embraced by his countrymen.

It will be important to keep in mind that nationalism as a shaping force in modern music primarily concerns musical material and expressive content. It is very different from chauvinistic patriotism in the political sphere. Many of the leading nationalist composers of the twentieth century have been internationalists in their social viewpoint. Charles Ives, for example, was an ardent supporter of the League of Nations following World War I. Béla Bartók, the most important nationalist composer of the century, was a staunch believer in the community of nations. In a letter of 1931 to Octavian Beu he clarified his beliefs:

> My own idea, of which I have been fully conscious since I found myself as a composer, is the brotherhood of peoples. . . . I try to the best of my ability to serve this idea in my music. Therefore I do not reject any influence, be it Slovakian, Rumanian, Arabic, or from any other source. The source must only be clean, fresh, and healthy.

THE FOLK SONG ARRANGEMENT

The phenomenon of nationalism gave rise to one important new musical genre: the artistic folk song arrangement. A work of this type consists of a preexistent folk song that is harmonized or accompanied in such a way as to reveal the originality and musical expressiveness of the arranger. Such works are normally for the medium of chorus or solo voice accompanied by piano, but arrangements may also be intended for one or more instruments without voice.

Music of this description became prominent in the late nineteenth century among composers living outside of central Europe. Edvard Grieg in Norway, Leoš Janáček in Bohemia, and Nikolai Rimski-Korsakov in Russia were all active as collectors and arrangers of their native folk songs. The genre received even greater attention in the twentieth century as an important and original medium for musical expression. As in the late nineteenth century, it experienced its principal currency outside of the "mainstream" of Western Europe, where German and Austrian music was dominant. Folk song arrangements of great originality appeared especially in Eastern Europe by Béla Bartók, Zoltán Kodály, and Karol Szymanowski, in Spain by Manuel de Falla, in Latin America by Alberto Ginastera and Heitor Villa-Lobos, in the United States by Charles Ives, Roy Harris, and Henry Cowell, and in England by Ralph Vaughan Williams, Frank Bridge, Percy Grainger, and Benjamin Britten. The French composers Maurice Ravel, Arthur Honegger, Darius Milhaud, and Joseph Canteloube also left important examples of the genre. Notably missing from this list are the leading German and Austrian composers of the early twentieth century, again suggesting that folk music as a stimulus to original composition was felt in large part as a rebellion against German hegemony in music.

Before going further with a discussion of this important new genre, it is necessary to ask, "What is folk song?" Even so simple a question can receive no easy answer. In general a folk song is one which is learned, performed, and passed on by ear rather than through musical notation. Folk songs exist among people who do not necessarily have musical training, and they are used primarily for diversion and entertainment in mundane situations—mothers singing to their children, people at work, soldiers preparing for conflict, or people expressing religious sentiments. Since these songs are learned by rote, they are susceptible to many changes in both words and music as they are passed on.

The musical style exhibited by folk songs is highly varied. Most are strophic in overall form and monophonic in texture. The melodies are easily sung, using the notes of the church modes, pentatonic scale, or major and minor keys. Very often the melodies outline primary chords in a key, suggesting a simple accompaniment. It is likely that the best-known folk songs are not very old. Most were probably composed in the nineteenth century by amateur or professional musicians, then taken up in an oral tradition following which the identity of the composer was quickly forgotten. Other songs, especially those preserved by peasants in isolated locations, may be considerably older, and these often do not suggest the simple harmonic profile described above. Béla Bartók researched both types and developed a great admiration for the latter. The former and better known type he termed "popular art music," which he considered inferior to the older music of peasant classes.

Bartók was also disdainful of the simple or pretentious harmonizations given to folk songs in most anthologies that appeared early in the century. In a scathing review of one such publication Bartók denounced the "bombastic nature and false pathos" of some of the harmonizations and the poverty of imagination in others. "The entire accompaniment," he wrote regarding one tune, "consists of nine chords. Of the nine, five are one and the same: the tonic triad in root position."

An example of Bartók's artistic originality in the genre of the folk song arrangement is his treatment of the Hungarian tune "Fekete föd" (Snow-White Kerchief) from Eight Hungarian Folksongs (published in 1922). The melody was one of many that the composer had himself noted down after hearing it performed by Hungarian peasants living in Transylvania. Its words utter a sad plaint of broken love and the tune is starkly simple: the four lines of the first stanza (all that Bartók uses) correspond to four musical phrases of equal length, repeated in the scheme A B A B. The rhythm consists of a chant-like parlando, performed with considerable flexibility of tempo. The notes of the melody are entirely confined to a pentatonic scale on the keynote E.

Bartók's harmonization (the first half of the song is shown in Example 9-1) perfectly captures the beautiful plainness of the tune, its lack of sentimentality, and its reduction to the essentials of expression. The piano introduction sweeps in billowing arpeggios over the notes of the tune's pentatonic scale; as the voice enters, the piano cautiously introduces a few tones outside of the five-note mode. The chords that are chosen are entirely triads and seventh chords, in keeping with the reigning simplicity of expression. Although E is clearly the tonic, Bartók entirely avoids the dominant chord, making subtle references instead to the tones and intervals of the melody rather than imposing conventional harmonic progressions upon it.

In the cynical and doctrinaire musical climate that emerged following World War II, the genre of the folk song arrangement waned, preserved mainly by the more traditionally minded composers such as Benjamin Britten, Aaron Copland, and Virgil Thomson. Luciano Berio's *Folk Songs* (1964), to be discussed in Chapter 16, are an exception in that they continue the high level of originality and imagination established by Bartók and his prewar contemporaries.

Example 9-1. Bartók, Eight Hungarian Folksongs, no. 1. Copyright 1922 by Universal Edition. Copyright assigned 1939 to Boosey and Hawkes, Inc. English version copyright 1955 by Hawkes & Son (London), Ltd. Reprinted by permission.

208

BÉLA BARTÓK
(*Nagyszentmiklós, 1881–New York,
1945*)

Bartók's parents were both amateur pianists who enthusiastically encouraged his first precocious steps as a musician. In 1894 he settled with his mother in Pozsony (also called Pressburg or Bratislava) where he studied piano with László Erkel and made the friendship of Erno Dohnányi. Like Dohnányi, Bartók later attended the Royal Academy of Music in Budapest to prepare for a career as a virtuoso pianist. His interest in composition was stimulated by a succession of composers whom he studied: Brahms, Wagner, Strauss, and Liszt. The last of these, according to Bartók, "revealed to me the true essence of composing."

His intense Hungarian nationalism drew his attention to folk music. Musical ethnology soon became a consuming passion, and, often in collaboration with Zoltán Kodály, he traveled in Eastern Europe, Asia Minor, and Northern Africa to collect peasant music. From 1907 until 1934 he taught piano at the Budapest Academy and concertized, but his work as a composer was several times put aside due to a lack of understanding for it. From 1934 to 1940 he received a stipend from the Hungarian Academy of Sciences to pursue ethnographic work, and, by this time, he received several important commissions for new music. He immigrated to the United States in 1940, living impecuniously in New York until his death in 1945.

SELECTED WORKS

Dramatic Music. *Duke Bluebeard's Castle* (opera, 1911), *The Wooden Prince* (ballet, 1916), *The Miraculous Mandarin* (pantomine ballet, 1919).
Orchestral Music. Suites (1905, 1907), Four Pieces (1912), *Dance Suite* (1923), *Music for Strings, Percussion, and Celesta* (1936), *Divertimento* (1939), Concerto for Orchestra (1943).
Concertos. Two violin concertos (1908, 1938), three piano concertos (1926, 1931, 1945, the third unfinished), Viola Concerto (unfinished, 1945).
Chamber Music. Six string quartets (1909, 1917, 1927, 1928, 1934, 1939), Sonatas for violin and piano (1921, 1922), Sonata for solo violin (1944),

Sonata for two pianos and percussion (1937), *Contrasts* (violin, clarinet, piano, 1938).

Piano Music. Bagatelles (1908); Dirges (1910); *Allegro barbaro* (1911); Sonatina (1915); Suite (1916); Studies Op. 18 (1918); *Improvisations on Hungarian Peasant Songs* (1920); *Out of Doors* (1926); Sonata (1926); *Mikrokosmos* (153 pieces, 1926–39).

Vocal Music. Choruses: *Cantata profana* (1930), *From Olden Times* (1935), Twenty-Seven Choruses (1935), folk song arrangements. Solo songs: two sets of five songs, Op. 15 and Op. 16 (both 1916); approximately ten collections of folk song arrangements.

EASTERN EUROPE: BARTÓK, KODÁLY, JANÁČEK, AND SZYMANOWSKI

The musical art of the peasant was a lifelong inspiration to Béla Bartók (1881–1945). It was the object of an intense and systematic study, and it provoked him to compose music of an originality and vitality unsurpassed in this century. Bartók's career was divided among three interests: musical ethnology, composition, and piano playing. The first of these was dominant. "The one thing which is as necessary to me as fresh air is to other people," he wrote to János Buşiţia in 1921, "is the possibility of going on with my studies of folk music in the countryside."

Folk music for Bartók offered the twentieth-century composer a model for natural expression:

> Pure folk music can be considered a natural phenomenon influencing higher art music just as bodily properties perceptible to the eye influence the fine arts or phenomena of life influence the poet. This influence is most effective for the musician who acquaints himself with folk music in the form in which it lives, in unbridled strength, amid the lower classes. . . . If he surrenders himself to the impact of this living folk music and to all the circumstances which are conditions of this life, and if he reflects in his works the effects of these impressions, then we might say that he has portrayed therein a part of life. [From "The Influence of Folk Music on the Art Music of Today," 1920.]

Bartók considered the peasant song an epitome of artistic perfection, equaled only by the work of an individual genius. Both were marked by conciseness, inner life, and total lack of sentimentality and superfluity. "Artistic perfection can only be achieved by one of two extremes: on the one hand by peasant folk in the mass, completely devoid of the culture of the town-dweller; on the other, by creative power of an individual genius. The creative impulse of anyone who has the misfortune to be born somewhere between these two extremes leads only to barren, pointless, and misshapen works."

Many of Bartók's musical materials were absorbed from peasant music, which he put to a profoundly original use. His works also reveal an awareness of his contemporaries, especially of the music of Stravinsky, Schoenberg, and the French Impressionists. His mature style is relatively homogeneous: Bartók's music of the 1920s is experimental in comparison to his later works, which are clearer in texture and more consonant in sonority. But his music did not undergo the far-reaching evolution of Schoenberg or Scriabin nor the volte-face to neoclassicism of Stravinsky.

His melodies usually adopt the tonal materials of peasant songs—especially pentatonic scales (pervasive elements in Bartók's music) or church modes. Rarely are they based upon major or minor scales. Bartók distinguished two rhythmic prototypes in Hungarian peasant tunes, both of which have analogies in his own music. The first is a chant-like "parlando-rubato" rhythm, as in the song "Fekete főd" illustrated in Example 9-1. The other is derived from peasant dances: it is strict in tempo but may contain changes of meter. The fast, driving rhythms with shifting accents of the *Allegro barbaro*, for example, are Bartók's adaptation of these dance rhythms. Bartók also found that certain dotted rhythms were common in peasant music, hence the "Scotch snap" so often heard in his works. In Bulgarian dance melodies he discovered a type of rhythm in rapid tempi in which the measure is asymmetrically divided. He used such meters, for example, in the last six *Mikrokosmos* and in the Scherzo of the Fifth String Quartet.

The harmonic palette chosen by Bartók is eclectic. Chords drawn from notes of a pentatonic scale, octatonic subsets (especially the major/minor tetrachord), and triadic tetrachords are common. Unlike Schoenberg and composers of his school, Bartók freely mixes these sonorities with triads and seventh chords. The issue of tonality was especially problematic for Bartók, since the folk songs that he used or imitated invariably were in a key while his harmonic practice suggested the free dissonance of atonality. Early in his career, Bartók seemed willing to accept a designation as an atonalist, whose essential characteristic was the free and equal treatment of all twelve pitch classes. By the 1930s, however, he rejected the concept of atonality and asserted that all of his music expressed key. It is plain, all the same, that common-practice tonality plays no important part in Bartók's style. The element of key instead resides in the assertion of a pitch class—often at the very end of a piece or movement—as central or cadential. Such focus upon a principal pitch is normally conveyed by the melodic line.

Bartók's Fourteen Bagatelles for piano Op. 6 (1908) illustrate his eclectic mixing of opposites—the tonality of folk song and atonality associated with new musical ideas. The composer's utter rejection of romantic overstatement is reflected in the brevity and spare texture of these pieces. The first piece (Anthology no. 4) contains conflicting key signatures: four sharps in the right hand are pitted against four flats in the left. The melody of the upper part outlines a C#-minor chord, with emphasis upon its third, E. The accompanimental left hand contains descending ostinato figures, which derive primarily from the Phrygian mode on C.

In the introduction to *Béla Bartók Masterpieces for the Piano* (1945), the composer comments upon the implications of the conflicting key signatures:

> This half-serious, half-jesting procedure was used to demonstrate the absurdity of key signatures in certain kinds of contemporary music. After carrying the key signature principle *ad absurdum* in the first piece, I dropped its use in all the other Bagatelles and in most of my following works as well. The tonality of the first Bagatelle is, of course, not a mixture of C-sharp minor and F minor, but simply a Phrygian coloured C major.

Bartók's assignment of the piece to C major is presumably based upon the final cadence, which comes to a rest upon the notes C and E. The primary integrative element of the work is not a key, but a three-note set which underlies the melodic motion in the right hand. This element of pitch organization is first encountered at the beginning of the second phrase (measure 3) in the notes G# C# D#; it gradually takes on more distinctive motivic shape, culminating in two related presentations in measure 16 (C# F# G#) and measure 17 (A B E). The line in measures 12–14 (represented below) is almost entirely constructed from interlocking forms of this trichord, which is marked by brackets:

E A B C# F# | E B F#   C# G# D# | A E B   C# F# G#

Bagatelle No. 8 (Anthology no. 4)—said by the composer to be in G minor—is in a ternary form whose three parts (mm. 1–15, 16–23, 24–32) are in progressively slower tempi. G-minor triads appear only in measure 10 and in the final bar, in the latter decorated by unresolved passing motion in an inner voice. The triadic tetrachords described in Chapter 3 play an especially large role in this piece.

The final two Bagatelles are given the titles "She is dead . . ." and "My dancing sweetheart. . . ." Both contain a melodic figure that

Bartók had earlier adopted as a motto for his friend and confidante Stefi Geyer, who had broken off their relationship only weeks before the Bagatelles were written. The contrasting and sardonic character of these pieces reflects Bartók's bitterness at this turn of events. "She is dead" is a lugubrious study in which the left hand alternates between two tritone-related minor triads, while the right hand intones a chromatic plaint. After the appearance of Geyer's motive (the ascending triadic figure in mm. 22–23), the melody dwindles off into tritones and moves to a somber conclusion.

"My dancing sweetheart" (Anthology no. 4) places Geyer's motive (mm. 9–12) into a grotesque waltz, alternately banal, directionless, and misshapen in form. In the transition to the reprise (mm. 151–78), a search for the arpeggiated motto is launched. The motive is recovered at measure 179, but, despite great fanfare, its motion remains harmonically unresolved. It hangs upon the leading tone C♯ and, in the last four measures, tumbles broken and lifeless to the tonic note D in the lowest register of the instrument.

Explicit folk song quotations are confined to the fourth and fifth Bagatelles, which exemplify the simplest of three ways in which Bartók used such melodies. The composer defined these three in his article "The Influence of Peasant Music on Modern Music" (1931): A folk tune may be quoted with the addition of an appropriate accompaniment, an original melody may be composed to imitate a folk tune, or the spirit of folk music may be evoked with no direct quotation or imitation. The fourth Bagatelle (Anthology no. 4) is an example of the first method. Here the melody of the Magyar song "Mikor guláslegény voltam" is harmonized by parallel triads and seventh chords from the Aeolian mode on D.

A much more daring attempt to merge folk song with original music using atonal harmony is carried out in the *Improvisations on Hungarian Peasant Songs* for piano Op. 20 (1920). In the seventh Improvisation (a work dedicated to the memory of Claude Debussy), the preexistent melody "Belli, fiam, Belli" is heard in octaves in measures 1–11 (Example 9-2). This tune, in Phrygian mode on C, returns varied and transposed a fifth higher in measures 15–21, and a final allusion to it at its original pitch is made in the last five measures. The melody illustrates the chant-like "parlando-rubato" rhythm that the composer found in the oldest Hungarian peasant songs.

Bartók's harmonization of the melody of this *Improvisation*—contrary to the fourth Bagatelle—is largely independent of the melody and of the mode upon which the tune is based. The chords consist primarily of four- and five-note octatonic subsets. Prominent among them is the major/minor tetrachord, a favorite harmony which Bartók attributed to "bimodality" or the simultaneous use of parallel

Example 9-2. Bartók, *Improvisations sur des chansons paysannes hongroises*
Op. 20, No. 7, measures 1–11. Copyright 1922 by Universal-Edition.
Renewal 1949. Copyright and renewal assigned to Boosey & Hawkes, Inc.
Reprinted by permission.

major and minor modes. This chord punctuates the opening and closing statements of the melody (mm. 2–3, 11) with a bell-like sonority.

Bartók's six string quartets span his entire career as a composer
and reveal a cross section of the various styles within his music as a
whole. The First and Second Quartets (1909 and 1917) are each in
three movements. The first adopts a post-Brahmsian style comparable to Schoenberg's First Quartet. The second is more closely related
to Bartók's later music, especially in its absorption of folk elements.
The Third and Fourth Quartets (1927 and 1928) are among his most
advanced and difficult compositions in their recondite motivic
work, dense counterpoint, and rhythmic energy. The Fourth and
Fifth Quartets share a similar design in which five movements are
laid out symmetrically: the first and fifth and second and fourth
movements of each share similar material. The Fifth and Sixth
Quartets (1934 and 1939) use a more relaxed texture and sonority
compared to Bartók's works of the 1920s.

The Third Quartet illustrates Bartók's third method of applying
folk material to art music. No folk songs are quoted or directly imitated, but the pentatonic element of peasant music is merged
nonetheless with an essentially chromatic language. The quartet is in
one movement, consisting of four connected parts which have the
relationship A B A' B'. The first of these four parts (pages 3 to 8 of the

miniature score) is intensely polyphonic and rigorously organized by the development of motives from the first twelve measures. There are no sectional repetitions within this part, and all subdivisions are linked by common motives. The passage from measures 35 to 42, a dialogue of disconnected chromatic fragments between the two violins, is a type of music often heard in Bartók, the prototype of which is the "Night Music" movement of the piano suite *Out of Doors* (1926).

In a lecture on "Chromaticism" given at Harvard University in 1943, Bartók described a type of melody that he had begun to use twenty years earlier, in which the initial pitches chromatically fill a small boundary interval. He attributed this type of chromaticism to the conflation of several diatonic modes. "This 'modal chromaticism' . . . is a main characteristic of the new Hungarian art music," he remarked. "Another and different characteristic, as you will probably remember, is the appearance of pentatonic melodic structures in our work, as a contrast, so to speak, to the modal chromaticism, although both may be combined."

The opening theme of the Third Quartet (Example 9-3) combines modal chromaticism and pentatonicism. The head motive consists of pitches that chromatically fill the interval from G to C (B#). The accompaniment in the lower strings is similarly a chromatic cluster D D# E. The theme is continued, however, by pentatonic motion: F G Bb G F C (simplifying Bartók's curious enharmonic notation).

In his lecture at Harvard, the composer described how a chromatic motive could be varied by splaying its intervals into a more diatonic shape. "This circumstance is very good indeed," he concluded, "because we will get variety on the one hand, but unity will remain undestroyed because of the hidden relation between the two forms." This relationship between themes is clearly exploited in the first part of the Third Quartet, as the chromatic motive of measures 2–4 blossoms into diatonic (or, more precisely, pentatonic) forms (Example 9-4).

The pentatonic content of these variants is divided with some strictness between "black key" collections (as in mm. 27–32) and those among white keys (mm. 87–92, for example). The pentatonicism of motives is also apparent in chords. The final chord of the

Example 9-3. Bartók, Third String Quartet. Copyright 1929 by Universal-Edition. Copyright and renewal assigned to Boosey and Hawkes, Inc. Reprinted by permission.

Example 9-4. Bartók, Third String Quartet. Copyright 1929 by Universal-Edition. Copyright and renewal assigned to Boosey and Hawkes, Inc. Reprinted by permission.

quartet (G♯ A♯ C♯ D♯) is a pentatonic subset, and the cadential succession of fourths and fifths in measure 33 states a complete pentatonic scale of the white-key type (Example 9-5).

But Bartók does not excessively prolong these passages of pentatonic content. They appear and then quickly recede into the tissue of chromatically developing variations, by which we perceive the work as organically alive and devoid of the predictable or commonplace.

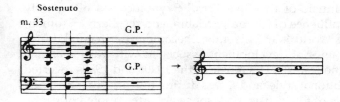

Example 9-5. Bartók, Third String Quartet. Copyright 1929 by Universal-Edition. Copyright and renewal assigned to Boosey and Hawkes, Inc. Reprinted by permission.

The second part of the quartet imitates the strict tempo and driving rhythms of Hungarian peasant music. It also displays Bartók's great resourcefulness in drawing diverse colors from the instruments of the string quartet. The final two parts (the last called a coda) are highly abbreviated and varied recapitulations of material from the first two.

Other Eastern European composers in the early twentieth century who used national idioms include Leoš Janáček (1854–1928), Zoltán Kodály (1882–1967), and Karol Szymanowski (1882–1937). Most of Janáček's music was composed in the twentieth century after the limited success of his opera *Jenůfa* (1904, later revised). His artistic outlook, however, was rooted in the nineteenth century and modeled on Smetana and Dvořák. His knowledge of folk music of his native Moravia helped him to develop a distinctively flexible and colorful lyric idiom which he used in his operas, including the starkly realistic *Jenůfa* and later in *The Cunning Little Vixen* (1923) and *The Makropoulos Affair* (1925). Among his instrumental works, the *Sinfonietta* is vividly orchestrated and direct in appeal.

Kodály's career was closely related to Bartók's from the time both studied composition with Hans Koessler at the Budapest Academy. They served subsequently on the faculty of the Academy, and they jointly undertook ethnomusicological research. Kodály's music is based almost exclusively on Hungarian peasant melodies, while Bartók availed himself of a wider variety of folk music. Kodály's adaptation of the folk idiom lacked Bartók's originality—he cleaved instead to a traditional harmonic and tonal style. Nevertheless, his music, steeped in the sounds and contours of folk song, is colorful and melodious. Among his best-known works are the opera *Háry János* (from which a popular orchestral suite was extracted), his orchestral *Dances of Galanta*, and oratorio *Psalmus hungaricus* (1923). Kodály is well known, especially in Hungary and America, for his innovative approach to teaching music to children.

The early music of the Pole Karol Szymanowski alternately reflected the influence of Chopin, Scriabin, and the German romanticists. During World War I his music became experimental, but it still followed lines of development associated with earlier French and German modernists. His music of the 1920s and 1930s reverted to a more traditional style, and it was during this time that he made his greatest use of folk music. Folk songs are often quoted outright, and the spirit of Polish folk dances is evoked in his mazurkas and other character pieces for piano.

SCANDINAVIA: SIBELIUS AND NIELSEN

Finland during the nineteenth century was a duchy of Russia, although it was allowed considerable autonomy by the Tsars. A movement for Finnish nationalism waxed throughout the century, and, when Tsar Nicholas II attempted to reassert Russian sovereignty in 1899, rebellion was narrowly averted. Finnish nationalism, however, did not come immediately to Jean Sibelius (1865–1957). His native language was Swedish, which remained for most of the nineteenth century the language of government and of the upper classes in Finland. While a student in Vienna in 1890–91, he struggled through the Finnish heroic poem *Kalevala*. His imagination and patriotism were thus fired, and he shortly completed a choral symphony, *Kullervo*, the first of many pieces inspired by this national epic.

The *Kalevala* is a saga of uncertain origin which deals with the exploits of three brothers inhabiting Kaleva, the land of heroes. It is divided into large sections, or "runes," each line of which is in the distinctive trochaic quatrameter imitated by Longfellow in his poem *Hiawatha*. The *Kalevala* is closely associated with other Nordic myths such as the Icelandic *Eddas* and the German *Nibelungenlied*, the latter drawn upon by Richard Wagner in his texts for *The Ring of the Nibelung*. Each emphasizes man's closeness to nature, his heroic deeds, and his relationship with the gods. The *Kalevala* was preserved and transmitted among folk singers in the region of Karelia in eastern Finland (now part of Russia). Its texts were transcribed and edited by several nineteenth-century folk enthusiasts, and its chant-like music was recognized as the oldest type of Finnish folk song.

Although Sibelius did not have a great interest in studying folklore, he traveled to Karelia in 1892 to meet runic singers and to transcribe their melodies. These he found to be extremely simple, almost recitational formulas, by which poetry like that of the *Kalevala* was intoned in a series of varied repetitions. It was not an artistically sophisticated music which Sibelius could easily assimilate into his own work.

JEAN SIBELIUS
(*Hämeenlinna, 1865–Järvenpää, 1957*)

Sibelius was born into a Swedish-speaking family and learned the Finnish language only as an adult. His early ambition as a musician was to be a virtuoso violinist, a goal he pursued at the Helsinki Conservatory from 1885 to 1889. There he met Ferruccio Busoni, who taught piano at the Conservatory, and he became a favorite student of the director of the school, Martin Wegelius. He subsequently studied for two years in Berlin and Vienna, where his interests turned decisively to composition under the tutelage of Robert Fuchs and Karl Goldmark.

From 1897 he received a stipend from the Finnish government in support of his work, and he was quickly recognized as the greatest modern composer of his nation. From 1904 until his death in 1957 he lived in Järvenpää near Helsinki; he traveled regularly in Europe and England and made one visit to America to receive an honorary doctorate from Yale University. He composed no major works after 1925.

SELECTED WORKS

Orchestral Music. Seven symphonies (1899–1924; an eighth symphony was destroyed); tone poems: *En Saga* (1892, rev. 1901), *Four Legends* (*Lemminkäinen and the Maidens of Saari*, 1895; The *Swan of Tuonela*, 1893; *Lemminkäinen in Tuonela*, 1895; *Lemminkäinen's Homeward Journey*, 1895, all later revised), *Finlandia* (1899), *Pohjola's Daughter* (1906), *The Bard* (1913), *The Oceanides* (1914), *Tapiola* (1925); incidental music for theater: *Pelléas et Mélisande* (1905), *The Tempest* (1926).
Concertos. Violin Concerto (1903, rev. 1905).
Chamber Music. String Quartet in D minor (*Voces intimae*) (1909), collections of pieces for violin and piano (five collections with opus numbers).
Vocal Music. Songs, choral music, part songs.

His national profile was revealed in other ways. The stories rather than the music of the *Kalevala* became for Sibelius a source of enduring inspiration. These tales would be celebrated in many of his tone poems. The four *Legends* Op. 22 relate the exploits of the hero Lemminkäinen as he woos the beautiful Kyllikki and recklessly shoots at the black swan that circles Tuonela, the land of the dead. *Pohjola's Daughter* Op. 49 recounts the tale of another hero, Väinämöinen, who tries to win the affection of a cunning maiden from the land of Pohjola. *Tapiola* Op. 112, Sibelius's last tone poem, depicts the brooding forests of the North, inhabited by the god Tapio.

Sibelius succeeded in translating the spirit of Finland and its people into a musical language without other recourse to folklore or to notable stylistic innovation. His works speak with great emotion to the Finns, capturing their love for their country and clarifying their national identity. Technical features of his music cannot alone explain this attachment, but it rests in part upon certain recurrent features that mark his work: its dark sonority, sudden bursts of light leading to dramatic climaxes, archaic modal textures, ostinatos, and pedal points.

Many of these features are heard in one of his most cheerful works, the Seventh Symphony Op. 105 (1924). This piece was first designated a "Symphonic Fantasy" because of its unconventional one-movement form. In its unabashed lyricism, it owes much to the symphonies of Tchaikovsky; in its unusual form, cautious pace, and epic climaxes, it is indebted to those of Mahler; and in its dense texture and motivic unity, it is connected to the works of Brahms.

The Seventh Symphony is not in any conventional instrumental form. Several lines of thought run through it and emerge alternately. It can be viewed in three large parts: an introductory exposition (mm. 1–93), development of a new theme (mm. 94–474), and epilogue (mm. 475 to the end). The development concerns a scherzando theme (Example 9-6) introduced at measure 94. Its motives are spun into endlessly varied shapes, borne along by ever greater rhythmic motion. A familiar device in Sibelius's orchestral music may be observed in measures 96–97 of this theme: the same motive is stated in octaves by the high and low strings, but the lower voices are slightly out of phase with the upper ones. The effect is to make the polyphonic texture denser and to blur the sense of pulse.

The development section is interrupted by two important episodes: first, the return at measure 222 (rehearsal L) of a theme in the brass heard earlier at measure 60; and, second, an exposition of new themes beginning at measure 261. The development resumes at measure 322, now involving the new themes as well as the older

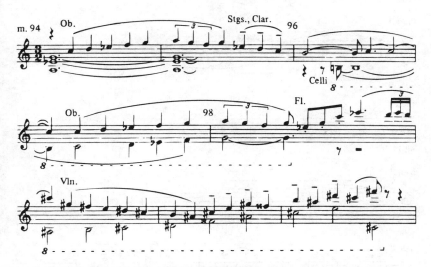

Example 9-6. Sibelius, Symphony No. 7. Copyright 1926 by Wilhelm Hansen, Copenhagen. Reprinted by permission.

one. A climactic epilogue begins at measure 475, recapitulating the brass episode from measures 60 and 222 and touching at the end upon a flute motive from measure 11.

The large quantity of melodic material in the Seventh Symphony can be reduced to three developmentally interrelated families of themes: those with stepwise diatonic motion (the opening of the work is a prototype), those outlining a triad (for example, the theme in the woodwinds and horns at measure 261), and themes that contain a turn figure. The last of these is the most important. Eight themes of this type are shown in Example 9-7 (the turn figure is bracketed in each). These turn figures are brought to a triumphant peroration near the end in a unison passage in the high strings (Example 9-8).

The harmonic language of the Seventh Symphony is influenced by the modal content of its lines. A resonant polyphony from measures 22 to 50, for example, is based upon the Mixolydian mode on G. The tonal plan of the work alternates between regions emphasizing G and C, with C emerging as the central tonality. Secondary areas a third away (such as the region in Eb major at rehearsal T) are also prominent.

Carl Nielsen (1865–1931) occupies a position in his native Denmark comparable to that of Sibelius in Finland, although Nielsen's music is not overtly nationalistic in theme or substance. His six symphonies exhibit several of Sibelius's trademarks: dense modal counterpoint, motivic interconnection of themes, and free

Example 9-7. Sibelius, Symphony No. 7. Copyright 1926 by Wilhelm Hansen Copenhagen. Reprinted by permission.

handling of dissonance within a tonal context. They are also marked by a dramatic rivalry between key areas, often producing a highly chromatic and dissonant texture. In the end, one key will emerge victorious over its rivals.

m. 504

Example 9-8. Sibelius, Symphony No. 7. Copyright 1926 by Wilhelm Hansen, Copenhagen. Reprinted by permission.

ENGLAND: VAUGHAN WILLIAMS AND HOLST

Serious attempts to record and preserve English folk song began early in the nineteenth century. They reached an apogee at the turn of the century in the work of Cecil Sharp (1859–1924). This indefatigable collector pursued authentic examples of folk music throughout England, and he then came to America in the hope of finding more primitive versions of songs and dances among descendants of English settlers. His work was an inspiration to English composers of the early decades of the century.

Foremost among England's musical nationalists was Ralph Vaughan Williams (1872–1958). Between 1903 and 1913 he was active as a collector of folk songs and English carols. which he arranged and published in several volumes. Like Bartók, he considered the folk song to be a model of artistic perfection. He demanded that national traits be evident in art music: "Art, like charity, should begin at home," he wrote. "If [a composer's work] is to be of any value it must grow out of the very life of himself, the community in which he lives, and the nation to which he belongs." He rejected aestheticism and contrived universality, preaching instead a utilitarian element in music that should grow from a diverse culture and human experience. Like his contemporary neoclassicists, he embraced traditional idioms, especially folk song, the Anglican hymn, and English music of the sixteenth and seventeenth centuries. "Why should music be original?" he queried. "The object of art is to stretch out to the ultimate realities through the medium of beauty. The duty of the composer is to find the *mot juste*. It does not matter if this word has been said a thousand times before as long as it is the right thing to say at that moment."

Vaughan Williams's assimilation of English folk music is revealed in his nine symphonies. The *Pastoral* Symphony (Symphony No. 3, 1916–21) is an especially important example of the applicability of modality and folk-like pentatonicism to the symphonic genre in the twentieth century. This work is in four movements. A serene first movement suggests the gentle melancholy of the countryside. Its pentatonic themes are accompanied by parallel root position triads. Several such streams of "enhanced melody" frequently overlap. The

RALPH VAUGHAN WILLIAMS
(*Down Ampney, 1872–London, 1958*)

Vaughan Williams's education as a composer was pursued alternately at the Royal College of Music in London under Hubert Parry and Charles Stanford and at Trinity College, Cambridge, from which university he received the degree of Doctor of Music in 1901. He also studied briefly in 1897 with Max Bruch in Berlin and in 1908 in Paris with Ravel, with whom he formed a warm friendship.

During the first decade of the new century, he devoted himself to folk song collecting and to editorial work on the *English Hymnal.* After four years of wartime service on the Continent he returned to London and was appointed to the faculty of the Royal College of Music and conductor of the London Bach Choir. He devoted himself unflaggingly to teaching and to his work as a composer until his death in 1958.

SELECTED WORKS

Operas. *Hugh the Drover* (1914), *Sir John in Love* (1928), *The Poisoned Kiss* (1929), *Riders to the Sea* (1932), *Pilgrim's Progress* (1936–49).

Ballets. *Old King Cole* (1923), *Job* (1930).

Orchestral Music. Nine symphonies (1909–57), *Fantasia on a Theme by Thomas Tallis* (1910).

Concertos. *The Lark Ascending* (violin and orchestra, 1914, rev. 1920); Concertos for violin (1925), piano (1931), and oboe (1944).

Chamber Music. Sonata for violin (1954), three string quartets, three piano quintets.

Songs. Numerous songs and cycles, including arrangements of folk songs.

Choral Music. *Toward the Unknown Region* (1906), *Five Mystical Songs* (1911), Mass in G (unaccompanied, 1922), *Sancta civitas* (1925), Magnificat (1932), *Five Tudor Portraits* (1935), *Dona nobis pacem* (1936), *Old Hundredth Psalm Tune* (1953), *Hodie* (1954), *Epithalamion* (1957).

second movement is slow and elegiac, making use of an unmeasured pentatonic melody, first on natural trumpet, then natural horn. The pungent intonation of valveless brass instruments was influential on Benjamin Britten, who called for similar effects in his Serenade and *Noye's Fludde*. The third movement is a scherzo with folk-like tunes heard in the two trios.

An unmeasured soprano or tenor vocalization introduces and concludes the finale of the *Pastoral* Symphony. This melody touches upon all notes of the C-major scale, but it focuses on A and E and otherwise emphasizes pentatonic segments. The first theme of the free sonata form that follows is also pentatonic, accompanied by root position major triads descending in whole steps. The second theme, in Dorian mode, is accompanied at first by a diatonic polyphony (Example 9-9). A development begins at measure 56 and a majestic recapitulation is heard at measure 110.

The symphony is distinguished by its unaffected melodiousness and simplicity. It avoids clear expression of a major or minor tonality—none is indicated in the title—but the melodic assertion of local

First theme
Strings

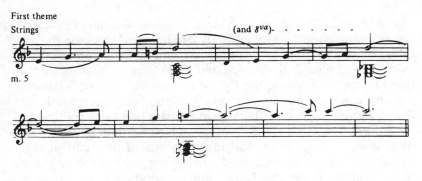

Second theme
Ob.

Example 9-9. Vaughan Williams, *Pastoral* Symphony, fourth movement, finale. Copyright 1924 by J. Curwen & Sons Ltd. U.S. copyright renewed 1952. Used by arrangement with G. Schirmer, Inc., U.S. agent for J. Curwen & Sons, Ltd., London.

tonics within a pentatonic or modal framework creates a fluctuating sense of key. Triads reign unchallenged among the accompanimental harmonies. They are applied almost solely to enhance the resonance of the melodic line; their content of pitches is not confined to any prevailing diatonic scale, nor do they suggest a key in a traditional way.

Gustav Holst (1874–1934) met Vaughan Williams in 1895, while both were students at the Royal College of Music. They formed a lifelong friendship and proceeded along similar paths as composers. Holst's music, like that of Vaughan Williams, reflects his interest in folk song and earlier English polyphony, the former seen in his popular Suites for military band. His fascination with Sanskrit literature is revealed in the texts of several early works. He is best known for the orchestral suite *Planets* (1917), which is skillfully orchestrated and powerful in its driving five- and seven-beat meters.

SPAIN: MANUEL DE FALLA

Spain in the 1500s—its "golden century"—was a center of European wealth and political power and a rival to Italy and France in the arts. She produced masters of sacred music, among them Tomás Luis de Victoria and Cristóbal Morales, and great instrumentalists such as the lutenist Luis Milán. But by the nineteenth century, Spain had become a musical province. Its artistic life had long been dominated by foreigners, especially Italians since Spain had close political ties with Italy. The Italian composer Domenico Scarlatti spent his last twenty-eight years in Madrid in the service of the Spanish royal family, and Italian opera gained a firm grasp on Spanish taste later in the eighteenth century. Native music dwindled into the confines of vigorous folk songs and dance, a brilliant school of guitar playing, and an Italianate genre of operetta called *zarzuela*.

The modern renaissance of Spanish music was brought about largely through the influence of Felipe Pedrell (1841–1922). This composer, pedagogue, and musicologist almost singlehandedly revived knowledge and appreciation of sixteenth-century Spanish art music and of his nation's vibrant musical folklore. He was also closely in touch with contemporary developments in European music, and he helped to launch the careers of three young protégés who became the outstanding figures in Spanish music of the early twentieth century: Isaac Albéniz (1860–1909), Enrique Granados (1867–1916), and Manuel de Falla (1876–1946).

Albéniz, a student of Liszt, was a virtuoso pianist whose cycle of Spanish character pieces *Iberia* (1906–1908) was widely admired.

MANUEL DE FALLA
(*Cádiz, 1876–Alta Gracia
[Argentina], 1946*)

Falla's native city of Cádiz is in the Andalusian region of southern Spain, a melting pot of Eastern and Western cultures whose folk music he would later celebrate. His family moved to Madrid in 1896, where he continued preparation as a concert pianist. He tried his hand at composing popular operettas, or *zarzuelas*, at which he was largely unsuccessful. His studies with Felipe Pedrell were a great encouragement to his career as a serious composer.

From 1907 to 1914 he lived in Paris where he made the acquaintance of most of the leading French composers of that time. He returned to Madrid in 1914, moving to Granada in 1919. There he was active in efforts to preserve the authentic *cante jondo*. He formed a close friendship with the poet and musical amateur Federico García Lorca. After the end of the Spanish Civil War he immigrated to Argentina.

SELECTED WORKS

Dramatic Music. *La vida breve* (opera, 1913), *El amor brujo* (ballet, 1915), *Three-Cornered Hat* (ballet, 1916–19), *El retablo de Maese Pedro* (for puppet theater, 1919–22), *Atlántida* (opera, incomplete, 1926–).
Orchestral Music. *Nights in the Gardens of Spain* (1911–15), Concerto for harpsichord and five instruments (1926).
Piano Music, *Pièces espagnoles* (1908), *Fantasía baetica* (1919), *Pour le tombeau de Paul Dukas* (1935).
Guitar Music. *Homenaje "le Tombeau de Claude Debussy"* (1920, also a version for piano solo).
Vocal Music. *Trois mélodies* (1909), *Seven Spanish Folk Songs* (1915), *Psyché* (1924), *Soneto a Córdoba* (1927).

Granados wrote a comparable set of piano works entitled *Goyescas*, in which he sought to translate into music the dramatic images of life portrayed by the eighteenth-century Spanish painter Goya. Granados later refitted this music as an opera of the same title.

By the turn of the century, Paris had emerged as a proving ground for the Spanish musical renaissance. Both Albéniz and Granados were active in France, where audiences relished their stylized portraits of their homeland. Bizet's *Carmen* and Chabrier's *España* initiated a series of works by French composers imitating Spanish life and customs. Spain was of particular fascination to Debussy, who translated the impressions that he garnered from pictures and literature into numerous piano works. These pieces and others by Ravel were played with fiery conviction in Paris by the Spanish virtuoso Ricardo Viñes.

Manuel de Falla also came under the wing of Pedrell, and he later followed Albéniz and Granados to Paris. There he made the friendship of Dukas, Ravel, and Debussy, who supported his efforts to meld impressionistic imagery with rhythms and accents of his native Andalusia. Falla particularly admired the Spanish character pieces of Debussy. "Here we are actually given Andalusia," he wrote regarding Debussy's *Soirée dans Grenade*. "The truth without the authenticity, as it were, for although not a single measure is taken from Spanish folklore, the whole piece, down to its smallest details, brings Spain to us."

Debussy's method of evoking Spanish colors without overt references to folk songs was Falla's model for most of his early works. These included sets of character pieces for piano, the opera *La vida breve*, the ballets *Three Cornered Hat* and *El amor brujo*, and the orchestral *Nights in the Gardens of Spain*. In all of them he sought the "truth" about his homeland without directly quoting folk tunes, a practice he deemed provincial. "The essential elements of music, the sources of inspiration, are nations and people," he wrote. "I am against music resting on authentic folklore documents. I believe, on the contrary, that one must start from the natural living fountainheads and use the substance of sonority and rhythm, not their outward appearance."

In his *Fantasía baetica* (1919), Falla educes the sonorous and rhythmic outlines of his native Andalusia, the region of southern Spain called Baetica by the Romans. In this virtuosic work for piano, Falla imitates the traditional Andalusian *cante jondo*, a genre sometimes called "flamenco." The *cante jondo* is a song accompanied by guitar in which the voice is metrically free, highly ornamented, limited in range, and often unfixed of intonation. These songs are tragic in mood and usually peppered by shouts from the audience and the chatter of castanets and clicking of heels.

All of these features are evoked in the *Fantasía*. It is a ternary work in which the middle "intermezzo" is a lyrical interlude between sections of vivid dissonance, driving dance rhythms, melodic ostinatos, and flamboyant accompanimental figuration. The piece has no central key, although most of the themes focus in modal fashion on some pitch, most often A or E. The sound of castanets and tambourins is captured by pointed dissonances on strong beats, as in Example 9-10. A passage from measures 115 to 149 imitates the traditional flamenco guitar prelude and tragic song or "copla." Guitar figuration is suggested here by a motive in fourths, which could be played on open strings if the instrument were tuned—as it often was by the native player—higher than usual (Example 9-11). The bitter and nasal plaint of the folk singer is evoked by dissonant grace notes, as in Example 9-12.

Fantasía baetica was one of Falla's last works of an overtly Spanish type. In the mid-1920s he turned toward a more abstract musical style, perhaps following the example of Stravinsky, who in these years was outspoken in his rejection of the regionalism that pervaded his own earlier music. In this new idiom, Falla composed *El retablo de Maese Pedro*, a work for puppets dramatizing a scene from Cervantes's *Don Quixote*; a chamber concerto for harpsichord,

m. 9

Example 9-10. Falla, *Fantasía baetica*, measures 9–11. Reprinted by kind permission of J & W Chester/Edition Wilhelm Hansen London Limited.

m. 115

Example 9-11. Falla, *Fantasía baetica*, measures 115–118. Reprinted by kind permission of J & W Chester/Edition Wilhelm Hansen London Limited.

m. 134

Example 9-12.   Falla, *Fantasía baetica*, measures 134–136. Reprinted by kind permission of J & W Chester/Edition Wilhelm Hansen London Limited.

strings, and winds; vocal music; and laments for several departed friends. His "Homages" to Dukas and Debussy—the former for piano and the latter for guitar—quote from music by these two composers whom Falla so greatly admired.

THE NEW WORLD

American music during the first half of the twentieth century was strongly nationalistic. There was a common view that artistic expression in the United States should be distinctive of the American experience, different from that of Europe. This viewpoint reflects American society and politics of the same time, when patriotism and isolationism were pronounced.

An attitude of idealistic separatism in the arts appeared first in literature in the nineteenth century. The essayist Ralph Waldo Emerson (1802–1882) saw for the American poet a very different mission than for the intellectuals of other nations. "Our day of dependence," he said in his 1837 lecture "The American Scholar," "our long apprenticeship to the learning of other lands, draws to a close. The millions that around us are rushing into life, cannot always be fed on the sere remains of foreign harvests. Events, actions arise, that must be sung, that will sing themselves."

Emerson's vision of uniqueness in the American intellectual was continued by Walt Whitman (1819–92), whose themes, techniques and attitudes about art became characteristic of the American style. Whitman found the substance of art in the institutions and stereotypes of American life: the common person, democracy, egalitarianism, nature, masculinity, and vigor foremost among them. In the preface to the first edition of his poetic anthology *Leaves of Grass* (1855), Whitman constructs an ideal of America and its art. Concerning the American poet he writes: "His spirit responds to his country's spirit . . . , he incarnates its geography and natural life and rivers and lakes. . . . Here the theme is creative and has vista. Here comes one among the well-beloved stonecutters and plans with decision and science and sees the solid and beautiful forms of the future where there are now no solid forms."

Most American composers of the early twentieth century embraced the self-conscious and separatist ideals of Emerson and Whitman, gradually shedding their reliance on European music and seeking a new and distinctly American alternative. The first important American composer who was unfettered by European traditions was Charles Ives, whose prophetic experimentalism accommodated an intensely American musical speech. Many of Ives's works recreate musical and spiritual recollections from his youth—the sounds of marching bands, gospel hymns, and cowboy songs—which were assembled into an eclectic diversity of styles that had little in common with the unified languages of European composers. His works will be discussed in Chapter 12.

The national impulse in American music is also encountered among the populist composers who will be surveyed in Chapter 11. Aaron Copland, Virgil Thomson, and Roy Harris are examples. These figures found a usable American image in several sources. Folkloristic musical elements—dances, religious songs, marches, and jazz idioms—were frequently quoted, as in Harris's *Folksong Symphony* (Symphony No. 4), and American tales were drawn on for such dramatic works as Copland's ballets *Billy the Kid, Rodeo,* and *Appalachian Spring*. More important still in creating an indigenous music was finding a style that could speak to and about the American consciousness. At the hands of Copland, Thomson, and Harris, this style was defined in terms of simplicity, naïveté, even primitivization. Thomson's opera *Four Saints in Three Acts* (1933) was a prototype for the charmingly unadorned music that quickly became synonymous with a distinctly American spirit in music.

Music by Latin American composers in the early decades of the century was strongly national in character, although it sometimes mixed folk styles with modern harmonic techniques. Heitor Villa-Lobos (1887–1959) joined Brazilian folk music to a mixture of conventional and modernistic accompaniments in his series of nine *Bachianas brasileiras* and sixteen *Chôros*. The music of Alberto Ginastera (1916–83) in the 1930s and 1940s was based upon the style of Argentinian dances and folk songs. In the 1950s and later, his works took on a more international and avant-garde character, as they used elements of serialism, aleatory techniques, and manipulation of textural masses.

The music of Carlos Chávez (1899–1978) reveals the profile of Indian culture in Mexico. His orchestral works are marked by a powerful use of percussion and other coloristic devices. His Mexican colleague Silvestre Revueltas (1899–1940) was fascinated by the rhythmic and orchestrational style of Stravinsky's *Rite of Spring*, which he imitated in his fancifully barbaric tone poem *Sensemayá* (1938).

The national movements that promised to reinvigorate music early in the twentieth century began to wane by the latter 1920s and 1930s. Stravinsky—whom Bartók had earlier identified as one of the most outstanding folklorists—now dismissed this movement: "What is so obvious in [the Five]," he wrote in his *Autobiography*, "as indeed in the modern Spanish 'folklorists,' whether painters or musicians, is that naive but dangerous tendency which prompts them to remake an art that has already been created instinctively by the genius of the people. It is a sterile tendency and an evil from which many talented artists suffer."

Stravinsky thus joined with Schoenberg, who had never considered folk music applicable to original composition. In an article "Folkloristic Symphonies," Schoenberg wrote: "The discrepancy between requirements of larger forms and the simple construction of folk tunes has never been solved and cannot be solved. A simple idea must not use the language of profundity. . . . Structurally, there never remains in popular tunes an unsolved problem, the consequences of which will show up only later. . . . There is nothing in them that asks for expansion."

Musical nationalism endured outside of Western Europe until after World War II, but in France and Germany it was outshone by a new mode of expression that was purged of regional color. We turn to this development in the next chapter on neoclassicism.

BIBLIOGRAPHY

Important statements by composers concerning musical nationalism may be found in *Béla Bartók Essays*, ed. Benjamin Suchoff (New York, 1976), Stravinsky's *Autobiography* (New York, 1936), Schoenberg's essay "Folkloristic Symphonies" in *Style and Idea*, ed. Leonard Stein (Berkeley, 1984), Falla's *On Music and Musicians* (London, 1979), Vaughan Williams's *National Music* (London, 1934), Copland's *Music and Imagination* (Cambridge, 1952), Ravel's "Contemporary Music," *Revue de musicologie*, 50 (1964), 208–21, and Milhaud's *Notes Without Music* (New York, 1953).

Halsey Steven's *Life and Music of Béla Bartók* (3d ed., rev. by Malcolm Gillies, 1993) is authoritative and powerfully written. A selection of the composer's correspondence is presented in his

Letters (Budapest, 1971). Elliott Antokoletz emphasizes Bartók's use of symmetric sets in his analytic study *The Music of Béla Bartók: A Study of Tonality and Progression in Twentieth-Century Music* (Berkeley, 1984). In his book *Music of Béla Bartók* (New Haven, 1992), Paul Wilson analyzes selected works using aspects of set theory and Schenker-like voice-leading diagrams.

The Music of Szymanowski by Jim Samson (New York, 1981) is an authoritative analytic survey of Szymanowski's music. The operas of Janáček are covered in studies by Erik Chisholm (New York, 1971) and Michael Ewens (London, 1977). Erik Tawaststjerna's *Sibelius* deals with this composer's life and works up to 1905; Robert Layton's *Sibelius* (New York, 1993) is a more general study. Elliott Schwartz's informative *Symphonies of Ralph Vaughan Williams* (New York, 1982) and Michael Kennedy's *Works of Ralph Vaughan Williams* (London, 1964) are good sources of information, as is Michael Short's very thorough *Gustav Holst: The Man and His Music* (Oxford, 1990). A brief guide to the music of Manuel de Falla is found in Ronald Crichton's *Falla* (London, 1982), and a selection of the composer's writings is in *Manuel de Falla: On Music and Musicians* (London, 1979).

10

Neoclassicism in France, Germany, and England

Rapid changes in musical style of the late nineteenth and early twentieth centuries were temporarily stayed by the First World War. The years after the war were a time of questioning and reevaluation in the arts in general. Had artistic expression progressed too far too fast? Were the war and its aftermath the results of an unhinged civilization to which artistic experimentation had unwittingly contributed?

For many observers, the issues that fueled the war could be overcome by artistic communication. According to their view, music had to seek a new universality. Such thoughts came to Paul Hindemith when he recalled a poignant moment during his wartime service, as he performed Debussy's String Quartet for his German commanding officer:

> When we had finished the slow movement, the officer who led the communications division came in with dismay and reported that just then news of Debussy's death had been received over the wire. We did not continue. It was as though life had been taken from our playing. We felt then for the first time that music is more than style, technique, and expression of personal feeling. Music then went beyond political boundaries, beyond national hatred and beyond the horror of war. At no other time has it appeared so clearly to me in which direction music had to unfold. [*Paul Hindemith: Zeugnis in Bildern* (Mainz, 1955), p. 8.]

Hindemith implies that music cannot be allowed to evolve beyond the understanding of the public. His words suggest that a damaging esotericism had already diminished the broad communicative role of music and that this art had to be called back to a simpler and more natural order.

In fact, most of the outstanding European composers after the war entered a phase of retrenchment or consolidation of their stylistic advances of the pre-war decade. Clarity and accessibility were the order of the day. Experimentation became much less important to the mainstream of musical development and was confined instead to outlying regions such as the United States or to the dilettantish activities of Dadaism or Futurism.

This desire to communicate directly to a larger audience was shared by contemporary painters and writers, whose message was often one of social or political satire. Several German painters of the 1920s such as George Grosz (1893–1959) and Otto Dix (1891–1969) put aside the abstractions of Expressionism and adopted instead a realistic manner dubbed "The New Objectivity." Their themes were often bitter social criticisms. German writers such as Bertolt Brecht (1898–1956) held similarly that social reform was a goal of art, and the musicians with whom he collaborated—Kurt Weill (1900–1950) and Hanns Eisler (1898–1962)—used a direct and popular style to facilitate the comprehension of their works.

Writings by Ferruccio Busoni after the war enunciated the new conservatism among musicians as emphatically as his earlier *Sketch of a New Esthetic of Music* (1907) had informed the pre-war avant-garde. In a letter of 1920 to the critic Paul Bekker, Busoni called for an era of "Young Classicism." "By Young Classicism I mean the mastery, the sifting and turning to account of all the gains of previous experiments and their inclusion in strong and beautiful forms." Young Classicism, Busoni predicted, would be marked by a renewed melodic emphasis, renunciation of subjectivity, and the "reconquest of serenity."

These and other classicizing directions were adopted by a large number of composers in Europe and America between the world wars. Their music assimilated and reinterpreted the forms, genres, and styles of European music of the eighteenth and nineteenth centuries. Triads and diatonic collections of pitches gained favor, and straightforward melody and homophonic textures were reasserted. Traditional instrumental and vocal types were emphasized, and compositional techniques of earlier times were revived in a modern guise. The particular musical language of an earlier composer was often imitated, and artistic arrangements of earlier masterworks won a new respect. These features collectively point to a style to be termed *neoclassicism*, and its appearance in the works of leading

The "New Objectivity": Otto Dix, *Two Victims of Capitalism* (Courtesy of the Otto Dix Stiftung, Vaduz.)

composers in France, Germany, and England in the 1920s, 1930s, and 1940s will be the subject of this chapter.

In retrospect we can see that the end of World War I marked the beginning of a new stylistic period in music. As with many other changes in taste in the history of music, this one was brought about primarily by a rebellion against the immediate past—against the late romantic language in both its German progressivist and French impressionist manifestations. Late romantic music was hyperexpressive, densely serious, and often grandiloquent. Neoclassical music, on the contrary, was cool and detached in its emotional content, often light and entertaining, and entirely life-sized in proportions. The romantic emphasis on innovation led in the decade before World War I to a virtual revolution in musical materials, most apparent in an expanded use of dissonance and the abandonment of traditional tonality. These innovative resources were not in themselves rejected after the war, but they were leavened by an eclectic style in which elements of traditional music were brought back and mixed together with the new.

FRENCH NEOCLASSICISM: STRAVINSKY AND THE SIX

The leading neoclassicist in France between the world wars was the Russian émigré Igor Stravinsky. The power and originality of his music in this new idiom carried the younger generation of French composers in its wake, much as the experimental style of the *Rite of Spring* had proved so compelling to European and American composers prior to the First World War. Stravinsky's neoclassicism endured from the early 1920s until the early 1950s, at which time he embraced chromatic serialism (to be discussed in Chapter 13).

During this period between the world wars, Stravinsky spoke emphatically of the necessity of tradition in music:

> Far from implying the repetition of what has been, tradition presupposes the reality of what endures. It appears as an heirloom, a heritage that one receives on condition of making it bear fruit before passing it on to one's descendants. [From *Poetics of Music*. See the Bibliography to Chapter 8 concerning the authenticity of this book.]

Stravinsky made many traditions bear fruit during his neoclassical period, including the Russo-Italian operatic style of the nineteenth century, the instrumental idiom of Bach, and the nineteenth-century lyric tradition of Rossini, Verdi, and Weber. But for the immediate past as represented by the music of Wagner he had only disdain, and his neoclassical works stand as a rejection of ultraromantic progressivism among German composers as well as a reaction against his own earlier milieu: French Impressionism and Russian nationalism.

Stravinsky's Octet (1922–23) was one of his earliest masterpieces in this new style. The work will illustrate what writers of the 1920s often referred to as the "international neoclassical style," an idiom associated with Stravinsky and younger French composers characterized by a detached coolness, regular or motoric rhythm, linear texture, hard or percussive sonority, classical forms, and modernistic dissonance and nontraditional tonality. It will also show that neoclassicism was at first primarily a rebellion against turn-of-the-century romanticism, rather than an attempt to revive earlier musical traditions. This three-movement work is scored for flute, clarinet, and pairs of bassoons, trumpets, and trombones, a medium that reflects Stravinsky's predilection at this time for small ensembles. His choice of woodwinds and brass rather than strings is also typical of his early neoclassical music. The winds provide Stravinsky with a clear, hard, and objective sonority, which conformed to the image he intended his music to convey. "My Octuor is made for an ensemble of wind instruments," he writes in the article "Some Ideas about my Octuor [Octet]" (1924). "Wind instruments seem to me to be more apt to render a certain rigidity of the form I had in mind than other instruments—the string instruments, for example, which are less cold and more vague."

In its linearity and rhythmic clarity, the Octet forms a marked contrast to the hyperemotive music of German and Austrian composers at the turn of the century as well as to the refined and evocative textures of the French Impressionists. "My Octuor is not an 'emotive' work, but a musical composition based on objective elements which are sufficient in themselves," he writes.

In order to dispel more completely the mists of romanticism, Stravinsky applies classical forms of absolute music: sonata form in the first movement, theme and variations in the second, rondo in the third, fugue in part of the second movement, and, in general, a terse and economic polyphony.

The centerpiece of the composition is the theme and variations. The theme (rehearsal 24–26) is entirely octatonic, and it does not have a strongly asserted keynote. The underlying chords begin and end with triads on D, and the theme concludes with a cadential progression from dominant to tonic in D major. Throughout the Octet, such dominant–tonic progressions serve to connect structural elements and to mark cadences, but they do not create traditional tonality nor do they organize large spans of the music.

The variations that follow all contain the theme in a recognizable though varied form. The first accompanies the theme by what the composer called "ribbons of scales"—a flurry of diatonic scales departing from different tonics. This variation returns as a refrain before the third and fifth variations. Each of the other variations takes on a different character: the second is a march, the third a waltz, the fourth a cancan, and the last a solemn fugue.

Beginning with the opera-oratorio *Oedipus rex* (1926–27), Stravinsky returned to a larger orchestra and a more conventional style of orchestration in which the string ensemble is again prominent. His music from this time emphasizes symphonic and dramatic genres.

The Mass (1944–48) reverts to a small wind orchestra, which accompanies a mixed chorus using children's voices on the higher parts. Although Stravinsky was a communicant of the Russian

Orthodox Church from 1926, the music of his neoclassical years is overwhelmingly secular. He was provoked to write a concerted Latin Mass, as he relates in *Expositions and Developments*, by his desire to provide music for use in the Christian liturgy which would be untainted by theatricality:

> Why, then, did I compose a Roman Catholic Mass? Because I wanted my *Mass* to be used liturgically, an outright impossibility so far as the Russian Church was concerned, as Orthodox tradition proscribes musical instruments in its services—and as I can endure unaccompanied singing in only the most harmonically primitive music.... My *Mass* was partly provoked by some Masses of Mozart that I found in a second-hand music store in Los Angeles in 1942 or 1943. As I played through these rococo-operatic sweets-of-sin, I knew I had to write a Mass of my own, but a real one. Incidentally, I heard Machaut's *Mass* for the first time a year after mine was composed, and I was not influenced in my *Mass* by any "old" music whatever, or guided by any example.

Although Stravinsky denies having adopted any models of earlier music, the treatment of voices is highly reminiscent of medieval and Renaissance polyphony. An alternation of imitative and homophonic textures suggests the Renaissance Mass, and the pungent alternation of perfect and imperfect consonances between the solo voices in the Gloria is reminiscent of harmonies in medieval organum.

The Credo (Anthology no. 23) stands as the centerpiece of this work. Its lengthy text is set as choral declamation where cadences and rests closely follow the punctuation and meaning of the words. Its declamatory rhythm conforms to the rhythm of the Latin words as they might be spoken. The composer remarked, "In making the musical setting of the Credo, I wished only to preserve the text in a special way. One composes a march to facilitate marching men; so with my Credo I hope to provide an aid to the text. The Credo is the longest movement. There is much to believe."

In the traditional manner of polyphonic Credos, the initial phrase "Credo in unum deum" ("I believe in one God") is sung in Gregorian chant by the celebrant. The composer specified the so-called "authentic" Credo melody (*Liber usualis*, p. 64, no. 1) for this purpose. The music that follows is unified by the recurrence of two prominent tetrachords, both of which are subsets of diatonic scales and which themselves contain triads. The first, designated in Example 10-1 as tetrachord A, is heard as the initial chord. It is scored so as to emphasize the root-position triad (E minor) which it contains. This chord is most prominent at the beginning and end of the movement.

The second tetrachord (tetrachord B in Example 10-1) is the familiar major seventh, based upon the root D in most occurrences. It

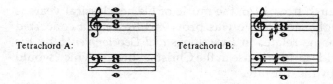

Tetrachord A: Tetrachord B:

Example 10-1. Cadential tetrachords in the Credo of Stravinsky's Mass.

characterizes the middle of the Credo, where it is heard at virtually all cadences. It is introduced in the bar before rehearsal 27.

The contrast of these two sonorities and the concentric tonal motion about E give the Credo a freely ternary form, which is diagrammed in Example 10-2. The *a cappella* fugato of the Amen relates subtly to tetra-chord B, which is equivalent to the set of pitches upon which the voices enter: F A C E. The music comes to a rest on the bass note G so that the tonal motion of the entire movement spans the same interval (E to G) heard in reverse order at the opening of the celebrant's chant.

An article published in 1920 by the critic Henri Collet refers to a group of younger French composers as the "Six" and relates their music to the influence of Erik Satie. The composers whom Collet cites are Darius Milhaud, Francis Poulenc, Georges Auric, Arthur Honegger, Germaine Tailleferre, and Louis Durey. Despite consid-erable differences in their music, they accepted this common desig-nation and collaborated for several years. Their mentors were Satie and Cocteau, with whom they shared the ideal of a simplified, anti-Wagnerian, and anti-Impressionistic music. The Six were not mod-ernists. In fact, modernism was decried in their broadsheet *Le Coq* as a danger second only to the overrefinement of Impressionism.

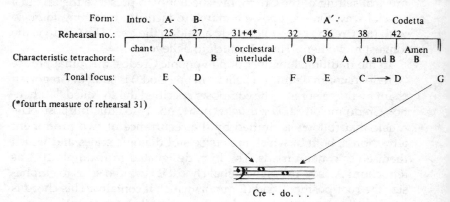

Example 10-2. Form and harmonic recurrence in the Credo of Stravinsky's Mass.

As these composers increasingly asserted their own artistic person-alities, their music generally remained in the neoclassical vein with an emphasis on melody, clear lines and textures, conventional forms, and diatonic or triadic sonorities. The music of Durey and Tailleferre remains relatively obscure, and Auric soon devoted himself to composing for film. Milhaud was the most innovative figure in the group; his application of polytonality and of jazz and Latin rhythms will be described at the end of this chapter. Although different in background and artistic personality, Poulenc and Honegger clearly represent the spirit of neoclassicism among native French composers between the world wars.

The music of Francis Poulenc (1899–1963) during the 1920s was closely allied to the direction of Satie and Cocteau in its eclecticism, witty simplicity, and spirit of the music hall. In the later 1920s his mature style emerged in a succession of songs for voice and piano, a medium in which he was also active as accompanist to the singer Pierre Bernac. Poulenc's songs are among the most distinguished twentieth-century contributions to this genre. They continue the tra-dition of the nineteenth-century French *mélodie*, a genre inspired by the lieder of Schubert and Schumann. Although they occasionally delve into modern dissonant harmonies and liberated tonal plans, their style conforms primarily to the romantic song.

Tel jour, telle nuit (1936–37), a cycle of nine songs drawing upon verse by Paul Eluard (1895–1952), shows Poulenc's great ability to elu-cidate modern poetry by musical means. Eluard's surrealistic writings were a continuing inspiration to Poulenc during the last thirty years of his life. The nine works selected by Poulenc for *Tel jour, telle nuit* forgo logical narrative in favor of free expression of the poet's thought and emotion. Poems celebrating love ("Je n'ai envie que t'aimer" and "Nous avons fait la nuit") alternate with verses depicting loneliness ("Le front comme un drapeau perdu"), joy ("Bonne journée"), vio-lence ("Figure de force brûlante et farouche"), and dreams ("Une ruine coquille vide"). Although these texts are not unified by a com-mon theme, Poulenc shapes them into a cycle by returning in the last song to the key and accompanimental figuration of the first.

The music in this cycle is unusually free in its handling of both tonality and dissonance. As in most of Poulenc's vocal music, an underlying sadness and nostalgia well up beneath its surface. His settings are finely tailored to the poetic structures and images. To his collaborator Pierre Bernac he said, "I recite the poem to myself many times. I listen, I search for the traps, at times I underline the text in red at the difficult spots. I note the breathing places, I try to discover the inner rhythm from a line which is not necessarily the

FRANCIS POULENC
(*Paris, 1899–Paris, 1963*)

Poulenc has written that his greatest childhood experiences in music were first hearings of works by Debussy and Schubert. Both composers would later provide models for his own work. He did not attend a conservatory; instead, he studied piano privately with Ricardo Viñes and, after his initial successes as a composer, composition with Charles Koechlin (1921–24). His early works are modeled on those of Erik Satie, but in the 1920s and 1930s his interest turned increasingly to the composition of songs, which were allied in style to French and German models of the nineteenth century.

He lived primarily in Paris, and he toured throughout Europe as accompanist to the singer Pierre Bernac. His later works include larger genres such as opera and dramatic monologues.

SELECTED WORKS

Operas. *Les mamelles de Tirésias* (1944), *Dialogues des carmélites* (1955), *La voix humaine* (1958).
Ballets. *Les biches* (1923), *Aubade* (1929).
Concertos. *Concert champêtre* (harpsichord, 1928); concertos for two pianos (1932), organ (1938), piano (1949).
Chamber Music. Sonatas for clarinet and bassoon (1922); horn, trombone, and trumpet (1922); violin (1943); cello (1948); two pianos (1953); flute (1956); oboe (1962); clarinet (1962).
Songs. Over 100 songs on texts by Max Jacob, Paul Eluard, Guillaume Apollinaire, and others.
Choral Music. Mass in G (1937), Motets (1939), *La figure humaine* (1943), Stabat mater (1950), Gloria (1959).

first. Next I try to set it to music, bearing in mind the different densities of the piano accompaniment" (from Pierre Bernac, *Francis Poulenc*, trans. Winifred Radford [New York, 1977], p. 39).

Arthur Honegger (1892–1955) was of a different artistic temperament from any of the other figures of the Six. His parents were Swiss and he proudly maintained Swiss citizenship throughout his life. He was educated in Zurich, where he developed a great admiration for Wagner and other German modernists. He saw no need for French composers to reject German music, as did Satie and Cocteau. In fact, he had little affinity for Satie, whose irreverent jesting was far from his own serious approach.

Among his better known compositions is the orchestral portrait *Pacific 231*. This work—one of many "mechanistic" pieces of music composed in France in the 1920s—is intended to capture the energy and dynamism of a steam locomotive. His operas and oratorios are his most ambitious works. The oratorio *King David* (1921) was his first success as a composer, and the oratorio *Joan of Arc at the Stake* (1935) enjoyed a huge popularity in France during the 1940s.

Joan of Arc was commissioned by Ida Rubinstein, a Russian expatriate who organized her own ballet company in Paris in 1927. Her commissions also led to Ravel's *Boléro* and Stravinsky's *Baiser de la fée* and *Perséphone*, the last of which shares with *Joan of Arc* a principal role for speaker and mime. *Joan of Arc* was written to a libretto by Paul Claudel, who also took an active part in its musical setting. Claudel's text recounts the life and death of the fifteenth-century heroine Joan of Arc, who resisted English domination of parts of France that had resulted from the Hundred Years War and who promoted the restoration of Charles VII to the French throne. Joan was captured by forces allied to England and turned over to an ecclesiastical court in Rouen to be tried on a charge of witchcraft and heresy. She was burned at the stake in 1431. Joan's legendary bravery and patriotism had a special meaning to the French during the period of German occupation from 1940 to 1944.

Claudel's poem takes the form of a flashback at the moment of Joan's death. At the beginning of the oratorio, she is shown chained to the stake, and her life is recounted by her confessor, Brother Dominic. In the final scene she is comforted by the Virgin Mary as she breaks loose from her fetters and ascends into heaven. Honegger's music is intensely dramatic; indeed, its range of expressive media is more akin to opera than to oratorio. The musical language is likewise diverse: polytriadic effects depict the chaos of the Prologue (added by the composer in 1945 to celebrate France's deliverance from the Germans), and a free, colorful dissonance

ARTHUR HONEGGER
(*Le Havre, 1892–Paris, 1955*)

Honegger was born to a German-Swiss family living in France, and he maintained lifelong contact with musical developments in all three nations. He attended the Zurich Conservatory from 1909 to 1911, where his fondness for the music of Bach and German moderns was strengthened. During the next two years, he was enrolled at the Paris Conservatory, after which he continued to study composition with Charles-Marie Widor and Vincent d'Indy.

In 1920 he became associated with the young French composers called the Six, a group with whom he had little in common. He frequently traveled to Switzerland to promote performances of his music, although he resided primarily in Paris.

SELECTED WORKS

Operas. *Judith* (opera or oratorio, 1925), *Antigone* (1927), *La belle de Moudon* (1933).

Oratorios. *King David* (1921), *Cris du monde* (1931), *Jean d'Arc au bûcher* (1935).

Orchestral Music. Five symphonies (1930–50), *Pastorale d'été* (1920), *Pacific 231* (1923), *Rugby* (1928).

Chamber Music. Three string quartets (1917–37); Sonatinas for clarinet and piano (1922), violin and cello (1932); Sonata for solo violin (1940), *Le cahier romand* (solo piano, 1922).

Miscellaneous. Songs, ballet scores, incidental music, popular songs, film scores.

alternates with simple triadic passages. Joan's child-like purity is captured by the use of folk song. The polyphonic choruses take their departure from those of Bach's *Passion According to St. John* as they depict the frenzied mob accusing Joan of heresy.

In the fourth scene Joan is turned over to a court populated by barnyard animals, playing upon the name of her judge, Cauchon, and the French word for pig, *cochon*. The use here of coarse French and corrupt Latin underscores the hypocrisy of the proceedings, as does Honegger's jazzy, commercial music. The work reaches its dramatic climax in the final scene, "The Burning of Joan of Arc." The chorus at first represents the crowd, denouncing Joan and praising the flames by which she is engulfed. The chorus then becomes an ensemble of angels celebrating her triumph. Joan's role is spoken and mimed, and she is accompanied by the singing of the Virgin Mary, who provides comfort and consolation. The music ends serenely on a D major/minor tetrachord.

GERMAN OBJECTIVITY: STRAUSS AND HINDEMITH

Just as Richard Strauss prefigured Expressionist opera in his *Salome* in 1905, he became a forerunner of postwar German neoclassicism with his opera *Der Rosenkavalier* in 1910. In this work Strauss put behind his foray with the avant-garde and returned to a style combining Mozartean clarity with his innate romantic lyricism.

The libretto of *Der Rosenkavalier* by Hugo von Hofmannsthal is based upon conventions of the seventeenth- and eighteenth-century French farce. Thus it has much in common with Mozart's *Marriage of Figaro*, a work that served both Strauss and Hofmannsthal as a model. The characters and comic situations of both are cut from the same cloth: youthful lovers thwarted at first by lecherous older men, intrigues complicated by disguises, and, in the end, young love winning out over all. Hofmannsthal weaves into this traditional comedy a more profound and touching story: the "Marschallin," Princess of Werdenberg, must endure the passing of her youth and innocence, symbolized by the loss of her lover Octavian to a younger rival.

After the success of *Der Rosenkavalier*, Strauss and Hofmannsthal began work on *Ariadne auf Naxos* (1911–12). Their original conception was most unusual—to interpolate an operatic divertissement dealing with the Greek myth of Ariadne and Theseus into a version of Molière's farce *Le bourgeois gentilhomme*. Strauss composed music for the opera and incidental music for the play. Later the opera was revised as an independent work (1916), and the incidental music was reshaped into an orchestral suite, *Der Bürger als Edelmann* (1920). Strauss's music evokes the atmosphere of the seventeenth century in numerous ways: the orchestra is reduced to chamber proportions, and a piano is used to imitate the harpsichord in accompaniment of recitatives. Strauss also quotes several melodies from the works of Jean-Baptiste Lully (1632–87), who had composed the original incidental music for *Le bourgeois gentilhomme*.

Paul Hindemith (1895–1963) is the greatest German neoclassicist of the years between the world wars. His career is typical of his generation: a youthful period of experimentation gave way shortly after the First World War to a more traditional artistic orientation. In his early music, Hindemith dabbled in many of the experimental approaches to composition of his day: atonality, Expressionism, jazz, parody, and satire. None of these, however, was true to his deeply serious and philosophical nature, which emerged in his music by the mid-1920s.

Hindemith held that music was functional and ethical. Its purpose was to communicate to the musically literate public and play a salutary role in society and culture. It was a composer's moral obligation to defend music's comprehensibility, which in the twentieth century seemed under attack by unrestrained modernity and unnatural abstraction. He was highly critical of atonal or twelve-tone composers, who, "attempting to replace with an apparent rationality what is lacking morally, develop an oversublimated technique which produces images of emotions that are far removed from any emotional experiences a relatively normal human being ever has. In doing so they advocate an esoteric *art pour l'art*, the followers of which can only be emotional imps, monsters, or snobs."

An outcome of his functional conception of art was the composition of what he termed *Gebrauchsmusik* or "useful" music. Such works were intended for students or amateurs, comparable in type to the keyboard sonatas of C. P. E. Bach written for dilettantes or for purposes of teaching. Several of Hindemith's early examples in this genre were published under the title *Music to Sing and to Play: For Amateurs and Music Lovers* (1928). His last major essay in *Gebrauchsmusik* was the *Plöner Musiktag* (1932), which consisted of a cycle of vocal and instrumental pieces to accompany daily student activities at a private school in the town of Plön. Hindemith considered them facile enough for student players and singers, but most are of considerable difficulty, as is virtually all of his music for amateurs.

Hindemith's song cycle *Das Marienleben* (*The Life of Mary*, 1923, rev. 1936–48) was the first important work in his mature style, which German writers typically refer to as "objective" rather than "neoclassical," the latter usually reserved for related developments in France. The text is a cycle of fifteen poems by Rainer Maria Rilke (1875–1926) of the same title. It deals with major events in the life of the Virgin Mary as they are told in Scripture and traditional Christian lore. Rilke fluctuates between simple lyrics and flamboy-

PAUL HINDEMITH
(Hanau, 1895–Frankfurt, 1963)

Hindemith began his musical career as a violinist at the Hoch Konservatorium in Frankfurt. He also received instruction there in composition from Arnold Mendelssohn and Bernhard Sekles. He was concertmaster of the orchestra of the Frankfurt Opera from 1915 to 1923. Between 1921 and 1929 he played viola in the Amar Quartet, an ensemble that he founded and that was devoted to the performance of modern music. He was brought to international attention as a composer by performances of his music at the Donaueschingen Festival.

From 1927 to 1937 he served on the faculty of the Staatliche Hochschule für Musik in Berlin. Here he discovered his great talent for teaching, and his interests broadened to include musical theory and performance of early music. From 1934 until his departure from Europe in 1940, his music was increasingly opposed by Nazi authorities, and, after several trips to Turkey as a musical consultant and a period of exile in Switzerland, he immigrated to America and accepted an appointment at Yale University. In 1951 he began teaching at the University of Zurich and attempted a new career as an orchestral conductor.

SELECTED WORKS

Dramatic Music. Operas: *Cardillac* (1926, rev. 1952), *Mathis der Maler* (1934–35), *Die Harmonie der Welt* (1956–57); ballet: *Nobilissima visione* (1938).

Orchestral Music and Concertos. *Kammermusik* (1921–27: seven works of which the first is for chamber orchestra and the others a cycle of concertos); *Konzertmusik* Opp. 48–50 (1930, three works), *Concerto for Orchestra* (1925); *Philharmonic* Concerto (1932); Symphony *Mathis der Maler* (1934); *Der Schwanendreher* (viola concerto, 1935); Suite *Nobilissima visione* (1938); Concertos for violin (1939), cello (1940), piano (1945), clarinet (1947), horn (1949), organ (1962); *Symphonic Metamorphoses on Themes of Carl Maria von Weber* (1943).

Chamber Music. Six string quartets (1918–45), two string trios (1924–33),
    Ludus tonalis for piano (1942), solo sonatas for orchestral instruments
    and piano, three piano sonatas, Suite "1922."
Songs and Choral Music. *Das Marienleben* (1923, rev. 1936–48), Mass (1963),
    Madrigals for unaccompanied chorus (1958), *Das Unaufhörliche*
    (oratorio, 1931), Six chansons for chorus (1939).
Theoretical Writings. *Unterweisung im Tonsatz*, three vols. 1937, 1939, 1970;
    Vols. 1 and 2 translated as *The Craft of Musical Composition*.

---

ant images. His Marian poems delve intensely into human emotions, ranging from suppressed joy in "Birth of Mary" to anger and
remorse in "Joseph's Suspicion" to self-pity in "Before the Passion."

The cycle is concluded by three poems "On the Death of Mary."
Hindemith's setting of the first of these three (Anthology no. 13) is
an example of the touching simplicity that he allied to Rilke's
poetry. The lengthy text is an account in free verse of Mary's last
moments on earth: her encounter with an angelic messenger, her
final meeting with the Apostles, and the legendary giving away of
her two cloaks.

The music is placidly detached from this dramatic text. The composer made no attempt at word painting or other graphic musical
expressions of the miraculous events of Mary's assumption. By its
very lack of graphic realism, the song captures the abstract unearth-
liness of this phase of Mary's existence. The musical form is that of
the baroque passacaglia—continuous variations upon a five-mea-
sure ground bass. The ground was intended by the composer to
suggest the majesty of Mary's departure. Other neoclassical elements of the setting reside in its rigidly contrapuntal texture, triadic
points of arrival and departure, and regularity of rhythm and phrasing. The continuous motor rhythms, especially apparent in the right
hand of the piano, enhance its relation to baroque music.

The song uses a ternary design, the outer parts variations upon
the ground. This ostinato line moves deliberately through intervals
of the fourth and fifth, typical of the ground bass in baroque music.
Its harmonic implications, however, are not realized in the chords of
the upper voices except at cadences. The upper-voices move instead
in rapidly changing diatonic patterns. The ground ends on the pitch
class G, which functions throughout the song as the main goal of
tonal motion.

The contrasting middle section (mm. 27–58), typical of many
baroque passacaglias, dispenses with the ground, although it continues in the form of continuous variations, now upon two motives

in the right hand of the piano shown in Example 10-3. These figures are varied by changing harmonizations in the piano and by a through-composed vocal line which focuses on the note G. The "tonality" of G is reaffirmed at the end of the song by motion to a concluding G-major triad.

In 1948 Hindemith completed a revision of *Das Marienleben* in which he sought to improve its vocal line and large-scale structure. The opening of the new version of "On the Death of Mary I" shows that the vocal line was completely rewritten to make it more diatonic and to bring its phrasing into agreement with the bass (Example 10-4). The middle section was simplified harmonically as well as being fitted with a new vocal melody.

In the introduction to the revised edition, Hindemith explains a symbolism of keys that guided him in revising the harmonic vocabulary of the entire cycle. Keys (or triadic areas) are used in the revised version to represent characters or spiritual qualities found in Rilke's poetry. These are based upon a central tonality of E, which represents Jesus. The remaining tonal centers are assembled into a series of increasingly distant relationship to E, corresponding to the diminishing importance of the characters or qualities that these keys represent. Closest to E is its dominant B, the symbol of Mary; next is the subdominant A, representing angels; C symbolizes eternity, and so forth through all twelve pitch classes. The G tonality of "On the Death of Mary I" points to idyllic contentment, bringing with it, as the composer writes in the introduction, "a shimmer of lyric softness."

The opera *Mathis der Maler* (*Mathis the Painter*, 1934–35) is Hindemith's masterpiece and the work that vaulted him to international recognition after its suppression by the Third Reich. The text, written by the composer, is a fictionalized account of the life of the painter Matthias (or Mathis) Grünewald (fl. 1500–1530). Using Grünewald's life as a pretext, Hindemith explored a subject of lifelong fascination to him: the role of the artist in culture and society. His work on the score came at the time of his greatest mastery. It was also the beginning of a period of intense concern with a theory of harmony and tonality, which would be formulated in the first

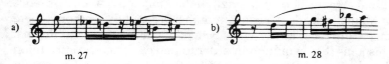

a) m. 27   b) m. 28

Example 10-3. Hindemith, "Vom Tode Mariä I" from *Das Marienleben* (1924 version). © B. Schott's Soehne, Mainz, 1924; © renewed. All rights reserved. Used by permission of European American Music Distributors Corp., sole U.S. agent for B. Schott's Soehne.

Example 10-4. Hindemith, "Vom Tode Mariä I" from *Das Marienleben* (1948 version). © by Schott & Co. Ltd. London 1948. All rights reserved. Used by permission of European American Music Distributors Corp., sole U.S. agent for B. Schott's Soehne.

volume of his *Unterweisung im Tonsatz (Craft of Musical Composition,* 1937) and have a profound influence on his music of the 1940s and 1950s.

The action takes place in Germany at the time of the Peasants' War (1524–25). Mathis is a painter in the service of Albrecht, Cardinal Archbishop of Mainz. He has taken a leave-of-absence from Mainz to work at a convent of the Order of St. Anthony; there he meets the rebel leader Hans Schwalb and his daughter Regina. Mathis joins the revolution in order to make a greater contribution to the people. But he is revulsed by their excesses and narrowly escapes execution after the rebels are put to rout.

In the sixth tableau, Mathis has fled into the forest with Regina, whose father, Schwalb, is dead. After reassuring her about the joys of heaven now partaken of by her father, Mathis has a dream in

Models for *Mathis der Maler*: Matthias Grünewald, *Meeting of St. Anthony and St. Paul the Hermit*, from the Isenheim Altarpiece. (Courtesy of the Musée d'Unterlinden, Colmar.)

which he is the legendary hermit St. Anthony. Mathis relives through Anthony the temptations which, according to legend, the saint endured in the desert. He also witnesses the legendary meeting of Anthony with St. Paul the Hermit, the latter represented in the dream by his patron Albrecht. Paul advises him to put aside his other interests and return to his work as artist, by which he can best serve God and man. The seventh tableau is a denouement in which the elderly artist puts away his painting tools and prepares to die.

Hindemith's characterization of Mathis is in part autobiographical. Mathis, like Hindemith, comes to learn the truly social and ethical purpose of art, which, far from being a diversion, is fundamental to man's higher nature.

Much of the scenery, text, and music of this opera was inspired by Grünewald's masterpiece: a series of nine altar paintings for the Order of St. Anthony in Isenheim, where the painter worked for a period early in the sixteenth century. Grünewald's polyptych portrays events in the lives of Christ and St. Anthony and a mannered "Concert of Angels" which lends its name to the overture of the opera. The paintings are now found in the Musée d'Unterlinden in Colmar, France, where they were studied by Hindemith during his work on the libretto.

In the panel depicting the meeting of Anthony and Paul (see illustration), the artist may have modeled the figure of St. Anthony upon his patron at the convent, Guido Guesi. The figure of St. Paul may be a self-portrait of Grünewald. Hindemith dramatized this iconography in the third scene of the sixth tableau, but with a reversal of roles, as he has Mathis imagine that he is Anthony, and his patron Albrecht appears as St. Paul. The symbolism is carried to a still higher level since Anthony (Mathis) also represents the composer Hindemith and, by implication, all artists.

The third scene of the sixth tableau is the climax of the opera, as Anthony, under the tutelage of St. Paul, comes to accept the importance of his creative work. Hindemith notes in the score that the scenery is to resemble Grünewald's painting of this legendary meeting. The scene is divided into four sections with an introduction:

Introduction: dialogue in recitative. Anthony tells Paul of the depths of his despair;

1. Paul's homily: arioso with refrain (six measures before rehearsal 85 to rehearsal G). Paul advises Anthony to return to his former profession.
2. Paul's peroration: aria in bar form and codetta (rehearsal G to rehearsal 97). Through artistic creativity, the individual is subsumed by service to God and man.

3. Epilogue: duet (four measures before rehearsal 98 to two measures before rehearsal 102). Man cannot escape his earthly calling, through which he best recognizes and appreciates heavenly power.
4. Coda: duet. Alleluia (a quotation of the Alleluia for the Feast of Corpus Christi).

The aria (rehearsal G) makes use of the traditional German "bar" form A A' B, thus accenting certain nationalistic overtones in the libretto; elsewhere in the opera the bar form is associated with German folk music. The following diagram of the aria also shows Hindemith's use of focal triads to articulate the aria's closed form:

Paul's Aria:	A–	A'–	B–	Codetta
Rehearsal:	G	95–2*	96–2	97
Triadic Focus:	D♭	D♭	E	(D♭)

(* two measures before rehearsal 95)

The key of D♭ is the central tonality of the entire opera, heard at the beginning of the first tableau and at the conclusion of the seventh. But in the sixth tableau it has a secondary role as lower neighbor to the triadic area of D, to which the music turns without break at the beginning of the duet. The magnificent coda of the duet, which paraphrases the Gregorian Alleluia for the Feast of Corpus Christi, ends on a luminous D-major triad (Example 10-5).

Hindemith's first compositional work on *Mathis der Maler* took the form of an orchestral suite, the Symphony *Mathis der Maler*. This piece received its premier performance in 1934 and served to prepare for a staging of the entire opera that was blocked at the eleventh hour by Nazi opposition. The three movements of the Symphony are titled "Concert of Angels" (later used as prelude to the opera and in music of the first scene of the sixth tableau), "Entombment" (used as an interlude in the seventh tableau), and "Temptation of St. Anthony" (used in the second scene of the sixth tableau). The music of the "Alleluia" at the end of the sixth tableau is added to form the conclusion of the Symphony.

TRADITIONALISM IN ENGLAND: BRITTEN AND TIPPETT

English composers did not in general participate in the European avant-garde of the first two decades of the century. The conservatively classical language popular there during the interwar period was an uninterrupted continuation of the romantic tradition brought into the twentieth century by composers such as Edward

Example 10-5. Hindemith, *Mathis der Maler*, sixth tableau. © B. Schott's Soehne, Mainz, 1935; renewed 1963. Used by permission of European American Music Distributors Corp., sole U.S. agents for B. Schott's Soehne.

Elgar and Frederick Delius. Their musical idiom was carried on by William Walton, Gustav Holst, and Ralph Vaughan Williams, none of whom placed primary emphasis on innovation or stylistic experiment.

The classical-romantic tradition of English music was carried to its greatest heights in the twentieth century by Benjamin Britten (1913–76). His music grew from the same soil as that of Vaughan Williams. Both used English folk song and both found inspiration in the music of Purcell and his English predecessors. Neither composer dispensed completely with traditional harmony, tonality, or concepts of form. But Britten went far beyond Vaughan Williams in establishing an original musical language within an essentially traditional framework.

Britten's music is primarily vocal and dramatic. His eleven operas are the greatest contributions to English-language opera since Purcell, and their number is augmented by several dramatic pieces for churches, numerous collections of songs, and a repertory

BENJAMIN BRITTEN
(*Lowestoft, Suffolk, 1913–
Aldeburgh, 1976*)

Britten began the study of composition with Frank Bridge, and he continued with John Ireland at the Royal College of Music in London from 1930 to 1934. Dismayed by the prospect of European hostilities, he immigrated in 1939 to Canada, later moving to the United States, where he remained until 1942.

After the end of World War II, he settled permanently in his native Suffolk. In 1948 he collaborated with the singer Peter Pears and writer Eric Crozier to found the Aldeburgh Festival, at which many of his works subsequently received their first performance. Until he was prevented by illness, Britten was active as a pianist and conductor, specializing in performances of his own music.

SELECTED WORKS

Operas and Other Dramatic Works. Operas: *Paul Bunyan* (1941, rev. 1976), *Peter Grimes* (1944–45), *Rape of Lucretia* (1946), *Albert Herring* (1947), *Let's Make an Opera* (including the opera *The Little Sweep*, 1949), *Billy Budd* (1951), *Gloriana* (1953), *Turn of the Screw* (1954), *A Midsummer Night's Dream* (1960), *Owen Wingrave* (1970), *Death in Venice* (1973). Dramatic works intended for performance in churches: *Noye's Fludde* (1957), *Curlew River* (1964), *Burning Fiery Furnace* (1966), *Prodigal Son* (1968).
Orchestral Music. *Sinfonietta* (1933), *Sinfonia da requiem* (1940), *Young Person's Guide to the Orchestra* (1946).
Concertos. Piano Concerto (1938, rev. 1945), Violin Concerto (1939, rev. 1958), Symphony for Cello and Orchestra (1963).
Chamber Music. Three string quartets (1941, 1945, 1975; also an early string quartet in D, 1931), Cello Sonata in C (1961), Suites for Cello (1964, 1967, 1972).
Songs and Song Cycles. *Our Hunting Fathers* (1936), *Les illuminations* (1939), *Seven Sonnets of Michelangelo* (1940), *Serenade* (1943), *Holy Sonnets of John Donne* (1945), *Songs and Proverbs of William Blake* (1965), *A Birthday Hansel* (1975).

Choral Music. *A Boy Was Born* (1933), *Ceremony of Carols* (1942), *Rejoice in the Lamb* (1943), *Saint Nicolas* (1948), *Spring Symphony* (1949), Missa brevis in D (1959), *War Requiem* (1961).

of choral music that is among the greatest of this century. His choice of texts was exceedingly broad, including poetry in Italian, French, and German as well as English verse from all eras. His religious music draws upon biblical stories, English carols and hymns, medieval lyrics, and Latin texts.

Britten's music before the 1950s continued the classicizing directions of Vaughan Williams. It was largely diatonic and triadic, and it expressed key in novel ways. His works created easily recognizable forms by refrains, strophic recurrences, and other repetitive patterns. Beginning with the opera *Billy Budd* (1951), Britten spoke with a more dissonant, nontriadic vocabulary and in more concentrated forms. His opera *Turn of the Screw* (1954) and most of his later works reflect a singular adaptation of aspects of the twelve-tone method.

Britten's early style is exemplified by the Serenade for Tenor, Horn and Strings Op. 31 (1943). The six songs of this cycle are framed by a Prologue for valveless French horn, repeated offstage as a concluding Epilogue. The poetry ranges from an anonymous medieval lyric to verses by Charles Cotton, Tennyson, Blake, Ben Jonson, and Keats. These texts are linked by references to night, death, love, and evil—all recurrent themes and images in Britten's music. Each of the songs utilizes a repetitive form and each focuses upon some triadic goal which acts as a tonic key.

The Dirge found as the fourth song of the Serenade (Anthology no. 14) sets a chillingly realistic poem of the fifteenth century in Scottish dialect (also used by Stravinsky in his Cantata of 1952). It tells of the horrors of hell that await those who have lacked Christian charity. Its nine stanzas are set vocally by a recurrent ostinato which outlines a G-minor triad. Just as the Last Judgment will be inexorable and pitiless, the ostinato relentlessly disregards the tortured plaint of the accompanying orchestral fugue.

Voice and orchestra are, however, interrelated by the principal motive of the ostinato—a rising and falling semitone shown in brackets in Example 10-6. The semitone figure is duplicated over a longer span of time by tonal motion underpinning the orchestral music. The orchestra begins on an E♭ triad; at the climax of the movement (rehearsal 17) it arrives on E, and it returns to E♭ for the concluding verse (rehearsal 20).

Example 10-6.   Britten, Serenade for Tenor, Horn and Strings Op. 31, Dirge. Copyright 1944 in U.S.A. by Hawkes & Son (London) Ltd. Renewed 1981. Reprinted by permission of Boosey & Hawkes, Inc.

Britten's first important opera was *Peter Grimes* (1944–45). Its central character, Peter Grimes, is a maladjusted loner who cannot adapt to society and who is finally destroyed by his environment. Like Wozzeck, Petrushka, and Schoenberg's Pierrot, he embodies the recurrent twentieth-century dramatic image of the antihero. The libretto of *Peter Grimes* was written by Montagu Slater, based on the poem *Borough* (1810) by George Crabbe. Grimes is a fisherman in a coastal village in England about 1830. He seeks respect from the townspeople and is distracted by their gossip. As the Prologue opens he is facing an inquest regarding the death of an apprentice who perished during a fishing expedition. Although the death is ruled accidental, Grimes is warned to take no other boys as apprentices.

Peter is supported by Ellen Orford, a widow and former schoolteacher, and by Balstrode, a retired fisherman. Ellen arranges for Grimes to obtain another apprentice, as she believes that only with such assistance can he be successful in his trade and establish a normal existence. But the townsfolk suspect that he is abusing his new assistant, and the men menacingly approach his cottage atop a cliff. Grimes forces the boy out a back door and down the steep cliff to his boat, but the apprentice loses his step and falls to his death.

After several days Grimes returns, totally deranged. He is met by Ellen and Balstrode; the latter tells him that he must take his boat to sea and scuttle it, committing suicide. Ellen is horrified, but Grimes does as Balstrode commands. As Grimes dies, the townspeople are seen once again about their daily activities.

The story can be understood on several levels. Most obvious among them is Grimes's implicit homosexuality, a theme addressed many times by Britten, most explicitly in his operatic adaptation of Thomas Mann's *Death in Venice* (1973). In this interpretation Ellen represents a "legitimate" heterosexual alliance, which Grimes desires alternately with a compulsion for boys, the latter invariably proving destructive. Balstrode is his conscience. He tries to put Grimes's aberrations in the best light until Grimes's split personality makes suicide appear the only alternative.

On a more abstract level, Grimes represents a twentieth-century everyman, torn between good and evil, compassion and brutality, acceptance and rebellion, society and isolation. He is destroyed by the conflicting, schizophrenic forces within his very nature and within society.

The opera is divided into a Prologue and three acts, each of two scenes. Orchestral interludes link these seven parts. The acts and scenes are made up from distinct (though connected) subsections or numbers, which include recitatives, arias, large ensembles, and choruses. The music within a number may be a concise closed form (as in the duet of the nieces, Act 1, rehearsal 67) or a through-composed *scena*.

Although Britten generally eschewed Wagnerian through composition, he makes important use of recurrent motives and recurrent sections to underscore parallelisms in the drama. A striking example is the return of the "dawn music" of Act 1, scene 1, at the end of the opera (from rehearsal 53), as Grimes's boat is seen sinking far at sea while the townspeople go about their daily routines.

The music is predominantly diatonic and triadic, freely creating keys or areas of triadic focus. These tonalities have dramatic functions. The opposition of keys in sharps and those in flats depicts the dichotomies that Grimes represents. This juxtaposition of flats and sharps is presented in the opening phrase of the opera (Example 10-7), which begins on a Bb triad but moves to an E-major collection at its end. The duet of Ellen and Peter at the end of the Prologue (rehearsal 9) pits Ellen's optimism (four sharps: E major) against Peter's resentment (four flats: F minor). At the end of the duet, however, he accepts her friendship and moves into her key of E.

At the beginning of the climactic second scene of Act 3 (rehearsal 47), Grimes's derangement is depicted by the bitriadic conjunction of D-seventh chords in the chorus with the Eb by which the tuba evokes a fog horn. Peter's music wanders between elements of both chords, showing that his schizophrenia is by then complete.

Example 10-7.   Britten, *Peter Grimes.* Vocal score by Erwin Stein Copyright 1945 in U.S.A. by Boosey and Hawkes Ltd. Renewed 1972. Reprinted by permission of Boosey & Hawkes, Inc.

Michael Tippett (1905–) worked along the same general lines as Britten during the earlier part of his career. His music prior to about 1945 was vigorously rhythmic and contrapuntal with an extended triadic tonality organizing large passages. He made poignant use of Negro spirituals in his oratorio *Child of Our Time* (1941). His works of the 1960s reflect more innovative trends in music after the Second World War in their greater chromaticism, dissonance, and conciseness. Several of these more recent pieces imitate jazz, and others (such as his *Songs for Dov*) are quotation collages.

POPULAR MUSIC OF THE NEW WORLD AND THE NEOCLASSICAL STYLE

Just at the time following World War I that the neoclassical rebellion against romanticism was being waged, dance music and jazz from the United States and Latin America poured into Europe, capturing the attention of general audiences as well as serious composers. In Paris jazz was heard from visiting American bands, who were eagerly joined by native musicians. The resourceful French pianist Jean Wiéner played jazz with the American Vance Lowry at the bar La Gaya, to which French composers of the 1920s flocked. Wiéner organized concerts in which new serious music alternated with authentic jazz. Interest in jazz among the leading younger composers was especially keen because popular music promised to be a powerful ally of their new idiom: it was entertaining, lifelike, direct—the perfect antidote to the dismal aftermath of war and to the waning excesses of romanticism.

Jazzlike genres, including ragtime, blues, New Orleans style jazz, and dance music, became a fund of new musical ideas that were readily drawn upon by neoclassical composers throughout the world. Ragtime is a style characterized by a syncopated melodic line with an accompaniment in regular rhythm. The term is usually applied to a genre of piano music akin to a slow march in its duple meter, multithematic and multisectional form, and percussive treatment of the instrument. Such "rags" enjoyed great popularity in America from about 1890 to 1915. Unlike early improvised jazz they were composed and published as sheet music.

A blues was originally an improvised African-American folksong that was constructed according to a strict plan. Each stanza of text had three lines: the second line simply repeated the first and the third commented upon or resolved a problem stated in the first two. The music consisted of a chain of variations upon the tune of the first stanza, which was supported by an accompaniment with an unvarying harmonic progression that moved through chords of the tonic, subdominant, and dominant. The singer typically slid between tones or expressively bent certain scale degrees downward by a semitone: lowering the third, fifth, and seventh degrees in major mode was especially common, and these altered tones came to be known as "blue notes." By the turn of the twentieth century, the blues form and style was taken over by instrumental ensembles and often used for dancing.

Unlike rags and blues, New Orleans jazz is a style rather than a genre. Its most characteristic feature is its medium: a small band of five to seven players, divided into two groups. One group (typically cornet, clarinet, and trombone) played the melodic material and the other (often piano, drums, banjo, string bass, or tuba), the accompaniment. Most of the New Orleans bands performed entirely by group improvisation, which led to intricate polyphonic textures.

In the 1920s classical composers throughout Europe and America imitated elements of jazz. Musicians in France had a special affinity for it. Satie wrote a ragtime in his ballet *Parade* in 1917; Stravinsky included both a ragtime and a tango (an Argentinian dance) in *L'histoire du soldat* (1918), which was shortly followed by his *Rag-Time* (for chamber orchestra, 1918) and *Piano-Rag-Music* (1919). Ravel imitated blues and ragtime in several works, as did the younger composers Honegger, Poulenc, and Auric and the Czech expatriate Bohuslav Martinů (1890–1959). Darius Milhaud (1892–1974) made especially imaginative adaptations of American jazz and Latin American popular dances. These will illustrate the natural alliance between popular music and the spirit of neoclassicism. Milhaud's knowledge of the music of Latin America was born in 1917 and 1918, when he served as an aide to the writer and diplomat Paul Claudel in Rio de Janeiro. "I was fascinated by the rhythms of this popular Brazilian music," he wrote in his autobiography *Notes Without Music*. "There was an imperceptible pause in the syncopation, a careless catch in the breath, a slight hiatus that I found very difficult to grasp. So I bought a lot of maxixes and tangos and tried to play them with their syncopated rhythms, which run from one hand to the other. At last my efforts were rewarded and I could both play and analyze this typically Brazilian subtlety."

The rhythms of the *maxixe*, samba, and the Argentinian tango are captured in his piano dances *Saudades do Brazil* (*Longing for Brazil*, 1920). Each of these is named for a place near Rio, and, in addition to their allusions to Latin American dance rhythms, each is an example of polytonality (see Chapter 3). "Botafogo" (Anthology no. 5) illustrates the unmannered spontaneity that Milhaud derived from Brazilian dances. The piece has the slow and lyrical quality of the *max-*

DARIUS MILHAUD
(*Aix-en-Provence, 1892–
Geneva, 1974*)

A youthful enthusiasm for the music of Debussy led Milhaud to embark upon the career of a musician. He studied at the Conservatory in Paris from 1909 to 1912, where he was in the counterpoint class of André Gédalge and the composition class of Charles Widor. He was secretary to the French writer and diplomat Paul Claudel, in whose service he sojourned in Brazil from 1917 to 1918 and later traveled to Scandinavia and England. He collaborated with Claudel on the ballet *L'homme et son désir* and other dramatic or vocal works.

In the early 1920s he was active with a group of young Parisian composers who had been dubbed the Six. His music was the most experimental of this group, as it delved into polytonality, adaptations of jazz, and other modernistic directions. He later collaborated with Paul Hindemith in the organization of music festivals in Baden-Baden and Berlin.

He immigrated to the United States in 1940 and taught at Mills College; in 1947 he returned to France to accept an appointment to the faculty of the Conservatory. Despite crippling arthritis, he frequently returned to America, where he taught at Tanglewood, Music Academy of the West, and Aspen.

SELECTED WORKS

Operas. *Le pauvre matelot* (1926), *Christophe Colomb* (1928), *Médée* (1938), *Maximilien* (1932), *Bolivar* (1943), *La mère coupable* (1964).
Ballets. *L'homme et son désir* (1917), *La création du monde* (1923), *Le train bleu* (1924).
Orchestral Music. Thirteen symphonies (1940–65), *Suite provençale* (1937), *Suite française*, (band 1945); concertos for diverse instruments.
Chamber Music. Eighteen string quartets, sonatas for diverse instruments.
Piano Music. *Le boeuf sur le toit* (piano duet, 1919, later rev. as ballet music), *Saudades do Brazil* (two books, 1920), *Scaramouche* (1939, two pianos).
Choral Music. *The Orestes Trilogy of Aeschylus: Agamemnon* (1913), *Les choéphores* (1915), *Euménides* (1916); *La sagesse* (1935), Jewish Sacred Service (1947), *Pacem in terris* (1963).

ixe or *lundú*. It is divided harmonically into two strata corresponding to the two hands, of which the right hand carries the melody. The middle section (mm. 27–42) contrasts with the outer ones by a change of tempo, figuration, and harmony. Here the two hands each state different pentatonic collections, the left hand confined to the black keys and the right hand mainly on the white. The outer sections, on the contrary, superimpose different diatonic scales (F minor and F♯ minor).

After the war Milhaud became familiar with ragtime and other popular American dance music, which he imitated in his "Caramel mou" for voice, dancer, and jazz ensemble. He did not experience true jazz until he visited Harlem in 1922. "The music I heard was absolutely different from anything I had ever heard before, and it was a revelation to me," he wrote in his autobiography. "Against the beat of the drums the melodic line criss-crossed in a breathless pattern of broken and twisted rhythms."

His recollections of improvised jazz were put to use in his ballet *La création du monde* (*Creation of the World*, 1923), written for the Swedish Ballet to a scenario by Blaise Cendrars. The story has obvious connections with Stravinsky's ballet *Rite of Spring*, which had caused a sensation in Paris a decade earlier. The setting is Africa, which for Milhaud made the use of jazz all the more appropriate. "There can be no doubt that the origin of jazz music is to be sought among the Negroes," he wrote in the article "The Jazz Band and Negro Music." "Primitive African qualities have kept their place deep in the nature of the American Negro and it is here that we find the origin of the tremendous rhythmic force as well as the expressive melodies born of inspiration which oppressed races alone can produce."

By the later 1920s, jazz had lost its appeal for Milhaud, as it had for many of the French composers who had earlier relished its vitality. Milhaud himself set out in several new directions. After this time his music often fell back upon a pleasant tune and comfortable rhythm suggestive of popular music, but lacking the "broken and twisted rhythms" that gave works such as *Création du monde* their distinctive power.

Musicians in Germany and Austria also adapted jazz idioms, although not always as ingenuously as their French counterparts. Ernst Krenek caused a sensation with his jazz opera *Jonny spielt auf* (1926), and the jazz band was imitated by onstage musicians in Berg's *Lulu*. The finale of Paul Hindemith's Piano Suite "1922" is a ragtime, where the composer instructs the player, "Pay no heed to what you learned in your piano lessons; don't worry whether the D♭ is played with the fourth or sixth finger. Play this piece wildly, but always strictly in tempo, like a machine. Consider the piano as a kind of percussion instrument and treat it accordingly." Hindemith wittily manipulates the percussive style of American ragtime, its synco-pated sixteenth-note rhythms, and its form (the customary trio enters at measure 51, a reprise at measure 80). But his treatment is other-wise a heavy parody—it is dense in texture and alternates ponder-ously between fourth chords and bitriadic formations. His ragtime in fact gives ample testimony to his distaste for popular music as art. In 1920 he wrote to his publisher Willi Strecker, "Would you be inter-ested in publishing foxtrots, Bostons, ragtimes and other junk? When I run out of any decent ideas I always write such things."

An especially important German adaptation of American popu-lar music was made by Kurt Weill (1900–50) in *Die Dreigroschenoper* (The Threepenny Opera, 1928), based on a text by Bertolt Brecht and Elisabeth Hauptmann that is itself an adaptation of John Gay's *Beggar's Opera* (1728). True to the spirit of neoclassicism, the work revives an earlier musical genre—*Singspiel* (or its English equiva-lent, ballad opera)—which it transforms by adding songs in the style of Tin Pan Alley and by music that is mildly modernistic. The orchestration, for example, is Stravinskian in its small proportions and emphasis on winds and brass, and the tonal plan of some of the music is more unstable than is the norm for popular music.

The story of the opera is pure social satire, a parody implying that modern society is thoroughly hypocritical and corrupt. Following an Overture, the opera consists of a succession of songs, one of which, the "Moritat vom Mackie Messer" (Ballad of Mack the Knife) has lived on as a true popular song. In one important respect, this work is entirely different from most other neoclassical pieces that appropriate jazz or popular musical styles. Weill not only meant to draw upon an existing popular style, but also to make the work popular, to make it entertaining for and understood by the public at large. In his essay "Opera—Where To?" (1929) he draws a fine distinction between artis-tic and popular music: the music of operas like *Die Dreigroschenoper* should not be popular per se, he writes. It should maintain the values of "high art," but at the same time it must have the same effect and communicability of popular music. In this distinction Weill has touched upon one of the central aesthetic issues of the modern period: the relationship between high and popular art. His conception of this relationship, which is to question any a priori distinction between the two, looks forward to the 1980s and 1990s when a blurring of the dis-tinction again became relevant to the mainstream of music.

Neoclassicism was a worldwide phenomenon that was not lim-ited to a few European countries. It found an especially fertile ground on which to grow in the United States, to which we turn in the next chapter.

BIBLIOGRAPHY

Neoclassicism as a style period in twentieth-century music is addressed in Scott Messing's *Neoclassicism in Music: From the Genesis of the Concept Through the Schoenberg/Stravinsky Polemic* (Ann Arbor, 1987). In his book *Remaking the Past: Musical Modernism and the Influence of the Tonal Tradition* (Cambridge, Mass., 1990), Joseph Straus deals broadly with aesthetic and technical questions raised by the reinterpretation of earlier music.

The bibliography to Chapter 8 recounts representative writings by and about Stravinsky. Stravinsky's essay "Some Ideas about My Octuor" (1924) is reprinted in Eric Walter White, *Stravinsky: The Composer and his Works* (Berkeley, 1979), Appendix A. Excellent studies of Poulenc have been written by Keith W. Daniel (*Francis Poulenc: His Artistic Development and Musical Style*, Ann Arbor, 1982) and Wilfrid Mellers (*Francis Poulenc*, Oxford, 1993). Arthur Honegger's *I Am a Composer* (London, 1966) is mainly a polemic on the lack of interest shown in modern music. Darius Milhaud's fascinating autobiography, written in 1949, is entitled *Notes Without Music* (London, 1952); also see the general study by Paul Collaer, *Darius Milhaud* (San Francisco, 1988). Paul Meylan's German-language study *Arthur Honegger* (Frauenfeld, 1970) gives untechnical descriptions of his works that will be useful to readers of German.

Paul Hindemith's *A Composer's World* (Garden City, N.Y., 1961)—based on lectures given in 1949 and 1950—is a detailed presentation of his aesthetic; it is the source of all quotations attributed to Hindemith in this chapter, unless otherwise indicated. Hindemith's music is discussed in concise but informative fashion in Ian Kemp's *Hindemith* (London, 1970), and his life is traced by Geoffrey Skelton in *Paul Hindemith: The Man Behind the Music* (New York, 1975). A detailed technical analysis, emphasizing *Mathis der Maler*, is provided by David Neumeyer in *The Music of Paul Hindemith* (New Haven, 1986). There is a large literature on the music of Kurt Weill. Concerning *The Threepenny Opera*, see Stephen Hinton, ed., *Kurt Weill: The Threepenny Opera* (Cambridge, 1990).

Detailed studies of the music of Benjamin Britten are found in Peter Evans's *The Music of Benjamin Britten*, rev. ed. (London, 1989) and Arnold Whittall's *Music of Britten and Tippett*, 2nd ed. (Cambridge, 1990). Also see Humphrey Carpenter's *Benjamin Britten: A Biography* (New York, 1992) and Britten's *Letters from a Life: The Selected Letters and Diaries of Benjamin Britten*, 1913–1976, ed. Donald Mitchell (2 vols., Berkeley, 1991).

The literature on early jazz is extensive. See Frank Tirro's scholarly *Jazz: A History* (2nd ed., New York, 1993) and Gunther Schuller's more speculative *Early Jazz: Its Roots and Musical Development* (New York, 1968). Concerning ragtime, Edward A. Berlin's *Ragtime: A Musical and Cultural History* (Berkeley, 1980) is clearly written and extensively documented.

11

Neoclassicism and Populism in American Music

Following World War I, fundamental changes appeared in American music. Prior to this time—in the last decades of the nineteenth and the early years of the twentieth centuries—music in the United States was dominated by European models. America's most prominent composers, including Horatio Parker (1863–1919), George Chadwick (1854–1931), Edward MacDowell (1861–1908), and Charles Griffes (1884–1920), studied in Germany, and their music later developed styles that they had discovered toward the end of the century on the Continent. MacDowell, the possessor of a great lyric gift, was influenced by programmatic trends in German music, and Griffes adopted the idiom of the French Impressionists and a stylized orientalism. Parker composed mainly choral works, among which his Latin oratorio *Hora novissima* (1892) is best known. Chadwick worked in both instrumental and vocal genres, and his symphonic and chamber music is occasionally touched by elements from American folk music.

After World War I, two branches appeared among American composers of serious music, both groups sharing a desire to be different, at least to some degree, from their European contemporaries. One group was more conservative and traditional. They often expressed their independence by adopting a nationalistic stance in their music, although they still went to Europe to receive their training and kept closely in touch with new musical styles abroad. These figures will be surveyed in this chapter. Another group made a cleaner break with Europe. They were more experimental in temperament, showing less interest in developing contemporary European styles such as neoclassicism. These musicians will be addressed in Chapter 12.

NEW DIRECTIONS

An important aspect of the change in American musical culture following World War I was a shift in influence away from Germany to France. During the later nineteenth century and in the early years of the twentieth, America's music, to a considerable extent, took its cue from Germany, not surprising since German music during these years exerted a dominance throughout the Western world. Germans worked at America's first schools of music, ambitious native composers went to Germany to finish their education, German players and conductors staffed America's orchestras, and German music was held in the highest esteem by American audiences.

But after the war German culture was not so highly regarded in the United States. The reasons for this change of taste were both political and stylistic. Germany and Austria had been the enemy during the war, and Germany's defeat began a period of economic hardship in the German-speaking world that made it an unlikely source for new ideas in the arts. Furthermore, Germany and Austria were virtually synonymous with the late romantic musical style, which by the 1920s was being rejected by younger composers around the globe.

America's new European model in the arts became France, beginning the affinity of Americans for French life, language, and culture that continues to exist in the present day. The new orientation toward France was strongly apparent in literature and painting as well as music. Young American writers including F. Scott Fitzgerald, Ernest Hemingway, Gertrude Stein, and e. e. cummings took up residence in Paris, a location that seemed more sympathetic for working out their disillusionment with society than their homeland. The American artists Alexander Calder (1898–1976) and Gerald Murphy (1888–1964) lived in France following World War I, and the bright light of French painting of the interwar period—the work of Georges Braque, Henri Matisse, and the Cubists—dazzled most of the leading American painters and sculptors.

French music now became central to American thought. Composers following World War I abandoned German conservatories for their advanced training, seeking instead French teachers. The most important of these was Nadia Boulanger (1887–1979),

mentor to American composers from the time of Aaron Copland to
that of Philip Glass. Boulanger taught at several schools of music in
Paris, meeting most of her American students at the American
Conservatory in nearby Fontainebleau. Her training was notori-
ously strict, emphasizing craft, music making, and early as well as
modern music. Her students were exposed to all types of new music
except for contemporary German works, for which she had little
affinity. The music of Stravinsky had a special importance for her,
and Stravinsky's international neoclassical style of the 1920s is generally associated with the work of her students. In assessing a new
piece she insisted primarily on the presence of a "long line." "It is
difficult adequately to explain the meaning of that phrase to the lay-
man," wrote her student Aaron Copland. "In mere words, it simply
means that every good piece of music must give us a sense of flow—
a sense of continuity from first note to last."

The attraction exerted by France on American composers
extended also to the influence of contemporary French musical
styles. The music of Stravinsky, who lived in France after the war,
hovered above the French-trained Americans, alternately imitated
and rejected by them. The music of Satie and the Six was also compelling to younger American composers, just as Wagner and
Brahms had been before the war. The dominant approach to music
in France between the wars, the international neoclassical style discussed in Chapter 10, became one of several primary directions for
Americans of the 1920s through 1940s.

At the same time, the need for a distinctive American, nationalistic
idiom in music was widely felt. Boulanger encouraged her American
students in this direction, being especially sympathetic to adaptations
of jazz. While Stravinsky tried his hand at jazz adaptations shortly
after the end of the war, he soon rejected all folklorism as a "naive but
dangerous tendency." The upshot for American music between the
wars was a pronounced conflict between internationalism and
regionalism, a split that also characterizes American politics of the
same time. The conflict became apparent in the music of the leading
composers in the United States as well as in their polemical essays.
Aaron Copland and Virgil Thomson—both known for their critical
writings—argued in favor of music that could embody the time when
and the place where it was written. Roger Sessions and Walter Piston,
on the contrary, adopted a more cosmopolitan neoclassical style,
which was often interpreted as devoid of a sense of place.

The split also came to reflect American society between the wars.
In the 1920s Americans basked in great economic prosperity, but in
the 1930s the country was cast into a devastating economic depression. The sassy modernistic spirit of neoclassicism that had made its
way to America in the 1920s seemed to many composers to be irrel-

evant to the America of the 1930s. In its place these composers often adopted a populist manner—accessible to a larger audience, less modernistic, and more clearly nationalistic and folkloric. The very same appeal to the common person was felt in American art of the 1930s, especially in the idealized visions of the American land and its working people by Thomas Hart Benton and Grant Wood.

In retrospect, the divisions represented by nationalism, internationalism, and populism in American music have become less apparent as the more general similarities unifying all of these directions have come more clearly into focus. Virtually all important American composers of these decades were influenced by an overarching spirit of the time, which asserted the need for a music that was antiromantic and that embraced traditional values and materials in a modernized form.

The prominence of symphony orchestras and symphonic genres is another important feature of American musical culture between

Idealized visions of rural America: Grant Wood, *Young Corn*. (Courtesy of the Cedar Rapids Museum of Art, Cedar Rapids School District Collection.)

the wars. Before World War I, America had relatively few outstanding orchestras. By 1940, however, the United States led the world in the number and quality of such organizations, which flourished not only in the major cities but in smaller ones including Pittsburgh, Cincinnati, and St. Louis. The rise of the symphony orchestra came from several factors: rivalry among patrons of the arts in different cities, the attractiveness of star conductors, and the orientation toward instrumental music in American schools and colleges. But whatever its origins the supremacy of orchestral music soon became a fact of life—still today as in the 1930s and 1940s—for American composers. The road to success was of necessity through the orchestral genres rather than through opera, chamber music, or other types of music available to the Europeans.

The great virtuosity and precision of the new American orchestras were exploited especially through the genre of the absolute, multi-movement symphony, which flourished among native-born composers between the world wars. This was not the case in Europe at the same time, when the traditional symphony had waned in importance. Emigré musicians in the 1930s and 1940s, including Hindemith and Stravinsky, composed major symphonic works upon arriving in America, knowing that they were central to success in their new homeland. Indeed, the tradition of the symphony, which reached its greatest heights in German-speaking lands in the eighteenth and nineteenth centuries, was carried on in the twentieth century primarily in outlying areas, especially the United States and Soviet Union.

In this chapter we shall encounter some of the most prominent composers in America of the 1920s through 1940s. Both their similarities and differences are pronounced. Virtually all were students of or in contact with Nadia Boulanger, and all aspired to develop a solid, craftsmanly technique in composition. All were influenced by the music of Stravinsky and modern music in France of the postwar years. But their attitudes toward regionalism and populism were different. Roy Harris, Aaron Copland, and Virgil Thomson pursued a type of music that would clearly embody aspects of their American homeland, and in the 1930s all wrote music in a populist, antielitist style. Walter Piston, Roger Sessions, and David Diamond, on the contrary, generally avoided the nationalistic idiom.

POPULIST COMPOSERS: COPLAND, HARRIS, THOMSON, AND BARBER

The music of Aaron Copland (1900–90) embodies virtually every important trend in American music of the interwar period. His works during these years are alternately neoclassical, populist, and overtly nationalistic, and, like all great composers, he often went

AARON COPLAND
(Brooklyn, 1900–New York, 1990)

Copland's youth in Brooklyn was spent, in his words, "in an environment that had little or no connection with serious music." His discovery of this art and of his own ability in it was at first self-guided. He received his advanced musical education in France from 1920 to 1924, mainly at the hands of Nadia Boulanger. His Symphony for Organ and Orchestra, commissioned by Mme. Boulanger, brought him to the attention of several influential American conductors.

Copland's music from the mid-1920s imitated jazz idioms in a style that was widespread at this time among many composers in Europe and America. He dispensed with this influence at about the same time as did the Europeans, but he continued to forge a distinctive American dialect in works that were alternately abstract or popular.

He lived abroad for much of the period before the Second World War, including several sojourns in Mexico arranged by his friend Carlos Chávez. He was associated as a teacher with the Berkshire Music Center and Harvard University, and he was active in the founding of the League of Composers and the American Composers Alliance.

SELECTED WORKS

Opera. *The Tender Land* (1954). Also film scores.

Ballets. *Billy the Kid* (1938), *Rodeo* (1942), *Appalachian Spring* (1944).

Orchestral Music. Three symphonies (1924, 1933, 1946), *Music for the Theater* (1925), *Statements* (1934), *El Salón México* (1936), *Outdoor Overture* (1938), *Quiet City* (1940, with obbligato trumpet and English horn), *Lincoln Portrait* (1942, with narrator), *Variations* (1957, arrangement of the Piano Variations), *Connotations* (1962), *Emblems* (1964, for band), *Inscape* (1967).

Chamber Music. *Vitebsk* (1929), Sextet (1937), *Fanfare for the Common Man* (1942, brass and percussion), Violin Sonata (1943), Piano Quartet (1950), Nonet (1960).

Piano Music. Piano Variations (1930), Sonata (1941), Piano Fantasy (1957).

Vocal Music. *Old American Songs* (1952, folk song arrangements), *Twelve Poems of Emily Dickinson* (1950), *Canticle of Freedom* (1955, chorus and orchestra).

Writings. *What to Listen for in Music* (New York, 1939), *Our New Music* (New York, 1941), *Music and Imagination* (New York, 1952).

beyond the existing styles of his day to create new syntheses. Following World War II, Copland daringly reformulated his musical language in a dissonant, chromatic, and partly serialized manner that seemed more relevant to postwar culture. In whatever vein he wrote, his musical imagination was marked by such a powerful originality as to make all of these trends appear to be entirely his own.

A common thread running through Copland's music is its Americanism. Works that simply quoted folk tunes seemed provincial to him. Instead, he sought "a music that would speak of universal things in a vernacular of American speech rhythms." Rhythm for Copland was the most distinctive part of America's musical profile. "What is the nature of this gift?" he asked.

> First, a conception of rhythm not as a mental exercise, but as something basic to the body's rhythmic impulse. This basic impulse is exteriorized with an insistence that knows no measure, ranging from a self-hypnotic monotony to a riotous frenzy of subconsciously controlled pounding. Second, an unparalleled ingenuity in the spinning out of unequal metrical units in the unadorned rhythmic line. And lastly, and most significant, a polyrhythmic structure arrived at through the combining of strongly independent blocks of sound [*Music and Imagination*].

After returning from France, where in the 1920s he pursued his musical education, Copland used jazz to capture this rhythmic vitality. After about 1930 he turned to a more complex manner that had its roots in the international neoclassical style. Works such as the Piano Variations (1930), Short Symphony (Symphony No. 2, 1933), and *Statements* for orchestra (1934) share with neoclassicism a dry percussiveness, modernistic dissonance and suppressed tonality, cosmopolitanism, and nonprogrammatic abstraction. But Copland's music of the 1930s often goes beyond French-inspired neoclassicism in its fragmented and angular lines, intensely dissonant harmony, and organic unity.

A celebrated example of this eclectic but still original style is the Piano Variations. The form of the work consists of a theme, twenty continuous variations (the beginning of each is marked in the score by a rehearsal number), and a coda. Much about the work suggests that Bach's *Goldberg Variations* were a model—its compact orderliness, its gradual increase in complexity, the diversity in character of each variation, and the overall division of the twenty variations into two equal groups. Just as Bach's variations relate to the theme through form and underlying harmonies, Copland's variations reveal a process of continual organic growth, going back ultimately to the first phrase of the theme in measures 1–3 (Example 11-1).

The composer asserted that he used a technique in these Variations drawn from Schoenberg's twelve-tone method. Copland was presumably referring to the systematic deployment throughout the entire composition of the notes and intervals of the opening line, E C D♯ C♯. These recur to flesh out the theme (measures 1–11), and they are present in often recondite variations in all that follows. Despite the difficulty and abstraction of the Variations, however, Copland still considered them distinctly American. "Their rhythmic life is definitely American and influenced by jazz, although there are no literal quotations," he said. The jazz influence is clear enough in variations 15 and 16, and elsewhere the changing meters and irregular rhythmic groupings within an existing meter suggest the American rhythmic impulse of which the composer spoke in *Music and Imagination*.

In the mid-1930s Copland began to write music of an entirely different type, intended to be accessible to the larger audiences created in America by the media of radio and film. It embodied a simpler and decidedly populist style that used American themes and folk materials rather than the subtle references in the Piano Variations to the American spirit.

> What I was trying for in the simpler works was only partly the writing of compositions that might speak to a broader audience. More than that they gave me an opportunity to try for a more homespun musical idiom. . . . This musical vernacular . . . was perhaps nothing more than a recrudescence of my old interest in making a connection between music and life about me [*Music and Imagination*].

Example 11-1.   Copland, Piano Variations. © 75
Copyright 1932 by Aaron Copland; Copyright Renewed. Reprinted by permission of Boosey & Hawkes, Inc., Sole Licensee.

Copland's works in his "simpler" style include three ballets—
Billy the Kid, Rodeo, and *Appalachian Spring*—several film scores and
operas, and the recitation *Lincoln Portrait. Appalachian Spring* (1944)
shows Copland's gift for a musical expression whose direct appeal
is devoid of banality. Its apparent simplicity is belied by the depth
and ingenuity of its structural relationships.

The choreography presents a young bride and groom beginning
their married life in rural Pennsylvania in the nineteenth century.
They are greeted by a helpful neighbor and a revivalist minister and
his following, with whom they share moments of tenderness alternating with rousing country dances. They pantomime their everyday activities, and, at the end, the bride willingly takes her place
among her neighbors. The scenario speaks of values widespread
among Americans in the 1930s and 1940s: a desire to be isolated
from the complications of life, a wish to be close to the earth and
frank in the expression of emotion, and a readiness to accept conventional social roles.

The music is perfectly suited to this story. It is best known in an
orchestral suite, which is a slightly shortened version of the original
score written for thirteen instruments. The music is predominantly
diatonic; its tonal plan progresses from A major at the beginning
through the dominant E major near the middle to C major at the
end. Many passages vividly illustrate the rhythmic characteristics
that Copland found in the American musical imagination. The
bride's dance at rehearsal 35 (1945 orchestral score) contains asymmetrical changes of meter governing a motoric eighth-note rhythm
reminiscent of passages from Stravinsky's *Rite of Spring*. A
polyrhythm created by "strongly opposing blocks of sound" is
heard at rehearsal 31 (Example 11-2). The opposition of these two
strata is enhanced by harmony, as the top strand dwells on the tonic
A-major chord, the bottom on E major.

To accompany a pantomime near the end of the ballet, Copland
quotes a Shaker hymn "The Gift to be Simple," which is then used as
a subject for variations. Both text and music of the hymn proclaim
the unadorned directness that reigns over the whole ballet. The
beginning of the hymn is shown in Example 11-3. Regarding the use

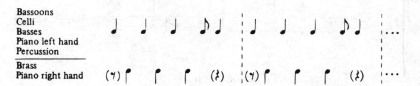

Example 11-2.   Polyrhythm in Copland's *Appalachian Spring.*

'Tis the gift to be sim - ple, 'tis the gift to be free, 'tis the

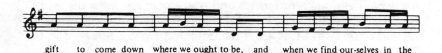

gift to come down where we ought to be, and when we find our-selves in the

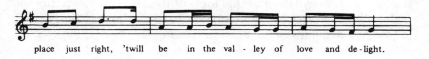

place just right, 'twill be in the val - ley of love and de - light.

Example 11-3. "'Tis the Gift to be Simple," from Edward D. Andrews's *The Gift to be Simple* (New York: J. H. Augustin, 1940). Used by permission of Dover Publications, Inc.

of preexistent melodies, the composer writes in *Music and Imagination*: "A hymn tune represents a certain order of feeling: simplicity, plainness, sincerity, directness. It is the reflection of those qualities in a stylistically appropriate setting, imaginative and unconventional and not mere quotation, that gives the use of folk tunes reality and importance."

Perhaps seeking the long line of which Boulanger spoke, Copland prefigures the full-blown appearance of the tune in the penultimate scene by triadic shapes underlying most of the earlier themes and motives. Those that unfold a triad in second inversion, beginning, that is, with an ascending fourth followed by a major third, are all the more closely related to the head motive of the hymn. The interval of the fourth alone has great importance in the contour of lines, as in a flute solo near the end (Example 11-4)—a melody that is developmentally related to numerous other themes and motives. Here the head motive of the hymn is varied by a concatenation of intervals of the fourth.

Example 11-4. Copland, *Appalachian Spring*. Copyright 1945 by Aaron Copland. Renewed 1972. Reprinted by permission of Boosey & Hawkes, Inc., sole licensee.

The Shaker hymn is also subtly related to the work's harmonic organization. The tune outlines only two harmonies, tonic and dominant. Copland superimposes these to form a bitriadic chord that is central to the entire work and also characteristic of Copland's music in general. It is first heard as a conflation of tonic A major and dominant E major in the strings in measures 4–6 (Example 11-5). Later it appears in various reorderings and transpositions, as at the end of the piece where the tonic C major is joined to its dominant G major. Several of the ways this set is manipulated are encountered in the first scene (measures 1–50). It is "inverted" in measures 34–38 so that the A-major triad is combined with its subdominant D major (Example 11-6). The oboe melody in measures 40–44 (Example 11-7) is a linear representation of this form of the set. The integration of materials in *Appalachian Spring* suggests that Copland's "simplicity" is confined to details of the musical surface.

The music of Roy Harris (1898–1979) is related to the populist trend in interwar American music also represented by Aaron Copland. Harris's music is geared to appeal to a broad American audience, it is nationalistic in its frequent use of folk song and in its quest for a characteristic American spirit, and it has an unselfconscious simplicity, drama, and emotionality. In genre it is overwhelm-

mm. 4-6

Example 11-5. Copland, *Appalachian Spring*. Copyright 1945 by Aaron Copland. Renewed 1972. Reprinted by permission of Boosey & Hawkes, Inc., sole licensee.

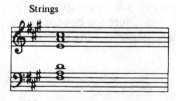

m. 35

Example 11-6. Copland, *Appalachian Spring*. Copyright 1945 by Aaron Copland. Renewed 1972. Reprinted by permission of Boosey & Hawkes, Inc., sole licensee.

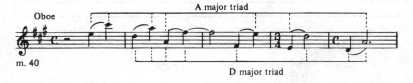

Example 11-7. Copland, *Appalachian Spring.* Copyright 1945 by Aaron Copland. Renewed 1972. Reprinted by permission of Boosey & Hawkes, Inc., sole licensee.

ing devoted to works for orchestra, chorus, and chamber combinations. Unlike Copland, Harris was never especially concerned with the international neoclassical style or with recent developments in music by Stravinsky or the French composers who were so influential upon American music of the 1920s and 30s. He was at first opposed to adapting jazz to serious music, although he wrote jazz pieces himself in his later years.

Harris's music underwent no striking stylistic evolution. It reveals the training of Boulanger in the frequent appearance of strict counterpoint and in a translucent style of orchestration that normally addresses the strings, woodwinds, brass, and percussion as distinct groups. His works are highly melodious, diatonic, pervasively triadic, but free and unstable in tonal plan.

Harris's approach to music was strongly nationalistic. In his article "Problems of American Composers" he becomes Whitmanesque in his depiction of the special qualities of America and its people:

> Our rhythmic impulses are fundamentally different from the rhythmic impulses of Europeans; and from this unique rhythmic sense are generated different melodic and form values. Our sense of rhythm is less symmetrical than the European rhythmic sense. . . . We do not employ unconventional rhythms as a sophistical gesture; we cannot avoid them.

The same sense of rhythm—manifest in the asymmetrical or unequal division of a meter—was found by Harris in America's folk music, which he studied and used in many of his compositions. "There will remain those composers," he wrote in "Folksong: American Big Business," "who have been deeply influenced by the finest, clearest, strongest feeling of our best songs. Because these songs are identified with emotions deeply implicit in themselves, such composers will be enriched and stimulated."

Harris's best known composition is his Symphony No. 3 (1938). Although it does not use folk song and has no overt programmatic content, it still exemplifies the type of music that the composer considered quintessentially American. The Symphony is in one move-

ROY HARRIS
(Chandler, Ok., 1898–
Santa Monica, Ca., 1979)

To his friend Aaron Copland, Roy Harris did not seem like a composer, "more like a farmer who had taken it into his head suddenly to become a composer of concert music." Harris was indeed a farmer and truck driver before turning to music. He was born in a log cabin in Oklahoma and grew up in California, isolated from a sophisticated musical culture or training. His path toward international recognition in music was primarily the outcome of his innate curiosity and natural artistic sensitivity.

Following encouragement from Howard Hanson and Copland, he traveled to Paris in 1926 to study with Nadia Boulanger. True to the pattern established by his American contemporaries, Harris was brought into prominence by Serge Kussevitsky, who in the 1930s premiered Harris's Symphonies Nos. 1 and 3 with the Boston Symphony Orchestra. The latter work was a major success and remains by far his most often performed composition.

Harris taught music at numerous colleges and universities, including the University of California, Los Angeles, and California State University, Los Angeles. Among his students was William Schuman.

SELECTED WORKS

Orchestral Music. Thirteen symphonies: No. 1, (*Symphony 1933*); No. 2 (1934); No. 3 (1938); No. 4, (*Folksong Symphony*, with chorus, 1940); No. 5 (1942); No. 6, (*Gettysburg*, 1944); No. 7 (1952); No. 8 (*San Francisco Symphony*, 1962); No. 9 (1962); No. 10 (*Abraham Lincoln Symphony*, for speaker, chorus, brass, amplified pianos, and percussion, 1965); No. 11 (1967); No. 12 (*Père Marquette*, 1969); and No. 13 (*Bicentennial Symphony 1976*, with chorus, 1975). Symphonic poems: *When Johnny Comes Marching Home* (1935), *American Creed* (1940), *Elegy and Dance* (1958).
Concertos. Concertos for piano (1944), two pianos (1946), violin (1949).
Chamber Music. Three string quartets (1929, 1933, 1937); Trio for piano, violin, and cello (1934); Quintet for piano and strings (1936); Sonata for

violin and piano (1942); Concerto for piano, clarinet, and string quartet (1926); Concerto for string sextet (1932).

Piano Music. Sonata (1928), Suite (1944), *American Ballads* (1945), Toccata (1949).

Music for Chorus. Symphony for Voices on Poems of Walt Whitman (1935), *Freedom's Land* (various versions, 1941–42), *Rock of Ages* (1944), *Blow the Man Down* (1946), *Take the Sun and Keep the Stars* (1944), *Folk Fantasy for Festivals* (1956).

ment. According to Harris's program notes for the premier performance with the Boston Symphony Orchestra in 1939, it consists of five connected sections, each suggesting a state of mind: the first, "tragic," the second (from rehearsal 15), "lyric," the third (from 21), "pastoral," the fourth (from the seventh bar of 41) "fugue-drama," the fifth (three before 57), "dramatic-tragic." Each of the five sections is distinguished by new thematic material and a distinctive tempo or rhythmic design, and continuity—the "long line" demanded by Boulanger—is provided by the carryover of themes from one section to the next. The five parts are laid out in a freely ternary design: the last section recapitulates motifs from the first two, also returning to the focus on the G-minor triad that begins the work. The Pastoral and Fugue constitute a contrasting middle section of the ternary form.

Each section of the Symphony is filled by a continuous melodic stream that is divided into many phrases having subtle similarities among themselves. It is indeed the melodic element that primarily holds the listener's attention. Harris's melodies (the opening one is shown in Example 11-8) are usually long and flowing; as in Example 11-8, they typically begin by outlining a major or minor triad with additional notes creating a pentatonic set. Ensuing phrases elaborate upon earlier ones by bringing in more tones and by changing the triadic focus.

Example 11-8.   Harris, Symphony No. 3. Copyright © 1939, 1940 (Renewed) by G. Shirmer, Inc. (ASCAP). Reprinted by Permission.

The triads suggested by the melodic motion are usually sounded in the accompaniment, but these almost entirely avoid circular harmonic progressions in any key. In the Pastoral section the simple triads of the accompaniment are enriched by a succession of bitriadic formations, especially those formed by a major and minor triad a third apart. The tonal plan of the symphony is free from traditional tonal organization. The triadic area on G begins and closes the symphony, and other areas defined by triads on C, E, A, and D are prominent.

The music of Virgil Thomson (1896–1989) is a pronounced representation of several important trends in American composition between the world wars: antiromantic sentiment, simplicity and reductiveness of materials, influence from modern French music, and the application of American folk song to an artistic musical idiom. In the music of Erik Satie, Thomson found a model for a musical style that was radically antiromantic, anti-German, and simplified in materials. Satie's works, he wrote in 1941, were "among the major musical values of our century."

> To the uninitiated they sound trifling. To those who love them they are fresh and beautiful and firmly right. . . . [Satie's music] wears no priestly robes; it mumbles no incantations; it is not painted up by Max Factor to terrify elderly ladies or to give little girls a thrill. Neither is it designed to impress orchestral conductors or to get anybody a job teaching school. It has literally no devious motivation. It is as simple as a friendly conversation and in its better moments exactly as poetic and as profound.

These were the qualities that Thomson wanted for his own music. His works of the 1920s echo French neoclassicism in their dissonance and freedom of tonality, but with far fewer notes than used by the neoclassicists and with a rhythmic style and texture that is often reduced to the minimum. As with American music in general of the 1930s and 1940s, his works gradually became more populist, tending to revive commonplace tonality, triadic harmony, melodious textures, and to apply familiar folk tunes, all in a hypersimplified idiom.

His best known composition is the opera *Four Saints in Three Acts* (1927–33), composed in France in collaboration with the American expatriate writer Gertrude Stein (1874–1946). In her poetry and prose Stein usually dispensed with conventional meaning or logical narrative in favor of allowing words and phrases to be appreciated for their sounds, impressions, and free associations. In *Four Saints* there is no narrative, instead banter, nonsense, and witty nonsequiturs among various saints (more than four) and their associates.

VIRGIL THOMSON
(*Kansas City, Mo., 1896–New York, 1989*)

Virgil Thomson's early years in Kansas City provided him with a fund of musical memories that he called on for the rest of his life. "When I reach down, I get Southern hymns and all those darn-fool ditties we used to sing—'Grasshopper sitting on a railway track'," he later recollected. To this vernacular musical background he added a sophisticated training, attending Harvard College (1919–23) and studying with Nadia Boulanger in Paris (1921–22). A confirmed francophile, Thomson returned to Paris in 1925, where he lived until 1940, making the acquaintance of most of the important musicians and writers who lived there during those years. In 1934 he scored his greatest success as a composer when his opera *Four Saints in Three Acts* (on a libretto by his friend Gertrude Stein) was staged in Hartford.

In 1940 he returned to America, working until 1955 as chief music critic for the *New York Herald Tribune*. His writings on music reveal a clear mind, an ease with words, and a remarkable understanding of music of all types. His compositions continued to receive attention. Music for the film *Louisiana Story* (1948) was awarded a Pulitzer Prize, and Thomson was also made a member of the French Académie des Beaux Arts and Legion of Honor.

SELECTED WORKS

Operas and Ballets. *Four Saints in Three Acts* (opera on a text by Gertrude Stein, 1933), *The Mother of Us All* (opera on a text by Gertrude Stein, 1947), *Lord Byron* (opera on a text by Jack Larson, 1968), *Filling Station* (ballet, 1937).

Orchestral Music. Two symphonies (*Symphony on a Hymn Tune*, 1928; Symphony No. 2, 1931), suites from film music (*The Plow That Broke the Plains*, 1942; *The River*, 1957; *Louisiana Story*, 1948), tone poems (*Wheat Field at Noon*, 1948; *The Seine at Night*, 1947; *Sea Piece with Birds*, 1952), concertos for cello (1950) and flute, harp, strings, and percussion (1954), Concertino for harp, strings, and percussion (1964).

Chamber Music. Two string quartets (1931, 1932), Sonata da chiesa (1926), Sonata for violin and piano (1930), Serenade for flute and violin (1931).

Piano Music. Four sonatas (1929–40), Etudes (1940, 1943, 1951), Five Inventions (1926).

Music for Solo Voice. Songs with various accompanimental media to poetry by Blake, Lowell, Stein, Sade, Hugnet, Racine, Campion, Shakespeare.

Choral Music. *Capital Capitals* (male voices and piano, 1927), Requiem Mass (with chamber orchestra, 1960).

Musical "Portraits." Approximately 150 aphoristic works for various instrumental combinations intending to capture in music a person whom the composer knew.

Writings. *The State of Music* (New York, 1939), *Virgil Thomson* (New York, 1966), *American Music Since 1910* (New York, 1971), several volumes of reviews reprinted from the *New York Herald Tribune*. *A Virgil Thomson Reader*, edited by John Rockwell (New York, 1981), provides selections from all of Thomson's major writings.

The music is reduced virtually to a trivial background. Typical of the neoclassical composer, Thomson alludes to musical conventions (here those associated with opera) but does not write opera in the conventional sense. The singing by soloists, ensembles, and choruses rapidly alternates among arialike passages, recitative, chanting, and speech. The accompaniment in the orchestra is based on the banal harmonic progressions of Baptist hymnody, occasionally quoting well-known tunes or (as in the Prelude before Act 4) stepping forth in a more artful way. Just as Stein's text is filled with recurring words and phrases, so too Thomson's music is highly repetitious. The music of the opening Prelude recurs at the end of the opera to create a rounded form. *Four Saints* is as far removed as possible from the romantic conception of opera as high art. It amounts instead to the "friendly conversation" that Thomson found approvingly in the music of Satie.

The music of Samuel Barber (1910–81) stands somewhat to the side of the mainstream of the French-oriented, neoclassical, or nationalistic music that dominated America between the world wars. Few of his early works reflect French neoclassicism; they stand closer to German music of the nineteenth century and extend the language of romanticism far into the twentieth. There is no sense of rebellion in Barber's music, either against the romantic period or against the European spirit and tradition of music. In terms of expressivity, however, Barber's music is squarely in the American idiom in its frank and uncomplicated presentation of emotion.

Viewed as a whole, his music represents several distinct styles. At first it was closest to the romantic manner. Near the end of World

SAMUEL BARBER
(West Chester, Pa., 1910–New York, 1981)

Even as a child growing up in the suburbs of Philadelphia, Samuel Barber sensed that his calling was to be a composer. A precocious development in music led to his entering the newly-founded Curtis Institute of Music at the age of only fourteen. There he studied composition with Rosario Scalero, under whose guidance he composed such works as the ever-popular Overture to *The School for Scandal*. By the mid-1930s this and other pieces for orchestra had attracted international attention, and they were taken up by Bruno Walter, Serge Kussevitsky, and Arturo Toscanini, among other conductors.

Following service in the Air Force during World War II, Barber settled in Mt. Kisco, New York, pursuing the career of a composer of music in all genres. In the 1950s he turned increasingly to vocal works, composing song cycles and, after 1958, operas. His opera *Antony and Cleopatra* was commissioned for the opening of the new Metropolitan Opera House in 1966.

Barber taught occasionally at schools including the Curtis Institute, although in general he lived as an independent composer. He was the recipient of two Pulitzer Prizes in music and an honorary doctorate from Harvard University.

SELECTED WORKS

Operas and Ballet. *Vanessa* (opera, text by Gian Carlo Menotti, 1957), *Antony and Cleopatra* (opera, text by Franco Zeffirelli after Shakespeare, 1966), *Medea* (ballet for Martha Graham, 1946, also titled *Serpent Heart* and *Cave of the Heart*).

Orchestral Music. Two symphonies (1936, 1944), three essays (1937, 1942, 1978), Overture to *The School for Scandal* (1931), Adagio for Strings (arrangement of the second movement of the String Quartet Op. 11, 1938), *Medea's Meditation and Dance of Vengeance* (music from the ballet *Medea*, 1953).

Concertos. Concertos for violin (1939), cello (1945), and piano (1962); *Capricorn Concerto* for flute, oboe, trumpet, and strings (1944).

Chamber and Piano Music. String Quartet (1936), Sonata for cello and
   piano (1932), *Summer Music* for woodwind quintet (1955), *Excursions* for
   piano (1942–44), Sonata for piano (1949).
Songs. *Dover Beach* (voice and string quartet, 1931), *Knoxville: Summer of
   1915* (voice and orchestra, 1947), *Hermit Songs* (1952–53), *Nuvoletta*
   (1947), *Mélodies passagères* (1950–51), other collections of songs for voice
   and piano on poetry by Joyce, Yeats, Hopkins, Agee, Horan, and others.

War II Barber began to take more obvious note of contemporary
musical developments. His *Capricorn Concerto* (1944) suggests the
baroque revival element of neoclassicism in its allusions to Bach's
Brandenburg Concertos, and his brilliant orchestral tone poem
Medea's Meditation and Dance of Vengeance revives the bacchanalian
atmosphere of Stravinsky's *Rite of Spring*. In his Piano Sonata (1949)
Barber dabbled with twelve-tone melodic materials, and in general
his postwar music is more chromatic and dissonant than earlier.

The German romantic spirit in Barber's music is clearest in his
early works from the 1930s. The String Quartet (1936), for example,
approaches its genre with the intensity, tonal language, and motivic
work of Beethoven. The second movement (Molto adagio), better
known in an orchestral arrangement that the composer made in
1938, takes its musical language from Wagner. The work is ingenious in its use of this style. The form of the movement consists of
free and continuous variations upon an initial harmonic and
melodic idea. The melodic line is passed from instrument to instrument, reaching a climax in the upper register and then returning
somberly to the opening presentation.

The beginning of the Adagio is illustrated in Example 11-9. In this
passage, the basic elements of Wagner's harmonic style are evident.
The essential harmony (here the dominant chord in the key of Bb
minor) is sustained while on the surface of the music there is considerable harmonic motion. This rich and complex overlay of chords
arises by voice leading in several lines. Some of these superficial
chords receive emphasis, for example, the luminous Ab major triad
in measure 4, but these are not immediately relevant to the underlying harmonic motion in Bb minor. As is often the case in Wagner, the
tonic chord is less in evidence than the dominant. The tonic Bb is
heard at cadences (measures 19 and 28), but it is never approached
by its dominant and it is sometimes bridged over by the melodic
lines. The movement ends on the dominant chord, lending an added
measure of poignancy to music that has long been admired for its
powerful and genuine expressivity.

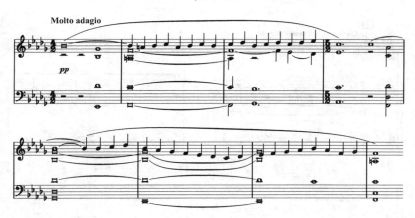

Example 11-9. Barber, String Quartet Op. 11, second movement. Copyright © 1949 (Renewed) by G. Schirmer, Inc. (ASCAP). Reprinted by Permission.

Music that is more in the simplified, naive mainstream of American composition is found in Barber's songs, especially in the much-admired orchestral song *Knoxville: Summer of 1915* (1947). The text is drawn from an autobiographical prose-poem by James Agee (1938, reprinted as a preface to Agee's novel, *A Death in the Family*). Here the author reflects with great nostalgia upon his childhood in Knoxville, Tennessee. He writes from the naive and childlike perspective, calling attention to mundane events and disconnected impressions, with a child's sensitivity but also a melancholy foreboding of the impermanence of life. The spirit of the text is indeed well suited to Barber's emotionality, both quintessentially American.

On the surface, this work is much simpler than the String Quartet, but beneath the surface it has a less traditional harmonic and tonal organization. In these respects, as well as in certain specifics of harmonic practice, it shows the influence of Copland. The simplicity is plain enough: the form of the song is based on clear sectional, thematic, and motivic repetitions. The opening section recurs in rondo fashion at rehearsal 12 and 25, between which several contrasting sections depict the mood and meaning of the text. Rhythm and meter are uncomplicated, the texture of the work is uncluttered, and triadic harmonies and diatonic melodies are the norm.

On the other hand, the tonal language is complex, far more modernistic than Barber's earlier use of romantic-era tonality. In every section of the song, two triadic areas alternate as local tonics: the two are related as are a major triad and its relative minor triad. An example is the alternation of A major and F♯ minor triads near the beginning of the song (Example 11-10). The two triads together are a subset of the pentatonic scale that is the source of every tone in the

Example 11-10. Barber, *Knoxville: Summer of 1915.* Copyright © 1949 (Renewed) by G. Schirmer, Inc. (ASCAP). Reprinted by Permission.

opening melody. Pentatonic fragments and related fourth and fifth chords recur throughout the song, lending it a Coplandesque, "American" flavor. A conflation of different triads is also prominent at the end of the song, where A major is brought together with E major, thus forming the "tonic plus dominant" bitriadic harmony so often used by Copland. The *Knoxville* song, characteristic of music of its time, alludes to tonality but does not use it in a traditional way.

In the late 1940s Barber's music began to depart from the lyrical, simplified, and traditional style represented by *Knoxville*, toward an idiom more characteristic of the postwar avant-garde. The Piano Sonata (1949) was one of the earliest pieces in this manner. The work could scarcely be more different from *Knoxville*. It is complex and bombastic, its emotionality is submerged beneath waves of notes, and it is intensely chromatic and dissonant, making use (especially in the third movement) of twelve-tone materials.

NEOCLASSICAL COMPOSERS: PISTON, SESSIONS, DIAMOND, AND OTHERS

The music of Walter Piston (1894–1976) represents a cosmopolitan, French-inspired neoclassicism. Overt Americanisms are generally absent, classical forms and genres are used, there is little that is overtly programmatic, and the basic materials are drawn from traditional

WALTER PISTON
(*Rockland, Maine, 1894–Belmont, Mass.,
1976*)

Walter Piston entered Harvard University in 1920, following his service in the U.S. Navy during World War I. After graduating in 1924, he traveled to Paris, where he continued his musical education with Nadia Boulanger and Paul Dukas and broadened his familiarity with modern composers. In 1926 he returned to the United States and began teaching at Harvard, remaining on its faculty until his retirement in 1960. In addition to composing, Piston was the author of widely used textbooks on harmony, counterpoint, and orchestration. His students at Harvard included Elliott Carter, Leonard Bernstein, Arthur Berger, and Irving Fine.

Piston received virtually all of the major awards and prizes available to an American composer. Among them are two Pulitzer Prizes and an honorary doctorate from Harvard.

SELECTED WORKS

Orchestral Music. Eight symphonies (1937–65), two suites (1929, 1948), Concerto for Orchestra (1933), Suite from the Ballet *The Incredible Flutist* (1939), *Three New England Sketches* (1959), Sinfonietta (1941), Serenata (1956).

Concertos. Concertos for violin (1939, 1960), two pianos (1959), viola (1937), flute (1971), and clarinet (1967); Variations for cello and orchestra (1966), Concerto for string quartet, wind instruments, and percussion (1976).

Chamber Music. Five string quartets (1933–62), two trios for violin, cello, and piano (1935, 1966), duos for viola and cello (1949) and cello and piano (1972), sonatas with piano for flute (1930) and violin (1939), Sonatina for violin and harpsichord (1945), Suite for oboe and piano (1931), Woodwind Quintet (1956), String Sextet (1964), Partita for violin, viola, and organ (1944), Improvisation for piano (1945), Passacaglia for piano (1943).

European music with a modern harmony and tonality. This description applies uniformly to works throughout Piston's long and productive career, with only temporary deviations. His early music from the 1920s and early 1930s is the most eclectic, touching alternately on evocations of jazz, motoric neobaroque rhythms, and an intensely dissonant counterpoint. In the 1940s he experimented with a form of twelve-tone composition. His choice of genres, typical of the American composer, emphasized orchestral works and chamber music.

Piston's eight symphonies reveal the composer's musical persona in breadth and depth. The Symphony No. 2 (1943) is typical. It is a three-movement work, large and serious in scope, and lacking in any overtly programmatic content. Everything is worked out with clarity, balance, restraint, and precision. The music is never allowed to become turgid; nothing unsettling happens. The first movement shows these features, characteristic of Piston's entire oeuvre. It has a clarity of form that is created by straightforward thematic and sectional repetition, frequent occurrence of cadences, clear distinctions among major themes, and regularity of rhythm and meter. The movement is in sonata form: the first themes consist of several related ideas linked into a great arch shape that reaches its peak at measure 44; the subsidiary theme (measure 55) is sprightly and syncopated. A development (from measure 94) concerns itself with the first themes, and a recapitulation beginning at measure 149 brings back all of the main ideas.

The opening of the main theme (Example 11-11) outlines an A-minor triad, the tonic of the entire symphony. Chromatic tones are increasingly added to the basic diatonic melody, and the underlying harmonies make only passing allusions to functional harmonies in A minor. The interval of the fourth is prominent in all of the main themes and fourth chords (especially three-note figures such as the woodwind chord A D G in measure 91) are prominent.

The texture of Piston's symphony balances homophony and polyphony, although the contrapuntal passages and the fleeting fugatos never become so complex or turgid as to obscure the

Example 11-11. Piston, Symphony No. 2, first movement. Copyright © 1949 (Renewed) by G. Schirmer, Inc. (BMI). Reprinted by Permission.

melodic line. Piston's orchestration—based on the nineteenth-century French style—always makes the orchestra sound coherent and pleasing. Melodic material is normally stated by only one of the main choirs of the orchestra; in loud or climactic passages, there is doubling among the choirs. In lightly scored passages, Piston favors soloistic woodwinds as the bearers of melodic material.

The Suite from the Ballet *The Incredible Flutist* (1939) is an example of Piston in a lighter and more accessible mood. This is music that approaches the conscious simplification and accessibility of the popular works of Copland, Thomson, and Harris. The ballet, written in 1938 and Piston's only venture into dramatic music, portrays village scenes in which the playing of a circus flutist stimulates love among the townspeople. The music has the same lack of pretense as the scenario. In 1939 Piston created a Suite from the ballet music, a work destined to be his most often performed. The "Tango of the Merchant's Daughters" is typical of music in this popular Suite. As with most music intended to be popular, it is constructed from the repetition of ideas rather than their variation. The main theme (Example 11-12) is heard six times, varied only in orchestration. The key of E♭ major is used here in an entirely traditional manner. The Tango is cast into a simple ternary form whose middle part has a colorful Latin rhythm.

The works of Roger Sessions (1896–1985) went against the grain of American musical culture between the world wars. The simple, reductive musical surfaces of Copland, Thomson, and Barber were never congenial to him. His music is instead complex, difficult to play and to sing, and challenging to the listener. He assiduously avoided the nationalistic stance that characterized the main stream of American music and also bypassed the general orientation toward

Example 11-12.   Piston, *The Incredible Flutist.* Copyright © 1939 by Arrow Music Press. Copyright Renewed and assigned to Associated Music Publishers, Inc. (BMI). Reprinted by Permission.

ROGER SESSIONS
(*Brooklyn, 1896–Princeton, 1985*)

Roger Sessions was a musical and intellectual prodigy, composing ambitious works even before entering Harvard College at the age of fourteen. There he studied music with Edward Burlingame Hill and Archibald Davison, later with Horatio Parker at Yale. His primary teacher was Ernest Bloch, whom he contacted in New York in 1919 and later followed to the Cleveland Institute of Music.

In 1924 he continued his education in Europe, in Paris, where he met Nadia Boulanger and Aaron Copland, as well as in Italy and Germany. Like many other American expatriate composers of the 1920s and 30s, his career was launched by the Boston Symphony Orchestra under Serge Kussevitsky, who conducted Sessions's Symphony No. 1 in 1927. From 1928 to 1931 Sessions helped to organize the "Copland-Sessions Concerts" of modern music in New York.

Throughout his long career, Sessions taught at many colleges and universities, primarily Princeton and the University of California at Berkeley. His students included Edward Cone, David Diamond, Milton Babbitt, and Leon Kirchner. He was also a voluminous writer on musical topics. Sessions was the recipient of awards and honors including two Pulitzer Prizes, the second in 1981 for the Concerto for Orchestra, his final major composition.

SELECTED WORKS

Operas. *Montezuma* (1963), The *Trial of Lucullus* (1947).
Orchestral Music. Nine symphonies (1927–78); Orchestral Suite from *The Black Maskers* (1923); concertos for violin (1935), piano (1956), violin, violoncello, and orchestra (1971); Concerto for Orchestra (1981).
Chamber and Piano Music. Two string quartets (1936, 1951), String Quintet (1958), Duo for Violin and Piano (1942), Sonata for Violin Solo (1953), three sonatas for piano (1930, 1946, 1965), *From My Diary* (1939–40, four pieces for which the composer intended the title *Pages from a Diary*), Three Chorale Preludes for Organ (1924–26).

Vocal Music. Mass for unison choir (1955), *Idyll of Theocritus* (soprano, orchestra, 1954), *When Lilacs Last in the Dooryard Bloom'd* (chorus, orchestra, solo voices, 1971).

Writings. *Questions About Music* (New York, 1970), *The Musical Experience of Composer, Performer, Listener* (Princeton, 1950), *Harmonic Practice* (New York, 1951). Essays by Sessions are reprinted in *Roger Sessions on Music: Collected Essays* (Princeton, 1979).

French musical culture following World War I. Sessions outlook was instead international, with a sympathy toward German modernism.

The development of Sessions's musical language in a larger sense followed a path that was well worn by his contemporaries. His music of the 1920s and 1930s (relatively small in quantity) exemplifies the international neoclassical style. It uses traditional genres, diatonic lines and triadic chords that are extended by chromatic inflections, familiar homophonic and contrapuntal textures, and regular, often motoric rhythms. Its expressiveness is subdued, avoiding programmatic associations or the overt evocation of moods.

In the 1940s his music gradually evolved toward more complex textures, more chromatic and dissonant collections of pitches, and less regular rhythm and meter. In the 1950s Sessions followed the international trend toward twelve-tone composition, which he adapted in a distinctive way producing music that reveals his admiration for the later works of Schoenberg. The discussion that follows will emphasize the earliest of these styles.

In a letter to Aaron Copland of August 24, 1926, Sessions chided his friend for his allegiance to an emerging American style and school. "You are quite aware, I know, that I feel a certain irony in regard to schools and groups, and, in music at least, a respect for individuals who stand by themselves in the most profound sense." Especially in his music of the 1920s and 1930s, Sessions seemed intent on remaining aloof from the mainstream of American music. This remoteness was not overlooked by his colleagues. In a review of 1947 of Sessions's Second Piano Sonata, Virgil Thomson remarked:

> Like all of this composer's music, it bears no clear marks of its national or local origins. It could have been written anywhere in the world— Buenos Aires, Vienna, Rome, or Melbourne—as easily as in Berkeley, California, where it was actually composed. . . . Its speech represents the international neo-Classic style at its most complete and eclectic.

Session's first Sonata for Piano (1927–30) will exemplify the eclectic neoclassicism of which Thomson spoke. This piece, Sessions's

most often performed early work, is in three primary movements—
Allegro, Poco meno mosso, Molto vivace—played without pause.
The Sonata begins with a lyrical Andante passage that returns
before each of the other movements. The composer's own description suggests a highly integrated form in both small and large
dimensions. He describes the initial Andante, for example, not as an
introduction but as an "exposition" of the slow movement, of which
the Allegro first movement is but an interruption.

In this Andante passage (the opening is shown in Example 11-13)
an important element of eclecticism in the neoclassical style is
clearly revealed: the tendency to allude to several elements of tradi-

Example 11-13.   Sessions, Piano Sonata No. 1 © B. Schotts Söhne, Mainz,
1931. © renewed. All Rights Reserved. Used by permission of European
American Music Distributors Corporation, sole U.S. and Canadian agent
for B. Schott's Söhne, Mainz.

tional music without adopting any of them outright. One such allusion is to tonality. The Andante refers clearly enough to B minor, whose tonic chord is heard at its beginning and end measures (24–25) and at the other structural junctures in the long melodic line in measures 9 and 17. Otherwise the passage has virtually no relation to the key of B minor: nondiatonic tones are copiously introduced and there is no evidence of controlling circular harmonic progressions. Occasionally there are allusions to cadential dominant–tonic motions, as in the approach to the new "tonic" C minor at the beginning of the Allegro first movement (measures 26–29), but this sonata is in no key in a traditional sense. The structural function of triads is to mark formal junctures in the work.

The Allegro first movement reveals other aspects of Sessions's neoclassicism. Its rhythm is motoric, clearly expressing a beat, although regular meter is dispelled by the constant alternation of duple and triple groupings of small rhythmic values. Typical of Sessions's treatment of the piano, the instrument is handled in a percussive and sharply accentuated manner. The form of the Allegro is based on easily perceived thematic recurrences: a string of themes is introduced in measures 27–120, a contrasting idea (tranquillo) is then produced, and the first themes recur mildly varied from measure 148.

The music of David Diamond (1915–) emphasizes the orchestra. Between 1941 and 1961 he wrote eight symphonies as well as tone poems and concertos. He also composed eight string quartets (1940–66), choral music, and songs. His career unfolded in a typical way. After attending the Eastman School of Music in the early 1930s, he traveled to France to study with Nadia Boulanger. His career was set in motion by performances of his symphonic music by Serge Kussevitsky and the Boston Symphony Orchestra, and he was the recipient of numerous grants. He later taught, primarily at the Manhattan School of Music and Juilliard School.

His early music is squarely in the international neoclassical style: diatonic, foursquare in rhythm and much oriented to the beat, but also abstractly contrapuntal, astringent in dissonance, and flexible in tonality. Typical of this style, his works avoid overtly American themes or materials. His symphonies of the 1940s became more traditional: more melodious in texture, more clearly tonal, and more triadic in harmony. These works, such as the admirable Symphony No. 2 (1943), take on a melancholy tone in their slow movements and an ebullient, toccatalike quality in the fast ones. The orchestration is much in the French-American style of the time, with the main choirs of the orchestra treated separately and often placed in a rapid-fire alteration or opposition.

Howard Hanson (1896–1981) also concentrated on the symphony, of which he wrote seven between 1922 and 1977. Hanson's idiom is closer to the romantic spirit of Sibelius than to the neoclassical style. The symphonies are programmatic, full of unconcealed emotion and expressivity and essentially romantic in their musical materials. Hanson was the director of the Eastman School of Music from 1924 until 1964. His book *Harmonic Materials of Modern Music: Resources of the Tempered Scale* (New York, 1960) contains an important and highly original exploration of the intervallic properties and relationships among sets of pitches drawn from the chromatic scale.

William Schuman (1910–92) composed ten symphonies from 1936 until 1976; the earlier ones suggest the international neoclassical style with clear and regular rhythm, linear textures, diatonic pitch collections, and an alternation of somber, melodious slow movements and toccatalike fast movements.

BIBLIOGRAPHY

Excellent surveys of music in the United States include Gilbert Chase's *America's Music*, 3d ed. (New York, 1987), Wilfrid Mellers's *Music in a New Found Land*, rev. ed. (New York, 1987), and H. Wiley Hitchcock's *Music in the United States: A Historical Introduction*, 3d ed. (Englewood Cliffs, N.J., 1988). The 1933 symposium *American Composers on American Music*, ed. Henry Cowell (New York, 1962), contains important statements by and about major American composers of the 1920s and 1930s. The Germanized taste of nineteenth-century American audiences is recounted in lively fashion by Joseph Horowitz in *Wagner Nights: An American History* (Berkeley, 1994), and Richard Crawford's Bloch Lectures, published as *The American Musical Landscape* (Berkeley, 1993), is especially authoritative.

The biographies of Aaron Copland by Arthur Berger (New York, 1953) and Julia Smith (New York, 1955) are considerably dated but a good starting point for information on this composer. Copland's own writings, invariably perceptive and skillfully written, are cited in the composer's biography earlier in this chapter. Essays from the journal *Modern Music* and other sources are reprinted in *Copland on Music* (New York, 1960). Also see Copland and Vivian Perlis, *Copland 1900 through 1942* and *Copland Since 1943* (New York, 1984; New York, 1989). Roy Harris's essay "Folksong: American Big Business" is found in *Modern Music*, 23/2 (1946):8–11, and "Problems of American Composers" is reprinted in *American Composers on American Music: A Symposium*, 149–66, ed. Henry Cowell (New York, 1962). Also see Don Stehman, *Roy Harris: An*

American Musical Pioneer (Boston, 1984) and Nicolas Slonimsky, "Roy Harris," *Musical Quarterly*, 33 (1947):17–37.

Any study of the music of Virgil Thomson must begin with a survey of his own criticial and autobiographical writings, which clearly enunciate his objectives as a composer and his place in the history of music. *A Virgil Thomson Reader*, ed. John Rockwell (New York, 1981) reprints excerpts and reviews from his long career as a critic. The life of Samuel Barber is admirably surveyed in Barbara B. Heyman's *Samuel Barber: The Composer and His Music* (New York, 1992), although this book does not contain an analysis of Barber's music. Concerning Walter Piston's life and works, see Howard Pollack, *Walter Piston* (Ann Arbor, 1982), Elliott Carter's important essay "Walter Piston," *Musical Quarterly*, 32 (1946):354–75, and Peter Westergaard's "Conversation with Walter Piston, *Perspectives of New Music*, 7/1 (1968):3–17. Biographical information on Roger Sessions is found in Edward T. Cone's "Conversation with Roger Sessions," *Perspectives of New Music*, 4/2 (1966):29–46 and in *Conversations with Roger Sessions*, compiled by Andrea Olmstead (Boston, 1987). A general study of Sessions is by Andrea Olsmtead, *Roger Sessions and His Music* (Ann Arbor, 1985). Session's books on music are surveyed in his biography earlier in this chapter.

12

Experimental Music in America

"America," wrote John Cage, "has an intellectual climate suitable for radical experimentation." Even in the interwar period, when traditional musical values in the form of neoclassicism and populism were dominant in America, there still existed an important experimental musical culture. The split between traditionalism and avant-gardism is also seen in American painting and literature of the same time. The dominant trend in painting in the 1920s and 1930s was a sentimental realism that was often highly regionalized, as in paintings by Grant Wood, Thomas Hart Benton, and some of the works Georgia O'Keeffe. At the same time a smaller number of important artists were working in more abstract styles, including Alexander Calder and Stuart Davis. In the 1930s Calder attracted attention with his "mobile" sculpture—suspended abstract shapes that were kept in constant motion by air currents.

During the 1920s and 1930s, the musical avant-garde in America became increasingly distinct from the neoclassicism or populism of composers such as Copland. The split between these camps was brought into focus by two important organizations of composers. The modernists were generally allied to the International Composers' Guild (1921–27) and its successor, the Pan-American Association of Composers (1928–34). Both organizations were founded by Edgard

Varèse, and Charles Ives, Wallingford Riegger (1885–1961), Carl Ruggles, and Henry Cowell were represented in their concerts. The League of Composers (1923–ca. 1946), on the other hand, was dominated by French-trained musicians of more conservative tastes. Aaron Copland was among its leaders and most notable composers.

While both groups made important contributions to American music between the world wars, the experimentalists laid the groundwork for developments in music in the United States after the Second World War, when the avant-garde returned to a position of leadership. Thus we turn in this chapter to the work of outstanding experimentalists in America prior to about 1945.

COMPOSERS IN NEW ENGLAND: IVES AND RUGGLES

Charles E. Ives (1874–1954) was the first important American modernist of the twentieth century. Although he possessed a good musical education and a respectable knowledge of European music, his culture and aesthetic were self-made. Working in nearly complete isolation from traditional musical institutions and bolstered by great independence of thought, he forged a style that was both intensely nationalistic and experimental in its materials.

Music for Ives was an art that expressed spiritual and ethical qualities. Its sources were in the human character rather than in abstract laws of sound and time. There was music to be found in human affairs and in people whom Ives admired. "Thoreau was a great musician," he wrote in *Essays Before a Sonata*, "not because he played the flute but because he did not have to go to Boston to hear 'the Symphony.'" Later in these *Essays* he exclaimed, "My God! What has sound got to do with music!"

Music that spoke from the soul with truth, sincerity, and universality was said by Ives to possess "substance." It was very different, he wrote, from the shallow "manner" of composers such as Wagner and Debussy, which too greatly emphasized form, technique, and aural sensuality. An assertive individualism aimed at financial or material advancement in music also diminished substance. For Ives the great artists of substance were Bach, Beethoven, and writers such as Emerson and Thoreau. Like Jean Cocteau, he proclaimed that art should be drawn from life, not from other works of art. Cocteau might also have envied Ives's assessment of Debussy: "Debussy's content would have been worthier his manner if he had hoed corn or sold newspapers for a living."

In order to imbue his own music with substance, Ives makes it depict the musical landscapes of his memory. Quotations of

CHARLES E. IVES
(*Danbury, Conn., 1874–*
New York, 1954)

The greatest influence upon Ives's career as a musician was his father, George Ives, a municipal band leader and free-thinking experimentalist. The musical impressions of his childhood—his father's experiments, traditional European music, and varieties of American popular music—would be a font of inspiration for all of his later work.

Ives attended Yale University from 1894 to 1898, where he studied music with Horatio Parker. Upon graduation he entered an insurance firm in New York City, beginning a career at which he was immediately successful. In 1907 he opened his own agency, which, by his retirement in 1930, had become the largest life insurance firm in the country.

From his college days until he suffered a heart attack in 1918, he worked with furious dedication as a part-time composer. From 1918 to 1922 he published at his own expense his *Concord* Piano Sonata, the rambling *Essays Before a Sonata*, and a collection of *114 Songs*. After completing work on the contents of this songbook in 1921, he virtually ceased composing. Ives's reputation grew steadily from this time, largely due to efforts of his friend Henry Cowell, who printed Ives's works in his periodical *New Music* and arranged for performances in Europe and America. Performances of the *Concord* Sonata in New York in 1939 by John Kirkpatrick brought additional attention to Ives's music. Ives was awarded the Pulitzer Prize in music in 1947 for his Third Symphony.

SELECTED WORKS

Orchestral Music. Four symphonies; fragmentary *Universe* Symphony; *Holidays* Symphony; *Robert Browning* Overture (1912); three orchestral suites ("sets"), the first subtitled *Three Places in New England*; band marches.

Chamber Music. Two piano sonatas (No. 2 subtitled *Concord, Mass., 1840–60*), miscellaneous works for organ including *Variations on America*, two string quartets, four sonatas for violin and piano, experimental music for chamber ensembles including *Central Park in the*

Dark (1906), *The Unanswered Question* (ca. 1906), *From the Steeples and the Mountains* (1901), and *Over the Pavements* (ca. 1906–13).
Songs. Approximately 200 songs, ca. 1886–1929. A collection of *114 Songs* was published privately by Ives in 1922.
Choral Music. *67th Psalm* (ca. 1894), *Three Harvest Home Chorales* (ca. 1898–1901), *The Celestial Country* (1898–99), *Let There Be Light* (1901).

marches, patriotic tunes, and revival hymns punctuate his works. These tunes were part of his background and soul, and they had to be expressed in his music if it was to be sincere and truthful. "If a man finds that the cadences of an Apache war dance come nearest to his soul," he wrote, "let him assimilate whatever he finds highest of the Indian ideal so that he can use it with the cadences, fervently, transcendentally, inevitably, furiously, in his symphonies, in his operas, in his whistlings on the way to work, so that he can paint his house with them." Ives sometimes tries to capture the powerful but unpolished renditions of country bands or revival singers. Other works are evocative musical impressions of scenes welling up in his memory—Central Park after dark, the Housatonic River at Stockbridge, or the sounds of church bells echoing through the mountains of New England.

His music achieved an emancipation of dissonance far in advance of its time. Dissonance was especially valuable to Ives as it matted the shallow surface of music. "Beauty in music," he writes, "is too often confused with something that lets the ears lie back in an easy chair." Ives's dissonant harmony is sometimes systematically constructed: it may draw upon collections of pitches such as whole-tone or pentatonic scales and use them in ways that preserve intervallic unity. In some works, on the contrary, Ives is not systematic in selecting pitches. In these pieces the musical element resides alternately in a vigorous manner of performance or in innovative manipulations of rhythm, space, color, and texture.

Ives was indeed chary of conventional notions of musical unity. "The 'unity of dress' for a man at a ball requires a collar; yet he could dance better without it," he writes. In works such as *The Unanswered Question*, superficial unity is dispelled by a texture consisting of several nonsynchronous streams of sound.

By the end of his apprenticeship at Yale University with Horatio Parker in 1898, Ives had mastered his own highly original musical language. Most of his compositions were written during the next two decades, after which he devoted himself to revising his earlier works and attempting to make them better known. Many pieces were left incomplete or in versions for different media, as Ives rarely composed for a specific performance.

His songs are among his finest music. They reveal the eclectic diversity of his work and contain a cross section of his many styles. The songs belong to three general types. First are those that are tonal, largely triadic, and often in simple repetitive forms. These include early pieces such as "Christmas Carol" and "Memories," settings of German, French, and Italian texts ("Feldeinsamkeit" is an especially handsome example), folk-like tunes ("Side Show" and "Charlie Rutlage"), marching songs ("Circus Band," "Son of Gambolier"), arrangements ("Watchman," "At the River"), and nostalgic narratives ("The Greatest Man"). Except for the earliest songs written under the eye of Horatio Parker, most of these works also contain passages of unconventional harmony, melody, or rhythm.

The second type of song is slow, static, mildly dissonant, and atonal. In this category are such examples as "The Innate," "Serenity," "Thoreau," "Indians," and "Afterglow." Third is a more bombastic, aggressively dissonant type, such as "Majority," "From *Paracelsus*," and "From *Swimmers*." These atonal songs make frequent use of whole-tone sets (as in "White Gulls"), tone clusters ("Majority"), and fourth chords ("The Cage").

Quotations from preexistent tunes may appear in any of the three types; they normally occur when the text of the preexistent melody is appropriate to the sentiments of the song in which it is used. Many of the songs freely combine features of two or more types.

An example of a work combining all three types is "From *Paracelsus*" (1921, Anthology no. 12). This song—a reworking of passages from the *Robert Browning* Overture (1912)—sets lines from Browning's closet drama *Paracelsus* (1835). The play fictionalizes thoughts of the sixteenth-century Swiss physician and mystic Philippus Aureolus Paracelsus, and it emphasizes Browning's philosophy of the proper relation of love and knowledge among mankind. Browning was greatly admired by Ives. An interest in transcendental philosophy and a belief that great art sprang from life and experience were shared by both men.

Ives's setting includes passages in each of the three styles described above. It begins with an energetic, dissonant flurry in the piano, settles into a progression in G major in the middle, and ends in dreamy, static atonality. This threefold division corresponds to the three stages in Paracelsus' enlightenment: he is first devoted to power (measures 1–15), then he perceives its limitations (measures 16–17), and finally he understands that power must be preceded by love (measures 17–20).

The opening is bombastically dissonant, marked by busy chromatic lines, chords moving in parallel by semitone, and abrupt disjunctions in register. The song has no stable meter, and its division into measures is free. Whole-tone or nearly-whole-tone harmonies are emphasized as well as pentatonic chords and diatonic sets (triads, seventh chords, and "white key" clusters). All of these harmonies may be observed in Example 12-1 (measures 10–12). The transition to a passage in G major is accomplished by bitriadic harmonies in measure 15, and the conclusion ("always preceding power . . .") uses whole-tone chords which finally resolve upon the note D.

"Charlie Rutlage" (before 1921, Anthology no. 12) is a predominantly tonal and diatonic song with an atonal middle section. The text, by the Montana rhymester D. J. O'Malley, perfectly embodies Ives's conception of art, as it brings together the mundane and the spiritual. On a typical day at work, the cowboy Charlie must suddenly confront his fate, as he is killed by his falling horse. The outer

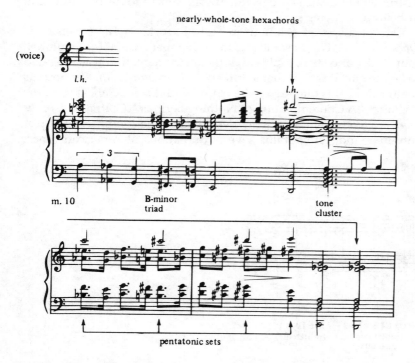

Example 12-1. Ives, "From *Paracelsus*." © 1935 Merion Music Inc. Reprinted with permission.

sections of the song are in a quirky folk-song style; the piece begins
in F major and passes quickly through C (measure 6), D (suggested
by its dominant, 8–12), Bb (13–16), and A (16–17). The vocal melody
begins with pentatonic motion (measures 1–7), which not only
enhances its flavor as folk song, but also connects it to pentatonic
harmonies later in the piece.

The middle part begins at measure 21 as the voice changes from
song to rhythmic narration. The piano spins out a static ostinato figure while the accompanist takes the part of Charlie, calling out
"Whoopee ti yi yo, git along little dogies!" to a variant of the opening pentatonic melody. Whole-tone chords and tone clusters bring
the music to a frantic climax as Charlie is killed by his falling horse.
Solemn pentatonic chords shown in Example 12-2 lead back to the
music of the beginning.

Ives's works for instruments include string quartets, violin
sonatas, and piano sonatas as well as experimental chamber music,
symphonies, and a fragmentary *Universe* Symphony in which creation, evolution, and heaven were to be depicted. Virtually all of his
instrumental music is programmatically linked to his philosophical
or historical interests.

One of his most original orchestral works is *The Unanswered
Question* (ca. 1906). This piece is for a chamber ensemble of trumpet,
four flutes, and strings, although the instrumentation was intended
to be flexible. It was at first subtitled "A Contemplation of a Serious
Matter" and was intended to be paired with *Central Park in the Dark*,
the latter "A Contemplation of Nothing Serious." *Central Park in the
Dark* is a lively orchestral work described by the composer as a "pic-
ture-in-sound." It contains several quotations of American tunes.

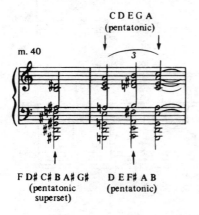

Example 12-2. Ives, *Charlie Rutlage,* © copyright 1939 by Arrow Music
Press, Inc. Copyright assigned 1957 to Associated Music Publishers, Inc.

The Unanswered Question does not contain quotations, but it exemplifies the contemplative, impressionistic sonority of much of Ives's best music, his adaptation of a philosophical program, and his technique of layering several loosely coordinated musical strata.

In the foreword to the score, the composer outlines the program of the work, which has to do with the "perennial question of existence" by which mankind is eternally confronted but to which no satisfactory answer can be found. The strings provide the backdrop of the continuum of time. They play serenely and continuously in G major with little definition of beat or meter. The other strata are not precisely coordinated: they react to one another in the free manner of a dialogue. The trumpet states a five-note non-triadic motive which poses the question of life's meaning. The flutes, which represent mankind, seek an answer, beginning softly and slowly, but becoming progressively louder and more animated. As their answers are frustratingly inadequate, they become increasingly shrill and densely chromatic. Example 12-3 shows the final chords of each of their first five statements, which move gradually from a diminished triad to a semitonal cluster. The flutes then gather for a "secret conference" (to quote the composer) and, realizing the futility of their quest, they mock the question derisively

Example 12-3. Ives, *The Unanswered Question.* Copyright 1953 by Southern Music Publishing Co., copyright renewed by Peer International Corp. International copyright secured. Reprinted by permission.

Example 12-4. Ives, *The Unanswered Question.* Copyright 1953 by Southern Music Publishing Co., copyright renewed by Peer International Corp. International copyright secured. Reprinted by permission.

(Example 12-4). But their noisy argument is to no avail as the trumpet returns with the unanswered question and the strings continue their endless melody.

Carl Ruggles (1876–1971) shared with his friend Charles Ives a stubborn Yankee individualism, an openness to experimental ideas, and an untiring fondness for dissonance. But their differences in style far outweigh their similarities. Ruggles was not an eclectic like Ives: he hewed to a unified language that banished diatonic structures and strove instead toward chromatic saturation. Ruggles did not use quotations of preexistent music, nor was his music as graph-

Thomas Hart Benton, *The Sun-Treader—Portrait of Carl Ruggles*. (Courtesy of The Nelson-Atkins Museum of Art, Kansas City, Missouri.)

ically programmatic as Ives's. Much of Ives's music depended upon a spirited performance rather than a precise rendition of notated pitches. But Ruggles's music is more consistently organized in pitch, making an accurate reading crucial to its effect.

Ruggles was an exceedingly meticulous worker. His first mature composition was the song "Toys," which he completed at the age 43. His oeuvre remained small, as he devoted himself increasingly in his later years to painting as well as to music. He is best known for a few orchestral works (of which *Sun-Treader*, 1932, is outstanding), the brass ensemble *Angels* (1921), songs, and four *Evocations* (1935–44, rev. 1954) for piano.

Evocation No. 4 will illustrate the austere simplicity, uncompromising dissonance, and strict pitch organization of all of his music. The revised version is dedicated to Charles Ives, a supporter of Ruggles, who died in the year that the revision was made. It shares with much of Ives's music a slow, wistful contemplativeness. The piece is in ternary form with an animated middle section beginning at measure 11 and a varied reprise at measure 25. Constantly changing tempi and meters and irregular divisions of the beat—characteristics of all of his music—create a "musical prose" akin to the work of Schoenberg. The piece is also Schoenbergian in its chromatic density, avoidance of triadic structures, and certain harmonic relations, but its spare texture and motivic sequences are unlike most of Schoenberg's music.

The texture of the work emphasizes line, which, the composer remarked, "is the basis of all music." Harmonies are built by sustaining melodic notes through a pedaling effect, which is also imitated in orchestral works such as *Sun-Treader*. The line that opens this *Evocation* (Example 12-5) illustrates a guiding melodic principle for Ruggles, by which a pitch class was usually not repeated until the tenth or eleventh note. He rarely constructed lines containing all twelve pitch classes in succession, as in the twelve-tone method, since this would amount, in his words, to "a dog chasing its tail." The opening motive (D G F♯ C♯ F C) is made so that its sequential repetition in the second measure (B E D♯ A♯ D A) will produce a recurrence of the first pitch class D as the eleventh note of the line. The chromatic aggregate is then completed by the next two notes, A and A♭.

The *Evocations* use a rudimentary serialism, suggesting that Ruggles was aware of Schoenberg's twelve-tone method. An example in *Evocation* No. 4 is the thirteen-note series of pitches in measures 15–18: G C F♯ F B♭ E E♭ A♭ D D♭ G♭ C B. This series is a concatenation of forms of its initial trichord (G C F♯), which is spun out by sequential repetitions. The series recurs in retrograde and with an inverted contour in measures 21–23, beginning with the note B-natural.

Example 12-5. Ruggles, *Evocation* No. 4 for piano. Revision of 1954, edited by John Kirkpatrick. Original version copyright 1943 by Carl Ruggles. Revised version copyright 1956 by American Music Edition. Reprinted by permission of Theodore Presser Co.

COMPOSERS ON THE WEST COAST:
COWELL, CAGE, HARRISON, PARTCH

The early works of Henry Cowell (1897–1965) were experimental studies in new musical resources. These include early applications of tone clusters on the piano, noise, and open or "elastic" forms. In the 1940s and 1950s, he produced most of his twenty symphonies, eighteen *Hymns and Fuguing Tunes*, music for Asian instruments, and numerous works in other genres, most of which adopt a more conventional style. Cowell was an active supporter of the music of Charles Ives, and Ives generously contributed to Cowell's periodical *New Music Quarterly* (1927–58), in which the scores of several major American composers were first published.

One of Cowell's most resourceful works of the experimental type is "The Banshee" (1925, Anthology no. 71). In this piece the performer produces both fixed and sliding pitches by manipulating strings inside the piano. These sounds suggest the cry of the banshee, a mythical creature in Irish folklore whose unearthly wail forecast death. Fixed pitches establish two recurrent motives. The first, heard in long values at the outset, imitates the funeral chant "Dies irae." The second (measures 8, 20, 33) is a short motive made from plucking the strings.

"The Banshee" illustrates the expansion of sources of sound that underlies the work of several other American experimentalists. Noise—sounds, that is, of unfixed pitch—had been used earlier by the Italian Futurist Luigi Russolo (1885–1947), but his music was never more than an obscure curiosity. The liberation of sound by Americans such as Cowell, John Cage, and Edgard Varèse, on the contrary, had a lasting impact on the history of musical style, as it laid the foundation for electronic and taped media of the 1950s and led to significant and widespread changes in musical structure.

Cowell referred to music made of noise and sliding pitch in his book *New Musical Resources* (1917–19, rev. ca. 1930):

> Natural sounds, such as the wind playing through trees or grasses, or whistling in the chimney, or the sound of the sea, or thunder, all make use of sliding tones. It is not impossible that such tones may be made the foundation of an art of composition by some composer who would reverse the programmatic concept. . . . Such a composer would build perhaps abstract music out of sounds of the same category as natural sound—that is, sliding pitches—not with the idea of trying to imitate nature, but as a new tonal foundation.

This "new tonal foundation"—which would be explored more by Cowell's student John Cage than by Cowell himself—had momentous significance. Not only did it admit to music a new and intriguing palette of sounds, but, more important, it diminished the importance of pitch and interval as the structural bases of music. Cowell helped to set in motion a new understanding of musical form, the ramifications of which would be worked out by major composers in Europe and America after the Second World War.

Cowell's experiments with sounds of variable pitch and noise were carried on by his student John Cage (1912–92). Cage's works of the early 1930s were chromatic contrapuntal studies, some of which used a type of serialism learned from the music of another of his teachers, Arnold Schoenberg. Cage's music from 1939 through the 1940s dwelled upon new sonorities and innovative ways of organizing them. He was a pioneer in the use of electronic gadgetry to pro-

JOHN CAGE (*Los Angeles, 1912–*
New York, 1992)

Cage's teachers of music included Richard Buhlig, Adolph Weiss, Henry Cowell, and Arnold Schoenberg. Beginning in 1937 he was active as an accompanist and composer for modern dance groups, and he later toured throughout the world as composer for the Merce Cunningham Dance Company. In 1942 he moved to New York where he quickly established a reputation as a leader of the avant-garde. His study of Zen with Dr. Daisetz Suzuki led to his "chance" music of the early 1950s, work that soon exerted an influence on both European and American composition.

Cage's interests were broad, extending not only to the modern arts but to other fields such as the study of mushrooms. He was associated with several American universities, including Wesleyan University, the University of Illinois, and the University of California, Davis.

SELECTED WORKS

Music for Prepared Piano. *Bacchanale* (1940), *Tossed as It Is Untroubled* (1943), *Perilous Night* (1943–44), *A Book of Music* (two prepared pianos, 1944), Three Dances (two prepared pianos, 1944–45), *Sonatas and Interludes* (1946–48).

Percussion Ensembles. *Imaginary Landscape* Nos. 1–5 (1939–52), *Construction* Nos. 1–3 (1939–41), *Double Music* (with Lou Harrison, 1941), *Credo in Us* (1942), *Amores* (1936–43 [movements 1 and 4 for solo prepared piano]).

Music for Other Conventional Media. *Seasons* (piano or orchestra, 1947), String Quartet in Four Parts (1949–50), Concerto for Prepared Piano and Chamber Orchestra (1950–51), *Music of Changes* (piano, 1951), *Music for Piano* (Nos. 1–84, 1952–56), *Aria* (solo voice, 1958), *Cheap Imitation* (piano, 1969).

Music with Tape or with Live Electronic Manipulation. *Williams Mix* (1952), *Fontana Mix* (1958–59), *Cartridge Music* (1960), *HPSCHD* (1967–69).

Aleatoric Music of Unfixed Medium. 4'33" (1952) (followed by a series of
works with durational titles), Variations (1–8, 1958–78), *Theater Piece*
(1960), Improvisations (1–4, 1975–80), Quartets 1–8 (1976–77).

duce musical sounds, and he refined Cowell's methods of manipulating strings within the piano. Several works for percussion ensemble emphasize metallic sonorities reminiscent of oriental music. In
pieces such as *Living Room Music* (1940), Cage instructs the percussionists to choose everyday household objects upon which to produce musical sounds.

His most resourceful new musical instrument was the "prepared"
piano, which he first used as a solo medium in *Bacchanale* (ca.
1938–40). Objects such as screws, bolts, erasers, and bits of plastic and
rubber were placed between the strings of the instrument according
to instructions of the composer. The piano was thus transformed into
a percussion ensemble which could produce tones of fixed pitch as
well as colorful noises. Cage's prepared instrument often approximated the sound of Balinese gamelans, which he had earlier imitated
in such percussion ensembles as his three *Constructions* (1939–41).

He matched these innovations in musical timbre with new structural principles. Increasingly, these were determined by rhythmic
or durational considerations rather than by harmony, motive, or
other configurations of pitches. In an article in *Modern Music* of
1942, Cage states:

> In writing for these sounds, as in writing for percussion instruments
> alone, the composer is dealing with material that does not fit into the
> orthodox scales and harmonies. It is therefore necessary to find some
> other organizing means than those in use for symphonic instruments.
> The sounds cannot be organized through reference to an underlying
> fundamental tone since such a tone does not exist. Each sound must
> be considered as essentially different from and independent of every
> other sound. . . . Because of the nature of the materials involved, and
> because their duration characteristics can be easily controlled and
> related, it is more than likely that the unifying means will be rhythmic.

In a lecture at Black Mountain College in 1948 on Erik Satie, he
pointed to the music of Webern and Satie as the earliest in which duration rather than pitch created basic formal patterns. He continued:

> If you consider that sound is characterized by its pitch, its loudness,
> its timbre, and its duration, and that silence, which is the opposite
> and, therefore, the necessary partner of sound, is characterized only

by its duration, you will be drawn to the conclusion that of these four characteristics of the material of music, duration, that is, time length, is the most fundamental.

Beginning with *Imaginary Landscape* No. 1 (1939), the basic designs of his music were prearranged successions of durations following simple numerical ratios. The *First Construction (in Metal)* (1939), for example, consisted of sixteen sections that were grouped according to the ratios 4:3:2:3:4. Such durational plans may have been suggested to Cage by the theories of Cowell, who speculated in *New Musical Resources* about the extension of simple integral ratios of the overtone series to all musical parameters.

In his earlier works using predetermined patterns of duration, the ratios that controlled large-scale form were duplicated on the small scale as well. In the *First Construction (in Metal)*, for example, each of the sixteen sections contains sixteen measures. These were grouped by similar instrumentation into a succession of four, three, two, three, and four measures, thus duplicating the large structure. In later works of the 1940s, however, Cage often dispensed with any logical preplanning of small-scale durations. He was content instead to lay out a strictly planned large structure and freely allow these durations to be filled by conventional musical sounds, noise, or silence.

Cage's most substantial work for prepared piano is *Sonatas and Interludes* (1946–48). This 70-minute cycle consists of sixteen sonatas, each in binary form A A B B, and four through-composed interludes. The composer sought to convey in them a panorama of emotions. "After reading the work of Ananda K. Coomaraswamy," he wrote, "I decided to attempt the expression in music of the 'permanent emotions' of Indian tradition: the heroic, the erotic, the wondrous, the mirthful, sorrow, fear, anger, the odious, and their common tendency toward tranquility."

Among these slow and quiet pieces, Sonata No. 5 (Anthology no. 9) is perhaps the most mirthful. Its large form is determined by a prearranged sequence of durations, which may be expressed in numbers of half notes:

A—				B—			Codetta	
‖:	18	¦	18	:‖‖:	18 ¦ 18	¦	9	:‖
		⎣——— 36 ———⎦			⎣——— 45 ———⎦			

As in the *First Construction (in Metal)*, these durations are reduceable to simple numerical ratios, here 4:4:5:5 (equivalent to 36:36:45:45).

The content of each subsection is not so precisely structured; indeed, it is improvisational in character. The pitches in both hands wander chromatically between the notes B and Eb. The sonorous image of this sonata—which is not directly revealed by its notation—resembles a duet between a drum-like left hand and bell sounds in the right. It is thus closely related to the sound of the gamelan.

Cage's music of the 1950s underwent a radical change, as he brought elements of chance into the compositional process and, under the influence of oriental philosophy, questioned the conventional acceptance of art as a form of communication. Both his ideas and music proved immensely influential in the decade after the Second World War, and his work of these years will be taken up again in Chapter 14.

Lou Harrison (1917–) shared much of the background of John Cage, with whom he was closely associated in the 1930s. Like Cage he was a student of Cowell and Schoenberg and active as a composer for dance. He collaborated with Cage in organizing and composing for percussion ensembles, and, like Cage, he was inspired by the sonorities of oriental music. His works contain innovative sources of sound (such as the tin cans so congenial to Cage) and a type of prepared piano in which tacks are inserted into the hammers of the instrument. He composed in conventional genres such as the symphony and concerto, music for percussion ensembles, and works imitating oriental media such as the gamelan.

Harry Partch (1901–74) was an entirely self-made musician. By 1928 he developed a unique technique and philosophy that is described in his book *Genesis of a Music*. The basis of his system is a microtonal scale that divides the octave into forty-three pitches, tones that can be realized on a variety of string, wind, and percussion instruments of his own making. Most of these are based on non-Western or ancient models, and they include devices that he dubbed with exotic names such as the "spoils of war" and the "eucal blossom." Performances of his works are often multimedia events in which dance and recitation play a role.

EDGARD VARÈSE

The French-born Edgard Varèse (1883–1965) may be considered an American composer not only because he spent most of his adult life in this country, but also because his experimental temperament and his eagerness to bring new sounds and formal procedures to music closely allied him to developments among native-born musicians.

EDGARD VARÈSE
(*Paris, 1883–New York, 1965*)

Varèse's youth was spent in Burgundy, a region to which he was greatly attached, in Turin, where he attended a scientific and technical school, and in Paris, where he pursued his musical education at the Schola Cantorum and Conservatory. In 1907 he moved to Berlin, attracted there by opportunities for modern music. His early compositions—all of which were subsequently lost or destroyed—were praised by Richard Strauss, Busoni, and Hugo von Hofmannsthal. He also began his career as an orchestral and choral conductor.

After wartime service in the French army, he immigrated in 1915 to America; he lived in New York for the remainder of his life except for frequent sojourns in France and Germany. He was co-founder of the International Composers' Guild (1921–27) and Pan-American Association of Composers (1928–34), both societies devoted to performances of modern music. In addition to private teaching in New York, he was temporarily associated with the faculties of Columbia University and the International Summer Courses for New Music in Darmstadt.

SELECTED WORKS

Orchestral Music. *Amériques* (1918–22), *Arcana* (1925–27).
Chamber Ensembles. *Offrandes* (with voice, 1921), *Hyperprism* (1923),
    Octandre (1923), *Intégrales* (1924), *Ionisation* (percussion ensemble, 1931),
    Ecuatorial (with voice, 1934), *Density 21.5* (solo flute, 1936), *Nocturnal*
    (with soprano and chorus, unfinished, 1961).
Works with Tape. *Déserts* (tape alternating with instruments, 1954), "Good
    Friday Procession in Verges" (for the film *Around and About Joan Miró*,
    1956), *Poème électronique* (1958).

Varèse, like his mentor Ferruccio Busoni, was a cosmopolitan. He resided alternately in France, Italy, Germany, and America, and he was sympathetic to the culture and musical traditions of all four nations. He was personally acquainted with many of the founders of modernism in France and Germany.

In 1921 Varèse and the harpist Carlos Salzedo founded the International Composers' Guild, which for six years sponsored concerts of modern music in New York City. The Guild was comparable in aim to the Society for Private Musical Performances, which had been organized by Arnold Schoenberg in Vienna three years earlier. Both groups were devoted to performing modern music by composers of all nationalities and styles. In his prospectus for the Guild, Varèse wrote, "The International Composers' Guild refuses to admit any limitation, either of volition or action. The International Composers' Guild disapproves of all 'isms'; denies the existence of schools; recognizes only the individual." Although their programs included works by several European neoclassicists (a movement opposed by Varèse), the Guild was associated primarily with music of the avant-garde. They brought to New York the first American performances of works by Schoenberg, Bartók, Stravinsky, and Varèse himself. In 1928 the Guild was superseded by the Pan-American Association of Composers, in which experimental directions were reinforced by the participation of Henry Cowell, Charles Ives, and the composer-conductor Nicolas Slonimsky.

Varèse's music falls into three chronological and stylistic areas. His works before 1914 consist of pieces for orchestra and an uncompleted opera, all of which were either lost or destroyed. Between 1918 and 1936, after his immigration to the United States, he completed nine works for orchestra or chamber ensemble which realize in conventional media his visionary ideas on musical form and content. After a period of almost two decades when no new works were completed, he pioneered the compositional use of taped electronic sounds.

Varèse emphasizes sound and rhythm, and he dispenses with conventional principles of meter, harmony, texture, and form. He was a crusader for new musical instruments: "I dream of instruments obedient to my thought," he wrote in the journal *391* in 1917, "which, with their contribution of a whole new world of unsuspected sounds, will lend themselves to the exigencies of my inner rhythm."

He hoped to replace conventional textures with mobile interplay among masses of sound. In a lecture in Santa Fe in 1936 he remarked:

> Music as I conceive it [consists in] the movement of sound-masses, of shifting planes. . . . When these sound-masses collide the phenomena of penetration or repulsion will seem to occur. Certain transmutations

taking place on certain planes will seem to be projected onto other planes, moving at different speeds and at different angles. There will no longer be the old conception of melody or interplay of melodies. The entire work will be a melodic totality. The entire work will flow as a river flows.

Rhythm was also to be liberated from its confinement to regular pulse and metric organization: "In my own works," he remarked in a lecture in 1959 at Princeton University, "rhythm derives from the simultaneous interplay of unrelated elements that intervene at calculated, but not regular time lapses." Varèse was inspired by science and technology, which is reflected in his choice of musical titles. But his works are written in a nonprogrammatic, nonreferential language:

> There is more musical fertility in the contemplation of the stars—preferably through a telescope—and the high poetry of certain mathematical expositions than in the most sublime gossip of human passions. However, there are no planets or theorems to be looked for in my music. Music being a special form of thought can, I believe, express nothing but itself. [From program notes to the first performance of *Intégrales*, 1925.]

The forms of Varèse's music are largely through composed, although most of his works contain localized repetitions and occasional recurrence of harmonies or motives on a larger scale. He rejected the notion that music should be shaped into a preestablished form or composed according to a formal system. Instead, each work establishes its own form, which results from a "process" by which an initial idea is spun into a unique shape by the motor of rhythm and other unspecified forces. "Form is a result—the result of a process," he stated in his Princeton lecture. "Each of my works discovers its own form. . . . There is an idea, the basis of an internal structure, expanded and split into different shapes or groups of sound constantly changing in shape, direction, and speed, attracted and repulsed by various forces. The form of the work is the consequence of this interaction. Possible musical forms are as limitless as the exterior forms of crystals."

The first movement of *Octandre* (1923, Anthology no. 24) illustrates several of these formal characteristics. This work, which is in three short movements, is for a chamber ensemble of eight different instruments. The medium shows Varèse's fondness for the small heterogeneous ensemble that emphasizes woodwinds and brass, but it is untypical in its lack of percussion instruments. The work is freely atonal and chromatic, and it does not consistently project any standard harmonic elements. The composer later stated in notes to *Déserts* (1954) that his music "was not based on any fixed set of intervals such as a scale or series, or any existing principle of musical measurement."

The movement is tied together by varied recurrences of a descending chromatic motive heard in the oboe in the first measure. The motive in its original contour returns at the end of the movement. This figure constitutes the "idea" of internal structure, about which Varèse spoke in his lecture at Princeton. It is freely transformed into blocks of sound—largely of chromatic content—which are juxtaposed, overlapped, or intersected. Typical of Varèse's instrumental music, the parts are often driven to extremes of register; they do not project a stable beat or meter, and their figures are repeated locally before moving on to a new "mass" of sound.

Varèse's music forms a bridge between the European avant-garde of the first two decades of the century and music after World War II. He helped to preserve the spirit of the avant-garde in a period when this movement was abandoned by many. His understanding of musical space as "open rather than bounded" became widespread after the Second World War, even if particulars of his style of "organized sound" were superseded by new musical ideas.

BIBLIOGRAPHY

Experimental music in America prior to World War II is surveyed by David Nicholls in *American Experimental Music, 1890–1940* (Cambridge, 1990) and John Struble in *The History of American Classical Music: MacDowell through Minimalism* (New York, 1995). Frank Rossiter's *Charles Ives and his America* (New York, 1975) is an outstanding study of the composer's life and cultural milieu. H. Wiley Hitchcock's *Ives* (London, 1977) is a short analytic survey. Stuart Feder's *Charles Ives: "My Father's Song"* (New Haven, 1992) is an important psychoanalytic study of the composer. Ives's own reminiscences or *Memos*, written in 1931 and 1932, have been edited with copious annotations by John Kirkpatrick (New York, 1972); this document served as the basis of the pioneering study of Ives by his friends Henry and Sidney Cowell (1955). Ives's writings are collected by Howard Boatwright in the volume *Essays Before a Sonata, The Majority, and Other Writings* (New York, 1962). The epilogue to his *Essays* is Ives's most important statement of his musical outlook.

An informative and amusing study of Ruggles is John Kirkpatrick's "Evolution of Carl Ruggles: A Chronicle Largely in His Own Words," *Perspectives of New Music*, 6 (1968), and Marilyn

Ziffrin's *Carl Ruggles: Composer, Painter, and Storyteller* (Urbana, 1994) is a broad biographical study. Henry Cowell's *New Musical Resources* (New York, 1969) was written in 1919, and it reveals the author's experimental spirit. It was influential on many later American composers, including Conlon Nancarrow. Cowell's music is surveyed by Hugo Weisgall in "Music of Henry Cowell," *Musical Quarterly*, 45 (1959). Also see the provocative article by Michael Hicks, "The Imprisonment of Henry Cowell," *Journal of the American Musicological Society*, 44 (1991):92–119.

Articles and lectures by John Cage are collected in numerous volumes, of which *Silence* (Middletown, Conn., 1961) is especially recommended. Cage's music has been studied in volumes by Paul Griffiths (London, 1981) and James Pritchett (Cambridge, 1993). Also see collections of essays edited by Richard Kostelanetz (*John Cage*, New York, 1970) and Marjorie Perloff and Charles Junkermann (*John Cage: Composed in America*, Chicago, 1994). The correspondence between Cage and Boulez, ed. Jean-Jacques Nattiez (Cambridge, 1993), is of considerable historical importance.

A detailed analytic study of the music of Varèse is provided by Jonathan W. Bernard in his *Music of Edgard Varèse* (New Haven, 1987). Louise Norton Varèse's engagingly written biography *Varèse: A Looking-Glass Diary*, Vol. 1 (New York, 1972) traces her husband's life and career to 1928. It is supplemented by several articles by his student Chou Wen-Chung: "Varèse: A Sketch of the Man and His Music," *Musical Quarterly*, 52 (1966) and "Open Rather Than Bounded," *Perspectives of New Music*, 5 (1966). Varèse's lectures at Santa Fe (1936), the University of Southern California (1939), Princeton (1959), and Yale (1962) are summarized in the article "Liberation of Sound," *Perspectives of New Music*, 5 (1966), and his illuminating "Conversation" with Gunther Schuller is recorded in the same journal, 3 (1965).

PART THREE

Music from 1945 to the Present

13

The Revival of the Avant-Garde

As Europe emerged from the chaotic aftermath of World War II, it appeared likely that neoclassicism would remain in the dominant position that it occupied before the war. Many of the leaders of modernism earlier in the century were now in retirement or in exile: Berg and Webern were dead, and Schoenberg had not established a following in America as he earlier had in Europe. Works by Hindemith and Stravinsky seemed destined to become the models for musical developments in the postwar years.

But the decade after the Second World War was instead a period of dramatic and far-reaching innovations in style which pushed neoclassicism far from the center of attention. The war thus had the opposite effect of the First World War, which had temporarily halted progressivism as an important trend in music. For many artists the legacy of the Second World War was a cynical view of the human condition and psyche that called for a clean slate. Elliott Carter remarked that his conversion from neoclassicism was provoked by his realization that violence was an unavoidable part of human nature. He says in *Flawed Words and Stubborn Sounds*:

Before the end of the Second World War, it became clear to me, partly as a result of rereading Freud and others and thinking about psycho-

319

analysis, that we were living in a world where this physical and intellectual violence would always be a problem and that the whole conception of human nature underlying the neoclassic esthetic amounted to a sweeping under the rug of things that, it seemed to me, we had to deal with in a less oblique and resigned way.

Similarly in Europe the leading younger composers ruthlessly dismissed the musical language of their forebears. Pierre Boulez, for example, proclaimed serialism to be the only path for future development. "I . . . assert that any musician who has not experienced—I do not say understood, but, in all exactness, experienced—the necessity for the dodecaphonic language is USELESS. For his whole work is irrelevant to the needs of his epoch" (from "Eventuellement," 1952).

Boulez's words suggest a new doctrinaire spirit that would be opposed to the eclecticism of prewar neoclassical or populist composers. The "needs of the epoch" to which he also referred were interpreted in most of the younger composers after 1945 as a demand for the reestablishment of control in music—clearly a reaction against the chaos of the war. For many, control was reasserted by an intensified application of serial methods; for others, automatized composition seemed to be the order of the day. An application of technology in the process of making music also appeared germane to the postwar spirit. The angst that spread throughout the world, as details of the Holocaust became known and as the threat of nuclear warfare became menacingly real, made composers suppress their expressive instincts and adopt a style of music that was depersonalized, abstract, difficult, even ludicrous. Much of the music that appeared after World War II poignantly embodied the sentiments of Theodor Adorno: "To write poetry after Auschwitz is barbaric!"

ATONALITY AND SERIALISM IN AMERICA

The evolution of style in music by Elliott Carter (1908–) mirrors the general transformation in American musical culture from cautious experimentation in the 1920s to neoclassicism in the 1930s to avant-garde innovations in the decades following the Second World War. Carter's mature style was formed in the late 1940s, when he dispensed with his earlier neoclassical populism—an idiom that he then dismissed as "music for a masquerade in a bomb shelter." Yet Carter also kept his distance from the experimental directions of American and European composers of the postwar era. He writes in traditional genres for conventional media, and he has not adopted techniques of serialism. He is especially chary of the emancipation of sound so congenial to American experimentalists since Varèse. "I don't believe in novelty of sound for its own sake," he said in *Flawed Words and Stubborn Sounds*.

Carter has been most resourceful in his attempts to establish a new temporal organization in music:

> The flow of the music [is] the most important thing; the "now" of any given point to me is only as significant as how it came to be "now" and what happens afterward. Therefore to me composing consists in dealing with the flow of music rather than with particular instants of sound, which is why I've never been so interested in remarkable sounds or effects of any kind for themselves alone, because they seem to evoke a very elementary past or future. [From *Flawed Words*.]

To explore the flow of music, he first dispensed with traditional temporal processes such as regular meter, a single common pulse in all parts, and regular divisions of the beat. He also eliminated the demarcation of time brought about by a thematic or motivic statement followed by its development. In place of these conventional ways of organizing time, Carter erected intricate contrapuntal textures consisting of distinct strata which progressively interchange features. Such compositions become, in his words, "large, unified musical actions or gestures."

Each line or stratum in a work by Carter normally begins with its own "personality," created by a unique combination of tempo, rhythmic figures, intervals, and expressive gestures. These personalities subsequently interact as characters in an inarticulate drama: they dominate momentarily or recede into the background, they take on the features of other characters, and they evolve within themselves.

The First String Quartet (1951) is one of Carter's earliest works in this mature style. It combines a three-movement and a four-movement shape. The more essential form consists of four connected parts: fantasia, allegro scorrevole, adagio, and variations. But the traditional pauses between movements occur, first, within the allegro section and then within the variations, thus creating an apparent three-movement cycle. The composer wished to avoid a pause at a major change of tempo since these are climactic moments in a work with almost constant changes of speed.

The First String Quartet is unusual among Carter's works after 1950 in its substantial amount of motivic development and recurrence. A large number of motives are introduced throughout the fantasia, for example, and these recur freely in different shapes in a through-composed continuum. The ongoing development is broken only by a brief reprise at measure 138 and by a climactic stretto

ELLIOTT CARTER
(*New York, 1908–*)

A fascination with the avant-garde compositions of Stravinsky, Scriabin, and Varèse led Elliott Carter toward the career of a professional composer. In 1924 he was introduced to Charles Ives with whom he maintained personal contact until the early 1930s. Carter attended Harvard University from 1926 to 1932, dividing his interests in music with the study of other arts and letters. On advice of his teacher, Walter Piston, he traveled to France in 1932 to study with Nadia Boulanger.

He returned to America in 1935 and became musical director of the newly formed Ballet Caravan. Subsequently, he held teaching positions in music and in the humanities at several American universities and conservatories. Among his many awards and honors is the Pulitzer Prize, which he received in 1960 for his Second String Quartet.

SELECTED WORKS

Orchestral Music and Concertos. *Holiday* Overture (1944); Variations for Orchestra (1953–55); Piano Concerto (1963–65); Concerto for Orchestra (1970); Double Concerto for Harpsichord and Piano and Two Chamber Orchestras (1961); Symphony of Three Orchestras (1976–77); Oboe Concerto (1987); Violin Concerto (1990).

Chamber Music. Four string quartets (1951, 1960, 1971, 1986); Brass Quintet (1974); Sonata for Cello and Piano (1948); Piano Sonata (1945–46); Eight Pieces for Four Timpani (1950–1968); Eight Etudes and a Fantasy for Woodwind Quartet (1950); Sonata for Flute, Oboe, Cello, and Harpsichord (1952–53); Duo for Violin and Piano (1974); *Night Fantasies* for piano (1979–80); *Penthode* for five groups of instruments (1985); *Riconoscenza* for solo violin (1984); Triple Duo for flute, clarinet, violin, cello, piano, and percussion (1983).

Songs and Vocal Ensembles. *A Mirror on Which to Dwell* (soprano, instruments) (1976); *Syringa* (mezzo-soprano, bass, instruments) (1978); *In Sleep, in Thunder* for tenor voice and chamber ensemble (1981).

beginning at measure 213, where several earlier themes are brought back simultaneously. This latter passage also functions as a transition to the second of four movements (allegro scorrevole) beginning at measure 356.

Important themes and motives are often presented simultaneously, each establishing a character of its own by intervallic contour as well as by its own tempo, dynamic level, playing technique, and expression. The passage beginning at measure 22 is an example of such a simultaneous exposition. Here, five important themes are heard (the one in the second violin had been introduced in measure 12). Each theme is extremely simple in rhythm, moving almost entirely by equal values. But each moves at a different pace with different expressive gestures. These are summarized in Example 13-1, where the rhythm of each theme is renotated in quarter notes.

After this expository passage, the pacing in each part begins a continuous process of change, which is carried on by metric modulations (see Chapter 5). Each of the five themes occasionally darts out in new guises and, having had its brief moment in the spotlight, recedes into the "flow" of passing time.

An antecedent of Carter's temporal and polyphonic idiom is found in the music of Charles Ives. Carter was acquainted with Ives in the 1920s in New York City, but he was later critical of the untutored quality of much of Ives's work. Ives's innovations in texture nevertheless became Carter's point of departure for all of his mature music. Perhaps in homage to this influence, Carter quotes the bass line of the opening of Ives's First Sonata for Violin and Piano as the cello theme in measure 27 of the First String Quartet.

Ives's *Unanswered Question* (discussed in Chapter 12) is an example of polyphonic stratification of distinct but interactive lines—a concept that reappears with greater abstraction in Carter's First String Quartet. Each of the three strata of *The Unanswered Question* has its own tempo and dramatic character. Like the lines of the First String Quartet, strata of *The Unanswered Question* reflect upon one another, for example, when the woodwinds sneeringly imitate the line of the trumpet. Ives's use of metric modulation in the *Robert Browning* Overture (see Chapter 5) prefigures its appearance in Carter's music.

Carter organizes his music to a considerable extent by recurring pitch-class sets. Usually one or more sets will emerge as central, made especially evident at important structural junctures. In the First String Quartet these focal harmonies are the two all-interval tetrachords equivalent to those shown in Example 2-21. These sets are prominent in the opening cello cadenza (Example 13-2). All-interval tetrachords were attractive to Carter as unifying sonorities

Example 13-1. Carter, First String Quartet, measures 22–30, five important themes. Copyright 1955, 1956 by Associated Music Publishers, Inc. All rights reserved. Reprinted by permission.

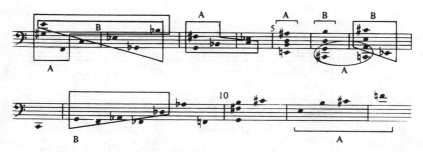

Example 13-2. Carter, First String Quartet, first movement, measures 1–12 (cello), rhythm omitted. Copyright 1955, 1956 by Associated Music Publishers, Inc. All rights reserved. Reprinted by permission.

precisely because they contain all of the interval classes. Each interval is subsequently assigned to one of the lines, helping to mold its distinctive personality. Just as the lines occasionally merge into a single stratum, the intervallic repertories of the lines occasionally come together in these focal harmonies.

In later music Carter availed himself of other sets with similarly comprehensive arrays of subsets. In the Piano Concerto, for example, he uses a hexachord as a referential harmony which has the unique property of containing all the possible types of equivalent trichords (of which there are twelve). One form of this "all-trichord" hexachord is C C♯ D E G G♯. The trichords that it contains are distributed within the different strata to reinforce their essentially distinctive characters.

In more recent compositions such as the Third String Quartet and Symphony of Three Orchestras, the central unifying harmony is a chord of all twelve notes between which each of the eleven intervals of the octave is stated once. The central all-interval harmony of the Third String Quartet is shown in Example 13-3 together with a realization of it (lacking the highest note A♭) in measure 15. Elsewhere the intervals of this chord are parceled out between the work's two "duos" (violin 2–viola and violin 1–cello) and among its various sections.

At the beginning of the Variations movement of his First String Quartet, Carter included a brief quotation from the Study No. 1 by Conlon Nancarrow (1912–), a composer who Carter admitted was "scarcely known even in America." The music of Nancarrow remained obscure until the 1970s, when it was recorded and caused a sensation in modern music circles both in the United States and abroad.

Nancarrow was born in Arkansas, studied music with Roger Sessions and Walter Piston, among others, and was active as a per-

Example 13-3.   Carter, Third String Quartet, central all-interval harmony
and realization in measure 15. © 1973 by Associated Music Publishers, Inc.
All rights reserved. Reprinted by permission.

former of jazz. In 1940 he emigrated to Mexico. Most of his music is
written for the medium of player piano, which allows him to construct contrapuntal studies of great rhythmic nuance and complexity.
He is the composer also of a smaller number of instrumental pieces,
including three String Quartets. The player piano Studies (of which
there are more than fifty, dating from the late 1940s) show the
American composer's resourcefulness with rhythm, and in their contrapuntal complexity they are akin to the music of Ives and Carter.

Study 3a, the beginning of what Nancarrow calls the "Boogie-
Woogie Suite," is a fantasy on the jazz idiom called boogie woogie.
This is a style of piano music popular in the 1930s and 1940s, usually
fast in tempo and percussive in manner, in which the player's left
hand reiterates a driving ostinato outlining a standard twelve-bar
blues harmonic progression (moving over the chords I IV I V I). The
right hand plays continuous variations upon the bass pattern, typically complex and fragmented. In Nancarrow's interpretation of this
idiom, the tempo is increased to breakneck speed, and the texture of
the work quickly becomes far more complex than is possible for a
pianist's two hands. In fact, by the end there are a total of eight distinct layers heard simultaneously, each with its own tempo, meter,
rhythm, and harmonic implications. Many of Nancarrow's other
Studies are more abstract than jazzlike, but virtually all of them

focus on the combination in strict counterpoint of lines with different meters, tempos, and rhythms.

After the completion of his opera *The Rake's Progress* (1951), a work based on the style of Mozart's Italian comic operas, Igor Stravinsky began an evolution toward a more chromatic idiom in which serialism would play an ever larger role. Between 1951 and 1957 he experimented with various approaches to serial composition which were intermingled with diatonic music of a more traditional type. His first completely twelve-tone work was *Threni* (1958), a choral piece whose texts are drawn from Lamentations. The twelve-tone method was also applied in other late works including *Movements* (for piano and orchestra, 1959), Variations (for orchestra, 1964), and *Requiem Canticles* (1966).

Stravinsky's adoption of the twelve-tone method was the last of his major changes of musical orientation. It was a transformation of compositional method also accompanied by a significant change of style, as his music became not only more chromatic but also more abstract and concise. Of many factors that contributed to this new language, probably the most decisive was Stravinsky's encounter in the early 1950s with the music of Webern. His assistant Robert Craft, who was instrumental in bringing Webern's music to Stravinsky's attention, wrote in the magazine *Score* (1957):

> In the years between 1952 and 1955 no composer can have lived in closer contact with the music of Webern. Stravinsky was familiar with the sound of the Webern Cantatas and of the instrumental songs at a time when some of these works had not yet been performed in Europe. The challenge of Webern has been the strongest in his entire life. It has gradually brought him to the belief that serial technique is the possible means of musical composition.

At the time of the premiere of *Pierrot lunaire* in 1912, Stravinsky was favorably disposed toward the music of Schoenberg and his circle, despite its stylistic differences with his own work. But by the 1920s, a personal estrangement arose between the two composers that permanently eliminated artistic contact between them. Schoenberg's death in 1951 removed whatever personal barriers may have existed between Stravinsky and Viennese serialism, and his "musical appetite" soon led him to digest and reinterpret this idiom as he earlier had done with the languages of Glinka, Tchaikovsky, Rimski-Korsakov, Bach, Weber, and Verdi.

The ballet *Agon* is a masterpiece of Stravinsky's transition to the twelve-tone method. Since its composition (1953–57) spanned virtually this entire period of change, it is a paradigm of the composer's stages from diatonic neoclassicism to twelve-tone serialism. The ballet has no narrative scenario; it is instead an abstract "competition" (suggested by the title) among twelve dancers. The number 12 is also evident in the large structure of the work, which consists of four groups each of three dances. The groups are connected by related transitional music.

The opening movement, "Pas-de-quatre," begins with nearly diatonic motion, progressing to a chromatic passage in the middle. This music, which was composed in 1953 and which is nonserial, is also used as a coda to conclude the ballet. The music of the interludes was likewise among the first composed, and, like the Pas-de-quatre, it progresses from the diatonic to the chromatic.

Dances from the middle two groups are adaptations of seventeenth-century dance genres: a saraband in stately triple time, a lively galliard, and three branles. These and the three movements of the final group exhibit different approaches to serialism: rows containing different numbers of notes are used, and their application to lines and chords is either strict or free in order.

An example of this mixed structure is the "Bransle gay," the second movement of the third major subdivision. The *branle gay* was an aristocratic social dance in France in the sixteenth and seventeenth centuries, given its name by the participants' swinging or shaking motions. In Stravinsky's adaptation, castanets keep a dance rhythm in triple meter, but the other parts mix duple and triple figures. The movement has a concise A B A' shape in which the B section begins at measure 321 and the reprise at measure 332. Pitches of the A section are strictly determined in order by a six-note row:

$$P_0: \quad B \quad D \quad C \quad F \quad Eb \quad Bb$$

The row is used in all four basic transformations and in numerous transpositions. Somewhat unusual in Stravinsky's serial music of this time is the distribution of notes from row forms into several parts rather than strict confinement in a single voice. Thus P_0 is divided among three instruments at its first entrance in measure 311 (Example 13-4).

The end of the B section (measures 328–31), on the contrary, departs from the row and uses instead the complementary hexachord of P_0 as an unordered pitch-class set. The derivation of this set from P_0 is illustrated in Example 13-5. The row of the preceding movement, "Bransle simple," is a transposed ordering of this complement. But the order established there is not observed in these measures, which return instead to atonal harmonic principles in which order is not dictated by a precompositional plan.

Example 13-4. Stravinsky, *Agon*, measure 311. © 1957 by Boosey & Hawkes, Inc. Reprinted by permission.

Example 13-5. Complementary hexachords in Stravinsky's *Agon*.

One final detail should be observed. The chord in the strings and harp that concludes the B section is made up from the complementary hexachord shown in Example 13-5, with the pitch class G♯ split off as a grace note in the cello. The resulting five-note subset is shown in Example 13-6. This chord has a decidedly "Stravinskian" sound, first, because it contains the familiar dominant seventh chord, but also because it is a five-note subset of the octatonic scale (which would be completed by adding the notes A♯, C, and D♯). Throughout his early serial music, Stravinsky finds many such ways of asserting diatonic and octatonic sets, which are the common property of all his periods and styles of composition.

The orchestral Variations are among Stravinsky's late works which most reflect the style of Webern. Like Webern's Variations for Piano Op. 27, this work contains no distinct theme. It consists instead of variations upon precompositional materials, including a twelve-tone row and configurations of rhythm and instrumentation. As in Webern's music there is great abstraction, conciseness, and a texture that projects short, disjunct figures with wide leaps and frequent changes of instrumental color.

(mm. 330-331)

Example 13-6. Stravinsky, *Agon*, measures 330–331. © 1957 by Boosey & Hawkes, Inc. Reprinted by permission.

The Variations are divided into twelve sections (at measures 1, 23, 34, 40, 47, 59, 73, 86, 95, 101, 118, and 130), and, as in *Agon*, the number 12 is also operative in other dimensions. There is virtually no motivic recurrence, development, or conventional variation, but the final section alludes to some of the rhythmic and textural figures of the opening. The second, fifth, and eleventh sections—which Stravinsky called "twelve-part variations" referring to their number of distinct voices—are rhythmically and metrically interrelated.

The Variations exemplify Stravinsky's techniques of twelve-tone composition in his late music. The basic series (as in works by Schoenberg) is conceived as a motivic shape, although this motive plays no further role in the piece. The series resembles those favored by Berg, since its first half is nearly diatonic:

P_0:   D   C   A   B   E   A♯   G♯   C♯   D♯   G   F♯   F.

But, unlike the twelve-tone works of Berg and unlike most of Stravinsky's earlier serial music, the Variations contain virtually no diatonic, triadic, or octatonic sets.

Stravinsky uses the series in all of its basic forms. He emphasizes the inversion of the untransposed retrograde, which in this series is identical to the row form RI_6. The basic row forms, however, are outweighed in importance by rotational forms, both the hexachordal transposition-rotations explained in Chapter 4 and transposition-rotations made from entire series.

Milton Babbitt (1916–) took his point of departure as a composer from the serial works of Schoenberg and Webern. He extended the principle of order in the twelve-tone method to encompass virtually all aspects of music. Pitch, point of attack, dynamics, register, and timbre are chosen by precompositional arrangements, which are themselves interrelated since they are all derived from the basic tone row. Babbitt's development of this closed system was facilitated by his use of a mathematical model to represent elements and operations of the twelve-tone system. Through this model he made great contributions to systematic analysis of twelve-tone music and suggested avenues for the analysis of all atonal music. Aspects of Babbitt's analytic and compositional methods are discussed further in Chapter 4 and Chapter 5.

Babbitt developed his brand of integral serialism independently of related phenomena among European composers of the late 1940s and early 1950s. Unlike the Europeans, who had departed from strict serialism by the late 1950s, Babbitt has maintained its methods to the present day. His music includes works for chamber ensemble and orchestra, songs, and pieces for tape with or without live performers. These works are usually abstract and concentrated studies which do not rely upon unusual colors, motivic development, or programmatic associations for their meaning. In *All Set* (1957) he imitates sounds and rhythms of a jazz ensemble, showing the flexibility of his serial procedures. In other works, such as his early string quartets, there is a homogeneity of rhythm that is a by-product of his method of serializing points of attack.

In several writings, Babbitt suggests that the listener must be able to perceive the intricate relationships that underlie his compositional method in order to understand his music. In his article "Who Cares If You Listen?" he points to the high degree of efficiency, determinacy, and autonomy of his music. He adds: "Compositions so rooted necessarily ask comparable knowledge and experience from the listener. Like all communication, this music presupposes a suitably equipped receptor." We shall return to works by Babbitt in the next chapter on electronic music.

SERIALISM IN EUROPE: STOCKHAUSEN AND BOULEZ

The expansion of serial composition among European composers following the Second World War is all the more remarkable since twelve-tone works by Schoenberg, Berg, and Webern had been virtually unavailable and unheard since the 1930s. European serialism after the war was catalyzed by two factors: the International Summer Courses for New Music in Darmstadt and the influence of Olivier Messiaen. The school in Darmstadt was founded in 1946 and soon became a meeting place for the emerging avant-garde. Here the music of Schoenberg and Webern was performed and studied. By the early 1950s integral serialism had become virtually synonymous with the compositional approach of its participants.

Also of importance to the onset of postwar European serialism was Olivier Messiaen, who was present in Darmstadt in 1949 and whose teaching attracted some of the outstanding younger composers of this period, including Karlheinz Stockhausen, Pierre Boulez, and Karel Goeyvaerts. Messiaen was not a serialist, but his great eclecticism and resourceful experimentation suggested procedures and styles that were then developed by his students in the serial idiom. His piano étude "Mode de valeurs et d'intensités" (1949) was especially influential. A mode for Messiaen is a preestablished, unordered set of musical elements, normally pitches. In this work he uses not only modes of pitch but also—as the title states—modes of durations and dynamics. Most important, the elements of these modes are linked together by a precompositional arrangement (see Chapter 4). A texture is produced in which traditional melody, accompanimental chords, and motivic developments are either absent or little in evidence. Instead, the music draws attention to individual notes, which burst forth in a panoply of sounds but which seem unconnected to any larger context.

Karlheinz Stockhausen (1928–) used the term *punctual* (or "pointillist") to describe the texture of this piece, by which he was greatly inspired. "Pointillist—Why?" he asked. "Because we hear only single notes, which might exist for themselves alone, in a mosaic of sound." Stockhausen found an even more pronounced pointillism in music by Webern, which, unlike Messiaen's étude, used silence to aid in the disruption of linear associations and which applied strict twelve-tone order to insure unity and continuity. The combination of pointillist textures and serial organization would guide Stockhausen's early works after 1951.

Kreuzspiel (*Cross Play*, 1951) was his first exploitation of serial pointillism. This work is for oboe, bass clarinet, piano, and percussion; it is in three connected sections, each marked by a change of tempo. *Kreuzspiel* is opened by an introduction (measures 1–13) which prefigures aspects of both the first section (motor rhythms in the drum-like tumbas) and second section (trichordal harmonies of the piano). The third section likewise combines features from the first two. The introduction and first section are found in Anthology no. 26.

In its rigorous application of serial procedures and elaborate preplanning, *Kreuzspiel* resembles Boulez's *Structures Ia* (see Chapters 4 and 5), which was also partly composed in 1951. Stockhausen uses simultaneous series governing the placement of attacks, dynamics, and register. A twelve-tone series controls the choice of pitches in the piano and woodwinds, but the composer does not use any of the classical transformations of the basic series associated with Schoenberg. Instead he employs forms made by shifting elements from the middle of a series progressively toward the outside. This process was inspired by Messiaen, who experimented with similar ways of permuting rows, which he called "interversion."

The "cross play" mentioned in the title refers to this method of generating row forms. It also alludes to the audible impression made by the piece, especially in its disposition of register and density. In the first section (measures 14–91), for example, the music begins with a relatively uncluttered texture of piano, tom-toms, and tumbas (conga drums). The notes in the piano are placed in either the very high or very low registers. By the middle (measures 50–70),

KARLHEINZ STOCKHAUSEN
(Cologne, 1928–)

Following the disruption of World War II, Stockhausen continued his musical and general education. In 1947 he enrolled at the Cologne Hochschule für Musik where he pursued mainly piano playing. He also attended lectures in the humanities at the University of Cologne. He studied composition briefly with Frank Martin in 1950 and earned his living as a jazz pianist. His career was furthered by the critic and composer Herbert Eimert, at whose urging Stockhausen first attended the International Summer Courses for New Music at Darmstadt in 1951. The following year he studied in Paris with Olivier Messiaen, during which time he was also an apprentice in the studio for *musique concrète* at the French Radio.

In 1953 he joined Eimert at the newly founded studio for electronic music of the North West German Radio in Cologne. He also studied phonetics with Werner Meyer-Eppler at Bonn University. He has frequently returned to Darmstadt to lecture on various subjects, and he regularly tours around the world to arrange performances of his music. He has been engaged since 1964 in a group for the performance of his own live electronic works.

SELECTED WORKS

Operas. *Licht* (cycle of operas for each day of the week, 1977–).
Orchestral Music. *Spiel* (1952, rev. 1973), *Gruppen* (1955–57), *Carré* (1960, with choruses), *Momente* (1961–64, various later realizations), *Hymnen* (1969, with tape, various versions), *Fresco* (1969), *Trans* (1971), *Inori* (1974).
Chamber Music. *Kreuzspiel* (1951), *Kontra-Punkte* (1952–53), *Klavierstücke* 1–14 (1952–88, some pieces later rev.), *Zeitmasse* (1955–56), *Zyklus* (1959), *Refrain* (1959), *Adieu* (1966), *Stimmung* (1968), *Amour* (1976); *Michaels Reise* for brass, winds, synthesizer, and percussion (1986).
Works for Tape (with or without instruments). *Gesang der Jünglinge* (1955–56), *Kontakte* (1959–60), *Telemusik* (1966).

Live Electronic Works. *Mikrophonie* I–II (1964–65), *Mixtur* (1964), *Prozession* (1967), *Kurzwellen* (1968, various versions), *Mantra* (1970), *Ylem* (1972).
Works for Unspecified Instrumentation. *Plus-Minus* (1963), *Aus den sieben Tagen* (1968), *Sternklang* (1971).

```

```

the texture has become dense and busy, with the woodwind instruments playing in the middle register. Toward the end of the section, the opening texture and registral extremes gradually return, but notes from the high register at the beginning have crossed into the low register and vice-versa. Music which thus mediates between extremes soon became a preoccupation for Stockhausen.

Kreuzspiel subtly evokes the free rhythms of jazz by its irregular accents and lazy ostinato in the tumbas. The choice of tom-toms, tumbas, wood block, and suspended cymbals also suggests the timbre of African music, an exotic element that was common to works by Messiaen and his students at this time. Like Stockhausen's later music, *Kreuzspiel* makes a large gesture in sound and time that has little to do with the grammar of thematic statement, development, and return so crucial to the musical language of earlier times.

Stockhausen continued to refine this idiom of serial pointillism in other works of the early 1950s, including *Formel* (1951), *Spiel* (1952), *Schlagtrio* (1952), *Punkte* (1952), *Kontra-Punkte* (1952–53), and the early *Klavierstücke* (1952–53). But his apprenticeship at the studio for *musique concrète* at the French National Radio in Paris in 1952 led him increasingly into electronic media of composition and toward new stylistic directions. We shall return to the works of this composer in the next two chapters.

The music of Pierre Boulez (1925–) from the time of his Sonatina for flute and piano (1946) applied twelve-tone procedures, which he had learned from his teacher René Leibowitz. Boulez's intricate rhythmic idiom, evocations of non-Western music, and fondness for pointillist textures stem in part from Olivier Messiaen, with whom Boulez had earlier studied at the Paris Conservatory.

Boulez quickly formed a rigid attachment to integral serialism. In his article "Schoenberg is Dead" (1952), he rashly dismisses the music of Schoenberg for its formal traditionalisms. "The confusion in twelve-tone works between the theme and the series," he wrote, "shows clearly enough his inability to foresee the world of sound brought into being by the tone row." Boulez may have overlooked the extent to which the row in Schoenberg's music influences all formal elements, a phenomenon that Boulez thought limited among

PIERRE BOULEZ
(*Montbrison, 1925–*)

Pierre Boulez began his advanced education in music in 1942 at the Paris Conservatory, where he studied with Olivier Messiaen among others. He was also tutored in twelve-tone techniques by René Leibowitz. In 1954 he collaborated in the founding of the Domaine Musical, a concert organization devoted to modern music which he subsequently conducted. His early compositions were heard at the Donaueschingen Festival and the International Summer Courses for New Music at Darmstadt. He has also been active as a writer of polemics on music and musicians. He took up temporary residence in Germany in 1958.

Boulez became internationally renowned as an orchestral conductor in the 1960s, and he served as musical director of the New York Philharmonic Orchestra from 1971 to 1978. He now resides in Paris where he is director of the Institut de Recherche et de Coordination Acoustique/Musique.

SELECTED WORKS

Orchestral Music. *Le soleil des eaux* (with voices, 1948), *Livre pour cordes* 1968, revision of *Livre pour quatuor*, 1949), *Pli selon pli* (soprano and orchestra, 1957–62, consisting of revisions of several earlier works, including three *Improvisations sur Mallarmé*); *Répons* (1980) for percussion, electronics and chamber ensemble.

Chamber Music. Sonatina for flute and piano (1946), *Le visage nuptial* (with voices, 1946), *Le marteau sans maître (1954, rev. 1957),* Domaines (1968, rev. 1969), *Éclat* (1965, later rev.), *e. e. cummings ist der Dichter* (chorus and chamber orchestra, 1970),*. . . explosante-fixe . . .* (1971), *Messagesquisse* (for celli, 1977); *Derivé* for chamber ensemble (1984); *Dialogue de l'ombre double* for clarinet and electronics; *Mémoriale* for flute and chamber ensemble (1985, based on *. . . explosante-fixe . . .*).

Piano Music. Three sonatas (1946, 1948, 1957), *Structures* for two pianos (two books, 1952, 1961).

prewar serialists to the works of Webern. It is also doubtful that Webern had any less allegiance to traditional forms than did Schoenberg.

Boulez's strictest essay in integral serialism was his *Structures Ia* for two pianos (1951–52). Here he achieved the elimination of traditional textures for which use he had berated Schoenberg. Aspects of the compositional technique of this work are surveyed in Chapters 4 and 5. But Boulez did not long remain a doctrinaire serialist. He soon evolved serial techniques in a very different direction from either Webern or his own contemporaries. In his article "Auprès et au loin" (1954), he suggests that the principle of order is not essential to serialism: "The serial phenomenon," he wrote, "is not constituted of the successive unfolding of the elements that it puts into relation. The series is not an order of succession." Serialism became for Boulez a private compositional approach that aided him in choosing compositional materials and in achieving certain stylistic goals, but that did not automate the order in which compositional choices were made. This flexible serialism led to music in which there was an even distribution of all chromatic pitch classes and registers, elimination of regular pulse and meter, a variety and apparent spontaneity of color, and elimination of textures of traditional homophony and polyphony. Strict serial organization of pitch cannot be found in his music after 1953 except in isolated passages.

Le marteau sans maître (*The Hammer Without Master*, 1954, rev. 1957) is Boulez's most widely imitated work in the postserial idiom. This is a setting of three surrealist poems by René Char (1907–88) drawn from an anthology of the same title. Boulez's setting joins an alto voice with varying combinations of alto flute, guitar, viola, vibraphone, xylorimba, and miscellaneous percussion. The work has nine movements of which four are vocal; the others are instrumental glosses upon the poetry, which are intertwined in this order:

1. Before L'artisanat furieux (instrumental)
2. Commentary I to Bourreaux de solitude (instrumental)
3. L'artisanat furieux (vocal/instrumental)
4. Commentary II to Bourreaux de solitude (instrumental)
5. Bel édifice et les pressentiments (vocal/instrumental)
6. Bourreaux de solitude (vocal)
7. After L'artisanat furieux (instrumental)
8. Commentary III to Bourreaux de solitude (instrumental)
9. Bel édifice variation (vocal/instrumental)

Each movement is uniquely orchestrated, ranging in complexity from a simple duet for flute and voice (third movement) to the climactic ninth movement where the voice, all pitched instruments, and most of the percussion are called into service. This finale dramatizes the relationship of voice and instruments that had been intimated earlier. Just as the narrator of the poem talks of being engulfed by the ocean's waves, the vocal line is swallowed up by the instruments and sings its last passage in a wordless vocalization.

Char's poetry is Expressionistic in its images of violence and death and surrealistic in its absence of logical continuity. The three short verses chosen by Boulez each consist of disconnected, often obscure allusions, which are juxtaposed without punctuation. Their images are interpreted by the composer in an exceedingly recondite manner. There are subtle word paintings and motivic cross references underscoring recurrences in the text: the setting of "Le marcheur s'est tu" ("the walker is silent") in the sixth movement, for example, recurs at the opening of the finale at the words, "J'écoute marcher dans mes jambes" ("I hear walking in my legs"). The vocal writing is extremely agile and diverse, sometimes calling for the singer's mouth to be closed or using Schoenberg's technique of speaking voice.

In fact, one important antecedent of this work is Schoenberg's *Pierrot lunaire*, which Boulez judged Schoenberg's masterpiece. *Pierrot* shares with *Le marteau* the medium of voice and small heterogeneous ensemble, and the poetry of the two is related by fantastic and lurid images. The third movement of Boulez's cycle uses the same combination of flute and voice as the seventh movement ("Der kranke Mond") of *Pierrot*.

The orchestration of *Le marteau sans maître* is highly virtuosic. Boulez combines in each movement instruments with certain similarities, such as the voice and flute in the third movement, both of which are instruments of breath having the same general range. The commentaries to "Bourreaux de solitude" (movements 2, 4, and 8) evoke the sound of the Balinese gamelan commonly found in Messiaen's music, and they also allude to the syncopated pulse of African drumming.

Structures of pitch in this work are derived from a twelve-tone row by a process which Boulez calls "multiplication." This method, which he also uses in many of his later works, does not produce serialized music in the Schoenbergian sense. A twelve-note series—E♭ F D C♯ B♭ B A C G♯ E G F♯—is the source of unordered sets which are the composer's basic materials, but the series itself does not appear.

In *Le marteau* Boulez begins by dividing the row into five segments; the notes are then placed into specific registers illustrated in Example 13-7. A segment is "multiplied" by another segment by constructing the intervals of one segment upon each pitch within the other. Duplicate pitches are then eliminated. In order to multiply

Example 13-7. Segmentation of the series in Boulez, *Le marteau sans maître.*

the first two segments shown in Example 13-7, for example, we build the minor seventh created by the first segment upon each of the four pitches of the second segment (Example 13-8). The result is a set with seven different pitch classes.

Boulez's use of this seven-note set may be observed in the third movement, "L'artisanat furieux" (Anthology no. 15). It appears in the figure in the alto flute in the first measure (note that the alto flute sounds a fourth lower than written). In each measure of the entire movement, pitches are determined by similar multiplications.

In *Le marteau* and in several of Boulez's later works, serial pre-planning governs the order in which one set follows another, but the order in which individual pitches occur is not predetermined. Beginning with the Third Piano Sonata (1957), Boulez's music admitted open forms, spontaneous choices by the performer, and other trappings of indeterminacy that will be outlined in the next chapter. It has retained the flamboyant virtuosity and abstruse refinement of *Le marteau*, and it repeatedly has returned to a literary text to provide formal models.

Numerous other European composers of the early 1950s began to write serialized music, usually allied to pointillistic textures inspired by the music of Webern. Bruno Maderna (1920–73) was associated with the Darmstadt summer courses from 1951, which provided him with a larger audience for his dodecaphonic compositions such as *Musica su due dimensioni* (1952) for flute and tape. Maderna was one of the most resourceful of the early composers of electronic music, and his later works often mix tape with live performances and theatrical gestures.

Maderna was joined at Darmstadt by his former student Luigi Nono (1924–90). Nono's *Polifonica–Monodia–Ritmica* for winds, piano, and percussion (1951) is a classic example of pointillist integral serialism. In the mid-1950s his music became primarily vocal, based upon

Example 13-8. Multiplication of segments.

texts that expressed his political and social views. His works remained in the vein of integral serialism until the late 1950s, after which he departed from serial procedures in order to tailor his style better to the understanding of workers and the disadvantaged proletariat.

Luciano Berio (1925–) studied serial procedures with Luigi Dallapiccola in America, but he returned to Italy to compose serialized works such as his orchestral study *Nones* (1954). He was one of the first Europeans to break with serial orthodoxy, which he eliminated in favor of electronic composition, exploitation of vocal resources, and chance procedures. Henri Pousseur (1929–) was a devoted follower of Webern in the early 1950s, seeking to extend both the styles and structural principles of Webern's music. His *Quintette à la mémoire de Webern* (1955) uses the row of Webern's Quartet Op. 22, in homage to this illustrious forebear. Pousseur's music of the later 1950s and 1960s was influenced by new directions associated with Stockhausen and Boulez, which allowed open forms to govern large-scale planning but which maintained Webernesque textures and sonorities on a smaller scale.

TEXTURAL COMPOSITION AND THE TRANSFORMATION OF SERIALISM

The vigor with which most of the leading European composers embraced serialism around 1950 was matched by the unanimity with which they eliminated these procedures after 1955. Boulez led the way as he dispensed with strict serialism almost immediately after *Structures Ia* in 1952, although he continued to defend the necessity of serialism of a more abstract kind.

Luciano Berio spoke for numerous composers of the late 1950s when he rejected the excessive emphasis on compositional method that serialism had provoked. "Even in itself," he wrote in "Poesia e musica" (1959), "serial procedure guarantees nothing. No idea is so miserable that it cannot be serialized." In its place he recommended "living and continuing contact with materials of sound." Later Berio was more outspoken in his rejection of serialism. He wrote in the *Christian Science Monitor* (1965): "Any attempt to codify musical reality into a kind of imitation grammar (I refer mainly to the efforts associated with the twelve-tone system) is a brand of fetishism which shares with Fascism and racism the tendency to reduce live processes to immobile, labelled objects, the tendency to deal with formalities rather than substance."

Henri Pousseur complained that the differentiation of elements which serialism should ensure was lost in a texture of sameness, which he termed "entropy." He wrote in "The Question of Order in New Music" (1966): "The rigorous serial procedures which determine all the detail do not seem to have a positive function. Far from establishing perceptible symmetries and periodicities, regularity in similarity and in differentiation—in other words, [in establishing] an effective and recognizable ordering of diverse figures—they seem instead to *hinder* all repetition and all symmetry or . . . all true *order*." He recommended that entropy be dispelled by combining serial preplanning with freely intuitive choice and elements of chance or mobile forms.

György Ligeti (1923–) complained in his article "Über musikalische Form" (1966) that serialism had led to a doctrinaire academicism that made it impossible for composers' methods to be evident in their music when performed. In an earlier article, "Metamorphoses of Musical Form" (1960), he argued that the overrefinement of serialism had reduced the importance of precise configurations of intervals, durations, and dynamics. Like Pousseur, Ligeti complained that these traditional elements were lost to entropy, making serial composition audibly identical to chance composition.

Ligeti's alternative was textural composition (see Chapter 6). In a work of this type, conventional textures made from lines and chords are replaced by masses of sound. Specific intervals, colors, rhythms, or pulse are no longer perceived as such; the sound mass instead becomes the elemental building block of a composition. Ligeti constructed textures, which he called "sound areas," in numerous ways: with tone clusters, hypercomplex polyphony, polyrhythms, noises, pointillistic textures, and improvisation by many performers. These innovations were directly based on the work of composers of electronic music in the 1950s. An important precursor was Iannis Xenakis, who attempt to duplicate random or "stochastic" processes in his music (see Chapter 15). In a stochastic piece by Xenakis, the number of sound events is so large that the nature of any one of them cannot be determined; the composer instead controls the behavior of the totality or mass of sounds. The result for Xenakis was an early form of textural composition. Other European composers, notably Krzysztof Penderecki, composed important textural works at about the same time as Ligeti. In the hands of all of these pioneers textural composition proved to be an intensely expressive avenue for new music that led composers away from doctrinaire serialism.

Ligeti's early textural compositions, such as the orchestral *Atmosphères* (1960), often consist of such massive polyphonic structures that the individual lines, intervals, and rhythms are "neutralized" and contribute solely to large blocks of sound, volumes, and colors. The form of such works is freely conceived, unique to each piece, and often derived from visual images or spatial conceptions. In later works, such as the third movement of the String Quartet No. 2 (1968), Ligeti experimented with ways of neutralizing rhythm by superimposing several different rhythmic strata, each having a mechanistic regularity. An overall beat or rhythmic organization is dispelled by the superabundance of different beats and rhythms. Ligeti has written that his attack upon conventional rhythm as a formal element was a reaction against the "oversensitization" of rhythm in serialized music of the 1950s.

An even more widespread technique by which European serialists of the early 1950s transformed their musical language was indeterminacy. We turn in the next chapter to this important innovation in modern music.

BIBLIOGRAPHY

The following books concerning general postwar developments in music in Europe and America are highly recommended: Elliott Schwartz and Daniel Godfrey, *Music Since 1945: Issues, Materials, and Literature* (New York, 1993); Paul Griffith, *Modern Music: The Avant Garde Since 1945* (New York, 1981); Glenn Watkins's imaginative *Pyramids at the Louvre: Music, Culture, and Collage from Stravinsky to the Postmodernists* (Cambridge, Mass., 1994); and Reginald Smith Brindle's concise *The New Music: The Avant-Garde Since 1945*, 2nd ed. (New York, 1987).

Elliott Carter's thoughts on music are expressed in essays and reviews that are collected in *The Writings of Elliott Carter*, ed. Else Stone and Kurt Stone (Bloomington, 1977). Also see Allen Edwards, *Flawed Words and Stubborn Sounds: A Conversation Elliott Carter* (New York, 1971). Carter's music through 1980 is analyzed by David Schiff in *The Music of Elliott Carter* (London, 1983). The serial music of Igor Stravinsky is described in sources mentioned in the Bibliography to Chapter 8. Also see articles on his late works by Milton Babbitt and Claudio Spies in *Perspectives on Schoenberg and Stravinsky*, rev. ed., ed. Benjamin Boretz and Edward T. Cone (New York, 1972) and Pieter C. Van den Toorn, *The Music of Igor Stravinsky* (New Haven, 1983). There is relatively little written to date on the music of Conlon Nancarrow. Selected piano studies are analyzed in Philip Carlsen's *The Player Piano Music of Conlon Nancarrow* (Brooklyn, 1988).

Throughout his career, Pierre Boulez has been a provocative essayist on modern music. See especially the writings collected in

Boulez on Music Today (London, 1971) and *Stocktakings from an Apprenticeship*, trans. Stephen Walsh (Oxford, 1991). An excellent cultural and analytic study is Dominique Jameux's *Pierre Boulez* (Cambridge, Mass., 1991). Stockhausen's writings are collected in the multivolume *Texte zur elektronischen und instrumentalen Musik*, some of which are translated in *Stockhausen on Music*, ed. Robin Maconie (New York, 1989). Maconie's study *The Works of Karlheinz Stockhausen*, 2nd ed. (London, 1900) is a good source of information about Stockhausen's music as is Michael Kurtz's *Stockhausen: A Biography* (London, 1992) about the composer's life. Jonathan Cott's *Stockhausen: Conversations with the Composer* (New York, 1973) is also very informative.

György Ligeti's article "Metamorphoses of Musical Form" appeared in *Die Reihe*, 7 (1960; English trans., 1965); his article "Über musikalische Form" is in *Forum*, 9 (1966). Ligeti's music is surveyed in a brief study by Paul Griffiths (London, 1983). Henri Poussuer's "Questions of Order in New Music" is found in *Perspectives of New Music*, 5 (1966), and Berio's articles "Poesia e musica" and "The Composer and His Work" are, respectively, in *Incontri musicali*, 1959, and *Christian Science Monitor*, 15 July 1965. Berio's music is concisely analyzed in David Osmond-Smith's *Berio* (Oxford, 1991).

Milton Babbitt's article "Who Cares If You Listen?"—a title that he disavows—first appeared in 1958. It is reprinted in *Comtemporary Composers on Contemporary Music*, ed. Elliott Schwartz and Barney Childs (New York, 1967). Andrew Mead's *Introduction to the Music of Milton Babbitt* (Princeton, 1994) is the most thorough study of its subject.

14

Indeterminacy

The years following World War II were marked not only by a recrudescence of serial composition, but also by an innovation of an opposite sort—indeterminacy. An element of a musical work is *indeterminate* if it is chosen by chance or if its realization by a performer is not precisely specified by notational instructions. These two situations will be called, respectively, "indeterminacy of composition" and "indeterminacy of performance." The term *aleatory* is also used to describe music of indeterminate construction, although some European writers have used this word to designate indeterminacy of a limited type which will be explained shortly.

Indeterminacy has proved to be one of the most radical innovations in musical composition of the entire twentieth century. If extensively applied, it eliminates style. It can remove all consistently distinctive features from the work of a composer and thus put his accomplishments at a distance from the listener. But few composers have achieved this effacement of style. Indeterminacy has instead served to further definite musical objectives: for John Cage it has intensified the importance of sounds and environmental noises; for Earle Brown it has increased the sensitive involvement of performers in musical decisions; for Pierre Boulez it has vivified musical materials that are otherwise subjected to complicated rational controls.

Like all important innovations in the history of Western music, indeterminacy had a substantial history prior to its emergence as an important compositional principle. In the eighteenth century, "composition" by random selection among precomposed musical units was a popular entertainment practiced by numerous musicians. Jazz improvisation is an example of a limited indeterminacy of performance.

Indeterminate composition in the twentieth century began among experimental American composers between the world wars. In Henry Cowell's *Mosaic* Quartet (String Quartet No. 3, 1934–35), the performers are invited to choose the order in which movements are played, thus permitting the work to take on different forms. Indeterminacy among Americans after the World War II represents an unbroken continuation of the experimental spirit which had informed musical culture in this country since the turn of the century. Indeterminacy was slower in coming to Europe and was ultimately accepted there with greater caution, perhaps because of a stronger sense of musical tradition there than in America.

American composers were guided toward indeterminate procedures by developments among their fellow painters and sculptors. The "action paintings" of Jackson Pollock (1912–56) were made by dripping or splashing paint upon a canvas, so that the result was to an extent the product of chance. The collages of Robert Rauschenberg

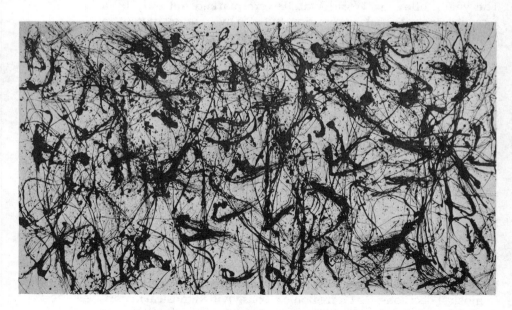

"Action painting": Jackson Pollock, *Number 32*. (Courtesy of the Kunstsammlung Nordrhein-Westfalen, Düsseldorf.)

The mobile poetic form: a page from Mallarmé's *Un coup de dés* (Paris, 1914).

(1925–) often combine sheets of newspaper to create random and con-flicting images. The mobiles of Alexander Calder use colorful metal-lic shapes connected by wires, whose overall form is changed spontaneously by currents of wind. In Europe, on the other hand, indeterminacy was inspired by trends in modern literature. Mallarmé's free distribution of lines in his poem "Un coup de dés" ("A throw of dice") invites the reader to take different routes about the page. This labyrinthine form was imitated by Pierre Boulez in several works. Syntactical discontinuities in the writings of James Joyce were similarly an inspiration to Luciano Berio, who used inde-terminacy of performance to capture Joyce's play of words and sounds.

INDETERMINACY IN AMERICA:
CAGE, FELDMAN, BROWN, AND WOLFF

In Chapter 12 it was shown that the early music of John Cage, like that of his fellow American experimentalists, emphasized unusual sounds and imaginative ways of presenting them. In these early pieces colorful noise and musical sounds were strewn within sys-tematically planned durations. Such music freely expressed the composer's tastes within the framework of preformed structures, or, to use his terms, it integrated "ideas of order" with "sponta-neous actions."

By 1950 Cage's philosophy of music had changed radically. He attributed his new viewpoint to an intensified awareness of Zen, mystic philosophy, and Eastern patterns of thought. From these sources he derived the idea that art must be part of a holistic reality. Art, which is a product of mankind, must imitate nature, since humanity and nature are essentially one. The common substance of nature and the art of music is sound. Its deployment in music must reflect its reality in nature, where it occurs with ceaseless abandon, unmotivated by the human will and not produced as a metaphor for any other meaning. The composer as a creator of beautiful objects should be replaced in importance by the listener, who, sensitized to sounds, is led to an awareness of the unity of all things.

Unmotivated sound would be the primary subject of Cage's music from 1950. In his lecture "Experimental Music" (1957), he spoke of the relation of sound to humanity and nature:

> If . . . it is realized that sounds occur whether intended or not, one turns in the direction of those he does not intend. This turning is psychological and seems at first to be a giving up of everything that belongs to humanity—for a musician, the giving up of music. This psychological turning leads to the world of nature, where, gradually or suddenly, one sees that humanity and nature, not separate, are in this world together; that nothing was lost when everything was given away. In fact, everything is gained. In musical terms, any sounds may occur in any combination and in any continuity.

Music for Cage became an activity in which the composer set in motion sonorous and visual processes whose outcome was unknown to him. Not all sounds in Cage's works are produced by performers. Random environmental noise—which Cage designated by the ironic metaphor "silence"—was also welcomed. "In this new music," he wrote, "nothing takes place but sounds: those that are notated and those that are not. Those that are not notated appear in the written music as silences, opening the doors of the music to the sounds that happen to be in the environment." His *4' 33"* (1952) is an essay in total silence, where, for the designated period of time, environmental noise reigns as the sole material of a work of music.

Cage sought to efface his personality from his music by strategies of chance. He relied especially on tosses of coins to guide him in selecting the elements of a composition. These exercises in chance were interpreted with the aid of the *I-Ching* or Chinese *Book of Changes*, a manual originally intended to dispense divine guidance according to the fall of yarrow sticks. In other works, random imperfections in a sheet of paper were used as a compositional guide. Music which is thus indeterminate of composition was not intended to be absurd or destructive of art. Cage expressed the hope that it would move the listener by the sublimity of sound. But the indeterminate work itself was not to be an object whose contemplation affected the listener. It was, instead, solely an occasion which could not possess or lack beauty. "Value judgments," wrote Cage, "are not in the nature of this work as regards either composition, performance, or listening."

Cage's *Music of Changes* for piano (1951) was one of the first pieces to reflect his new artistic orientation. This work is partially indeterminate of composition. Most elements were selected by chance, but the larger context of sounds and textures continued to reflect his own tastes.

The structure *of Music of Changes*, as in Cage's earlier works, is articulated by a sequence of numbers, in this case 3, 5, 6¾, 6¾, 5, 3⅛. These quantities refer to durations, which are operative in large and small dimensions. On the small scale, they determine the number of measures of 4/4 time before a change of tempo can occur. A section is concluded when the numerical sequence of measures has run its course, that is, in 29⅝ measures. The total number of sections is likewise 29⅝, which are divided into four movements also corresponding to the numerical sequence: the first movement has three sections; the second, 11¾ (combining 5 and 6¾,); the third, 6¾; and the finale 8⅛ (combining 5 and 3⅛).

The first section of the fourth movement (Anthology no. 9) illustrates this durational microstructure and the way in which it is animated by Cage's procedures of chance. The passage consists of 29⅝ measures of 4/4 time, divided by opportunities for new tempos into groups of 3, 5, 6¾, 6¾, 5, and 3⅛ measures. Notated sounds consist of chords, rapid figures, harmonics, and noises produced by the pianist striking the instrument in unorthodox ways. These are selected by procedures of chance, as are silences, durations, densities of texture, tempi, and dynamics. Since these procedures of chance sometimes generate unplayable configurations, Cage allowed the pianist then "to employ his own discretion."

Despite its indeterminacy of composition, *Music of Changes* still reflects the composer's musical preferences. His choices are all made from among a limited and carefully preplanned range of possibilities. He was assured, for example, that there would be an ample measure of silence in this work—it is almost Webernesque in sparseness— since the charts from which sounds were selected contained as many silences as sounds per se. The charts were also constructed so that Cage was assured that there would be a fairly even distribution of all twelve pitch classes and that the harmonic units—chords and short figures—would project primarily clusters of semitones. While Cage relinquished control over details of composition, his style is still in evidence at a higher level of construction.

In the later 1950s, Cage became dissatisfied with this apparent con-
tradiction of his aesthetic, and he sought ways to banish his preferences more thoroughly from his music. *Music of Changes* was
dismissed as "inhuman" and "a Frankenstein monster" for the strictness with which it dictated the actions of the player. Henceforth, he
adopted an increasingly less specific notation. His series of Variations
(1958–78) largely dispenses with precise notation and provides only a
general impetus for producing sounds. In these and other such works
from the 1960s, Cage's effacement of his style is virtually complete.

Thus Cage confided to the performer a larger role in the ultimate
shape and impact of a work. In a lecture on "Indeterminacy" given
at Darmstadt in 1958, he surveyed the roles of the performer in
music of this type. The performer, he said, might be comparable to a
painter who is asked to color a given sketch. Or he might be called
upon to give to a work its outer form or expressive content, "for
form unvitalized by spontaneity brings about the death of all the
other elements." He might be comparable to a photographer taking
one of an infinite number of pictures of a piece, or he might be asked
to react spontaneously to other performers like a traveler who must
catch an unannounced departing train. Any of these roles is prefer-
able, he concluded, to the conventional duty of performers, who,
like laborers, do simply as they are told.

Cage eschewed this last "intolerable" circumstance by recourse to
graphic notations. Graphic notation communicates pitches, durations, dynamics, textures, or other musical elements by symbols that
usually are visually analogous to the sounds they represent. These
symbols will often be mixed with standard notational elements.
Graphic notation is inherently imprecise, conveying only the outline
of a preconceived musical image. Since conventional notation is specific by comparison, virtually all modern music that is indeterminate of performance makes some use of graphic techniques.

There has yet to develop any significant standardization among
composers or performers of graphic systems, so we shall rely for the
remainder of this chapter on a few examples from works of prominent composers to illustrate their diversity and meaning. Cage's
Concert for Piano and Orchestra (1957–58), for example, consists of a
large and fantastic repertory of graphic notations. These may be
realized in any number and in any order. Most use conventional
staffs and noteheads, but some are entirely abstract. One of the latter is shown in Example 14-1, regarding which the composer
explains: "Any pitch area having at least 20 chromatic tones. Space
vertically = frequency. Horizontally = time. Horizontal lines = duration of single tones. Vertical lines = clusters or legati. Points = short
single tones."

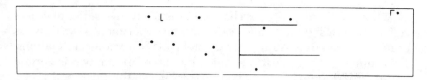

Example 14-1. Cage, *Concert for Piano and Orchestra.* © 1960 by Henmar Press Inc. Reprinted by permission.

Cage also promoted indeterminacy of performance by allowing variable forms and media. The graphs of *Concert for Piano and Orchestra*, for example, may be played in any order or quantity, either one at a time or several simultaneously by more than one pianist. The soloist(s) may be joined by any number of orchestral instruments *ad libitum*. This variable or "mobile" form was an approach to indeterminate performance that was more thoroughly explored by Cage's American contemporaries such as Earle Brown, and it was the main type of indeterminacy to be adopted by European musicians in the later 1950s and 1960s.

Cage's ideas and methods proved especially influential upon a group of musicians with whom he was associated in New York in the early 1950s, including Morton Feldman, Earle Brown, and Christian Wolff. All of these figures emphasized indeterminateness of performance rather than indeterminateness of composition, and all made important contributions to styles of graphic notation. The music of Morton Feldman (1926–87), like that of Cage, relies upon spontaneous sounds. Nearly all of Feldman's music is marked by a quiet and nearly immobile interplay of sounds and textures, usually emanating from conventional instruments and voices. His methods of obtaining these pictures in sound are very different from Cage's, since they place greater emphasis on his compositional instincts rather than on routines of chance. His early music, such as the series of *Projections* (1950–51) and *Intersections* (1951–53), uses graphic scores which allow performers to choose dynamics and pitches within specific ranges, but which control duration, texture, and continuity.

Feldman's later compositions are conventionally notated though largely unchanged in style. *Madame Press Died Last Week at Ninety* (1970), for example, is characteristically slow, repetitive, and inarticulate. It is more conventional in form than the graphic scores, as it uses motivic recurrences and is framed by the same six-note chord in the celesta at the beginning and end.

The music of Earle Brown (1926–) prior to 1952 was conventional in notation, reflecting partially serial or freely atonal structures. In

1952 his notational practices changed drastically. In a series of works collectively designated *Folio* (1952–53), he experimented with ways of notating relative durations by noteheads of various elongations. This "time-notation" as it was called by the composer, was in certain variations adopted by many composers later in the 1950s and 1960s. Brown's *1953* for piano uses time notation together with other elements of indeterminacy, as the pages can be read with either side up and with any combination of treble and bass clefs. An excerpt is illustrated in Example 14-2.

Other works from this collection are almost totally indeterminate in both composition and performance. *December 1952*, for example, consists of a matrix of horizontal and vertical lines and blocks shown in Example 14-3. These visual symbols are intended solely to be a stimulus to spontaneous decisions by the player(s), as their design does not necessarily represent any preconceived interpretation. "The composition may be performed," the composer notes in the preface, "in any direction from any point in the defined space for any length of time and may be performed from any of the four rotational positions in any sequence." Its appearance also reveals Brown's interest in modern art, especially in the geometrical studies of Pieter Mondriaan (1872–1944) and his Dutch contemporaries.

In later music, however, Brown retreated from the "conceptual mobility" of *December 1952*. He sought instead a middle ground of determinacy and indeterminacy, which would result in what he called "open" or "mobile" forms. Works such as the String Quartet

Example 14-2. Brown, "1953" from *Folio*. Copyright 1961 by Associated Music Publishers Inc. Reprinted by permission.

Example 14-3. Brown, *December 1952.* © 1961 by Associated Music Publishers, Inc. All rights reserved. Reprinted by permission.

(1965) consist of precomposed sections of varying degrees of notational specificity. These are selected and placed into order by the instrumentalists, either freely or under guidelines by the composer. The performers are admonished in the preface to the score to make rational and sensitive choices and to respond to the decisions of their fellow players:

> What I am trying to imply is not only a great responsibility on the part of the performers to perform the work "as written" but also an intense awareness of ensemble and individual flexibility, the material as written and within this concept of performance relativity.
> I would like to think that an intensified sense of human and sonic presence and intuitive performance contact can be extended beyond the "normal" precision-goal of most chamber music performing, into an area of immediacy of action, reaction, and flexibility, while maintaining the basic shape and character of the work.

By telling the performers to maintain "the basic shape and character of the work," Brown reveals his intention to establish a style—a distinctive compositional profile. Brown's music seeks to vivify this style by engaging the performers in a more intense and spontaneous participation. His concept of mobile forms, more than the

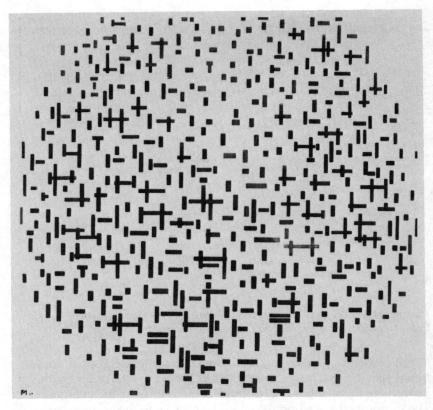

Models for graphic musical notation: Pieter Mondriaan, *Composition with Lines*. (Courtesy of the Rijksmuseum Kröller-Müller, Otterlo, The Netherlands.)

chance procedures of Cage, would prove analogous to formal developments among European composers of the late 1950s and 1960s.

Christian Wolff (1934–) came under the influence of Cage from the beginning of his work as a serious composer. His music is highly indeterminate of performance, intended primarily to allow the performers "freedom and dignity." By the late 1950s he developed a notation that not only guided the players in their choice of pitch and texture, but also provoked a rhythmically diverse interaction among them by their cueing one another.

Cage's experiments in indeterminacy of the 1950s were carried into new areas in the 1960s by figures such as La Monte Young, George Brecht, and the Englishman Cornelius Cardew. The first two were part of a group in New York called Fluxus, which in the early 1960s sponsored "events" or "happenings" mingling theater, comedy, and random sounds. We shall pick up the thread of these developments again in Chapter 17.

The spirit of Fluxus was also present in the work of Cornelius Cardew (1936–81). Cardew's group for free improvisation called AMM gave way in 1969 to his Scratch Orchestra, in which untutored musical and improvisational activities were substituted for the traditional values and background of an orchestra of trained musicians.

INDETERMINACY IN EUROPE:
BOULEZ, STOCKHAUSEN, BERIO, AND LUTOSLAWSKI

Although composition by chance, mobile forms, and graphic notation played a substantial role in works by major European composers of the 1960s and beyond, the influence of indeterminacy in Europe was moderated by a strong commitment to serialism and a more traditional view of the composer's role. Indeterminacy offered European serialists a way to overcome a major drawback of their idiom: its sameness. The maximal differentiation of pitch, duration, register, and color that was insured by integral serialism ironically produced not the effect of variety, but one of homogeneity and statistical uniformity. Even the most devoted of Europe's serialists recognized that this "entropy," as the phenomenon was often called, tended to produce monotony and a style different from what was intended.

Indeterminacy began to make inroads among European composers by the late 1950s, largely through the influence of John Cage, who lectured at Darmstadt in 1958, and Karlheinz Stockhausen, whose inexhaustible experimentation touched upon numerous indeterminate methods. Among the major European composers, indeterminacy never became an end in itself. It was instead an instrument by which distinctive and relatively traditional styles could be realized. Graphic notation was used by György Ligeti in the organ piece *Volumina*, for example, to accomplish the interplay of textures that was basic to his style. In works by Mauricio Kagel, improvisation by performers served to uncover new sounds and theatrical modes of expression. Luciano Berio's indeterminate notation in his cycle of *Sequenzas* liberated the instrumentalist's virtuosity.

This limited application of indeterminacy has been called "aleatory" by European writers such as Boulez and Lutoslawski, to distinguish it from the more extensive applications of chance among American composers. The term aleatory is defined in this restrictive sense by Werner Meyer-Eppler in his article "Statistic and Psychologic

Problems of Sound": "A process is said to be aleatoric if its course is determined in general but depends on chance in detail."

We shall now survey some of the aleatoric aspects of music by four major European composers of the postwar decades: Pierre Boulez, Karlheinz Stockhausen, Luciano Berio, and Witold Lutosławski. The first three began their compositional careers as serialists; Lutosławski turned to serialism in the late 1950s. By the 1960s all four composers had devised musical languages in which indeterminate techniques played a role.

Of these four figures, Pierre Boulez maintained the strongest allegiance to serial composition. But after his most doctrinaire essay in integral serialism—the first book of *Structures* for two pianos (1952)—he gradually shifted toward freer modes of expression. By the time of his Third Piano Sonata (1957) and second book of *Structures* (1961), he had incorporated some cautious opportunities for mobile forms.

Boulez explained his apparent volte-face in several polemics written in the late 1950s. In the article "Alea" (1958), he condemns composers of music by chance, referring no doubt to Cage and his circle:

> Chance . . . masks a basic weakness in compositional technique, it [is] a protection against the asphyxia of invention, the resort to a more subtle poison that destroys every last embryo of craftsmanship. I would willingly call this experiment—if experiment it be, since the individual does not feel responsible for his work, but merely throws himself by unadmitted weakness, by confusion, and for temporary assuagement into puerile magic.

But Boulez also attacks an excessive attachment to serial preplanning: "Schematization, quite simply, takes the place of invention; imagination—an auxiliary—limits itself to giving birth to a complex mechanism. . . . As for the imagination, it is careful not to intervene after things are under way. . . . We plunge into statistical lists that have no more value than other lists."

He proposes to eliminate both extremes of aleatory and serialism, replacing them with a style that admits limited elements of chance in a context also mixing serial procedures and intuitive choices. The form of a work should thus resemble a labyrinth: "The work must provide a certain number of possible routes," Boulez wrote in the article "Sonate, que me veux-tu?" "with chance playing a shunting role at the last moment." By the use of mobile forms and optional passages, he created works that were analogous to a "moving, expanding universe" in which the outer form would be renewed upon each performance. "We have respected the 'finished' aspect of the occidental work, its closed cycle," he wrote in "Alea," "but we have introduced the 'chance' of the oriental work, its open development."

These features are much in evidence in the Third Piano Sonata. In this work Boulez took his departure from language and literature, which not only provided a model for variable form but also suggested ways in which the instrumental sonata could be expressive and intelligible. In the literary works of James Joyce and in some of the poetry of Stéphane Mallarmé, he found a spontaneous variability of syntax and order that opened new dimensions of meaning. He imitated these free structures by allowing the performer to choose the order in which some elements of the composition could be played.

The work is made from building blocks that are put into a syntax at the moment of performance. These formal elements are themselves based upon models from verbal expression. The sections of the Sonata are given titles drawn in part from phonetics, rhetoric, and literature. The entire work consists of five movements, each of which the composer calls a "formant"—a term from phonetics referring to a primary acoustical element of spoken sound. The formants carry titles such as "Trope" and "Strophe." Boulez uses all of his powers of artifice in this work to make the instrumental sonata intelligible by analogy to primitive verbal expression.

The second formant, "Trope," illustrates Boulez's idea of the formal labyrinth. The movement has four sections—Text, Parenthesis, Commentary, and Gloss—whose titles develop the rhetorical metaphor. The player can begin with any of the four sections, continuing in order through the cycle. He can also elect to place the Commentary after the Gloss rather than before. In Parenthesis and Commentary, he may freely elect to perform or omit optional passages enclosed in brackets, and some pitches are indeterminate of duration. Otherwise, the sonata uses a freely serialized method.

Its style is consistent with most of Boulez's music. The surface is adorned with a busy, virtuosic filigree. Traditional lines and chords are entirely absent, replaced by an ornate counterpoint of attacks, registers, and densities. There is no consistent pulse, rhythmic pattern, or meter; instead, the passage of time is marked by an interplay of freely developing motions and colors.

Until the early 1960s, Karlheinz Stockhausen's music followed the same general evolution as that of Boulez. Both composers moved from strictly serial composition to an idiom where serial procedures were mingled with limited indeterminacy of performance and mobile forms. But Stockhausen has since proved to be of a more experimental temperament than the other postwar serialists. He has moved with startling swiftness through many developments in contemporary music including surrealistic theatrical music (e.g., *Originale*, 1961), verbal scores of "intuitive music" (*Aus den sieben Tagen*, 1968), minimalist pieces (*Stimmung*, 1968), and innovative uses of electronic media. We focus now upon several works characteristic of his music of the later 1950s and early 1960s which use indeterminate features of performance.

Piano Piece XI (1956) is Stockhausen's earliest example of a composition in mobile form, and it immediately provoked Boulez to compose the closely related "Constellation" movement of his Third Piano Sonata. Stockhausen's piece consists of nineteen brief passages in conventional notation. The player begins with any one of these "groups" and moves randomly to any others. Each group is played with a unique combination of tempo, dynamics, and style of attack, which is determined by indications attached to the end of the previous passage. When a group is played for the second time, certain changes are made (primarily transpositions at the octave), and the piece ends when the player lights upon a group for the third time.

Piano Piece XI exemplifies what the composer referred to as "group" composition, which several years before had replaced the "punctual" style of early works such as *Kreuzspiel*. In punctual music, the listener is confronted by relatively undifferentiated arrays of single notes, short figures, and silences—constellations, that is, of individual points of sound, each with its own pitch, loudness, register, and duration specified by interrelated series. Group composition, on the other hand, introduces differentiation into these otherwise static and homogeneous works. A group consists of a passage of short duration which is made distinctive by some musical characteristics such as a particular tempo, interval, contour, or timbre. Longer groups are called "moments."

In Piano Piece XI the structure of pitches in each group is fairly similar, but the distinctiveness of the group is insured by the unique combination of tempo, attack, and dynamics that the player must observe. There is no logic to the overall form or sense of direction in the succession of groups, which causes the listener to focus all the more upon present time—represented by the musical process of a group or moment—rather than upon linearly connected musical arguments. This emphasis upon the present is underscored by the composer in his article "Moment Form" (1960):

> Musical forms have been composed in recent years which are far removed from the schema of dramatic form. These new forms neither drive toward a single climax nor toward several such planned and anticipated climaxes. In them the customary stages of introduction, transition, tension, and relaxation are not represented by a developmental curve encompassing the entire work.... In these new forms

every "now" is not simply the result of what has gone before nor an upbeat to what follows or to what is expected, but instead a personal, independent, centralized entity existing for itself. These are forms in which a moment is not a point on a time line, not a particle of a measured duration, but rather forms in which the concentration on the now—on every now—makes vertical slices which penetrate across the horizontal presentation of time into a timelessness which I call eternity.

A work closely related to the mobile form of Piano Piece XI but larger and more dramatic in conception is *Momente* (*Moments*, 1961–64, several later versions). Here the brief groups of the Piano Piece are expanded to larger units or "moments." The large and diverse medium, which includes soprano solo, four choruses, brass, percussion, and two organs, creates visual effects suggesting a symbolic drama.

Its form consists of a succession of moments that can be rearranged and reconstituted at each new performance. Each moment is distinguished by an emphasis upon melody (synonymous with monodic or heterophonic textures), timbre (or homophonic textures), or rhythm (or polyphonic textures). Some moments are tinted by allusions to other moments, and some transitions between moments also make allusions to moments already heard or yet to come.

The timbral resources of *Momente* are broad and imaginative. The chorus not only sings but makes other sounds by clapping hands, talking, and stamping feet. These noises serve both to mediate between instrumental and vocal sounds—a type of homogenization of sources of sounds that occupied Stockhausen in many compositions—and also mediate between noisy audience reactions which greeted many of his works and sounds normally produced by the performing artists.

Zyklus (*Cycle*, 1959), for solo percussionist, differs from both Piano Piece XI and *Momente* in that its sections are organized into a definite succession. It is nevertheless mobile in form since the player can begin with any of the seventeen sections of the work and proceed through the remainder of the cycle.

As is often the case in works by Stockhausen, the title designates a form or procedure that is operative on several levels. Cyclical form is reinforced visually by the circular disposition of instruments, which requires that the percussionist move steadily around the circle as he proceeds through the formal cycle. *Zyklus* in fact consists of an intricate web of simultaneous cycles, each governing some musical element or process and each subjected to the rational control and coordination characteristic of Stockhausen's earlier serial compositions. One such cycle controls the number of attacks of nine of the thirteen instruments as the player progresses through the various sections. Another cycle establishes the degree of determinacy or indeterminacy of events in a section, and so forth.

Example 14-4 shows two of these sections, divided by the double horizontal line, and it also illustrates Stockhausen's techniques of graphic notation. The music can be read as shown or turned upside down. The section at the top is maximal in indeterminacy. Notes in the part for tom-toms, for example, are freely and densely sprinkled into its measure-like divisions. The section at the bottom, on the contrary, is maximal in determinacy in that it establishes relatively simple, discrete rhythmic figures and sonorities. Its notation is still approximate, but much less so than the random configurations at the top.

By the late 1950s the music of Luciano Berio, like that of Stockhausen and Boulez, had departed from strict serialism to a more distinctive style which admitted limited mobility of form and indeterminacy of performance and which relied upon graphic notation. Berio had a deep interest in the human voice and its ability to convey emotions in addition to a wide spectrum of musical colors. His methods of manipulating the voice were much influenced by Stockhausen, especially by *Gesang der Jünglinge* (see Chapter 15), in which Stockhausen attempts to mediate between vocal and synthetic sounds and to obliterate any absolute distinctions between them.

Berio responded with a series of works that combined the voice with diverse media and that exploited its sonorous capacity and ability to convey emotions on a primitive and abstract plane. His *Thema (Omaggio a Joyce)* (1958) used readings from Joyce's *Ulysses*, which were taped, modified electronically, and reconstituted into a montage of recognizable words and senseless vocal sounds. In an article "Music and Poetry: An Experiment" (1959), Berio told of his intention to create in this work a new relationship of word and tone: "My real goal was neither the juxtaposition nor jumble of two diverse systems of expression, rather, it was intended to establish a relationship of continuity between them, enabling the transition from one to another to be unnoticeable."

In *Circles* for voice, harp, and percussion (1962), Berio transplanted the techniques of *Thema* to a nonelectronic medium. This work is a setting of three poems by e. e. cummings, the first two of which are recapitulated in varied shapes to create an A B C B' A' form. This layout of materials is strongly directed toward the climactic middle section. In this focal passage the parts are graphically indeterminate, as the voice explodes into fragmented noises that approximate the timbres of the instruments. To reinforce this

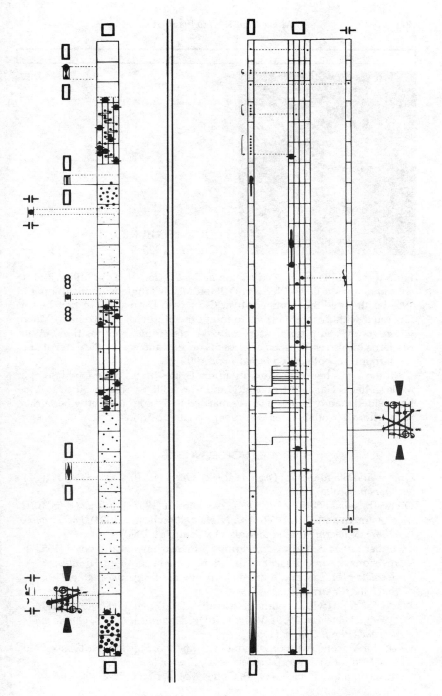

Example 14-4. Stockhausen, *Zyklus.* © Universal Edition (London) Ltd., London 1961. Used by permission of European American Music Distributors Corp., sole U.S. agent for Universal Edition.

LUCIANO BERIO
(Oneglia, 1925–)

Berio received his musical education at the Conservatory in Milan, and he subsequently studied with Luigi Dallapiccola at Tanglewood. Beginning in 1954 he attended the Summer Music Courses at Darmstadt. In 1955 he collaborated with Bruno Maderna to found the Studio di Fonologia in Milan, where both composers later realized electronic compositions. With Maderna he also established a series of concerts and a periodical devoted to modern music, both called *Incontri musicali*.

In the 1960s he lived primarily in the Unites States, where he taught at Mills College, Harvard University, and The Juilliard School. Since 1972 he has resided mainly in Italy. He was married to the soprano Cathy Berberian, with whom he collaborated on numerous compositions.

SELECTED WORKS

Operas and Stage Works. *Passagio* (1962), *Opera* (1970), *La vera storia* (1982), *Un re in ascolto* (1984).

Orchestra. *Nones* (1954), *Allelujah* I (1955) and II (1957), *Sinfonia* (1968, fifth movement added in 1969), *Voci* (viola and orchestra, 1984), *Formazioni* (1987), *Rendering* (based on music by Schubert, 1990).

Chamber Music. *Sequenzas* for various solo instruments and voice (1957–); revisions of some *Sequenzas* for different media, entitled *Chemins*; *Serenata I* for flute and fourteen instruments, *Tempi concertati* (1959), *Sincronie* for string quartet (1964).

Works for Tape (with or without instruments). *Thema (Omaggio a Joyce)* (1958), *Différences* (1959), *Visage* (1961), *Laborintus II* (1965), *Questo vuol dire que* (1969), *Ofanim* (1988).

Works for Voice(s) (with or without instruments). *Epifanie* (1961, based on *Quaderni* for orchestra), *Circles* (1962), *Cries of London* for unaccompanied voices (1974), *Coro* (1976), *Recital I (for Cathy)* (1972).

similarity of vocal and instrumental sounds, the percussionists blurt out nonsense syllables and the singer—in a theatrical gesture reminiscent of many works by Stockhausen—moves to a new position closer to the instruments and begins to play upon wood chimes. Example 14-5 shows this climactic passage and Berio's freely suggestive notation.

Berio's idiom owes much to the electronic and instrumental works Stockhausen of the 1950s but it is based on a much more intuitive groundwork. While Stockhausen's music often is inspired by a scientific or philosophical model, Berio's is informed by direct contact with his sources of sound. His music goes beyond Stockhausen's in its immediacy of impact and resourceful handling of the voice.

Works such as *Circles* opened the way for many related works of the 1960s and 1970s, especially by composers in America where Berio resided during much of this time. Several of the works of George Crumb—*Ancient Voices of Children* (1970), for example—are a continuation of Berio's liberation of vocal technique.

The music of Witold Lutosławski (1913–94) prior to 1958—including his First Symphony (1941–47), Overture for string orchestra (1949), and Concerto for Orchestra (1954)—is reminiscent of the style of Béla Bartók. It makes a colorfully dissonant use of the orchestra, its themes reflect the physiognomy of Eastern European folk song, and its textures create a rhythmically vivacious, asymmetrical polyphony. Lutosławski's Funeral Music for string orchestra (1958) was his first work to apply a highly novel version of the twelve-tone method, through which his music was more thoroughly irradiated by the chromatic scale and made even more severely linear and contrapuntal.

In 1961, beginning with his orchestral *Jeux vénitiens* (*Venetian Games*), Lutosławski turned to controlled aleatory to free both the rhythmic and textural dimensions of his music. The composer has attributed this change of style and compositional method to his encounter in 1960 with John Cage's *Concert for Piano and Orchestra*: "While listening to it, I suddenly realized that I could compose music differently from that of my past. That I could progress toward the whole not from the little detail but the other way round—I could start out from the chaos and create order in it gradually" (from Steven Stucky, *Lutosławski and his Music* [Cambridge, 1981], p. 84).

Lutosławski devised a music that he termed "aleatoric counterpoint," in which pitches in all instrumental and vocal parts are precisely notated and rhythms are improvised by the player within certain guidelines. The effect is usually a vivacious and busy polyphony in which the particular notes, intervals, and lines are subsumed into a texture. Passages of aleatoric counterpoint nor-

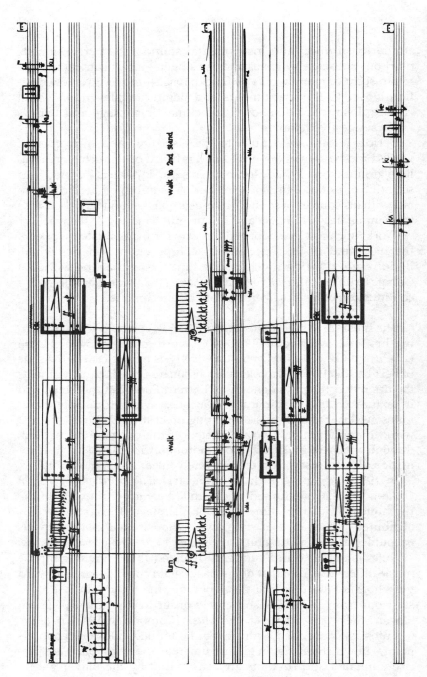

Example 14-5. Berio, *Circles*. © 1961 by Universal Edition (London) Ltd., London. Used by permission of European American Music Distributors Corp., sole U.S. agents for Universal Edition.

mally alternate with conventionally notated passages, and each block-like section projects a distinct texture that is linked to its neighbors in subtle ways. Lutosławski refined the style of *Jeux vénitiens* in music composed later in the 1960s and 1970s, including Three Poems by Henri Michaux for orchestra and twenty-part chorus (1963), String Quartet (1964), Symphony No. 2 (1967), and *Livre pour orchestre* (1968).

BIBLIOGRAPHY

A history of indeterminacy in the twentieth century is recounted by Michael Nyman in *Experimental Music* (New York, 1974). Reginald Smith Brindle's *New Music* (New York, 1981); Paul Griffiths's *Modern Music* (New York, 1981); and David Cope's *New Directions in Music*, 4th ed. (Dubuque, 1984) are also recommended.

Graphic notations by contemporary composers are illustrated in the anthology *Notations*, ed. John Cage and Alison Knowles (New York, 1969), in Smith Brindle's *New Music* (cited above), and in Erhard Karkoschka's *Notation in New Music*, trans. Ruth Koenig (London, 1972). There have been several noteworthy attempts to collect, categorize, and standardize modern notational practices. Kurt Stone's *Music Notation in the Twentieth Century* (New York and London, 1980) is especially authoritative, and the reader is also referred to the Proceedings of the International Conference on New Music Notation in *Interface*, 4 (1975) and to Gerald Warfield's *Writings on Contemporary Music Notation: An Annotated Bibliography*, Music Library Association Index and Bibliography Series, No. 16 (Ann Arbor, 1976).

John Cage has been an eloquent spokesman for his ideas on music. His most important lectures and articles are reprinted in *Silence* (Middletown, Conn. 1961), which was the first of several anthologies of his writings. Other statements by Cage are found in Richard Kostelanetz, ed., *John Cage* (New York, 1970); a brief analytic survey of his music is provided by James Pritchett in *John Cage* (Cambridge, 1993).

Earle Brown discusses his ideas on mobile forms in "Form in New Music" (1965), reprinted in *Source*, 1 (1967). Morton Feldman reveals his impatience with European composers of indeterminate music in "Pre-determinate/Indeterminate," *Composer*, 19 (1966).

Writings by and about Pierre Boulez and Karlheinz Stockhausen were surveyed in the bibliography to Chapter 13. Boulez's attitudes toward indeterminacy are discussed in "Alea" (1958), English translation in *Perspectives of New Music*, 3 (1964), and in "Sonate, que me veux-tu?" (which deals specifically with his Third Piano Sonata), *Perspectives of New Music*, 1 (1963). Stockhausen's article "Momentform" appears in German in his *Texte zur elektronischen und intrumentalen Musik*, Vol. 1 (Cologne, 1963).

Luciano Berio's ideas on the relationship of verbal and musical expression are sketched in his articles "Poesia e musica: un'esperienza," *Incontri musicali*, 3 (1959); "Form" in *The Modern Composer and His World*, ed. John Beckwith and Udo Kasemets (Toronto, 1961); and "The Composer and His Work," *Christian Science Monitor*, July 15, 1965. The last of these is a diatribe against serialism. While there is no comprehensive study of Berio's music, David Osmond-Smith's *Berio* provides a brief analytic account.

Lutosławski's life and works are traced by Steven Stucky in his *Lutosławski and His Music* (Cambridge, 1981). Also see Lutosławski's "About the Element of Chance in Music" in *Three Aspects of New Music* (Stockholm, 1968). Werner Meyer-Eppler's article "Statistic and Psychologic Problems of Sound" is found in *Die Reihe*, 1 (1955; English trans., 1958).

15

Electronic Music

The climate for renewed experimentation in music after the Second World War was intensified by a revolution in technology. Of several new avenues opened to the composer by postwar scientific research, none was more enticing than the prospect of using tape recorders and electronic equipment for the production and manipulation of sound. By approximately 1950 these new devices had given birth to *electronic music*, a medium in which the generation of musical sounds and their modification, storage, and reproduction are due, at least in part, to electronic means. We shall limit our definition of electronic music to those compositions in which the *original* conception is for these electronic media.

Electronic music was built upon technical and aesthetic foundations of earlier twentieth-century music. A direct precedent was the increased emphasis on diverse sounds. A fondness for unusual sound is especially evident in the experimental idiom of Americans such as Cowell, Varèse, and Cage. Their application of noise to music was also prefigured by experimental compositions of Italian Futurists such as Luigi Russolo, Russian Constructivists such as Alexander Mosolov, and French and German Dadaists during the years following the First World War.

Experimental use of noise and microtonal scales led to the invention of primitive electronic musical instruments, some of which attracted the attention of major composers. One of the earliest such devices was the "Telharmonium," invented by the Massachusetts technician Thaddeus Cahill around 1906. This electronic keyboard instrument transmitted sounds over telephone lines. It was mentioned by Ferruccio Busoni in his *Sketch of a New Esthetic of Music* as a means by which Busoni's theory of microtonal scales could be easily realized.

Among many electronic instruments that followed, the *ondes Martenot* ("Martenot's waves") proved to be the most important. This monophonic keyboard instrument, named after its inventor Maurice Martenot (1898–1980), produces a glassy tone that can be varied in dynamics and vibrato. It is tuned to the pitches of the chromatic scale, but it can also slide between notes. It was used by numerous French composers including Varèse, Messiaen, and Boulez.

Most types of electronic music depend not only on electronic devices for the production of sounds, but also on electronic means for their storage and reproduction. Disc recordings and film soundtracks were used experimentally as compositional media by several composers in the 1920s and 1930s. A typical experiment by artists at the Bauhaus school of design in Dessau involved drawing on a film soundtrack, which was then played by cinematic audio equipment. But the development of the magnetic tape recorder around 1950 was the decisive technological advance that made electronic music a practical reality.

Shortly after electronic music came into its own in the late 1940s, it branched into five basic media:

1. *musique concrète*: recorded music whose sounds are produced naturally or by conventional instruments;
2. pure electronic music: recorded works whose sounds are produced by electronic devices;
3. recorded music combining electronic and concrète sounds;
4. live performance plus recorded sounds;
5. live electronic music: live performances whose sounds are immediately modified by electronic means.

These media did not unfold chronologically. Each was in existence by the early 1950s or before. By 1970 there had occurred a decisive shift away from recorded electronic music toward those types involving live performance, as the traditional spontaneity and theatricality of the concert proved desirable to most composers and listeners.

We shall now survey each of these five media and trace within each the musical styles, compositional or structural features, and studio equipment which they have produced.

MUSIQUE CONCRÈTE

"Concrete" music was the invention of Pierre Schaeffer (1910–), a broadcaster and engineer at the Radiodiffusion-Télévision Françaises in Paris in the 1940s. In 1948 he composed a series of five études in which recorded sounds of everyday objects or musical instruments were manipulated, edited, and reassembled on phonograph discs for radio broadcast. He later termed such music "concrete" because he worked directly with sources of sounds rather than abstractly through the medium of musical notation.

The first of these studies, "Étude aux chemins de fer" ("Railroad Study"), is made, as the title suggests, from the sounds of a locomotive. The sounds are not modified, but are juxtaposed and reassembled in an attempt to imbue them with musical structure. The ascending and descending interval of the fourth of the locomotive's whistle recurs as a formal element, and the clatter of train tracks creates rhythm and meter. In other studies Schaeffer obscured his sources of sound by manipulating phonograph equipment. Timbre and pitch, for example, were altered by changes in the speed of playback, hybrid sounds were created by abutting different parts of different sounds, and entirely new contours of sound were obtained by playing a recording backward. The final version of a work was made by superimposing, mixing, splicing, and otherwise editing these prerecorded elements. With the introduction of tape recording equipment (at first opposed by Schaeffer), these manipulations and techniques of reassembly were greatly expanded and facilitated.

Schaeffer's music was normally referential: the origins of its sounds were usually recognizable. This realism was dissipated in 1949 when he began a collaboration with Pierre Henry (1927–). Henry possessed the musical training which Schaeffer lacked, and the works that they composed jointly—beginning with *Symphonie pour un homme seul* (1949–50, later rev.)—reveal greater possibilities inherent in this medium. *Le voile d'Orphée* (*The Veil of Orpheus*, 1953) was extracted and revised by Henry from the opera *Orphée* (1953). The former is called a "cantata," and it combines vocal sounds with unidentifiable noises. The voice becomes intelligible at the climactic reading of a Greek Orphic hymn. Its dramatic and energetic use of sound— reminiscent of the instrumental works of Edgard Varèse—goes far beyond the referentialism of Schaeffer in its powerful abstraction.

The original studio for *musique concrète* at the French Radio run by Schaeffer and Henry was expanded in 1951, when it became known as the Groupe de Recherches de Musique Concrète; it was again reorganized in 1958 as the Groupe de Recherches Musicales. Varèse, Messiaen, Boulez, and Stockhausen worked there briefly. The most successful collaborator was Iannis Xenakis (1922–), who composed a series of works which he called "electro-acoustic" music between 1955 and 1962. Xenakis was trained as an architect and mathematician, and he used his knowledge of statistics to develop a type of music in conventional media which he termed *stochastic*. In composing such works, Xenakis first makes decisions regarding the medium and basic musical materials and processess. The details of composition are then worked out automatically by mathematical formulas or computer programs which guarantee a random or "stochastic" distribution of events. In his *musique concrète*, however, Xenakis found that natural sounds were already random, thus allowing him to bypass the recondite methods that underlie his instrumental compositions. *Concret P-H* (1958), for example, uses the highly amplified sounds of burning charcoal, which emits a sparkling gossamer of noise. Other works such as *Bohor* (1962) (using the startlingly rich sounds of oriental jewelry and musical instruments) derive their shape from slowly evolving densities, which are manipulated by editorial techniques into dramatic soundscapes.

Pure *musique concrète* did not produce masterpieces beyond the essays of Henry and Xenakis. It was superseded by the flexible resources of synthetically generated sound, which was more compatible with serial organization demanded by many of the younger composers of the 1950s. *Musique concrète*, nevertheless, was the earliest important medium of electronic music. It demonstrated the usefulness of recorded sounds—especially those of the human voice—and it initiated technical processes and studio techniques that were adopted and developed by composers in other media.

In the early 1950s in New York City, Vladimir Ussachevsky (1911–90) and Otto Luening (1900–) used early tape recorders to produce works related to French *musique concrète*. Their medium—sometimes called "tape music"—differs from *musique concrète* since it takes its departure from a notated instrumental composition. This composition is recorded on tape and then manipulated by simple techniques such as change of speed, addition of reverberation, and the "feedback effect." Feedback is obtained and stored by dubbing the sounds on a tape as it crosses the playback head onto the same tape at the recording head a small distance away. The effect is a shimmering network of echoes. Ussachevsky's *Sonic Contours* (1952) uses a composition for piano in a tuneful and diatonic style, which is recorded and manipulated primarily by feedback. The works of Ussachevsky and Luening were the first important essays in electronic music in America. But like the idiom of their French contemporaries, tape music soon gave way to more sophisticated styles and apparatuses.

PURE ELECTRONIC MUSIC

The distinguishing feature of this medium is the source of its sounds, which are synthesized by electronic devices rather than recorded from live sources as in *musique concrète*. The term "elektronische Musik" was coined around 1950 by German pioneers of such music in order to distinguish it from works of their French counterparts. While our modern notion of electronic music has become considerably broader than this one medium, we shall now use the term "electronic" music in the more restrictive sense of recorded works whose sounds are electronically produced.

The technology for creating electronic signals which are convertible to sounds of fixed or variable pitch had been known since the early twentieth century. Research into the nature of musical sounds and the ways in which they can be simulated electronically was carried on in the early 1950s by the German scientist Werner Meyer-Eppler (1913–60) and musicians Robert Beyer and Herbert Eimert (1897–1972). These three figures were instrumental in founding the first studio for "elektronische Musik" at the North West German Radio in Cologne in 1951. Their studio was brought to great prominence beginning in 1953 by the work there of Karlheinz Stockhausen, which culminated in his electronic masterpieces *Gesang der Jünglinge* (1955–56) and *Kontakte* (1959–60). The studio was used later by Ernst Krenek, Henri Pousseur, Gottfried Michael König, György Ligeti, and other prominent composers. Stockhausen's first works at the studio in Cologne were two *Electronic Studies* (1953 and 1954). These were built entirely from electronic sounds devoid of overtones, and their construction reflects the serialized procedures of composition that were embraced by Stockhausen at this time. The composer also developed a notation for these works giving sufficient technical information for the music to be independently realized.

The compositional procedure of musicians at Cologne or at any of a number of other studios that were founded in Europe and America in the 1950s was divided into three broad phases. Composition began by generating electronic signals that could be converted by loudspeakers into musical sounds. These signals were

Milton Babbitt seated at the RCA Synthesizer (late 1950s). Courtesy BMI Archives.

The Electronic Music Studio of Nordwestdeutscher Rundfunk (NWDR), Cologne, in the mid- 1960s.

then modified to obtain more varied characteristics; finally, they were reassembled on tape in a musically satisfying order or mixture. There are several electronic devices that produce signals corresponding to sounds with different colors. The "sine-wave" generator produces pitches of glassy sound without overtones. It was this most basic signal that was preferred by Stockhausen in his early *Electronic Studies*. The "sawtooth-wave" generator produces a nasal pitch with all overtones, and the "rectangular-" or "square-wave" generator, a hollow tone with only odd-numbered harmonics. A "white-noise" generator produces a sound without definite pitch, suggesting the rush of a waterfall, and an "inharmonic" generator can produce bell-like sounds with irregular overtone patterns.

Devices that modify these basic sound elements include "modulators," by which two incoming signals interact to produce a new signal. The *ring modulator* is the most common of these instruments; it produces sums and differences of the incoming frequencies, which can create a sound of wild distortion. "Filters" change the color of a tone by reducing the audibility of some of its overtones, and "reverberators" are devices that introduce echoes. Ostinatos and other such periodic repetitions are easily obtained by placing a musical phrase on a loop of tape. The electronic composition is then assembled by combining these modified signals in the desired order, relative prominence, and texture.

Composition of electronic music in the 1950s was often a tedious exercise in splicing and mixing tape. But studio procedures were greatly simplified in the 1960s by the invention of *synthesizers*, which allowed the composer to generate a sequence of sounds and to combine several manipulations of these source signals in a rapid and facile manner. The first important such tool was the RCA Electronic Music Synthesizer, developed by Dr. Harry F. Olson in the mid-1950s and turned over to the Columbia-Princeton Electronic Music Center in New York in 1959. With this machine composers encoded on paper tape the succession of sounds they desired, each of which were given a specific pitch, volume, color, articulation, and duration. The device then realized the sounds and recorded them on tape in as many as four channels.

The RCA Synthesizer was of the greatest use to a composer such as Milton Babbitt, since it allowed complete precision in realizing the numerical relationships that underlay serial structures. Babbitt's *Composition for Synthesizer* (1961) and *Ensembles for Synthesizer* (1964) consist entirely of synthesized sound on tape. Both works are serialized and limited to the tonal resources of the traditional twelve-tone scale. A filigree of brief motives, massive chords, and rapid-fire bursts of sound alternate to create a great sense of space and motion.

Babbitt's more recent electronic music reflects the general trend of the 1970s toward works combining tape with live performance.

Although Babbitt has been the major composer to use the RCA Synthesizer, the device has helped to produce many other works by numerous musicians. *Time's Encomium* (1968–69) by Charles Wuorinen was realized in part by this machine. The work, over a half-hour in duration, uses the twelve tempered pitch classes and serialized structures favored by Babbitt. But it relies more heavily upon sonorous effects. Synthesized sounds, for example, alternate with the same passages electronically modified, most obviously by the addition of reverberation.

Electronic composition was made widely available in the 1960s by the introduction of modular, voltage-controlled synthesizers, which were marketed under such trade names as Moog, Buchla, and ARP. These devices have little in common with the RCA Synthesizer. They consist of several electronic components or "modules," each of which produces an electronic signal. These signals can take on different functions: they can be converted by a loudspeaker to audible sound or they can act upon ("control") the performance of other modules. This latter capability was revolutionary in the ease with which it allowed electronic sounds to be altered. For example, a module producing a pitch can be made to change its frequency simply by applying a "control voltage" to it. The initial pitch can take on a vibrato, tremolo, or other such modifications by the application of other types of voltage signals. Indeed, the possibilities for interaction among modular components provide the composer with a greatly expanded repertory of sounds and greater ease with which they can be obtained.

Music composed with such synthesizers has been both abstract and representational. A series of works by Morton Subotnick (1933–) realized on the Buchla synthesizer is of the more abstract type. The composer seeks to express in them some image contained in their title. *Silver Apples of the Moon* (1967), *The Wild Bull* (1968), *Touch* (1968), *Four Butterflies* (1974), and *Sky of Cloudless Sulphur* (1978) are examples. Subotnick's music is very direct, as it uses splashy sounds, spatial gyrations, and elements of conventional music such as rhythms of jazz.

The modular synthesizer is perhaps most widely known for its use in recreating works of the classical masters, such as Walter (Wendy) Carlos's adaptations of music by Bach on the Moog Synthesizer in a recording entitled "Switched-On Bach." Such electronic transcriptions of preexistent works are also found in a recording of 1955 made by the engineers of the RCA Synthesizer (RCA Victor LM 1922), in which electronic music was interpreted not as a distinctive idiom but as a means by which preexistent works could be performed.

Computer technology has had several applications to electronic music. In the early 1960s computer programs for sound generation were devised that allowed composers to bypass traditional electronic studios and rely instead on increasingly widespread and sophisticated computer hardware. The style of music first realized by computer programs, such as *Quartets in Pairs* by J. K. Randall and *Changes* by Charles Dodge, was virtually indistinguishable from the type of music that could be realized in the classic studio. But by the early 1970s the dramatic advances in computerized simulation of speech led to computer music of a more distinctive type. Charles Dodge's *Speech Songs* (1973) and *The Story of Our Lives* (1974) use such programs to create works which imaginatively evoke simulated readings of modern poetry.

RECORDED MUSIC WITH ELECTRONIC AND CONCRETE SOUNDS

Electronic music since 1950 has increasingly mixed its styles and media. In the early 1950s, composers both in the Parisian studio for *musique concrète* and at the studio for electronic music in Cologne were generally devoted to a single medium. Stockhausen and his colleagues at Cologne, for example, at first avoided the use of sounds recorded acoustically and even rejected all electronic sounds except the elemental sine-wave tone.

But the earliest masterpieces of electronic music and, indeed, the true maturity of the genre resulted from a freer combination of methods and philosophies. Music made from both concrete and electronic sounds allowed composers to combine the dramatic power of the style of Pierre Henry with the fastidious refinement and structure of the early *Electronic Studies* of Stockhausen. By the later 1950s this mixed medium was exploited by several composers in major works. The concrete sound that was most desired was the human voice. It was a sound with unparalleled power to fix a listener's attention and unique in its ability to express meaning precisely.

The medium of taped music combining vocal and electronic sounds was popularized by a single work, Stockhausen's *Gesang der Jünglinge*. This was perhaps the first masterpiece of electronic music, and it was soon followed by several other works of a similar type. In the following discussion, we shall deal with Stockhausen's *Gesang* and two related pieces: Varèse's *Poème électronique* (1958) and Berio's *Visage* (1961). The three are in very different styles, each reflecting the different artistic personalities of these composers. Stockhausen's *Gesang* is refined and philosophi-

The modern electronic music studio: synthesizers and computer interconnected by MIDI. Photo by Tom Prutisto.

cal; Varèse's *Poème*, direct and dramatic; and Berio's *Visage*, human and emotional.

Stockhausen's *Gesang der Jünglinge* is a thirteen-minute work using recorded sounds of a boy soprano singing and speaking texts from the apocryphal "Song of the Three," the hymn of praise to God sung by Shadrach, Meshach, and Abed-nego upon being cast into the blazing furnace of King Nebuchadnezzar. To these vocal sounds, the composer adds a virtuosic array of electronic sounds of the sine-wave type, filtered white noise, and sounds of an impulse generator. These materials are used in a construction that mixes aleatoric elements with highly abstracted serial procedures. The piece is divided into six sections or "textures," but the distinctions between them are scarcely perceptible except in the quiet and sparse third texture, from 2' 52" to 5' 15.5".

It was Stockhausen's intention in *Gesang der Jünglinge* to "mediate" between the vocal and electronic sounds: words of the voice are sometimes broken into noises that seem to merge with the electronic sounds; at other times, distinct German words appear, especially the phrases "lobet den Herrn" and "preiset den Herrn," both meaning "praise the Lord," which recur as formal and programmatic elements. The voice is often compounded into choral effects, and the impact of the work is greatly enhanced by the skillful manipulation of spatial contrasts.

Edgard Varèse's lifelong interest in technology, new musical instruments, and sound as the primary element of music came to fruition late in his career in the electronic medium. His first work involving tape was *Déserts* (1954), in which an ensemble of winds, brass, and percussion alternates with taped sounds. The electronic portions of this piece were begun in the manner of the "tape music" of Luening and Ussachevsky, in which an instrumental ensemble was recorded and enhanced by electronic means. The tape was completed at the studio of the Groupe de Recherches de Musique Concrète in Paris in 1954.

Varèse's only work entirely in the medium of tape is *Poème électronique*. It was commissioned by the Philips Corporation for use at the World's Fair in Brussels in 1958 in a tent-like pavilion designed by the architect Le Corbusier (1887–1965). Varèse's music, composed on three channels, was played continuously over 400 loudspeakers in the pavilion to accompany abstract visual projections.

The work is highly eclectic in its sources of sound. Purely electronic sounds were synthesized at the Philips Laboratories in Holland in 1957; these were subsequently combined with recorded sounds of bells, organ, excerpts of percussion music from his own earlier works, and, of great dramatic significance, an eerie wail of a human voice. As in most of Varèse's music, *Poème électronique* is tied together by recurrences of a short motive, in this case a high-pitched figure sliding upward between three chromatic tones. The work is slowly paced, which increases its dramatic impact in a way that has the opposite effect of Milton Babbitt's later high-speed studies on the RCA Synthesizer. Varèse's dramatic use of sound reaches its climax with the entrance of the voice in an unearthly moan. Despite the absence of a text, the voice vividly conveys dramatic meaning by its tortured sound and by the serene vocalization at the end. "I wanted it to express tragedy—an inquisition," the composer later remarked.

Most works in the electronic medium by Luciano Berio were composed during the years 1955 to 1961, when he collaborated with Bruno Maderna at the Studio di Fonologia Musicale in Milan. His *Thema (Omaggio a Joyce)*, a taped work assembled from readings in James Joyce's *Ulysses*, was a turning point in his style as a composer. Most of his compositions from this time, whether performed or taped, employ the voice in a dramatic and unorthodox fashion.

Visage combines electronic sounds with those of a solo soprano. Its dramatic treatment of the voice surpasses Varèse's *Poème* by thrusting the voice into a position of greater prominence and by allowing it to rush headlong through a whole gamut of emotions. The form of *Visage* is shaped by a gradual disintegration in the voice and in the vivid personality or "visage" that it represents. At the beginning the singer utters sounds of fear, satisfaction, joy, and sadness in a dizzying soliloquy accompanied by electronic commentary. By the end of the piece, however, the voice has been completely obliterated and swallowed up by electronic noise. The work is unified by recurrences of the word *paroles* ("words"), which is the single intelligible vocal utterance.

Many other composers have been attracted to the medium of taped music which combines electronic and recorded sounds. *Events* (1963) by Mel Powell (1923–) uses three different readings of Hart Crane's poem "Legend," which are manipulated with the addition of electronic sounds. The vivid imagery and dislocated syntax of the poem invite the highly dramatic and collage-like realization. *Sonic Seasonings* by Walter Carlos is a sort of *Pastoral* Symphony of electronic effects. It mixes sounds recorded in nature, instrumental passages, and electronic noises into a vivid depiction of the four seasons.

LIVE PERFORMANCE WITH TAPED SOUNDS

Music in media that we have now surveyed—electronic works, that is, which are entirely contained on tape—either eliminates the performer or relegates him to the role of an unseen maker of sounds. Such music has had no precedent in history. The performer had earlier been the indispensable medium by which the composer's thoughts were conveyed to the audience, and since the nineteenth century the performer had in fact rivaled the composer as the central figure in musical creation.

Some composers at first relished the opportunity to repossess this creative territory and bypass the performer altogether. Taped music allowed them direct contact with the audience and helped to eliminate the inevitable imperfections of live performances and interpretations that were not faithful to the composer's intent. But it soon became plain that these advantages were outweighed by the loss of spontaneity and of the drama of live performance. By 1970 music entirely on tape had lost favor, as composers of electronic works sought to revive the concert as a relevant musical event.

Live performance with coordinated taped sounds offered a straightforward compromise. This type of music had been composed since the early 1950s. Bruno Maderna's *Musica su due dimensioni* (1952, rev. 1958) combined solo flute with sounds on tape, and Varèse's *Déserts* called for an alternation of wind and percussion ensemble and recorded sounds. Vladimir Ussachevsky and Otto Luening collaborated on several works of the mid-1950s for tape and orchestra, including *A Poem in Cycles and Bells* (1954). Their *Concerted Piece for Tape Recorder and Orchestra* (1960) places taped sounds in the role of soloist in a traditional concerto.

By the 1960s this hybrid medium had branched into several styles. Milton Babbitt combined live music for soprano with taped sounds in three works, *Vision and Prayer* (1961), *Philomel* (1963), and *Phonemena* (1969–70). The first of these is a setting of poetry of the same title by Dylan Thomas. The electronic sounds were realized on the RCA Synthesizer and are organized serially. The voice is treated in a restrained fashion, alternating between recitation and conventional singing.

Berio's *Questo vuol dire che* (1969), on the other hand, merges tape with chorus and uses vocal techniques that are much more unconventional. This work combines folk texts in three languages and nonsensical vocal noise. Electronic music by Luigi Nono also combines tape and voice, but in his works the voices are vividly intelligible and serve to emphasize the message of socialism and struggle against economic and political tyranny, which is the purpose of his music. *La fabbrica illuminata* (1964), for example, combines a tape (made from vocal sounds and noises from a factory) with a soprano protesting against the degrading existence of laborers.

Electronic compositions of Mario Davidovsky (1934–) and Jacob Druckman (1928–) include series of works for instrumental performers and tape. Davidovsky has composed eight such pieces, which he calls *Synchronisms* (1963–74). The taped sounds are derived in part from the instruments that they accompany. The related series *Animus* (1966–69) by Jacob Druckman includes three pieces, combining tape with trombone, voice and percussion, and clarinet. His *Synapse→Valentine* (1970) uses double bass and tape in a similar way.

Druckman's *Animus III* (1969) for tape and clarinet enhances the performing situation by an amusing theatrical encounter between player and tape. In a note to the score, the composer outlines the story: "The clarinetist enters in the person of an arch-virtuoso, self-confident almost to the point of arrogance. During the sixteen minutes of the work, there is a gradual dissolution of the personality of the player. The person who leaves the stage at the end of the work is dissociated and hysterical to the point of insanity." The taped sounds suggest both a rival musician—whose abstract "virtuosity" plants seeds of self-doubt within the clarinetist—and the audience, who respond to his playing by laughter and rude gestures.

LIVE ELECTRONIC MUSIC

This medium, in which sounds produced in live concert situations are immediately manipulated by electronic devices, has been the primary area of concentration and innovation in electronic music since 1970. It has brought about close contact between "serious" composers and performers and rock musicians, a development that will be traced in Chapter 17. The medium has also been essential to a group of American composers often designated as "minimalists": Philip Glass, La Monte Young, Terry Riley, and Steve Reich. Their music will also be considered in Chapter 17.

Live electronic music harks back to experimental compositions by John Cage in the 1930s. His series of five *Imaginary Landscapes* (1939–52) calls for diverse electronic instruments, including phonograph recordings, radios, phonograph cartridges, and oscillators. Cage's *Cartridge Music* (1960) was the first important piece in which sounds were modified electronically on the spot. Like Cage's other works in electronic media after 1952, this piece is indeterminate of composition and performance. Any number of players attach phonograph cartridges and contact microphones to any sound-producing materials, and the noises that result are varied by amplifiers and reproduced on loudspeakers.

Cage's experiments were developed with remarkable diversity in a series of compositions by Karlheinz Stockhausen beginning with *Mikrophonie I* (1964). This is a work in "moment form" (see Chapter 14) in which the sonorous events of each moment are precisely notated. Two performers produce sounds on a large tamtam, two other players position microphones, and two players control filters and amplifiers.

Stockhausen's *Mixtur* (1964) for orchestra and *Mikrophonie II* (1965) for chorus and Hammond organ use ring modulation to modify performed sounds, a technique to which he returned in *Mantra* (1970) for two pianos and percussion. *Solo* (1965–66) is for one instrumentalist whose music is recorded on a tape loop as it is performed. The recorded sounds and newly performed sounds are progressively added to the tape, building up ostinatos of increasing complexity.

Stockhausen was active from 1964 as a performer, touring with an ensemble devoted to realizations of his own music. *Prozession* (1967) was written for this group. It is a lengthy work improvised by players on keyboard, string, and percussion instruments from excerpts drawn from Stockhausen's own earlier compositions. The music is then modified by on-the-spot filtering and amplification. *Kurzwellen* (1968) is similar except that the players improvise upon music they hear on radios.

Other composers who have worked in the medium of live electronic music include Max Neuhaus and Morton Subotnick. Neuhaus's recording entitled "Electronics and Percussion" (Columbia MS 7139) includes realizations of music by Earle Brown,

Sylvano Bussotti, and John Cage; his interpretations apply techniques of amplification and feedback. Recent compositions by Morton Subotnick such as *The Wild Beasts* (1978), *After the Butterfly* (1980), and *Axolotl* (1980) combine live instrumental performance with an imaginative application of the voltage controlled synthesizer. While Subotnick and others had earlier used the synthesizer to produce manipulations of electronic sounds on tape, in these works he uses a tape of sounds to control the synthesizer, which in turn modifies the sounds of the performer. Subotnick first composes music for the performer using standard notation. This music is played and picked up by a microphone by which it is relayed to the synthesizer for modification and reproduction through loudspeakers. The modification of sounds is guided by a "gesture sketch" made by the composer in the form of a tape of sounds of varying pitch and loudness. This tape is not audible at the performance, but instead serves to trigger the synthesizer to modify the performed music. These "ghost electronics," to use Subotnick's term, are an extension of the traditional modulators found in the classic electronic music studio and used widely in the live electronic idiom. But they are capable of a much wider range of manipulation of the incoming signal, as they can produce changes in its volume, direction, pitch, rhythm and attack, and timbre.

RECENT DEVELOPMENTS

The history of electronic music in the 1980s and 1990s is characterized by powerful opposing forces. On one side is the development of a staggering array of equipment that allows for relatively inexpensive access to electronic music and unprecedented applications to all types of electronic media, especially the live electronic option. Applications of the computer to music have been especially resourceful. But despite this explosion of available equipment and technology, electronic music has lost ground in contemporary serious musical culture at the hands of two opposing circumstances. The most critical of these is the more conservative and traditional taste in serious music of the present day; the other is an ever-stronger alliance between electronics and commercial music. Electronic music in the 1950s and 1960s was provoked and sustained by widespread support for unlimited experimentation in the arts and by a sense that change and exploration were necessary. As will be discussed further in Chapters 16 and 17, these sentiments are no longer strongly felt. The new music that is most often performed in prestigious national or international settings in the present day partakes largely of traditional musical values. Electronics, on the contrary, suggest experiment, innovation, and academicism—qualities that for the time being are unwelcome. The challenge of commercial music is scarcely less daunting to the development of electronic music. To a considerable extent, the new equipment for electronic music—keyboard synthesizers, MIDI technology that allows for the integration of equipment, computer-driven music synthesizers that provide for acoustic sampling—is most directly applicable to the popular or commercial musical world. The modern music synthesizer can "sample" (record digitally) familiar instruments and quickly and cheaply reassemble their sounds as a commercial musical product that approximates the sound of a band or orchestra. Live or interactive electronic effects produced by MIDI are the stock in trade of the modern rock concert. But what is their application to serious music? Although fascinating answers are provided by individuals still imbued by the experimental spirit, no generally accepted response has emerged.

All the same, the 1980s and 1990s have produced exciting new electronic works. Many of these have stemmed from the Parisian studio called IRCAM (Institut de Recherche et de Coordination Acoustique/Musique), directed by Pierre Boulez. Boulez's own *Répons* (1981 with later versions) is a much-performed live electronic work using the resources of the studio. In this lengthy composition a group of soloists (percussionists and pianists) plays and partly improvises from positions throughout the auditorium, "responding" aurally to the playing of each other and of a chamber orchestra. Their playing is manipulated in real time by electronic equipment to produce a dazzling array of sounds. The work produces the same sense of the unexpected, virtuosity, and alternative musical textures as the composer's earlier music.

The American composer Tod Machover (1953–) developed ingenious ways to enrich the medium of live electronic music. In works such as *Bug-Mudra* for guitars, percussion, and electronics (1990) and *Begin Again Again . . .* (1991) for cello and electronics, Machover has devised ways for the physical gestures of the performers, in addition to the sounds emanating from their instruments, to control the manipulation and creation of new electronic sounds.

BIBLIOGRAPHY

Two excellent surveys of electronic music are Elliott Schwartz's *Electronic Music: A Listener's Guide*, rev. ed. (New York, 1975) and Paul Griffith's *Guide to Electronic Music* (New York, 1979). Also see Jon Appleton and Ronald Perera, eds. *The Development and Practice of*

Electronic Music (Englewood Cliffs, N.J., 1974); Charles Dodge and Thomas A. Jerse, *Computer Music: Synthesis, Composition, and Performance* (New York, 1985); and Peter Manning, *Electronic and Computer Music*, 2nd ed. (Oxford, 1994). A thorough bibliography of the early literature on this subject is found in Lowell Cross, *A Bibliography of Electronic Music* (Toronto, 1968). Current developments in computer applications to music are found in the *Computer Music Journal* (1977–); also see Wayne Bateman's *Introduction to Computer Music* (New York, 1980). Hubert Howe's *Electronic Music Synthesis* (New York, 1975) is a detailed introduction to studio techniques and use of the synthesizer. A history of the early days of electronic music is given by Lowell Cross in "Electronic Music, 1948–1953," *Perspectives of New Music*, 7 (1968): 32–65.

Stockhausen's "Origins of Electronic Music," *Musical Times*, 112 (1971): 649–50, seeks to assert the priority of European developments in this medium over American initiatives. Stockhausen's article "Actualia," *Die Reihe*, 1 (1955; English trans., 1958) deals with aspects of *Gesang der Jünglinge*. Otto Luening gives a lively account of his introduction to electronic media in his memoirs, *The Odyssey of an American Composer* (New York, 1980). Studies of works by other composers of electronic music are surveyed in the bibliographies to Chapters 12 and 13. Recorded examples of sounds and their modification by control voltage are found on "The Nonesuch Guide to Electronic Music," Nonesuch HC 73018.

A discography of works cited in this chapter follows:

Babbitt	*Composition for Synthesizer*, Columbia MS 6566
	Ensembles for Synthesizer, Columbia MS 7051
	Phonemena, New World NW 209
	Philomel, Acoustic Research AR 0654
	Vision and Prayer, CRI SD 268
Berio	*Visage*, Candide CE 31027
Boulez	*Répons*, IRCAM Records 0001
Cage	*Cartridge Music*, Time 58009
Carlos	*Sonic Seasonings*, Columbia PG 31234
	Switched-On Bach, Columbia MS 7194
Davidovsky	*Synchronisms* Nos. 1–3, CRI SD 204
	Synchronisms No. 5, CRI SD 268
	Synchronisms No. 6, Turnabout TV 34487S
	Synchronisms No. 8, Vox SVBX 5307
Dodge	*Changes*, Nonesuch H 71245
	Speech Songs CRI SD 348
	The Story of Our Lives, CRI SD 348
Druckman	*Animus III*, Nonesuch H 71253
Henry	*Orphée*, Philips 839 484 LY (with Pierre Schaeffer)

	Le voile d'Orphée, Ducretet-Thomson DUC 8 LDG 1497
Machover	*Bug-Mudra*, Bridge BCD 9022
Maderna	*Musica su due dimensioni*, Compagnia generale del disco ESZ 3
Nono	*La fabbrica illuminata*, Wergo 60038
Powell	*Events*, CRI 227 USD
Randall	*Quartets in Pairs*, Nonesuch H 71245
RCA Electronic Music Synthesizer	*Sounds and Music of the RCA Electronic Music Synthesizer*, RCA Victor LM 1922
Schaeffer	*Étude aux chemins de fer*, Ducretet-Thomson DUC 8 LDG 1497
	(with Pierre Henry): *Symphonie pour un homme seul*, London DTL 93121
Stockhausen	*Gesang der Jünglinge*, DGG 138811
	Kontakte, DGG 138811
	Kurzwellen, DGG 139 461
	Mantra, DGG 2530 208
	Mikrophonie I and II, Columbia MS 7355
	Prozession, Candide CE 31001
	Solo, DGG 137 005
	Studie I, II, DGG LP 16133
Subotnick	*After the Butterfly*, Nonesuch N 78001
	Axolotl, Nonesuch N 78012
	Four Butterflies, Columbia M 32741
	Silver Apples of the Moon, Nonesuch H 71174
	Sky of Cloudless Sulphur, Nonesuch N 78001
	Touch, Columbia MS 7316
	The Wild Beast, Nonesuch N 78012
	The Wild Bull, Nonesuch, H 71208
Ussachevsky	*Sonic Contours*, Desto DC 6466
	(with Otto Luening): *Concerted Piece for Tape Recorder and Orchestra*, CRI 227 USD
	(with Otto Luening): *Poem in Cycles and Bells*, CRI 112
Varèse	*Déserts, CRI SD 268*
	Poème électronique, Columbia MS 6146
Wuorinen	*Time's Encomium*, Nonesuch, H 71225
Xenakis	*Bohor*, Nonesuch H 71246
	Concret P-H, Nonesuch H 71246

16

Eclecticism

Composers throughout the twentieth century have discovered sources for their own musical speech in the works of others. Despite the pronounced originality of much of the music of this century, there has been nonetheless a broad reliance upon preexisting styles and upon frequent borrowings from earlier music. Making the process of borrowing a basic premise of a composition suggests the notion of *eclecticism*—the creation of an artistic work by selecting elements from multiple preexisting sources and models. In the twentieth century the eclectic spirit in music has appeared in two principal guises: the use of several distinct styles in a single work and the quotation of passages from multiple existing musical sources.

Eclecticism has been a significant element of the art of music since its early history. Bach, for example, was notably eclectic, both for quoting and for manipulating different styles. He incorporated traditional Lutheran hymns in many original works for the church and alluded in his instrumental music to such distinct styles as that of the French clavecinists and the instrumental idiom of Vivaldi.

Eclecticism was less prominent among composers of the classical and early romantic periods because of the widespread acceptance of a common and uniform stylistic language. The use of a homogeneous, unified style continued to be widespread in the early twentieth century. Schoenberg spoke in favor of this objective when he argued against mixing triadic harmonies with the dissonances that characterized his atonal musical language. "The simple chords of the earlier harmony do not appear successfully in this environment," he wrote in his *Harmonielehre*. Only a few major figures early in the century, notably Charles Ives, allowed multiple styles and diverse quotations of existing music into their compositions.

By the 1920s and 1930s, as the unified German romantic language was increasingly banished, an eclectic music that mixed several distinct styles gained in prominence. It was a feature of neoclassicism during the interwar period, when composers revived styles associated with the baroque and classical periods and mixed them with a modernistic harmony and tonality. But the broadened historical interests of the neo-classicists still gave rise to an essentially uniform musical character. In the decades immediately following World War II, a unified style in music—most often abstract, depersonalized, dissonant, and chromatic—was also insisted upon in international modern music circles.

By the 1970s, however, an eclectic spirit in music became pronounced among modernist composers around the world. This new direction suggests a change of taste in music, a reaction against the dogmatism of the postwar decades and its tendency to ignore earlier developments in music history. On the contrary, important composers from this time embraced and celebrated the whole history of music and brought into their compositional arsenals ideas from non-Western cultures as well. Their nondogmatic viewpoint concerning style is seen most vividly in the technique of using multiple styles or quotations in a single work. Such eclecticism offers contemporary composers a link with their cultural forebears, a ready way to make their music more accessible and to imbue it with meaning.

Quotations from existing musical works have served many purposes for the twentieth-century composer. Early in the century they tended to be isolated elements introduced for the sake of parody or programmatic allusion. The music of Wagner, especially the opera *Tristan und Isolde*, was very often cited for these effects. The opening of the opera is quoted by Debussy in the piano piece "Golliwogg's Cake Walk" parodying Wagner's hyperemotional rhetoric. In the opera *Das Nusch-Nuschi* (1920), Paul Hindemith quotes from King Mark's music as an ironic reference to the plight of a character who is to be castrated for indiscretions with an emperor's wives. *Tristan* was quoted by Alban Berg in his string quartet *Lyric* Suite as a secretive reference to his love for Hanna Fuchs-Robettin.

Beginning in the 1960s the use of quotation began to exceed its earlier ironic or referential function, indicating a new spirit of eclecticism and a rejection of postwar musical abstraction. Rather than isolated allusions with clear meaning, quotations were frequently made from sources far separated in time and in an enigmatic profusion. Such new works began to resemble *collages*, artworks in which unrelated materials are glued to a surface to form a single composition. The quotation-collages of Bernd Alois Zimmerman (1918–70), including his opera *Die Soldaten* (1964), *Monologe* for two pianos (1964), and *Photoptosis* for orchestra (1968), pile together quotations from all eras of musical history into a mass of provocative but ununified sound. Mauricio Kagel's *Ludwig Van* (1969) is a mad hodgepodge of themes from the music of Beethoven. Michael Tippett's *Songs for Dov* for tenor and chamber orchestra (1969–70) quotes from music by Beethoven, Wagner, Musorgski, and Tippett's own earlier music.

The works discussed in this chapter thus herald the beginning of a new period in the history of twentieth-century music. Its onset occurred in the 1960s but its full impact was not apparent until the 1970s. Like other stylistic changes in modern music, it was brought on by a reaction against an existing state of affairs, represented by the postwar avant-garde. Whereas postwar experimentation tended to be doctrinaire in style, depersonalized in expressivity, and abstractly difficult, the new spirit characterized by eclecticism was emotive, unpredictable, and accessible to a larger audience. We turn in this chapter to notable eclectic composers in Europe and America who were in the van of this new style. The eclectic composers of the 1970s were much indebted to the works of Olivier Messiaen (1908–92), who pointed the way toward an original and provocative music that was based on multiple quotations and allusions.

OLIVIER MESSIAEN

Throughout his long and productive career, Messiaen made use of a grand multiplicity of existing musical sources, which he transformed, often beyond recognition, to produce a uniformity of style that was uniquely his own. In the preface to his *Technique of My Musical Language* he enumerates some of his favorite sources: "birds, Russian music, Debussy's *Pelléas et Mélisande*, plainchant, Hindu rhythmics, the mountains of Dauphiné, and, finally, all that evokes stain-glass window and rainbow." But the listener is not immediately aware of these borrowed elements since the composer transforms and reconstitutes them in his own distinctive manner. In his *Technique* Messiaen refers to this process of transformation as a "deforming prism" through which all of his source materials must pass.

The varied and often exotic sources of Messiaen's works are chosen both for their musical values and for their contribution to an elaborate

OLIVIER MESSIAEN
(*Avignon, 1908–Clichy, 1992*)

Messiaen attributed his artistic sensitivity to his parents. His father was a scholar of English literature; his mother, a poet. His desire to pursue the career of a musician stemmed from a childhood hearing of *Pelléas et Mélisande*. Messiaen attended the Conservatory in Paris from 1919 to 1930, during which time he studied composition with Paul Dukas and became a celebrated organist. He collaborated with André Jolivet, Daniel Lesur, and Yves Baudrier in the group "Young France," which from 1936 called for a music of renewed depth as an alternative to the superficial lightness of French neoclassicism.

During the Second World War Messiaen spent two years in Silesia as a prisoner of war, during which he composed his *Quartet for the End of Time*. Since 1942 he taught various subjects at the Conservatory in Paris and held private composition classes. He long served as organist at the Church of the Holy Trinity in Paris.

SELECTED WORKS

Orchestral Music. *Turangalîla Symphonie* (1946–48), *Réveil des oiseaux* (1953), *Oiseaux exotiques* (1956), *Chronochromie* (1960), *Sept Haïkaï* (1962), *Couleurs de la cité céleste* (1963), *Et exspecto resurrectionem mortuorum* (1964), *Des canyons aux étoiles* (1974).

Chamber Music. *Quatuor pour la fin du temps* (1940), *Le merle noir* (flute and piano, 1951).

Piano Music. Preludes (1929), *Visions de l'amen* (two pianos, 1943), *Vingt regards sur l'enfant Jésus* (1944), *Cantéyodjayâ* (1948), "Mode de valeurs et d'intensités" (1949), *Ile de feu* I and II (1949) *Catalogue d'oiseaux* (1956–58), *La fauvette des jardins* (1972).

Organ Music. *L'ascension* (1934), *La nativité du seigneur* (1935), *Les corps glorieux* (1939), *Messe de la pentecôte* (1950) *Livre d'orgue* (1951), *Méditations sur le mystère de la sainte trinité* (1969).

Songs. *Poèmes pour Mi* (1936), *Chants de terre et de ciel* (1938), *Harawi* (1945).

Choral Music. *O sacrum convivium!* (1937), *Choeurs pour une Jeanne d'Arc* (1941), *Trois petites liturgies de la présence divine* (1944), *Cinq rechants* (1949), *La transfiguration de notre seigneur Jésus-Christ* (1963–69).

symbolism that all of his music embodies. Three broad and interrelated subjects inform his work: premises of the Catholic faith, human love, and nature. Messiaen has stated that the last two are symbols of divine love, which underlies his understanding of Christianity.

Messiaen's music is in many respects a continuation of the modern school of French and Russian composition of the late nineteenth and early twentieth centuries. Like Scriabin and Rimski-Korsakov, Messiaen vividly associates colors with certain chords and tonalities. Like Stravinsky, Scriabin, Rimski-Korsakov, Debussy, and Ravel, he often exploits the harmonic resources of the octatonic scale. This is one of seven symmetric sets that he calls "modes of limited transposition" and uses in most of his works. Like Debussy and Ravel, he frequently evokes the percussive sonorities of the oriental gamelan.

Messiaen's music is relatively consistent in style, except for a period in the early 1950s when he experimented with pseudo-serial techniques and pointillist textures (see Chapter 13). His treatment of rhythm and meter—one of the most distinctive aspects of his music—is discussed in Chapter 5. In general, the element of time in his work is not organized by subdividing a steady beat or regular metric group. Rhythms are instead spun from small values into freely varied larger shapes.

Harmonies are generally derived from Messiaen's modes of limited transposition, which are sets of between six and ten pitch classes dividing the octave symmetrically. These modes are atonal sets: they do not necessarily relate to a keynote, and they are subject to free reordering and transposition.

Mode 1: C D E F♯ G♯ A♯ (C)
Mode 2: C C♯ D♯ E F♯ G A A♯ (C)
Mode 3: C C♯ D E F F♯ G♯ A A♯ (C)
Mode 4: C C♯ D D♯ F♯ G G♯ A (C)
Mode 5: C C♯ D F♯ G G♯ (C)
Mode 6: C C♯ D E F♯ G G♯ A♯ (C)
Mode 7: C C♯ D D♯ E F♯ G G♯ A A♯ (C)

The first mode is a whole-tone scale, which Messiaen uses infrequently, and the second mode—his most characteristic pitch resource—is the octatonic scale. His harmonies sometimes emphasize dissonant chords with triadic components, which he attributes to the "addition" of dissonant notes to familiar chords. Messiaen also states that his music typically asserts a keynote perceptible over spans of varying length, but his work makes no significant use of common-practice tonality.

In the rhythmic dimension, Messiaen has frequent recourse to preexistent sources. He was especially fond of the 120 rhythmic patterns or "talas" that had been assembled in a treatise by the ancient Hindu theorist Sharngadeva. Other rhythms are derived from the metric feet of Greek poetry. In his orchestral work *Chronochromie*, Messiaen uses rhythms derived from permutations of the numbers 1 to 32. Each integer represents a duration of the same number of thirty-second-note values. He refers to these permutations as "interversions" and uses the rhythmic patterns derived from them in several later pieces.

Messiaen asserts in his *Technique* that melody is the primary factor in his music. "Supremacy to melody," he writes, "the noblest element of music." The most striking of his melodic borrowings are his imitations of bird song. From his youth, he had studied and transcribed the songs of birds, which were applied in his music from 1941. The bird songs are first passed through his deforming prism, as their calls must be reinterpreted in the twelve traditional pitch classes and approximated in register, color, and rhythm. Bird song offered Messiaen not only a "found object" of great musical interest, but it also symbolized for him the music of God as He is revealed in nature. Messiaen also appropriates plainchant, motivic fragments from traditional Indian music, and paraphrases of motives from works by which he was inspired, especially from Musorgski's *Boris Godunov* and Debussy's *Pelléas et Mélisande*.

Couleurs de la cité céleste (*Colors of the Celestial City*, 1963) synthesizes most of Messiaen's earlier eclectic procedures. This work, written for clarinets, brass, piano, and percussion, is based upon five passages from the Revelation of John, the last book of the New Testament. These passages emphasize the colors that John so vividly describes in his vision of Jerusalem—colors that Messiaen seeks to evoke by combining his instrumental forces into blocks of sound.

The composer describes his manipulation of sound and color in the preface to the score:

> The form of this work relies entirely on colors. Melodic or rhythmic themes and masses of sounds and timbres are transformed like colors. Within their constantly changing shapes can be found (by analogy) warm and cold colors, complementary colors influencing their neigh-

bors, colors washed out toward white or compressed toward black. These transformations can be compared to characters acting on several superimposed stages, who simultaneously unfold their different stories.

The form of this one-movement piece consists in an alternation of five types of music: bird songs, quotations from Gregorian alleluias, slow-moving chords evoking colors, music depicting the abyss, and passages based on Indian and serial-derived rhythms. These sections are distinctly separated by changes of tempo, by intervening silence, and by their own harmonic and melodic character. The total effect is of a mosaic that is put together arbitrarily, or, as Messiaen writes in the preface, "The work does not end, never having truly begun. It turns on itself, interlacing its temporal blocks as in a cathedral's rose window, made from flamboyant and invisible colors."

The harmonic language of *Colors* does not rely primarily upon the modes of limited transposition. Although these sets occur in passing, the composer dwells more upon chords and constellations of pitches embracing the entire chromatic set, reflecting his experiments with integral serialism of a decade earlier. The three "color chords" at rehearsal 11 (Example 16-1) will illustrate this emphasis on the aggregate. All twelve pitch classes are found in the verticalities of each measure. These chords are labeled in the score "yellow topaz, clear green chrysoprase, and crystal," after the colored gems mentioned in Revelation. It may be observed also that the chord heard on the downbeat of the second measure of rehearsal 11 (see Example 16-2) is a form of Messiaen's mode 4.

Messiaen quotes four plainchant Alleluias, each chosen because of the appropriateness of its text to images from Revelation. These chants illustrate different ways in which Messiaen uses preexistent sources. The Alleluias for the Feast of Corpus Christi and Dedication of a Church are quoted intact, although they are harmonized in an atonal manner. The Alleluia for the Eighth Sunday after Pentecost, on the other hand, is quoted in contour, but with intervallic distortions (Example 16-3). The Alleluia for the Fourth Sunday after Easter is entirely distorted and used as a *Klangfarbenmelodie* divided between bells, horn, clarinets, and piano (Example 16-4).

The quotations from chant and color chords alternate with quotations of bird songs, the latter dispensing with brass and using hard and bright sounds evocative of the oriental gamelan. A middle section (rehearsal 42 to 62) applies five rhythmic patterns derived from the talas of Sharngadeva, and this passage also interlaces rhythms based on interversions of the numerical series used by Messiaen in *Chronochromie*.

Example 16-1. Messiaen, *Couleurs de la cité céleste*, non-transposing score. Copyright by Alphonse Leduc, Paris. Owners and publishers for all countries. Reprinted by permission.

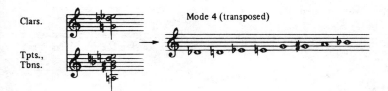

Example 16-2.   Messiaen, *Couleurs de la cité céleste*. Copyright by Alphonse Leduc, Paris. Owners and publishers for all countries. Reprinted by permission.

PETER MAXWELL DAVIES

While Messiaen's musical sources are unparalleled in their diversity, the various means of application of preexistent materials are more exhaustively explored by Peter Maxwell Davies (1934–). Davies has focused largely upon Gregorian chant and works of medieval and Renaissance composers who have themselves adapted preexistent material. *Alma redemptoris mater*, composed in the year of his graduation from the Royal Manchester College of Music (1957), sets the tone for most of his later works in its adaptation of a work of Renaissance polyphony. This chamber piece is dependent on John Dunstable's motet of the same title, which is based on the Marian antiphon "Alma redemptoris mater." Davies's use of his model is highly abstract, mirroring structural principles of Dunstable's motet rather than quoting or paraphrasing.

Davies's assimilation of early music has produced artistic arrangements of works by Buxtehude, Dunstable, Purcell, and others as well as pieces in which the model is only dimly perceived. He often reinterprets ways in which early composers used preexistent

a) Alleluia Magnus dominus

b) Piccolo Trumpet

Example 16-3.   Messiaen, *Couleurs de la cité céleste*. Copyright by Alphonse Leduc, Paris. Owners and publishers for all countries. Reprinted by permission.

a) Alleluia Christus resurgens

b)

Example 16-4. Messiaen, *Couleurs de la cité céleste.* Copyright by Alphonse Leduc, Paris. Owners and publishers for all countries. Reprinted by permission.

material, such as cantus firmus or parody techniques, or he imitates other structural principles of medieval and Renaissance music such as isorhythm, metric prolations or proportions, and varied canonic devices. His *Antechrist* (1967) for instrumental ensemble includes a complete quotation of an anonymous medieval motet, "Deo confitemini—Domino," which is surrounded by music abstractly derived from this motet. *Psalm 124* weaves three Renaissance works into a freely dissonant counterpoint.

Ave maris stella (1975) for instrumental sextet takes its title from plainchant. This source is heard only at the very end of Davies's lengthy piece, and most of the music is drawn from a matrix of numbers and pitch classes recalling the procedures of integral serialism. This "magic square" determines nondodecaphonic series of pitches and series of numbers dictating durations. Davies returned to the same matrix in his Symphony No. 1 (1973–76).

Regardless of its sources or preplanned compositional structures, the music of Davies is highly varied in style. Most works are freely chromatic and atonal with a considerable use of triadic sonorities and tonality by assertion. Other works (such as the carols from *O*

Magnum Mysterium) are pseudo-modal, imitating the texture of Renaissance polyphony but much freer in treatment of dissonance. A series of compositions written around 1969 evoke foxtrots and other popular music. One such work is the orchestral *St. Thomas Wake* (1969). Three separate styles interact in this piece: a pavane by John Bull (played on harp) from which Davies borrowed his title; foxtrots played by a dance band; and "serious" symphonic music played by orchestra. Material from the pavane is developed by both orchestra and dance band.

Also around 1969 Davies worked in "multimedia" or theatric music—an important development in the postwar era to be discussed further in Chapter 17. His pieces of this type include *Eight Songs for a Mad King* (1969), to be discussed presently, *Vesalii icones* (1969) for dancer and instrumental ensemble, and *Missa super l'homme armé* (1968, rev. 1971) for speaker and instrumental ensemble.

Eight Songs for a Mad King dramatizes the insanity of the English monarch George III (1738–1820) during the last decade of his life. George was an amateur player of harpsichord and flute and a great devotee of the music of Handel. During this period of mental incompetency, he is known to have sought diversion by teaching birds to sing. The work consists of eight texts written by Randolph Stow (which incorporate lines thought to have been spoken by the king). These are sung or declaimed by a character acting the part of the monarch, and they depict his interests, obsessions, and reflections upon his plight. Four of the six instrumentalists sit in bird cages, representing the birds that the king coaches to sing.

The seventh song, "Country Dance" (Anthology no. 17), finds the king regaling the people of Windsor by a mad rendition of the tenor recitative "Comfort Ye, My People" from Handel's *Messiah*. His mood suddenly turns grim, as he grabs a violin from one of the caged performers and rails on the evils of the world. Toward the end he smashes the violin—representing his soul—and dissolves into a wrenching, disconnected monologue. Davies treats the Handelian recitative in the style of a cocktail pianist, which gives way to a foxtrot as the king encourages the merrymakers of Windsor. As the king's momentary lucidity gives way to tortured ravings, the music descends into a cacophonous din.

In the eighth and final song ("The Review: A Spanish March") King George solemnly pronounces his obituary. He leaves the stage howling, and, as a final recollection of beatings which he had received, he is followed offstage by a bass drum played with leather whips.

GEORGE ROCHBERG

"I think borrowing is one of the essential traditions of music, an ancient one. And if you are a borrower, as I am, then I see nothing to prevent borrowing from oneself." This excerpt from an interview in *Soundpieces* (1982) underscores the conversion to eclecticism of George Rochberg (1918–). His works of the 1950s and early 1960s, including Twelve Bagatelles (1952), Symphony No. 2 (1956), and Piano Trio (1963), combine serialism with the grandiloquent styles of Mahler and early Schoenberg. By the mid-1960s he had rejected serialism. He writes:

> I had become completely dissatisfied with [serialism's] narrow terms. I found the palette of constant chromaticism increasingly constricting, nor could I accept any longer the limited range of gestures that always seemed to channel the music into some form or other of expressionism. The over-intense manner of serialism and its tendency to inhibit physical pulse and rhythm led me to question a style which made it virtually impossible to express serenity, tranquillity, grace, wit, energy. [From liner notes to Nonesuch Records, H 71283.]

Rochberg's flight from serialism had an aftermath different from the general collapse of European serialism of the late 1950s. The Europeans moved from serialism into other avant-garde areas—indeterminacy, theater, and composition with textures among others—but Rochberg looked to the nineteenth century for usable alternatives.

The music of Charles Ives pointed his way. In the Second String Quartet (1961), Rochberg adapted Ives's multilayered polyphony in which strata are partially distinguished by different tempi. Ives's music also had a far-reaching effect on Rochberg in its eclectic combination of diverse styles and preexistent music. These features were refined by Rochberg in the quotation-collages *Contra mortem et tempus* (1965) and *Music for the Magic Theater* (1965, rev. 1969), in which music by Ives, Varèse, Webern, Mahler, Beethoven, and Mozart mingle in order "to project an almost cinematic series of shifting ideas and levels."

By the time of the Third String Quartet (1971–72), another new idiom—which he termed "multi-gestural"—was in place. Here the composer adopts a different preexistent style in each movement. These styles may evoke the language of a single earlier composer, as in the third movement, which recalls the quartets of Beethoven in its expansion into the very high and low registers. Other movements represent a conflation of several styles, including those of the earlier twentieth century.

Such multigestural music, writes Rochberg, "makes possible the combination and juxtaposition of a variety of means which denies neither the past nor the present." His basic language, nevertheless, became common-practice tonality, which he embraced wholeheartedly as a flexible means to a unified and comprehensible musical speech. Accordingly, Rochberg makes little attempt to reinterpret tonality as did many neoclassicists between the world wars. He does not seek such expressions of originality: "I have had to abandon the notion of 'originality,' " he writes, "in which the personal style of the artist and his ego are the supreme values."

The Sixth String Quartet (1978) is one of Rochberg's most successful eclectic works. Its first and fourth movements (Fantasia and Serenade) are atonal, each touching briefly upon familiar styles of the early twentieth century (including those of Webern and Bartók). The second and fifth movements (Scherzo and Introduction/Finale) are in the keys of Bb and G, and the finale is especially indebted to the finales of Beethoven's quartets. The central third movement (Anthology no. 29) is in the form of variations upon material from a canon by Johann Pachelbel (1653–1706). The borrowed material consists of a basso ostinato of four measures length and the head motive of the leading canonic voice (Example 16-5).

This subject is elaborated not as a canon but as a chaconne, that is, by continuous variations upon either or both lines. The variations move stylistically from the idiom of the baroque (measures 1–12), through the elegant tunefulness of the classical period (measures 13–24), into the early-romantic period (measures 25–45), finally coming to an emotional climax with the language of Mahler and his post-Wagnerian contemporaries (measures 45–72). The final variations are reflective upon all of the preceding, ending with fragments of the primary material.

GEORGE CRUMB

George Crumb (1929–) has developed a distinctive approach to composition that brings together quotations of Western music and elements from music of the Orient. Most of his works contain an intricate symbolism, and all are informed by the liberation of sound stemming from electronic music.

Example 16-5. Pachelbel, Canon in D.

Beginning with *Night Music I* (1963), Crumb repeatedly uses the surrealistic poetry of Federico García Lorca (1899–1936) in works for solo voice and diverse instruments. These vocal pieces owe much to the style and innovative treatment of voice of Luciano Berio, as was seen in Chapter 14, for example, in Berio's *Circles*. But while Berio's pictures in sound symbolize the flux of human emotions, Crumb's tend to dwell upon dark subjects and the stark elemental images evoked by Lorca's poetry.

Crumb's *Black Angels* (1970) is for a string quartet in which each instrument is amplified and reverberated to produce a surrealistic aura. The four instrumentalists also play on a variety of percussion instruments, crystal glasses, and other implements. *Black Angels* was written during the years of the Vietnam War, and it expresses Crumb's belief that deviltry was then much afoot and locked in battle with godly forces. His musical treatment also suggests that these opposing elements are often combined inextricably in the same substance, epitomized by the satanic figure of the black angel. Numbers are the primary symbols of these inseparable opposites: 7 and 3 represent elements of good; 13, evil. The durational patterns that express these quantities frequently illustrate that 13 can be constituted by groups of 7s and 3s. Symbols of evil also include quotations of the chant "Dies irae," use of the tritone (the "devil in music"), and imitations of the "devil's trill" occurring in Tartini's violin sonata of the same title. Forces of good are represented by natural sounds of insects, triadic harmonies, and the ethereal tones of crystal glasses.

The quartet is divided into thirteen sections that are grouped in three parts, numbers that again show the interpenetration of good and evil. Part 1 ("Departure," sections 1 through 5) represents the descent of the soul from a state of divine grace; part 2 ("Absence," sections 6 through 9), the spiritual vacuum of the godless; and part 3 ("Return," sections 10 through 13), redemption. This arch-like shape is articulated by three sections of special importance—the first, seventh, and thirteenth—each of which is called a Threnody. Some of the sections recapitulate or "echo" earlier music.

In this work, as in Crumb's music in general, an aura of mystery is created by unusual sounds and an exotic mixture of styles and quotations. The sixth section, "Pavana lachrymae" (Anthology no. 27), quotes the theme of the slow movement of Schubert's String Quartet in D minor, which was taken by Schubert from the introduction to his song "Death and the Maiden." The music is converted into a dirge-like pavane in which the strings imitate a consort of viols. A solo violin inserts sounds of insects, thus creating a composite image of life and death.

The next section is the central Threnody, the diabolical "Black Angels!" Here evil reigns: the strings begin with superimposed tritones, and they continue with inventions upon Tartini's devil's trill. Yet the spiritual void is not entirely without hope, as the symbols of God are also in evidence. The movement occurs as the seventh in the cycle of thirteen, and the basic harmonic element—the trichord. D#–A–E—represents a conflation of thirteen semitones (D# to E) and seven semitones (A to E).

BERIO, PENDERECKI, AND HENZE

The works of Luciano Berio are of such diversity that they fall into several major styles of postwar music. Among them is eclecticism. Berio's *Folk Songs* (1964) are in the genre of the artistic folk-song arrangement so favored earlier in the century. This collection of songs in several different languages is arranged for voice and chamber ensemble. "Black Is the Color of My True Love's Hair" (Anthology no. 16), a song in folk style written by John Jacob Niles (1892–1980), is set for voice, viola, harp, and cello. The melody is repeated virtually unchanged in its three stanzas. It is in Aeolian mode on D, and Berio imitates the irregular rhythms of a free vocal rendition of the well-known tune. The harp adds a modal accompaniment. Its first two stanzas move through a descending diatonic scale; the third stanza (rehearsal 5) finds the descending scale in the upper staff of the harp part, supported by chords drawn from the mode. The viola imitates "a wistful 'country dance fiddler.' " Its introduction to the first verse is free in rhythm and meter and plays upon the prevailing mode with twangy double stops and pungent dissonances. It accompanies the vocal stanzas without rhythmic coordination.

Berio's most important eclectic work is the third movement of his *Sinfonia* (1968, rev. 1969). The symphony, originally in four movements with a final fifth movement added in 1969, is for large orchestra and eight solo voices. Its texts consist of disconnected phrases from various sources, primarily *Le cru et le cuit* by Claude Lévi-Strauss in the first movement and Samuel Beckett's *The Unnamable* in the third movement. The second movement, "O King," is a tribute to Martin Luther King in which the words consist solely of sounds from King's name, which gradually become perceptible as such.

The third movement is assembled from diverse quotations. As a musical backdrop the orchestra plays a version of the entire third movement (scherzo) of Mahler's Second Symphony. Into this continuum the composer floats quotations from music that relates in different ways to the Mahler work. "The whole point of this section of *Sinfonia*," Berio writes, "[is as] a documentary on an *objet trouvé* recorded in the mind of the listener." Berio mentions eighteen different composers whom he quotes, but the most prominent are Ravel (*La Valse, Daphnis et Chloé*), Debussy (*La Mer*), Richard Strauss (waltzes from *Der Rosenkavalier*), and Stravinsky (*Rite of Spring*). The movement by Mahler chosen by Berio is of significance. This scherzo was adapted by Mahler from his own earlier song "Des Antonius von Padua Fischpredigt" for use in the Second Symphony. Berio thus carries the process of quotation into a more abstract cycle, gaining a corresponding richness of allusion.

The music of Krzysztof Penderecki (1933–) in the 1950s was mainly serial, but by 1960 he had followed the general European development in which serialism was replaced by other avant-garde directions. His alternative to serialism was analogous to that of Ligeti and Lutosławski in its manipulation of masses of sounds, each characterized more by its texture and volume than by particular collections of pitches or intervals. Penderecki focused with great resourcefulness upon innovations in sound, including expanded sonorities of voices and conventional instruments. New playing techniques were often notated by a combination of conventional and graphic means.

The *St. Luke Passion* (1965) marked a turning point in Penderecki's work toward an idiom that combined in an eclectic manner composition with masses of sound and various stylistic ideas from earlier music. This lengthy and slowly paced work utilizes three mixed choruses, boys' chorus, soloists, speaker, and large orchestra. It combines free twelve-tone serialism, triadic textures, and slowly evolving masses of sound. These elements are sprinkled with quotations from chant and references to the BACH motive, the latter in homage to the passion music of J. S. Bach.

Hans Werner Henze (1926–) was one of the large number of European composers associated with the Darmstadt Summer Courses in the 1950s who helped to revive serial composition. Like virtually all of these musicians, he subsequently dispensed with strict serialism and developed his own distinctive language. Henze's music has maintained close stylistic contacts with the atonal idiom of the Viennese modernists—especially with Berg, whose lyrical treatment of the voice, wide and expressionistic range of emotion, and rich, triadically based dissonant harmony characterize Henze's musical language.

By the mid-1960s Henze's use of Bergian atonality was modified by a pronounced eclecticism. By this means he sought to increase the accessibility of his music in order to convey its political and social message. Most of Henze's vocal works from this time deal with the oppression of workers by political and economic establishments. An example is *Voices* (1973), a collection of twenty-two songs in various languages for soprano or tenor, orchestra, and electronics. Some of the songs ("Heimkehr" and "Gracia") adopt the styles of Schoenberg, Berg, and Webern; others parody popular music such as the cabaret song ("Recht und Billig"), the spiritual ("The Worker"), marches, and Italian serenades.

SCHNITTKE AND GUBAIDULINA

Alfred Schnittke (1934–), Sofia Gubaidulina, and Arvo Pärt were among the leading Eastern Bloc composers who emerged in the 1980s as celebrities on the international modern music scene. Schnittke had long been prominent as an avant-garde composer in the Soviet Union, teaching since 1961 at the Moscow Conservatory. After experimenting with several Western avant-garde techniques, he moved away from doctrinaire modernism by adopting what he called "polystylism": the juxtaposition in a work of several seemingly unrelated styles. Works of the 1970s and 1980s such as the Piano Concerto (1979), Sonata for Cello and Piano (1978), and the early symphonies and string quartets juxtapose the seemingly unrelated: bombastic dissonance beside serene Renaissance polyphony, jazz and Beethoven, Mahler next to the intentional triteness of Shostakovich. The genres that Schnittke uses—primarily symphonies, concertos, string quartets, sonatas, oratorios, and operas—also suggest a rejection of postwar avant-gardism. So too his treatment of form, which is based on traditional procedures such as thematic development and reprise and patterns created by large sectional recurrences.

Schnittke has stated that his polystylism comes from an attempt to reveal the totality of his musical experience through a great synthesis:

> Contemporary reality will make it necessary to experience all the musics one has heard since childhood, including rock and jazz and classical and all other forms, combining them into a synthesis. [*Tempo*, 151 (1984).]

Schnittke's String Quartet No. 3 (1983) illustrates this synthesis, which involves not only multiple styles and quotations but also a return to a classical conception of continuous and far-reaching motivic development. The work is in three connected movements, all interrelated by a cyclic treatment of themes. The basic materials and processes are given out in the expository first movement (Andante). At the very outset (Example 16-6) the composer makes three quotations in different styles: first, a cadential figure from Orlando di Lasso's motet "Stabat mater dolorosa"; second, the head motive from the primary subject of Beethoven's *Grosse Fuge*, op. 133; and third, the motive D E♭ C B, which in its German spelling (D S C H) is the personal motto of Dimitri Shostakovich, based on musical letters from his name and used by Shostakovich in his String Quartet No. 8 among other late works.

The remainder of the first movement consists of perpetual variations upon these motives. The process of development is seen even within the three motives themselves, since the Shostakovich motto

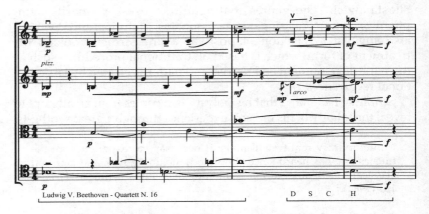

Example 16-6. Schnittke, String Quartet No. 3, first movement.
© Copyright 1984 by Universal Edition A.G., Wien. Reprinted by Permission.

is plainly a variant of the Beethoven quote (Example 16-6). The process of variation, which continues throughout the quartet, transforms the older materials from their original disparate style ever closer to a uniformly dissonant and chromatic context. The process of development entails not only the linear motivic shapes but also their harmonic implications. Beethoven's head motive (B♭ B A♭ G) and the Shostakovich motto form equivalent four-note octatonic subsets. Other octatonic subsets then recur prominently as chords throughout the work (see the six-note chord in measure 10 or the complete octatonic scale formed by the tones in measure 16).

Schnittke's Quartet still breathes the air of postwar modernism: it is a difficult and abstract work. But it also makes notable concessions to a new and more relaxed taste that had emerged in modern music during the 1970s. It does so by presenting the listener with elements that are known—passages made entirely from triads, isolated cadential progressions, evocations of Renaissance styles, and easy-to-follow recurrences of motives.

The same mixture of modernism with an eclectic assortment of known elements characterizes the music of Sofia Gubaidulina (1931–). Her career is often compared with that of Schnittke. They were both educated at the Moscow Conservatory and worked in the genre of film, also composing avant-garde pieces which in the 1960s were not officially accepted in the Soviet Union. Gubaidulina's music exhibits many aspects of postwar modernism: improvisation, graphic notational techniques, sound effects and textures, and Webernesque spareness. Her most important works tend to be long and slowly paced, but she deviates from the spirit of postwar modernism by making virtually all of her music intensely personal, expressive, even programmatic.

The eclectic element is not so prominent in her oeuvre as it is in Schnittke's, but it is still clearly present in a piece such as *The Seven Words* for cello, bayan, and string orchestra (1982). The bayan is a Russian accordion, which in this work is put to use to produce sounds and suggestive effects ranging from an organ to grotesque breathing. Each of the seven movements depicts one of the seven phrases said by Jesus on the cross, according to the Gospels. Although no voices are used, the music vividly depicts their content and emotion. Two motives are quoted from Heinrich Schütz's oratorio *The Seven Words*, and these create the formal basis of the work by recurring in variations throughout. Gubaidulina's highly unified composition mixes the style of Schütz with a variety of modernistic sonorous techniques, an eclecticism that serves the expression of the religious idea underlying the work.

BIBLIOGRAPHY

Olivier Messiaen surveys aspects of his early compositional style in *The Technique of My Musical Language*, trans. John Satterfield, 2 vols. (Paris, ca. 1956). His music is studied by Robert Sherlaw Johnson in *Messiaen* (Berkeley, 1989), by Paul Griffiths in *Olivier Messiaen and the Music of Time* (Ithaca, 1985), and briefly by Roger Nichols in *Messiaen*, 2nd ed. (Oxford, 1986). Messiaen's interviews with Claude Samuel are translated under the title *Music and Color* (Portland, Ore., 1994).

Paul Griffith's *Peter Maxwell Davies* (London, 1982) surveys music by this composer through 1981, and the volume also contains interviews with Davies and Davies's own notes on selected pieces. *Peter Maxwell Davies: Studies from Two Decades*, ed. Stephen Pruslin (London, 1979) is a collection of essays on various works.

George Rochberg's writings usually focus upon twentieth-century compositional materials and styles rather than upon his own music. "The New Image of Music" (1963), for example, surveys the liberation of sound and texture in modern music in general, and "Reflections on the Renewal of Music" speaks to his dissatisfaction with the doctrinaire attitudes of modernists such as Boulez. These and others essays are collected in *The Aesthetics of Survival: A Composer's View of Twentieth-Century Music* (Ann Arbor, 1984). Also see the interview with Rochberg in Cole Gagne and Tracy Caras, *Soundpieces* (Metuchen, N.J., 1982).

George Crumb is also interviewed in *Soundpieces*. An analytic assessment of harmony in selected works is made in Thomas R. de Dobay's "The Evolution of Harmonic Style in the Lorca Works of Crumb," *Journal of Music Theory*, 28 (1984). Crumb's life and work is briefly surveyed in Edith Borroff's *George Crumb: Profile of a Composer* (New York, 1986). Writings by and about Luciano Berio are included in the Bibliography to Chapter 14. Penderecki's music is studied in Wolfram Schwinger's *Krzysztof Penderecki: His Life and Work* (London, 1989).

Alfred Schnittke and Sofia Gubaidulina are interviewed by Claire Polin in "Interviews with Soviet Composers," *Tempo*, 151 (1984). Schnittke's music is surveyed in Ivan Moody's article "The Music of Alfred Schnittke," *Tempo*, 168 (1989), and the aesthetic and historical implications of his polystylism are explored in John Webb's "Schnittke in Context," *Tempo*, 182 (1992) and Hugh Collins Rice's "Further Thoughts on Schnittke," *Tempo* 168 (1989).

17

Recent Music in Europe and America

During the two decades following World War II, modernism was the dominant force in music. It was characterized by innovation and experiment with a tendency toward abstraction and depersonalization. Serialism at this time was rekindled into a bright but short-lived flame, and from its ashes grew other unprecedented ideas of what music could be.

But by the 1970s it became clear that postwar modernism was waning, to be challenged by a new taste in serious music. Whereas the recondite structures of the older style were often placed under the heading "academic," the new manner was quite the opposite: relaxed, traditional, eclectic, entertaining. After decades of exploration of new musical resources, composers in the new idiom sought to bring into their music things that were known—styles, materials, and values from elsewhere throughout the history of music.

Clearly, there was a desire to communicate to a larger audience than before. The composer Philip Glass was a proponent of this new accessibility: He dismissed Boulez and other postwar modernists as "these maniacs, these creeps who were trying to make everyone write this crazy creepy music." Glass continued:

There was a time when there wasn't this tremendous distance between the popular audience and concert music, and I think we're approaching that stage again. For a long while we had this very small band of practitioners of modern music who described themselves as mathematicians, doing theoretical work that would someday be understood. I don't think anyone takes that very seriously anymore. [From Robert Palmer's liner notes to *Einstein on the Beach*, CBS Records, M4 38875.]

The change of style in the 1970s has proved different from most changes in the past, even different from major changes of taste earlier in the twentieth century. First of all, music of the new type has existed side by side with a continuation of modernism, the very style which it rejects. Many of the leading modernists from the 1950s and 1960s—Boulez, Carter, and Lutosławski among them—have continued to write important new works in the modernist idiom, and these figures have argued strongly against the new manner. Important younger composers have emerged in the 1970s and 1980s who have resisted the new tendency, adhering unabashedly to modernist ideas. This has proved especially the case in Europe, where such figures as Wolfgang Rihm (1952–) and Harrison Birtwistle (1934–) have unheld the values and idiom of the postwar avant-garde. Even among composers in the new manner since the 1970s, there has not appeared any one widespread, homogeneous style, as happened in the 1920s under the banner of neoclassicism.

In this chapter we conclude our survey of music in the twentieth century by considering several important directions in style that have emerged since the 1970s and prominent composers who have helped to create the new idiom.

MINIMALISM

The American tradition of experiment in music fostered a new and distinctive style in the 1960s in the works of four composers: La Monte Young (1935–), Terry Riley (1935–), Philip Glass (1937–), and Steve Reich (1936–). Their idiom, which has been widely influential since that time, is often called *minimalism*, despite the inadequacy of any single term to describe their diverse styles. The unifying features of their music include repetition and ostinato (hence "minimal" in compositional materials), diatonic melody and harmony, controlled improvisation, and extended lengths. Minimalism has proved a distinctively American phenomenon by its emphasis on sound per se, by its relationship to non-Western music and to modern visual arts, and by its links with earlier American experimentalists such as John Cage. Minimalism was born in the 1960s as a modernistic, experimental type of music, which invoked improvisation, absurdity, and a strong current of social and musical rebellion. Its evolution in the 1970s and 1980s, however, turned to a more traditional, even populist direction—evidence of the general stylistic transformation of music during these years.

Young at first wrote twelve-tone music, but his direction as a composer changed after he met Cage at Darmstadt. He followed Cage to the New School for Social Research in New York, where he produced Cage-like happenings with the multimedia group Fluxus. His works with Fluxus include fifteen *Compositions 1960*. Each consists of a *verbal score:* a brief written statement instructing the performer in some activity or musical gesture. Number 7 of this series, for example, shows the notes B and F♯, which are "to be held for a long time." Number 2 instructs the performer to build a fire in front of the audience; number 10, to "draw a straight line and follow it."

Young found his mature style in 1964 in *The Tortoise: His Dreams and Journeys*. This work is an open-ended situation for improvisation within certain boundaries. Prior to the performance of part of the piece (Young has given subtitles to many partial realizations), the players and singers decide which upper partials of a given fundamental pitch will be sounded. The fundamental is begun as a drone, usually played on electronic equipment, and the instrumentalists and singers then add and sustain the harmonics. With the aid of amplification, a certain resonance or color is obtained, which is the objective of the music. Rhythm is freely created as the performers enter and drop out, but melody in the traditional sense is entirely absent.

Like all of the minimalists, Young is involved with the performance of his own music. In the mid-1960s he created a group called the Theater of Eternal Music to perform his works. Ideally, this group should perform in what Young has called a Dream House—a permanent environment in which his harmonies would be ever present.

Although the music of La Monte Young is little accessible outside of live performances by his own ensemble, its concept has been influential both on his American colleagues and on certain Europeans. Karlheinz Stockhausen's *Stimmung* (1968) uses pitch resources in a similar way. This lengthy work calls for six voices to sing exclusively the fundamental B♭ and five of its upper partials. Young's music was especially influential on Terry Riley among younger American composers. Riley, who performed with Young in the 1960s, discovered in Young's music the refreshing attractiveness of consonant sonorities and a way of extending simple materials into lengthy works.

Riley at first devoted himself to long solo concerts in which he improvised on saxophone and keyboard instruments with the support of live electronic and tape equipment. His first success as a composer was *In C* (1964). This piece consists of fifty-three short figures, each having a precise rhythm and a contour based on notes of a C mode (with occasional F#'s and Bb's). An eighth-note pulse on the note C is established by one player, which runs throughout the composition as a point of reference for rhythm and pitch. Any number of instruments in the soprano register begin with repetitions of the first figure, moving gradually and in general coordination with the other players through the entire set of fifty-three. The listener's impression is of a mesmerizing regularity, but with subtle interactions of figures and a gradual evolution of rhythm, harmony, and color.

In later works such as *Rainbow in Curved Air* (1969) and *Poppy Nogood and the Phantom Band* (1968), Riley returns to his improvisations on saxophone and keyboard, enhanced by live electronic techniques and tape delay. These soliloquies share with *In C* the use of regular rhythmic pulse and diatonic or modal melody and harmony. The live electronic medium helps to enrich their texture and reinforce their repetitiveness, all of which ally them to the atmosphere of rock. Riley is indeed more an improvisor in a semipopular style than a composer: "I put my music down on a tiny sheet of paper," he writes, "and spend all of my time playing."

His more recent compositions, however, dispense with the aura of rock and evoke traditional Indian music instead. "Embroidery"— one of three *Songs for the Ten Voices of the Two Prophets* (1982)—is improvised on an electronic music synthesizer that imitates the sounds of the tabla and sitar. Riley adds a nasal cantillation with traditional Indian ornaments and slides between tones. The words refer to Eastern art and, obliquely, to drugs.

Indian music was an inspiration to all of the minimalists. Its customary use of drones has a clear parallel in the music of Young; its continuous repetitions of rhythmic figures or talas and improvisation within scalar types or ragas is echoed in music by Riley, Reich, and Glass.

The additive rhythmic process of Indian music was the point of departure for the music of Philip Glass composed after the mid-1960s. Glass's music relies upon repetition of a limited number of musical elements which are spun out in the manner of an Indian tabla player improvising upon a tala. His early works in this vein are monophonic exercises in improvised rhythms and lines. In *1 + 1* (1968) the player is instructed to tap on an amplified table top, improvising upon combinations of two rhythms shown in Example 17-1. These two figures are to be put together into gradually evolving patterns that Glass calls "arithmetic progressions." In Example 17-2 we see one such pattern, where five of the eighth-note values are separated by a steadily increasing number of the figure containing two sixteenths and an eighth.

Glass's more recent music is written to be performed solely by his own ensemble of amplified keyboards and woodwinds, which is sometimes expanded to include voices and strings. It is accordingly richer in texture. The opera *Satyagraha* (1979) calls for a conventional orchestra.

The six pieces in his recording "Glassworks" (CBS 37265, 1982) are exemplary in their comfortable and consonant sonorities, simple harmonic changes, and regular pacing, which banish complexities of structure or meaning. Regular rhythms, standard harmonic progressions, and high levels of amplification link his music to rock, which may in part account for the immense popularity of his concerts with a public not otherwise involved with serious music. We shall return shortly to Glass's *Einstein on the Beach*, in which his musical style is applied to modern theater.

The music of Steve Reich has undergone a more pronounced evolution than has that of Young, Riley, or Glass. His career as a composer was launched in 1964 by his experiments in *musique concrète* made from taped words and phrases. Reich at first intended to enhance the melodious nature of certain speaking voices by creating ostinatos and other such manipulations of their words, while preserving their comprehensibility. One such experiment led to his discovery of a *phase process*, which can be observed in his early tape piece *Come Out* (1966). From the words of a youth arrested in riots in Harlem, Reich selected the phrase "come out to show them," which is played repeatedly on a tape loop in two channels. One channel gradually moves ahead of the other—it comes out of "phase"—which ultimately distorts the words beyond comprehension but creates slowly changing rhythms and new melodic fragments by the interplay between channels.

Beginning with *Piano Phase* (1967), Reich transferred the phase process from the medium of tape to live instrumental music. Two pianists play a short repeated figure in unison; one player then gradually increases tempo, moving out of phase with the other pianist.

and

Example 17-1. Rhythmic elements in Glass's *1 + 1*.

Example 17-2. Rhythmic elaborations in Glass's *1 + 1*.

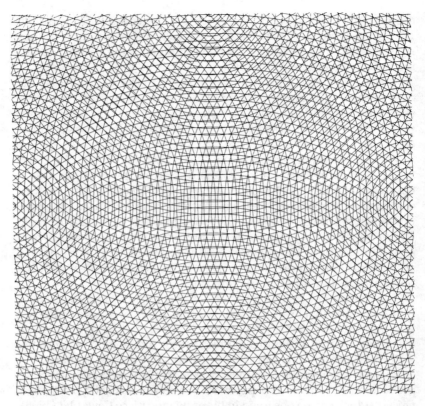

"Conceptual" art: Sol LeWitt, "Arcs from Corners and Sides." (Courtesy of the artist.)

Eventually the two return to a unison. A series of instrumental phase pieces followed: *Violin Phase* (1967), *Four Organs* (1970), *Phase Patterns* (1970), and *Drumming* (1971). The last of these is Reich's longest and most elaborate essay to explore the phase process.

Phase music is entirely the result of allying the initial material to a process which, when set in motion, automatically generates the form and substance of the work. It is closely analogous to a contemporary movement in the visual arts in America sometimes called "conceptual" art. "Arcs from Corners and Sides" by Sol LeWitt (1928–) is made from a minimum of materials—semicircular arcs—and a plan by which the arcs radiate from the four sides of a square. The design that results is enriched by other symmetrical patterns created by areas of varying densities of lines. These additional patterns are the unexpected result of the artist's concept.

Phase pieces by Reich contain similar "secondary" rhythms and melodic fragments. The composer refers to these as the "mysteries" of an otherwise automated idiom. "These mysteries," he writes in "Music as a Gradual Process" (1968), "are the impersonal, unintended, psycho-acoustic byproducts of the intended process. These might include submelodies heard within repeated melodic patterns, stereophonic effects due to listener location, [or] slight irregularities in performance, harmonics, or difference tones." For these secondary patterns to be audible, the instruments or sounds must be of the same timbre, which lends Reich's music of this period a sameness of sound that he would avoid in later pieces.

Reich has reinforced the secondary rhythms and melodies in some works by instructing other players to double them—underlining them, as it were, for the audience. An example is found in a passage from *Violin Phase* illustrated in Example 17-3. In this work violins 1–3 repeatedly play the same phrase. But by the point illustrated in Example 17-3 the second violin has moved two beats ahead of violin 1; violin 3 is four beats ahead of violin 1. Among several secondary rhythms or melodic fragments that are created by this phasing differential is the recurrence of low C♯ in the rhythm shown in the lowest staff. The fourth violin may play this resultant pattern in order to reinforce its audibility.

Clapping Music (1972, Anthology no. 28) is based on the phase principle. The first performer repeats the pattern shown in measure 1 throughout the piece. The second performer begins in unison, but, while maintaining the same pattern, leaps ahead by an eighth-note value in coordination with the upper part. The second player continues to increase his lead over the first player until he has completed an entire cycle and returned to unison, whereupon the piece

Example 17-3. Reich, Violin Phase. © 1979 by Universal Edition (London) Ltd., London. Used by permission of European American Music Distributors Corp., sole U.S. agent for Universal Edition.

ends. In each measure save the first and last, different secondary rhythmic patterns will be heard.

After 1973 Reich's music took several different directions, but he has not returned to the phase processes of his earlier works. *Music for Mallet Instruments, Voices and Organ* (1973) uses other processes together with a richer texture. This piece consists of three strata: voices and organ, bells, and marimbas. The first group plays sustained chords and the last two set up rhythmically active, repetitive patterns. The texture of *Music for Mallet Instruments* is further elaborated in *Tehillim* (*Psalms*, 1981). This work, a setting of four passages from Hebrew Psalms for four sopranos and orchestra, has little in common with the repetitiveness of minimalism. Its first and fourth sections use canon and repetition of larger musical units. The slow third section is less repetitive and more chromatic than diatonic. But the texture of the work is reminiscent of Reich's earlier music in its overlay of slow-moving chords and animated lines. Its continual division of beats into metric groups of twos and threes is reminiscent of the music of Stravinsky from the time of *Les noces*.

Minimalism has proved enormously influential among other American and European composers of the 1980s. In England, Gavin Bryars and Michael Nyman have allied minimalist elements to a continuation of the improvisational spirit of Cage and Cardew. Music by the Dutch composer Louis Andriessen (including *De Staat, De Tijd*, and *Hoketus*) uses minimalistic ostinatos, and Glenn Branca and Paul Dresher have fused minimalistic styles to the media of rock.

The music of John Adams (1947–) calls upon conventional media—orchestra, chamber ensembles, and solo piano—to realize his adaptation of minimalism. His *China Gates* for piano (1977) consists of a succession of "gates" or changes of mode, each of which punctuates a static ostinato. Each section is divided into three strata—a bass pedal point and two lines in the upper register made from repetitions of short figures. The pitch content of each gate is strictly confined to one "mode" or diatonic set. Adams's postminimalistic operas will be taken up later in this chapter.

A SEARCH FOR THE KNOWN

The rebellion against the abstraction and difficulty of postwar modernism among composers and audiences in the 1970s coincided with a great revival of interest in early music. For the first time, masterpieces from the Middle Ages through the early baroque period were

explore aural phenomena

performed by truly excellent professional ensembles and recorded in large numbers. For composers of this time, the entire history of music seemed to be thrown open, enticing them to borrow upon a vast fund of styles.

The music of Arvo Pärt (1935–) took its departure from church music of the Middle Ages and Renaissance. In fact, Pärt's entire career is instructive of the change in musical taste of the postwar decades. He was born in the Soviet Republic of Estonia, receiving his training in the capital city of Tallinn. In the 1960s he wrote twelve-tone music, then an accepted approach in international modernist circles. Feeling constrained by this technique, he then turned to eclecticism, which proved equally unsatisfying to him. Finally, in the 1970s, he discovered the beauty of Gregorian chant and Renaissance vocal polyphony, which he has since reinterpreted in his own highly distinctive music. After this change, his career blossomed, leading to his emigration from Estonia, first to Vienna, then to Berlin.

Most of Pärt's music since the 1970s uses Latin liturgical texts in settings for chorus with or without instruments. He has composed several Masses, numerous motets, antiphons, and Magnificats, a *Stabat mater* (1985), *Te Deum* (1986), and a lengthy setting of the *St. John Passion*, as well as numerous works for instruments. A clearer contrast between these pieces and postwar modernism would be difficult to imagine. The materials of Pärt's music are simplified to the point of primitivization. Forms are created by sectional and motivic repetitions that sometimes resemble minimalistic ostinati. His music is intensely expressive, although quiet and severly understated; it uses diatonic pitch collections and triads, and it is static in the melodic and harmonic dimension, almost never revealing familiar large tonal progressions.

The idea underlying his music is spiritual—partly religious, partly meditative. Pärt has written that the relentless progress of style, especially in music following World War II, only obscured the eternal spiritual content of music. His words suggest that changes of style in music are futile and counterproductive.

What we find in the world is already here. Ideas are always around us. Suddenly we find one and say: "Aha! There it is!" But it was always right there. . . . I have long pondered the meaning of the words "Pleni sunt coeli et terra majestatis tua" [Heaven and earth are full of Thy glory]. It's really the music of angels, which has always-existed, which Mozart heard and wrote down, the same music of angels that the Gregorian monks wrote down, still sung today in church. Mankind alone cannot write such music. What he can do is already well known and it doesn't satisfy us. His greatest problem is

the difficult access to eternal ideas, difficult because he is so susceptible to change. [*Neue Zeitschrift für Musik* 151/3 (1990):16].

Pärt's *Berlin Mass* (1990) will exemplify the composer's provocative reinterpretation of Renaissance music. The work is appropriate
for use in the traditional Catholic liturgy, especially for the Feast of
Pentecost (three optional movements are proper to that occasion). It
calls for chorus accompainied in different versions by organ or
orchestra. The Credo movement is an especially ingenious parody
of Renaissance procedures, which are carried to a point of exaggeration and subtly mixed with modern ideas. Like a movement in a
Renaissance Mass, there is no tempo indication, no regular meter,
and exclusively simple rhythmic figures. There is not a single tone
that deviates from the diatonic, E-major collection. The text strictly
governs the changing meters, rhythm, and placement of rests
(which come at the end of each unit of thought or grammatical
phrase). The work's form is created by continual mosaiclike recurrences of a few motives, especially those heard in the first six measures (Example 17-4). There is no attempt to depict the meaning of
isolated words or ideas from the text.

In this Pärt seems intent upon holding the listener's attention
with a bare minimum of materials and sense of change. The motives
and harmonies dwell on a single chord, the E-major triad, which,
except for polyphonic motion weaving between its three tones, is
ever present. Entirely unlike early music, however, the polyphonic
movement of parts is not governed by a strict treatment of dissonance. The sustained E-major triad is constantly altered, even at
important cadences, into pungent dissonant shapes. The alternation
among triads and carefully chosen dissonances is a basic premise of
the music, but this alternation does not drive the music forward as
in traditional harmony.

The romantic period of music history, like the Middle Ages and
Renaissance, was an attractive source of inspiration for composers
of the 1970s and 80s seeking the known. This was a time in which
romantic works themselves were receiving renewed attention:
Leonard Bernstein's recordings of Mahler's symphonies initiated a
revival of interest in this composer, and Pierre Boulez, when named
conductor of the New York Philharmonic Orchestra in 1971, chose
first to focus on the works of Liszt.

Neoromanticism has been an especially important trend in
American music since the later 1970s. The works of David Del
Tredici (1937–) are widely acclaimed examples. Del Tredici was
trained as a concert pianist, and his early music is for the medium of

Example 17-4. Pärt, *Berliner Messe*, Credo. © Copyright 1990, 1991 by
Universal Edition A.G., Wien. All Rights Reserved. Used by permission of
European American Music Distributors Corporation, sole U.S. and
Canadian agent for Universal Edition A.G., Wien.

keyboard. His compositions between 1959 and 1966 consist mainly
of settings of the poetry of James Joyce. Since 1968 he has dwelled
almost exclusively on music for soprano and orchestra inspired by
Lewis Carroll's *Alice's Adventures in Wonderland* (1865) and its sequel
Through the Looking Glass (1872). These include *Pop-Pourri* (1968), *An
Alice Symphony* (1969), *Adventures Underground* (1971), *Vintage Alice*
(1972), *Final Alice* (1976), *Child Alice* (1981),*Virtuoso Alice* (1984), and
Haddocks' Eyes (1986).

The later *Alice* pieces are wholeheartedly romantic. Although they
are not based on the idiom of any single nineteenth-century forebear,
they reflect Mahler's diverse world of sound and sudden alterna-
tions of the mundane and the ecstatic. They also incorporate some of
the sonorities of late-nineteenth- and early-twentieth-century
Russian orchestral music. Del Tredici's idiom has much in common
with Wagner, including a fairy-tale subject symbolizing realms of
human emotion, slow pacing and substantial length, and the use of
themes and motives with dramatic associations. Like Schumann, Del
Tredici avails himself of musical figures or mottos with autobiographical significance, and he unifies his works by a technique of
transformation of themes reminiscent of Liszt. His application of harmony and tonality is based on late-nineteenth-century techniques.

Final Alice tells of Alice's trial from the concluding chapters of *Alice's Adventures in Wonderland*, with the interpolation of related verses. The libretto is laid out as a narrative in which orchestral music, recitations, and arias alternate. The melody of the first aria recurs in Lisztian transformations, and other musical figures return as leitmotives with specific dramatic meaning. At the very end, Del Tredici adds his own musical signature; thirteen repetitions of a motto are counted by the soloist in Italian from *uno* to *tredici* (thirteen), the last number making explicit the identity of the composer.

The first part of the cycle *Child Alice* (completed in 1981) is entitled *In Memory of a Summer Day* (1980), a work for which Del Tredici won the Pulitzer Prize. Its three connected movements create a ternary shape. The first part consists of an orchestral introduction and the song "Simple Alice," the latter a strophic setting of Carroll's poem that prefaces *Through the Looking Glass*. An orchestral march and trio, "Triumphant Alice," follow as the middle part, which programmatically depict some untold fable. The concluding aria "Ecstatic Alice" recapitulates much of "Simple Alice," but in a more ebullient mood.

It was the composer's intention in this work to focus not upon the adventures of Alice, but, instead, to capture the bittersweet nostalgia of Carroll as he reflected upon the happy hours spent with the child Alice Liddell and her sisters, during which his fantastic tales were first spun. In the song "Simple Alice" we encounter Alice in the innocence with which she is recalled by Carroll. The aria "Ecstatic Alice," on the other hand, portrays Carroll's passionate love for the child Alice. Del Tredici indulges here in the hypothesis that Carroll had formed an erotic attachment to Alice Liddell. This idea—the substance of which is historically unlikely—is the composer's typically romantic statement that things are not what they seem.

Neoromanticism also appeared among Polish composers of the 1970s and 1980s, notable especially since many of these figures had earlier been among the most modernistic anywhere in the Eastern Bloc. Krzysztof Penderecki and Henryk Górecki (1933–), for example, departed from their textural and eclectic experiments of the 1960s to adopt an overtly romantic manner. Penderecki's Violin Concerto (1976), Symphony No. 2 (1980), *Polish Requiem* (1980–84), and *Te Deum* (1980) are examples. The last of these was composed to honor the election of the composer's countryman John Paul II as Pope, and it has the breadth and massive affirmation of music of the late nineteenth century.

Górecki's works of the 1950s and early 1960s were squarely in the modernist manner that flourished at that time in Poland. He was known especially for textural or sound mass compositions. In the

1970s he experimented first with eclecticism, then with neoromanticism. An example of the last of these is his Symphony No. 3 (*Symphony of Sorrowful Songs*, 1976) for soprano and orchestra. It evokes the Mahleresque romantic symphony in its merging of the genres of song and symphony, its considerable length and slow pacing, its somber tone and dark orchestration, and its intensity of expression. The music uses traditional homophonic and contrapuntal textures, it is rigidly diatonic, and it is highly repetitive. It is telling of the taste of the present day that the symphony attracted little attention when it was written. But in the 1990s, as modernism was pushed ever further from the center of attention, a recording of the work became a genuine hit, achieving some of the greatest sales ever in the history of classical music recordings.

The search for a larger audience was especially compelling for American composers of the 1980s and 1990s. As earlier in the century, the orchestra was the primary medium available for this objective. Most American orchestras during these decades appointed "composers-in-residence" to write new works, oversee modern music activities, and to review new compositions. The works written and performed were rarely multimovement symphonies so favored by American musicians between the world wars, but instead shorter character pieces. The style of such compositions by John Adams, Joan Tower (1938–), John Harbison (1938–), and Ellen Taaffe Zwilich (1939–), and others has shown considerable uniformity through an adoption of known musical materials reworked in a mildly modernistic way. Adams's *Short Ride in a Fast Machine* (1986) is typical of this new and virtually orthodox genre. The five-minute composition, written for the Pittsburgh Symphony, is based on a minimalistic ostinato. It is brightly orchestrated, ebullient in rhythm, and traditional in textures and harmony. It rises to a well-prepared climax at the end, at which point it refers to the well-known orchestrational and melodic style of Copland. The piece as well as its entire genre is a product of its time.

THEATER

Musical genres that were allied to theatric arts prior to the twentieth century were limited primarily to opera and ballet. In this century there has been a great expansion in the ways that music has been combined with other dramatic forms of expression, and we shall refer to these innovative hybrid genres as *theatric* or *multimedia* music.

multimedia

Traditional opera has not had the importance in this century that it experienced in earlier times. Most opera companies have chosen to base their repertories upon the more popular works of the eighteenth and nineteenth centuries rather than to risk large sums to mount untried pieces. Furthermore, the alliance of dramatic narratives to avant-garde musical styles has not been notably successful outside of atonal Expressionist opera.

The most important operatic composers after the Second World War have conservatively maintained traditional lyric textures and sonorities. The three outstanding figures of this era are Benjamin Britten, whose opera *Peter Grimes* was discussed in Chapter 10, Hans Werner Henze (see Chapter 16), and Gian Carlo Menotti (1911–). Menotti was born in Italy but has lived primarily in the United States since the 1920s. He has composed in many genres, including works for chorus, songs, ballet scores, and other instrumental music, but he is best known as a specialist in operatic composition. Menotti writes his own libretti, which usually make a direct appeal to the emotions of the audience. His themes have included social satire (*The Unicorn, the Gorgon and the Manticore*, 1956), comedy (*The Telephone*, 1947), verismo tragedy (*The Consul*, 1950), biblical stories (*Amahl and the Night Visitors*, 1951), and political criticism (*Tamu-Tamu*, 1973). These texts are set to music in a tuneful fashion. Menotti has not aimed at an innovative musical language, but, in his best works, he achieves a direct and effective dramatic style.

New modes of musical theater were evident early in the twentieth century, at least in part as reactions against the giganticism of Wagnerian music drama. Stravinsky's *L'histoire du soldat* is a fable acted out by a few players, a dancer, and a narrator with incidental music. Manuel de Falla's *El retablo de Maese Pedro* uses puppets to present a story from Cervantes's novel *Don Quixote*. Schoenberg's *Pierrot lunaire* imitates the ambience of the German artistic cabaret: an actress in costume projects the fantasies of the clown Pierrot by recitation in the eerie "speaking voice."

Multimedia music played an especially large role after the Second World War in the experimental arts in America, where the genre took on greater abstraction than in Europe. The forefather of multimedia music in America was the resourceful Harry Partch (see Chapter 12). Beginning in the 1940s Partch composed what he termed "corporeal" works—pieces combining instrumental music, mime, costume, and recited poetry—which deal with subjects ranging from Greek mythology to human dramas of the Great Depression.

The abstract multimedia event or "happening" became fundamental to the work of John Cage after 1952. In his lecture "Composition as Process" (1958), Cage referred to the importance of visible actions in the experience that his music was intended to frame: "[My recent compositions] are occasions for experience, and this experience is not only received by the ears but by the eyes too. An ear alone is not a being. I have noticed listening to a record that my attention moves to a moving object or a play of light."

The content of Cage's theatric music from the 1950s is largely indeterminate: *Theater Piece* (1960), for example, instructs up to eight performers to devise their own independent program of activities based upon general guidelines. *4'33"No. 2* (1962) consists similarly of a verbal score which guides the performers in meaningless exercises in sight and sound. Cage's purpose in these works is to mirror the indeterminate appearance of a natural event, or, in his words, "produce a kind of chaos characteristic of nature." His *Europeras* (1991 and later), produced with great interest in Germany, are made from a random selection of arias, accompaniments, stagings, and texts from the history of opera. They are both parodies of and tributes to the genre.

Cage's verbal scores were models for the Fluxus group in New York in the early 1960s. Among composers active in this movement such as La Monte Young, Takehisa Kosugi, and Nam June Paik, Cage's celebrations of nature dissolved into a comedy of the absurd. Kosugi's "Music for a Revolution"—one of a number of works of "danger music"—instructs the performer to "scoop out one of your eyes five years from now and do the same with the other eye five years later." Young's "Piano Piece for David Tudor no. 1" has the player "bring a bale of hay and a bucket of water onto the stage for the piano to eat and drink. The performer may then feed the piano or leave it to eat by itself. If the former, the piece is over after the piano has been fed. If the latter, it is over after the piano eats or decides not to."

The theater pieces of Philip Glass—including *Einstein on the Beach* (1976), *Satyagraha* (1979), *Music/Theater No. 1: A Madrigal Opera* (1980), *Akhnaten* (1983), *CIVIL warS* (1984) and *Hydrogen Jukebox* (1990)—represent more monumental and artistic contributions to American theatric music. These works approach the genre of opera except for their lack of dramatic narrative and traditional singing. *Einstein on the Beach* and *CIVIL warS* are collaborations with Robert Wilson, who devised their scenarios and staging. Wilson's theater is nonliterary; it derives from modern dance and visual arts. His themes are often based upon the lives of great figures from the past—Einstein, Freud, Stalin, Albert Speer, Queen Victoria, Lincoln, and others who significantly reshaped the course of history. His works are not created by dialogue or narrative; they rely instead on a collage of disjunct and symbolic images.

In *Einstein on the Beach*, Wilson manipulates three images that have cryptic relevance to the life of the physicist Albert Einstein

(1879–1955): a train, trial, and spaceship. Each recurs several times during the work's nine scenes, and each is supplemented by subsidiary images—a bed in the trial scene, a field connected with the spaceship, a prison associated with the trial, and a figure representing Einstein himself, who plays the violin and observes the other activities on stage. The actors also dance in two scenes and recite incongruous or illogical speeches.

Glass's music is highly structured. It consists of figures derived from a few simple harmonic progressions, which are distributed through the nine scenes in varied recurrences. Continuity is promoted by a so-called Knee Play, which connects each act and functions as a prologue and epilogue. The Knee Plays consist of related stage activities by two actors and recurrent music that derives from themes heard within the different acts.

Glass's ensemble of electric keyboard instruments and woodwinds is augmented by a solo violinist and by a chorus that counts rhythmically and sings in solfège (perhaps reflecting Glass's years of training with Nadia Boulanger). The music is minimalistic, as it consists of repetitive ostinatos made from relatively few pitches, spun out by a steady rhythmic motion gathered into asymmetrical meters. The ostinato figures are entirely diatonic, and they generally outline simple harmonic progressions. They undergo gradual changes—such as rhythmic extensions and contractions—that give the music a sense of organic life. The music does not express the poetic content of the images on stage; in fact, it could be allied to any scenario. It is a further abstract image which contributes to the totality of Wilson's "living theater."

The most widely noted new theatric works in America since the late 1980s were by John Adams, specifically, his operas *Nixon in China* (1987) and *The Death of Klinghoffer* (1991) and the song-play *I Was Looking at the Ceiling and Then I Saw the Sky* (1995). Each deals with current social, political, or historical issues, and, taken as a whole, their music documents the ongoing postwar movement away from experiment toward traditional or populist values. *Nixon in China*, on a libretto by Alice Goodman, deals with Richard Nixon's historic visit to China in 1972 and with the conflicting thoughts and aspirations of the people involved. The music of the opera—especially in comparison to the experimental approaches in musical theater of the preceding decades—is traditional: descriptive, familiar in its division into arias, choruses, and ensembles, and relaxing in its diatonic tonal language. Only Adams's use of ostinati and other trappings of minimalism reveal the time when the work was composed. The European development of new genres of theatric music has been more orderly and structured than the American. Peter Maxwell Davies has been one of the most active composers of multimedia music. His *Eight Songs for a Mad King*—discussed in Chapter 16—dramatizes the insanity of George III by a series of straightforward musical and visual symbols. *Vesalii icones* is a set of fourteen dances in which the dancer portrays images from both the Christian stations of the cross and the anatomical drawings of Andreas Vesalius. *Miss Donnithorne's Maggot* (1974) returns to the spirit of the *Eight Songs* in its portrayal of the ravings of the jilted Miss Donnithorne.

Most of the works of Stockhausen since 1970 have incorporated theatricalities. His earliest such work was *Originale* (1961), his answer to Cage's *Theater Piece* of the previous year. *Originale* is an elaboration upon Stockhausen's *Kontakte* (for tape, pianist, and percussionist), which is performed amid the incongruous activities of a film crew, recording technician, child playing with blocks, newspaper salesman, and other actors. His later works of a theatrical type include *Ylem* (1972), in which instruments act out the movements of interstellar bodies by exploding at the big bang of a gong and taking their places throughout the cosmos of the auditorium. *Inori* (1974), for orchestra and mime, is a musical and gestural realization of thirteen attitudes of prayer from various cultures.

The Argentine composer Mauricio Kagel (1931–) has specialized in theatrics since 1960. His *Sur scène* (1960) places music itself—played by pianists and percussionists—into a dramatic role. It interacts thus with a lecturer, mime, and the commentary of a singer. The spirit of Fluxus is evident in Kagel's *Pas de cinq* (1965), which consists solely of five performers walking about the stage. *Variationen ohne Fuge* (1971–72) dramatizes borrowings among composers, perhaps as a satire upon the contemporary trend toward eclecticism. The work consists of an orchestration of passages from Brahms's Variations and Fugue on a Theme by Handel Op. 24. During the thirteenth variation, an actor impersonating Brahms enters the auditorium and sits on the conductor's podium. He subsequently delivers a monologue on Hamburg, Brahms's place of birth. As the orchestra continues with another variation, an actor representing Handel enters and sits by Brahms. The orchestra then plays Handel's theme upon which Brahms made his variations, and the two actors depart arm in arm.

INTERACTIONS WITH ROCK

After the First World War, jazz idioms were eagerly adopted by composers of serious music in order to vivify their work. Assimilations of jazz waned in the 1930s and 1940s, but they were revived in music by the American composer Gunther Schuller (1925–) in the 1950s. Schuller coined the term "third stream" to designate an idiom in which jazz and concert music were combined. In works such as his *Concertino* (1959), *Conversations* (1959), and *Variants* (1960), jazz ensembles interact with orchestra or string quartet; other pieces such as his *Seven Studies on Themes of Paul Klee* (1959), Concerto for Orchestra (1965–66), and the opera *The Visitation* (1966) contain passages in which the classical orchestra plays in the style of jazz.

Popular musicians of the twentieth century have also incorporated aspects of art music. George Gershwin (1898–1937) was a pioneer in attempts to synthesize the realms of popular and serious composition, and contemporary performers such as Peter Nero and the group Emerson, Lake, and Palmer have availed themselves of the classics.

Since the mid-1960s, music of the avant-garde has been increasingly reflected in rock music. The Beatles led the way to a varied style of rock that admitted musical elements from many sources. Their songs "Good Day Sunshine" and "Being for the Benefit of Mr. Kite" applied changing, asymmetrical meters, which made such pieces unsuitable to accompany dancing. The Beatles' music demanded to be heard primarily as artistic expression. They were especially resourceful in applying modern techniques of electronic and taped music. High levels of amplification and feedback produce a backdrop of noise in works such as "Tomorrow Never Knows," which helps to express a recurrent theme in their songs: the seemingly new realms opened by drugs or hallucinatory experiences. "Revolution 9" is a milestone in rock, as it merges diverse elements of speech, electronically manipulated noise and music, and spatial effects into a lengthy collage. This piece has no sung text and little that would identify it as rock rather than as serious avant-garde composition. The recurrent words "number nine" lend it a cryptic focus and meaning.

The Beatles were the first great eclectics of rock. Not only did they use styles from the avant-garde, but they also incorporated elements of earlier classical and non-Western music. Songs such as "Penny Lane" and "For No One" use obbligato solos by orchestral instruments—the piccolo trumpet and French horn, respectively—lending to these numbers a flavor of the baroque. Tunes such as "Love to You" and "Within You Without You" use media of traditional Indian music. The use of electronic media is still much alive in rock, ranging from predictably deafening levels of amplification to more imaginative techniques of tape delay and application of the synthesizer. Extensive electronic manipulations underlay music of Brian Eno, David Bowie, and the German group Tangerine Dream.

An increasingly widespread area in which rock musicians have benefited from serious avant-garde composition is their adoption of minimalist styles. Minimalism has a natural alliance to rock in its diatonic or modal melody, sustained pulse, and ostinato-like repetition of brief melodic fragments and harmonic progressions. The minimalists did not borrow from rock; theirs was instead an original development within the experimental tradition of American serious music. Philip Glass has emphasized this relationship: "When you talk about concert musicians, you're talking about people who actually invent language. They create values, a value being a unit of meaning that is new and different. Pop musicians package language" (from Robert Palmer's liner notes to *Einstein on the Beach*, Records, M4 38875).

Echoes of minimalism may be heard in music by many contemporary rock groups—Tangerine Dream, Talking Heads, Pink Floyd, and The Police among them. "Synchronicity" (1983) by The Police is an example. At the beginning of this song, the percussion establish a repetitive figure recalling a work by Riley or Glass. This line is then elaborated by a rock rhythm and vocal overlay.

The Talking Heads represent a continuation of the eclectic spirit of the Beatles. Their work is fructified by contacts with ethnic music and the avant-garde. "I Zimbra" from the album *Fear of Music* (1979) uses African drumming and a Dadaist poem, elaborated upon by a minimalistic ostinato. "Memories Can't Wait" from the same recording uses discordant streams of sounds to accompany its hallucinatory words.

A novel combination of rock and serious music is achieved by Laurie Anderson (1947–). Her album *Big Science* (1982) contains music from a multimedia work *United States I–IV*, in which music, recitation, and visual projections depict aspects of life in this country. The music is essentially enhanced narration, often using a device called a Vocoder by which speech sounds are modulated by other signals. Anderson has an engaging way of delivering her texts, which are accompanied by diverse types of music. Her album *Mister Heartbreak* (1984) is more abstract in its verbal message, and it relies upon sounds of the jungle in its accompaniment.

EPILOGUE

In his book *Music, the Arts, and Ideas* (1967), Leonard Meyer advances the hypothesis that music of the later twentieth century will remain in a "dynamic steady state" in which relatively small variations in style will be observed, but from which no strongly unified practice will emerge. The nearly thirty years that have elapsed since his prediction have apparently borne out Meyer's thesis. We seem to live in a time of pluralism of musical styles, each with its own adherents.

But will the perception of this era be altered in the future? Will coming generations see the unstable multiplicity of styles that seem now so apparent? There is a great likelihood that they will not. Contemporary music will by then have experienced a most powerful catharsis: the test of time. Works of new music may now attract attention for various reasons: an ingenious construction, a novel or engaging style, or the forceful personality and promotional work of the composer. But music endures for other reasons, even though these are intractably difficult to define. Among them no doubt are a quality of sound that captures the imagination of the sensitive listener, the composer's mastery of his language, and the substance of what he wishes to communicate.

Now in the last decade of the twentieth century, we have reached a point when we can begin to see the effects of time at work in music composed earlier in the century. Some composers who were well known in their own era are now forgotten; others endure by repeated performances of their work. Musicians today continue to study and perform, for example, the music of Arnold Schoenberg. There is a mastery and substance to it that goes deeper than a thorny surface that continues to baffle many listeners. Schoenberg's music has nonetheless endured, and it now makes a living and lasting contribution to our culture.

But regardless of what judgments will eventually be made upon the music of our own century, our task of understanding the culture in which we live is no less vital and challenging. It demands of us a broad-minded perspective, a conscientious study of its major works, a sensitivity to its shaping forces, and a curiosity about art that refuses to be quenched.

BIBLIOGRAPHY

A survey of minimalism and of the earlier works of Riley, Reich, Young, and Glass is given by Michael Nyman in *Experimental Music: Cage and Beyond* (New York, 1980). Wim Mertens's *American Minimal Music*, trans. J. Hautekiet (New York, 1983), also deals with these four figures and adds philosophical and ideological interpretations of their music. Also see the interviews with Reich and Glass in Cole Gagne and Tracy Caras, *Soundpieces* (Metuchen, N.J., 1982), which also contains lists of works by these composers. Articles on English and European minimalists are found in *Contact*, 21–23 (1980–81). Steve Reich's ideas behind his music are expressed in articles collected in his *Writings About Music* (Halifax, 1974). Glass's *Music by Philip Glass*, ed. Robert T. Jones (New York, 1987), deals primarily with Glass's early operas, including *Einstein on the Beach*.

John Rockwell's *All-American Music: Composition in the Late Twentieth Century* (New York, 1983) contains chapters on Philip Glass, Laurie Anderson, the Talking Heads, David Del Tredici, and other serious and popular American musicians. It contains a useful bibliography. Regarding music for theater, see Richard Kostelanetz's anthology *Theatre of Mixed Means* (New York, 1968). Eric Salzman's *Twentieth-Century Music: An Introduction*, 3d ed. (Englewood Cliffs, N.J., 1988) surveys minimalism, contemporary popular music, and musical theater.

Leonard Meyer's *Music, the Arts, and Ideas* (Chicago and London, 1967) is a collection of essays dealing with various aspects of contemporary music, including a broad discussion on the processes by which musical styles evolve and on the purpose and understanding of experimental music.

Index